French Devotional Texts
of the Middle Ages

FRENCH DEVOTIONAL TEXTS
OF THE MIDDLE AGES

A Bibliographic Manuscript Guide

Second Supplement

Compiled by
KEITH V. SINCLAIR

GREENWOOD PRESS
NEW YORK • WESTPORT, CONNECTICUT • LONDON

Library of Congress Cataloging-in-Publication Data

Sinclair, Keith Val.
  French devotional texts of the Middle Ages : a bibliographic
manuscript guide. Second supplement / compiled by Keith V. Sinclair.
       p.   cm.
  Includes indexes.
  ISBN 0-313-26276-4 (lib. bdg. : alk. paper)
  1. Catholic Church—Prayer-books and devotions—French—
Manuscripts—Catalogs.   2. Devotional literature, French—
Manuscripts—Catalogs.   3. Manuscripts, French—Catalogs.
I. Title.
Z6611.T3S56 Suppl. 2
[BX2183]
016.242'0944—dc19   87-32273

British Library Cataloguing in Publication Data is available.

Library of Congress Catalog Card Number: 87-32273
ISBN: 0-313-26276-4

First published in 1988

Greenwood Press, Inc.
88 Post Road West, Westport, Connecticut 06881

Printed in the United States of America

The paper used in this book complies with the
Permanent Paper Standard issued by the National
Information Standards Organization (Z39.48-1984).

10 9 8 7 6 5 4 3 2 1

CONTENTS

PREFACE

As the Title Page and the Contents Page proclaim, this volume includes additional information concerning incipits 2375-5375 which has come to our attention since 1979.

The fifteen hundred new incipits 5376-6875 are derived from two sources: monographs and articles by scholars in the field on the one hand, and my own readings of literary and religious works as well as visits to libraries, on the other.

In 1982-1983 Dr Pierre Rézeau of Strasburg published two volumes entitled Prières aux saints en français à la fin du moyen âge which constitute a singular advance in our knowledge of Medieval French devotional texts. His work groups for the first time the numerous short compositions in prose and in rhyme in honour of designated saints. These hagiographical treasures are critically edited from fifteenth and sixteenth-century manuscripts or early printed copies of Books of Hours and Prayer-Books. Reference is made in this Supplement to Dr Rézeau's Saints as well as to the numerous devotional compositions in MS. Metz 600 of which he had given a detailed account in 1977.

The bulk, however, of the fifteen hundred incipits published in the present volume have come to light in the course of my own research. Firstly, my incursions into medieval literary works. Epic poetry and mystery plays have not been exhausted as genres in which prayers are commonplace, and a sprinkling of new texts are included from among such compositions. The emotive structure of Gréban's Mystère de la Passion is anchored in an ocean of prayer. Mortals of his creation continually utter praises, thanksgiving or lamentations to the Almighty and at times they employ for their orisons highly sophisticated and rhythmical forms such as the rondeau and fatras. Some unexpected, but welcome discoveries in literary works are an adaptation of Manasseh's prayer incorporated by Guillaume de Machaut into his Confort d'Ami (6627); a confession text by Octavien de Saint-Gelais (6457); a prayer to the Cross by one of the protagonists of the Dit des Trois Morts et Trois Vifs (6322); Credo and Pater Noster renditions in a translation of Caton (5961, 6462); and two emotional outpourings of high spirituality in Grosseteste's Château d'amour (5822, 5898).

Among the listings in the Supplement the reader will find additional examples of prayers associated with the Mass and with the Elevation and Communion aspects, in particular. Also included are what appear to be unica for the Hymns Christe qui lux es et dies (6717), Patris sapientia (6455), Panque linqua gloriosi certaminis (5548), Salvatoris mater pia (5765) and Ut queant laxis (6535). These may be set alongside additional paraphrases of the Ave maris stella, the Magnificat, the O gloriosa domina and the Te Deum.

The tract on the Articles de la foy, also called Codicile, by Jean Chapuis is recorded among the new incipits, as is a much shorter Codicile in 88 lines attributed to Jean de Meun. A study of St Edmund of Abingdon's Mirour de seinte Eglyse has brought to light comments in French on the Hours of the Cross which have parallels with other versions that stand alone in the manuscripts.

I have completed a reading of all the French works by Jean Gerson and many devotional compositions have, not unexpectedly, been unearthed. His Sermons, above all, are testimony to his rhetorical manipulation of devotional pauses to enhance the oratorical impact of his preaching.

Progress towards finalising certain entries has been slow indeed. This is especially true of the compositions that survive in large numbers of manuscripts. It will be recalled that an object of each entry in the F.D.T.M.A. was to make the codicological outline complete in terms of the manuscript foliations. It is now realised that to await until every codex can be examined would logically mean the omission for many years of hundreds of orisons. Clearly, a compromise was needed between the absolute and the ideal on the one hand, and the reality and research time available on the other. The compromise that has been struck is one that allows a prayer to be listed without every known manuscript being designated. The formulaic phrase "Screening of mss is incomplete" is designed to alert the reader to this state of affairs.

The other source of texts that are included in this Supplement is my own field work, periods when I abandoned the domestic armchair of piety in order to become the humble seeker of the evidence of past devotional practices amidst the medieval documents of the great repositories of the world. It is principally the libraries of the United States that I frequented for the purposes of this volume and it was during the seventies that the largest number of visits were made.

The focus on American collections was sharpened in the thirties when Seymour de Ricci and W.J. Wilson published their three-volume Census of manuscript holdings. The W.H. Bond and C.A. Faye Supplement, that appeared in 1962 enables the researcher to trace the majority of sales and purchases of manuscripts that had occurred in the intervening years. But, as I observed in the Avant-Propos of my Prières Supplement, these catalogues rarely mention French prayers individually. Yet another Supplement, now that a quarter of a century has passed, is certainly a desideratum and it could be more useful to researchers if it detailed all the small, often anonymous compositions, that occur so often in medieval codices. However that may be, American scholars have begun to publish descriptive catalogues of select collections, as well as articles and monographs about important manuscripts. We may cite as examples of this activity that are relevant for our devotional texts: Erwin Panofsky's paper on the De Buz Hours (1949); Anneliese Funke's paper on a Book of Hours for

Rennes Use (1957); John Plummer's iconographical and codicological study of the Hours of Catherine of Cleves (1966); J.D. Farquhar's notice about a Châlons-sur-Marne Horae (1968); Karen Gould's monograph on the Psalter and Hours of Yolande de Soissons (1978); and Lilian M.C. Randall's paper on MS. Walters 219 (1981).

It is probably now more comprehensible to the reader why it was necessary for me to visit American libraries in person. By naming the ones I have worked in, other scholars will know which manuscript holdings have been investigated for French prayers and which ones still remain to be visited. For convenience, I adopt a geographical progression from West to East across the United States: Berkeley and Los Angeles Libraries of the University of California; at Camarillo, the Library of St. John's Seminary, now housing by bequest the great Doheny private collection; at San Marino, the Huntington Library; in the Chicago area visits were made to the three principal repositories of medieval manuscripts, the University of Chicago Library, the Newberry Library and the Art Institute.   In Washington D.C. I inspected the modest medieval manuscript holdings in a comparatively short time, while the codices at the Walters Art Gallery were so numerous that I needed to make repeated visits to record their textual riches.   In Philadelphia I visited the Art Museum, the Free Library and the University of Pennsylvania Library.   The Art Museum and the University Library at Princeton have important manuscripts.   In New York City I paid numerous calls on the librarians at Columbia University, the Public Library, the Pierpont Morgan Library, and the Cloisters.   Being close to where I was employed at the University of Connecticut, New Haven saw me as a frequent pilgrim to the Beinecke Library at Yale University. Further North in Massachusetts, I ranged westwards to Williams College and North to Wellesley College at Wellesley, Clark University at Worcester, the Boston Public Library, the Isabella Gardner Museum and, of course, across the Charles River to the Houghton Library at Harvard College.   The small collection of ancient documents at Brown University in Providence was also well worth an excursion.

Among the multiplicity of manuscripts of interest that I encountered in the United States are three that are particularly noteworthy for the number of unrecorded French devotional texts they contain.   Brown University MS. C. 28. b. 4 is a small Horae of the second half of the fifteenth century, all in French.   Pierpont Morgan MS. 78 is also a Book of Hours from the same century with contents mainly in Latin. Its principal interest resides in the liturgical texts in French transcribed by a later hand into the blank spaces on the folios.   The third codex I have in mind to mention is Yale University 498 blandly catalogued, after its own title page, Manuel de dévotion.   This is the correct designation, being the one bestowed on the collection of prayers by the compiler himself.   Circumstantial evidence derived from statements made in select prayers has enabled me to determine that the compiler's name was Pierre, that he was a priest, that he was a royalist in the context of the Wars of Religion and that he was writing in Toulouse.   In a study in preparation I hope to be able to date the prayer-book to within a ten-year period.

All in all, these three manuscripts have probably contributed about five-hundred incipits to the present collection.   To this number must be added those of yet another prayer-book I discovered on the Continent of Europe at Roubaix where it had been incorrectly described as a Book of Hours.   It is a fifteenth-century compilation, prepared for Jacques de Luxembourg.

May I be excused if I repeat for my new readers' benefit the principles that govern a text's inclusion in the F.D.T.M.A. They remain much the same as I outlined on p. vii of the previous volume which was published in 1982. The incipits are those of prose or verse compositions in the French vernacular which express praise, adoration, veneration, supplication or gratitude to God, the persons of the Trinity, the Virgin Mary and Saints or Biblical Personages. I confess I have wavered in my attention to texts that may be considered ancillary to Devotion, but more recently, I have been persuaded by arguments put to me by Professor Ruth Dean that compositions of this nature could usefully find a place in the F.D.T.M.A. Sonet, after all, did include several versions of the Commandements de la Loy in his Répertoire (see Prières, 1978, p. 195).

The reader who is familiar with the alphabetical order of the incipits in the previous volumes will remember that the key to the order is in the first word of the prayer. Dialect differences of pronunciation and scribal blunders, however, would produce, if they were followed to the letter, the alienation of many incipits, one from another and cause the researcher to believe he is in the presence of distinctly different compositions. The examples of the forms of Beaus, Beals, Beauz, Beaus, Bials, Biels and of Dieus, Dé, Deu, Dieu, are to the point. In such cases, a form has been selected as a flag to which the others are attached, the incipit then being ordered according to the next word. Irrespective of this manoeuvre, and in practice with past procedure, inserts such as dit-il, font ils, dist Roland etc. are totally ignored for alphabetical ordering, whatever their position in the incipit.

It is always a pleasure to express my indebtedness to scholars far and wide for their interest and encouragement: Emeriti Professors Félix Lecoy, and Claude Schaefer, Paris, Emerita Professor Ruth Dean, New York, Professor D.D.R. Owen, St. Andrews, and Dr Pierre Rézeau, Strasburg, and the late Neil Ripley Ker, in retirement in Scotland.

It must be to the Librarians and Curators that I owe my greatest debt for their indulgence and cooperation with my cataloguing endeavours. Many have already been named in the introduction to my Prières I and II and my F.D.T.M.A. I and II. If I repeat names and add new ones here, it is to recall special considerations extended to me: Anthony S. Bliss, Bancroft Library, Berkeley; James Davis, Special Collection, University of California Research Library, Los Angeles; Dr Mary L. Robertson, Huntington Library, San Marino; Rev. Dr Ephrem Compte O.P., Los Angeles; Thomas Kren, J. Paul Getty Museum, Malibu; Professor Boyd W. Rayward, Dean of the Graduate Library School, University of Chicago; Robert Rosenthal, Special Collections, University of Chicago Library; Dr Anselmo Carini, Department of Prints and Drawings, Art Institute of Chicago; Dr John A. Tedeschi, Special Collections, Newberry Library, Chicago; Peter van Wingen and Thomas Burney, Special Collections, Library of Congress; Dr Lilian M.C. Randall, Walters Art Gallery, Baltimore; Dr John Plummer and William Voelkle, Pierpont Morgan Library, New York; Rudolph Ellenbogen, Rare Books Division, Columbia University; Paul R. Rugen and Joseph Rankin, Special Collections, New York Public Library; Roger S. Wieck, Houghton Library at Harvard College, Cambridge.

In the United Kingdom, Phyllis P.M. Giles and Paul Woudhuysen, Fitzwilliam Museum, Cambridge; S.M. Simpson, National Library of Scotland, Edinburgh; Dr J.T.D. Hall, Edinburgh University Library;

Philip S. Vainker, Glasgow Museums and Art Galleries; Theresa Thom, Grays Inn Library, London; Professor Andrew Watson, School of Library, Archive and Information Studies, University College, London.

My visits to the Cabinet des Manuscrits at the Royal Library in Brussels were always made pleasurable by renewing contacts with M. Georges Dogaer, M. Pierre Cockshaw and Madame Marguerite Debae.

In France I have been assisted in person, and occasionally by correspondence, by the following curators and librarians to whom I renew my expression of gratitude: Marie-Noëlle Icardo, Bibliothèque Méjanes, Aix-en-Provence; Françoise Bruno, Bibliothèque Municipale, Douai; A. Coisy, Bibliothèque Municipale, La Rochelle; Patricia Droulers, Bibliothèque Municipale, Metz; R. Saint-Pé, Bibliothèque Nationale et Universitaire, Strasburg; Geneviève Deblock, Ecole Nationale Supérieure des Beaux-Arts, Paris; Pierre Gasnault, Bibliothèque Mazarine, Paris; François Avril, Cabinet des Manuscrits, Bibliothèque Nationale, Paris.

At the James Cook University in Townsville, I am a heavy user of the interlibrary loan services and I should like to thank Mr John Penbrook, Dr John Kennedy and Ms Janelle Rawlinson for their assistance in procuring titles and articles from other libraries.

Ms Anne Douglass typed the manuscript and Mrs Joy Evans cheerfully met the challenges of its complex layout. I am in great debt to them for the successful outcome of the project.

K.V. Sinclair
Townsville, February 1985.

P.S.   Regrettably, the delays in the publication of this <u>Supplement</u> mean that no account will be found in it of P. Rézeau, <u>Répertoire d'incipit des prières françaises à la fin du moyen âge</u>, Geneva, 1986, a copy of which I have just received from the author.

Townsville, January 1987.

BIBLIOGRAPHY

Items mentioned in the edition and reference points for the texts are listed in the Bibliography. Other titles may be found in the bibliographic sections of Sonet, Répertoire; Rézeau, Saints I and II; Sinclair Prières I and II; Sinclair, FDTMA I and II.

Ahsmann, H.P.J.M. Le Culte de la Sainte Vierge et la littérature française profane du moyen âge. Paris: Picard; Nimeguen: Dekker-Van de Vegt and Van Leeuwen, 1930.

Altona, J. Gebete und Anrufungen in den Altfranzösischen Chanson de geste. Marburg: Elwert, 1883.

Aspland, C.W. A Medieval French Reader. Oxford: Clarendon, 1979.

Aubry, P. Les plus anciens monuments de la musique française. Paris: Welter, 1905.

Aubry, P. Le Roman de Fauvel, manuscrit inédit de la Bibliothèque Nationale fr. 146. Paris: Geuthner, 1907.

Auracher, T.M. "Der sogenannte poitevinische Pseudo-Turpin nach den Handschriften mitgetheilt." Zeitschrift für Romanische Philologie 1 (1877): 259-336.

Bartsch, K. Chrestomathie de l'ancien français. 12th ed. by L. Wiese. Leipzig: Vogel, 1920.

Bastin, Julia. Recueil général des Ysopets. 2 vols. Paris: SATF, 1929-1930.

Bayot, A. Gormond et Isembart, reproduction photocollographique. Brussels: Misch and Thron, 1906.

Bayot, A. Gormont et Isembart, fragment de chanson de geste du XIIe siècle. 3rd ed. Paris: Champion, 1931.

Bec, P. "Lyrique profane et paraphrase pieuse dans la poésie médiévale (XIIe-XIII^{e}s.)." In Jean Misrahi Memorial Volume. Studies in Medieval Literature, ed. by H.R. Runte et al. Columbia S.C.: French Literature Publishing Coy, 1977: 229-39.

Bec, P. La Lyrique française au moyen âge (XIIe-XIIIe siècles). 2
    vols. Paris: Picard, 1977-1978.

Bechmann, E. "Drei Dits de l'Ame aus der Hs. Gall. oct. 28 der
    Königlichen Bibliothek zu Berlin." Zeitschrift für Romanische
    Philologie 13 (1889): 35-84.

Becker, H.J. "Ein Gebetsrotulus des 15. Jahrhunderts:
    liturgiewissenschaftliche Randbemerkungen zu Aufbau, Inhalt und
    Herkunft von Clm 28961." Gutenberg Jahrbuch, 1976: 57-63.

Bédier, J. and Aubry, P. Les Chansons de Croisade. Paris: Champion,
    1909.

Belanger, J.L.R. Damedieus: The Context of the French Epic: The
    Loherain Cycle viewed against other early French Epics. Geneva:
    Droz, 1975.

Boca, L.N. Li Romans de Baudouin de Sebourg. 2 vols. Valenciennes:
    Henry, 1841.

Bond, W.H. and Faye, C.U. Supplement to the Census of Medieval and
    Renaissance Manuscripts in the United States and Canada. New
    York: Bibliographical Society of America, 1962.

Bornäs, G. Trois contes français du XIIIe siècle tirés des Vies des
    Pères. Lund: Gleerup, 1968.

Borodina, M.A. and Mal'kevic, B.A. Rukopisno enasledie V.F. Sismareva
    v Arkive Akademii Nauk SSSR. Moscow and Leningrad, 1965.

Bouly de Lesdain, Anne-Marie. "Les manuscrits didactiques antérieurs
    au XIVe siècle. Essai d'inventaire." Bulletin de l'Institut de
    Recherche et d'Histoire des Textes 13 (1964-1965): 57-79;
    14(1966): 43-82.

Brandin, L. "La Destruction de Rome et Fierabras." Romania 64(1938):
    18-100.

Brayer, Edith and Bouly de Lesdain, Anne-Marie. "Les Prières usuelles
    annexées aux anciennes traductions françaises du psautier."
    Bulletin de l'Institut de Recherche et d'Histoire des Textes 15
    (1967-1968): 69-120.

Brayer, Edith. "Manuscrits français du moyen âge conservés à
    Leningrad." Bulletin de l'Institut de Recherche et d'Histoire
    des Textes 7 (1958): 23-31.

Brayer, Edith. "Livres d'heures contenant des textes en français."
    Bulletin d'Information de l'Institut de Recherche et d'Histoire
    des Textes 12 (1963): 31-102.

Brayer, Edith. "Catalogue des textes liturgiques et des petits genres
    religieux." In Grundriss der Romanischen Literaturen des
    Mittelalters, edited by H.R. Jauss et al. 2 vols. Heidelberg:
    Winter, 1968-1970, 2: 19-53.

Brown, C. English Lyrics of the XIIIth Century. 2nd ed. Oxford:
    Clarendon, 1950.

Buchon, J.A. Branche des Royaux Lignages. Chronique métrique de Guillaume Guiart. 2 vols. Paris: Verdière, 1828.

Buffum, D.L. Le Roman de la Violette ou de Gérart de Nevers par Gerbert de Montreuil. Paris: SATF, 1929.

Cahn, W. and Marrow, J.H. "Medieval and Renaissance Manuscripts at Yale: a Selection". Yale University Library Gazette 52 (1978): 173-284.

Calkins, R.G. "Medieval and Renaissance Illuminated Manuscripts in the Cornell University Library". Cornell Library Journal 13 (1972): 3-95.

Caluwé, J. de. "La Prière épique dans la tradition manuscrite de la Chanson de Roland." Senefiance 10: 147-86.

Carnahan, D.H. The Ad Deum Vadit of Jean Gerson published from the ms. B.N. f.fr. 24841, Urbana: University of Illinois, 1917.

Castedello, W. Die Prosafassung des Bataille Loquifer und des Moniage Renouart. Halle: Hohmann, 1912.

Chailley, J. "Une signature inédite sur une prière du XVe siècle." Senefiance 10: 67-72.

Champion, P. Histoire poétique du XVe siècle. 2 vols. Paris: Champion, 1923.

Chaurand, J. Fou, Dixième Conte de la Vie des Pères. Geneva: Droz, 1971.

Chesney, Kathleen. "A Fifteenth-Century Miscellany: Notes on ms. Douce 252." In Studies in French Language and Medieval Literature presented to Mildred K. Pope. Manchester: Manchester University Press, 1939. 61-70.

Chesney, Kathleen. Fleurs de Rhétorique from Villon to Marot. Oxford: Blackwell, 1950.

Chesney, Kathleen. More Poèmes de transition. Notes on the Rondeaux of a Taylorian Manuscript. Oxford: Blackwell, 1965.

Chesney, Kathleen. "Two Collections of Early Sixteenth-Century French Rondeaux." Medium Aevum 40 (1971): 157-71.

Christ, K. "La Règle des fins amans. Eine Beginenregel aus dem Ende des 13. Jahrhunderts." In Philologische Studien aus dem Romanisch-Germanischen Kulturkreise Karl Voretzsch zum 60. Geburtstage dargebracht. Halle: Niemeyer, 1927: 173-213.

Colliot, Régine. Adenet le Roi, Berte aus grans piés. Etude littéraire générale. 2 vols. Paris: Picard, 1970.

Colombani, D. "La Prière du coeur dans les Miracles de Nostre Dame de Gautier de Coinci." Senefiance 10: 73-90.

Combarieu, Micheline de. "La Prière à la Vierge dans l'épopée." Senefiance 10:91-120.

Couraye du Parc, J. La Mort Aymeri de Narbonne, chanson de geste.
    Paris: SATF, 1884.

Craig, Barbara M. La Creacion, la Transgression and l'Expulsion of the
    Mistere du Viel Testament. Lawrence: University of Kansas, 1968.

Cremonesi, Carla. Lirica francese del medio evo. Milan: Istituto
    Editoriale Cisalpino, 1955.

Crosland, Jessie. Guibert d'Andrenas, chanson de geste. Manchester:
    Manchester University Press, 1923.

Curzon, H. de. La Règle du Temple. Paris: Renouard, 1886.

Delaisseé, L. "Problèmes de méthode en histoire de la miniature: le
    livre d'heures d'Isabeau de Bavière." Scriptorium 4 (1950):
    252-60.

Delisle, L. "Notice sur un recueil de traités de dévotion ayant
    appartenu à Charles V." Bibliothèque de l'Ecole des Chartes 30
    (1869): 532-42.

Dembowski, P.F. Jourdain de Blaye (Jordains de Blaivies), chanson de
    geste. Chicago, Chicago University Press, 1969.

Dembowski, P.F. Ami et Amile, chanson de geste. Paris: Champion, 1969.

Deschaux, R. "La Piété populaire à la fin du XVe siècle vue à travers
    le Calendrier des Bergers." Senefiance 10: 211-221.

Dickman, A.J. Le Rôle du Surnaturel dans les chansons de geste. Iowa
    City: Champion, 1925.

Dominguez Rodriguez, Ana. Libros de horas del siglo XV en la
    Biblioteca Nacional. Madrid: Fundacion Universitaria Espanola,
    1979.

Droz, Eugénie. "Notice sur un Recueil de Louanges." Romania 49 (1923):
    48-62.

Dupire, N. Les Faictz et Dictz de Jean Molinet. 3 vols. Paris: SATF,
    1936-1939.

Egbert, D.D. "The Western European Manuscripts, Princeton University,
    Garrett Collection." Princeton University Library Chronicle 3
    (1942): 123-30.

Fahlin, Carin. Chronique des ducs de Normandie par Benoît. 3 vols.
    Uppsala: Almqvist and Wicksell, 1951-1967. Third vol. by O.
    Södergård.

Farquhar, J.D. "A Book of Hours from Châlons-sur-Marne." Scriptorium
    22(1968): 243-9.

Ferrari, Mirella. Medieval and Renaissance Manuscripts at the
    University of California, Los Angeles. A Preliminary
    Description. Los Angeles: University of California. 1978.

Forshaw, Helen P. (Sister Mary Philomena). "St. Edmund of Abingdon's Meditations before the Canonical Hours." Ephemerides Liturgicae 78 (1964): 33-57.

Forshaw, Helen P. "New Light on the Speculum Ecclesie of St. Edmund of Abingdon." Archives d'histoire doctrinale et littéraire du moyen âge. 38 (1971): 7-33.

Förster, W. Aiol et Mirabel und Elie de Saint-Gille, zwei Altfranzösische Heldengedichte. 2 vols. Heilbronn: Henninger, 1876-1882.

Frappier, J. Les Chansons de geste du Cycle de Guillaume d'Orange. 2 vols. 2nd ed. Paris: Société d'Edition d'Enseignement Supérieur, 1955-1967.

Frénaud, G. La Passion Nostre Seigneur. Sermon Ad Deum Vadit prononcé par maistre Jehan Gerson en l'église Saint-Bernard de Paris le vendredi saint 1403. Paris: Wittmann, 1947.

Funke, Anneliese M. "A Book of Hours of Rennes." Boston Public Library Quarterly 9 (1957): 195-205.

Gallagher, E.J. A Critical Edition of La Passion Nostre Seigneur from MS. 1131 from the Bibliothèque Sainte-Geneviève, Paris. Chapel Hill N.C.: University of North Carolina, 1976.

Garel, J. "La Prière du plus grand péril." In Mélanges de langue et de littérature médiévales offerts à Pierre Le Gentil. Paris: Société d'Edition d'Enseignement Supérieur, 1973: 311-18.

Gastoué, A. Le Cantique populaire en France. Lyon: Janin, 1924.

Gautier, L. La Chevalerie. 3rd ed. Paris: Delagrave, 1895.

Gelzer, H. Der Altfranzösische Yderroman nach der einzigen bekannten Handschriften. Dresden: Gesellschaft für Romanische Literatur, 1913.

Gieber, R.L. La Vie saint Jehan-Baptiste. A Critical Edition of an Old French Poem of the Early Fourteenth-Century. Tübingen: Niemeyer, 1978.

Giraud, P.E. and Chevalier, U. Le Mystère des Trois Doms joué à Romans en MDIX, d'après le manuscrit original. Lyon: Brun, 1887.

Glorieux, P. Jean Gerson. Oeuvres complètes. 10 vols. Paris: Desclée, 1961-1973.

Gould, Karen. The Psalter and Hours of Yolande de Soissons. Cambridge (Mass): Medieval Academy of America, 1978.

Gröber, G. Grundriss der Romanischen Philologie. 2 vols. Strasburg: Trübner, 1888-1902.

Gros, G. "De la Ballade des Pendus à la Complainte des Trespassés de Jean Molinet, permanence d'un thème." Senefiance 10: 315-335.

Guessard, F. and Chabaille, P. Gaufrey, chanson de geste. Paris: Vieweg, '859.

Guessard, F. and Larchey L. Parise la duchesse, chanson de geste.
    Paris: Vieweg, 1860.

Ham, E.B. Girart de Rossillon, poème bourguignon du XIVe siècle.
    London: Oxford University Press, 1939.

Henry, A. Chrestomathie de la littérature en ancien français. 6th ed.
    2 vols. Bern: Francke, 1978.

Henry, P. Les Enfances Guillaume, chanson de geste du XIIIe siècle.
    Paris: SATF, 1935.

Herbert, J.A. "A New Manuscript of Adgar's Mary Legends." Romania. 32
    (1903): 394-421.

Higman, F. Guillaume Farel, le Pater Noster et le Credo en Françoys.
    Geneva: Droz, 1982.

Hill, Betty. "British Library MS. Egerton 613." Notes and Queries n.s.
    25 (1978): 394-409, 492-501.

Hoepffner, E. Oeuvres de Guillaume de Machaut. 3 vols. Paris: SATF,
    1908-1921.

Hofmann, K. Amis et Amiles und Jourdains de Blaivies. Zwei
    Altfranzösische Heldengedichte der Kerlingischen Sagenkreis.
    2nd ed. Erlangen: Deichert, 1882.

Holden, A.J. Le Roman de Rou de Wace. 3 vols. Paris: SATF, 1970-1973.

James, J.A. Octavien de Saint-Gelais. Le Séjour d'honneur. Chapel Hill
    N.C.: University of North Carolina, 1977.

Järnström, E. Recueil de chansons pieuses du XIIIe siècle. Helsinki:
    Société de littérature finnoise, 1910.

Järnström, E. and Långfors, A. Recueil de chansons pieuses du XIIIe
    siècle. Helsinki: Société de littérature finnoise, 1927.

Jeffery, B. Chanson Verse of the Early Renaissance. 2 vols. London:
    Tecla, 1971 and 1976.

Jodogne, O. Le Mystère de la Passion d'Arnoul Greban. Brussels: Palais
    des Académies, 1965.

Joüon des Longrais, F. Le Roman d'Aquin ou la Conqueste de la
    Bretaigne par le roy Charlemaigne, chanson de geste du XIIe
    siècle. Nantes: Société des Bibliophiles Bretons, 1880.

Katz, Blanche. La Prise d'Orange according to ms. A1, Bibl. nat. fr.
    774. New York: King's Crown Press, 1947.

Keller, H.A. von. Romvart. Beiträge zur Kunde Mittelalterlicher
    Dichtung aus Italienischen Bibliotheken. Paris: Renouard;
    Mannheim: Bassermann, 1844.

Ker, N.R. Facsimile of British Museum MS. Harley 2253. London: Early
    English Text Society, 1965.

Ker, N.R. Medieval Manuscripts in British Libraries. 3 vols. Oxford: Clarendon, 1969-1983.

Kessler, H.L. "A Book of Hours from the Atelier of Willem Vrelant." Scriptorium 18 (1964): 94-99.

Koch, Sister Marie-Pierre. An Analysis of the Long Prayers in Old French Literature with Special Reference to the Biblical-Creed-Narrative Prayers. Washington, D.C.: Catholic University of America Press, 1940.

Koenig, V.F. Le Comte de Poitiers, roman du XIIIe siècle. Paris: Droz, 1937.

Labande, E.R. "Le Credo épique." In Recueil de travaux offert à M. Clovis Brunel. 2 vols. Paris: Société de l'Ecole des Chartes, 1950; 2: 62-80.

Laborde, A. de. Les principaux manuscrits à peintures conservés dans l'ancienne Bibliothèque Impériale Publique de Saint-Pétersbourg. Paris: Société française de reproductions de manuscrits à peintures, 1936-1938.

Lacombe, P. Livres d'heures imprimés au XVe et au XVIe siècle, conservés dans les bibliothèques publiques de Paris. Catalogue, Paris: Imprimerie Nationale, 1907.

La Grange, Marquis de. Hugues Capet, chanson de geste. Paris: Franck, 1864.

Långfors, A. "Notice sur deux livres d'heures enluminés du XVe siècle." Mémoires de la Société Néophilologique d'Helsingfors 5 (1909): 481-504.

Långfors, A. Les Incipit des poèmes français antérieurs au XVIe siècle. Paris: Champion, 1917.

Långfors, A. Le Roman de Fauvel par Gervais du Bus. Paris: SATF, 1919.

Larmat, J. "Prières au cours de tempêtes en mer." Senefiance 10: 347-60.

Lecoy, F. "Farce et jeu inédits tirés d'un manuscrit de Barbantane." Romania 92 (1971): 145-99.

Legge, M. Dominica, "St. Edmund's Merure de seinte Eglise." Modern Language Review 23 (1928): 475-6.

Legge, M. Dominica. "St. Edmund on the Hours." Modern Language Review 29 (1934): 72-4.

Legge, M. Dominica. Anglo-Norman in the Cloisters. Edinburgh: Edinburgh University Press, 1950.

Legge, M. Dominica. "Wanted - an Edition of St. Edmund's Merure." Modern Language Review 54 (1959): 72-4.

Legge, M. Dominica. Anglo-Norman Literature and its Background. Oxford: Clarendon, 1963.

Le Grand, L. Statuts d'Hôtels-Dieu et de léproseries. Recueil de textes du XIIe au XIVe siècle. Paris: Picard, 1901.

Legros, Huguette. "Les Prières d'Isembart et de Vivien, dissemblances et analogies: la fonction narrative de la prière." Senefiance 10: 361-73.

Lemaire, J. Meschinot, Molinet, Villon: témoignages inédits. Etude du Bruxellensis IV. 541, Brussels: Archives et Bibliothèques de Belgique, 1979.

Leroquais, V. Les Livres d'heures manuscrits de la Bibliothèque Nationale. 3 vols. Paris: Imprimerie Nationale, 1927.

Le Verdier, P. Guillaume Tasserie, Le Triomphe des Normands. Rouen: Société des Bibliophiles Normands, 1908.

Lodge, R.A. Etienne de Fougères. Le Livre des Manières. Geneva: Droz, 1979.

Looten, chanoine. "Note sur un livre d'heures de Jacques de Luxembourg." Bulletin du Comité flamand de France 6(1920): 147-65.

Malmberg, B. Le Roman du comte de Poitiers, poème français du XIIIe siècle. Lund: Gleerup, 1940.

Mandach, A. de. Chronique dite saintongeaise: texte franco-occitan inédit Lee. Halle: Niemeyer, 1970.

Martineau-Genieys, Christine. Edition des Lunettes des Princes de Jean Meschinot. Geneva: Droz, 1972.

Masson, Anne-Louise. Jean Gerson, sa vie, son temps, ses oeuvres. Lyon: Vitte, 1894.

Matzke, J.E. Les Oeuvres de Simund de Freine, Paris: SATF, 1909.

McCulloch, Florence. "The Funeral of Renart the Fox in a Walters Book of Hours." Journal of the Walters Art Gallery 25-26 (1962-1963): 8-26.

Meiller, A. Jehan du Prier dit le Prieur, Le Mystère du roy Advenir. Geneva: Droz, 1970.

Melander, G. Guibert d'Andrenas, chanson de geste. Paris: Champion, 1922.

Merk, C. Josef. Anschauungen über die Lehre und das Leben der Kirche im Altfranzösischen Heldenepos. Halle: Niemeyer, 1914.

Meyer, P. and Longnon, A. Raoul de Cambrai, chanson de geste. Paris: SATF, 1882.

Mitchneck, S.R. Yon or La Venjance Fromondin, a thirteenth-century chanson de geste of the Lorraine Cycle. New York: Institute of French Studies, 1935.

Mölk, U. and Wolfzettel, F. Répertoire métrique de la poésie lyrique française des origines à 1350. Munich: Fink, 1972.

Moldenhauer, G. "Nachweis älterer Französischen Handschriften in Portugiesischen Bibliotheken." ASNS 151 (1927): 69-76.

Morawski, J. Les Diz et proverbes des Sages. Paris: Presses Universitaires de France, 1924.

Mortier, R. Les Textes de la Chanson de Roland. 10 vols. Paris: Geste Francor, 1940-1949.

Mourin, L. Six Sermons français inédits de Jean Gerson. Paris: Vrin, 1946.

Naetebus, G. Die Nicht-lyrischen Strophenformen des Altfranzösischen, Leipzig: Hirzel, 1891.

Neuhaus, C. Adgars Marienlegenden nach der Londoner Handschrift Egerton 612. Heilbronn: Henninger, 1886.

Nitze, W.A. Robert de Boron, le Roman de l'Estoire dou Graal. Paris: Champion, 1927.

Omont, H. Fabliaux, dits et contes en vers français du XIIIe siècle. Facsimilé du ms. 837 de la Bibliothèque Nationale. Paris: Leroux, 1932.

Orth, M.D. "Geofroy Tory et l'enluminure. Deux livres d'heures de la Collection Doheny." Revue de l'Art 50 (1980): 40-7.

Ouy, G. "Simon de Plumetot (1371-1443) et sa bibliothèque." In Miscellanea codicologica F. Masai dicata MCMLXXIX. ed. P. Cockshaw et al. 2 vols. Ghent: Story-Scientia, 1979; 2: 353-81.

Panofsky, E. "The De Buz Book of Hours." Harvard Library Bulletin 3 (1949): 163-82.

Paris, G. and Raynaud, G. Le Mystère de la Passion d'Arnoul Gréban, publié d'après le ms. de Paris. Paris: Vieweg, 1878.

Paris, G. Orson de Beauvais, chanson de geste du XIIe Siècle. Paris: SATF, 1899.

Payen, J.C. Le Motif du Repentir dans la littérature française médiévale. Geneva: Droz, 1967.

Pellechet, Marie. Notes sur les livres liturgiques des diocèses d'Autun, Chalon et Mâcon. Paris: Champion, 1883.

Perdrizet, P. Le Calendrier parisien à la fin du moyen âge. Paris: Belles-Lettres, 1933.

Perrier, J.L. Le Siège de Barbastre, chanson de geste du XIIe siècle. Paris: Champion, 1926.

Piaget, A. and Picot, E. Oeuvres poétiques de Guillaume Alexis, prieur de Bucy. 3 vols. Paris: SATF, 1896-1908.

Picot, E. Le Livre et mistère du glorieux seigneur et martir Saint Adrien, publié d'après un manuscrit de Chantilly. Mâcon: Protat, 1895.

Picot, E. Notice sur Jacques le Lieur échevin de Rouen et sur ses Heures manuscrites. Rouen: Cagniard, 1913.

Plummer, J. Liturgical Manuscripts for the Mass and Divine Office. New York: Pierpont Morgan Library, 1964.

Plummer, J. The Hours of Catherine of Cleves. London: Barrie and Rockliff, 1966.

Plummer, J. The Last Flowering. French Paintings in Manuscripts 1420-1530 from American Collections. New York: Oxford University Press and Pierpont Morgan Library, 1982.

Pope, Mildred K. and Reid, T.B.W. The Romance of Horn by Thomas. 2 vols. Oxford: Anglo-Norman Text Society, 1955-1964.

Porter, L.C. La Fatrasie et le fatras. Geneva: Droz, 1960.

Preston, Jean. "Medieval Manuscripts at the Huntington. Supplement to Dr Ricci's Census." Chronica 21 (1977): 2-9.

Randall, Lilian M.C. "Games and the Passion in Pucelle's Hours of Jeanne d'Evreux." Speculum 47 (1972): 246-57.

Randall, Lilian M.C. "Originality and Flair in an early 15th Century Book of Hours: Walters 219." Gesta 22 (1981): 233-42.

Raynaud, G. Elie de Saint-Gille, chanson de geste. Paris: SATF, 1879.

Régnier, C. Les Rédactions en vers de la Prise d'Orange. Paris: Klincksieck, 1966.

Régnier, C. La Prise d'Orange, chanson de geste de la fin du XIIe siècle, 3rd ed. Paris: Klincksieck, 1970.

Reinhold, J. "Die Franko-Italienische Version des Bovo d'Antone." Zeitschrift für Romanische Philologie. 35 (1911): 554-607, 683-714; 36 (1912): 1-32.

Rézeau, P. "La Tradition des prières française médiévales. A propos d'un livre d'heures et de prières des Célestins de Metz (Metz, Bibl. mun., ms. 600)." Revue d'histoire des textes, 7 (1977): 153-84.

Rézeau, P. "Les Prières en français adressées aux saints dans les livres d'heures du XIVe au XVe siècle." Senefiance 10, 431-447.

Rézeau, P. Les Prières aux saints en français à la fin du moyen âge. 2 vols. Geneva: Droz, 1982-1983.

Ricci, Seymour de, and Wilson, W.J. Census of Medieval and Renaissance Manuscripts in the United States and Canada. 3 vols. New York: Wilson, 1936-1940.

Rivière, J.C. Les Poésies du trouvère Jacques de Cambrai. Geneva: Droz, 1978.

Roach, Eleanor. Le Roman de Mélusine ou Histoire de Lusignan par Coudrette. Paris: Klincksieck, 1982.

Robbins, H.W. Le Merure de seinte Eglise by Saint Edmund of Pontigny. Lewisburg: Robbins, 1925.

Robertson-Mellor, G. The Franco-Italian Rolands (V4). Salford: University of Salford, 1980.

Roncaglia, R. Poesia dell'età cortese. Milan: Nuova Accademia Editrice, 1961.

Roques, M. "L'Interpolation de Fauvel et le Comte d'Anjou." Romania 55 (1929): 548-551.

Roques, M. Jehan Maillart. Le Roman du comte d'Anjou. Paris: Champion, 1931.

Rosenberg, S.N. and Tischler, H. Chanter m'estuet. Songs of the Trouvères. London: Faber and Faber, 1981.

Rosenfeld, H. "Die Münchner Gebetsrolle Clm 28961: zur Buch- und Frommigskeitsgeschichte des 15. Jahrhunderts." Gutenberg Jahrbuch, 1976: 48-56.

Rossi, Marguerite. "La Prière de demande dans l'épopée." Senefiance 10: 449-75.

Runnalls, G.A. Le Mystère de saint Christofle (Bibliothèque Nationale, Réserve Yf 1606). Exeter: Exeter University, 1973.

Sakari, A. "Un livre d'heures médiéval se trouvant en Finlande." Neuphilologische Mitteilungen 73 (1972): 402-8.

Saly, Antoinette. "Le Thème de la descente aux enfers dans le Credo épique." Travaux de linguistique et de littérature ... Strasbourg 7 (1969): 47-63.

Santucci, Monique. "Les Prières dans les Faictz et Dictz de Molinet." Senefiance 10: 495-514.

Scheler, A. La Mort du roi Gormond, fragment unique d'une chanson de geste inconnue. Brussels: Olivier, 1876.

Scheludko, D. "Neues über das Couronnement Louis." Zeitschrift für Französische Sprache und Literatur 55 (1931): 425-74.

Scheludko, D. "Ueber das Altfranzösische Epische Gebet." Zeitschrift für Französische Sprache und Literatur 58 (1934): 67-86, 171-99.

Schläger, G. and Cloetta, W. "Die Altfranzösische Prosafassung des Moniage Guillaume." ASNS 97 (1896): 101-28, 241-82; 98 (1897): 1-58.

Senefiance 10 = La Prière au moyen âge (littérature et civilisation). Aix-en-Provence: Publications du C.U.E.R.M.A., 1981.

Sennewaldt, Clotilde. Les Miracles de sainte Geneviève, neu herausgegeben nach der einzigen Handschrift 1131 der Pariser Bibliothek Sainte-Geneviève. Frankfurt-am-Main: Diesterweg, 1937.

Sinclair, K.V. <u>Prières en ancien français. Nouvelles références,</u>
<u>renseignements complémentaires, indications bibliographiques,</u>
<u>corrections et tables des articles du Répertoire de Sonet.</u>
Hamden CT: Archon, 1978.

Sinclair, K.V. "The Need for a new critical edition of an important
Devotional Text by Guillaume Alexis." <u>Romance Notes</u> 20
(1979-1980): 429-33.

Sinclair, K.V. "Anglo-Norman Bidding Prayers from Ramsey Abbey"
<u>Mediaeval Studies</u> 42 (1980): 454-62.

Sinclair, K.V. <u>French Devotional Texts of the Middle Ages. A</u>
<u>Bibliographic Manuscript Guide.</u> 2 vols. London and Westport CT:
Greenwood Press, 1979-1982.

Sinclair, K.V. "Chancellor Gerson's Epitome of the Oratio Fidelium."
<u>Annuale Mediaevale</u> 21 (1981): 134-8.

Sinclair, K.V. "Une nouvelle Vie rimée de saint Jean-Baptiste en
ancien français." <u>Romania</u> 103 (1982): 529-46.

Sinclair, K.V. Review of <u>Senefiance</u> 10. <u>Zeitschrift für Romanische</u>
<u>Philologie</u> 99 (1983): 568-72.

Sinclair, K.V. "Anglo-Norman at Waterford. The Mute Testimony of MS.
Cambridge, Corpus Christi College 405." In <u>Medieval French</u>
<u>Textual Studies in Memory of T.B.W. Reid.</u> London: Anglo-Norman
Text Society, 1984: 219-38.

Sismarev, V.F. "Quelques traces de la librairie du Roi René dans le
fonds manuscrit de la Bibliothèque Publique." <u>Leningrad.</u>
<u>Publichnaia Biblioteka. Srednevekou'e v rukopisiakh.</u> 2 (1927):
143-92.

Soleil, F. <u>Les Heures gothiques et la littérature pieuse aux XVe et</u>
<u>XVI</u>^e <u>siècles.</u> Paris: Augé, 1882.

Sonet, J. <u>Répertoire d'incipit de prières en ancien français.</u> Geneva:
Droz, 1956.

Spanke, H. <u>G. Raynauds Bibliographie des Altfranzösischen Liedes neu</u>
<u>bearbeitet und ergänzt.</u> Leyden: Brill, 1955.

Spaziani, M. <u>Antica lirica francese.</u> Modena: Società Tipografica
Modenese, 1954.

Spencer, Eleanor P. "Dom Louis de Busco's Psalter." In <u>Gatherings in</u>
<u>Honor of Dorothy E. Miner,</u> ed. Ursula E. McCracken, Lilian M.C.
Randall, Richard H. Randall Jnr. Baltimore: Walters Art Gallery,
1974: 227-40.

Stengel, E. <u>Hervis von Metz, Vorgedicht der Lothringer Geste.</u> Dresden:
Gesellschaft für Romanische Literatur, 1903.

Stimming, A. <u>Der Anglo-Normannische Boeve de Haumtone.</u> Halle:
Niemeyer, 1899.

St. John's Seminary, Camarillo. Catalogue of Books and Manuscripts in the Estelle Doheny Collection, Los Angeles. 3 vols. Los Angeles: Edward L. Doheny Memorial Library, 1955.

Subrenat, J. "Quatre Patrenostres parodiques." Senefiance 10: 515-47.

Suchier, H. Les Narbonnais. 2 vols. Paris: SATF, 1898.

Tarbé, P. Romancero de Champagne. 2 vols. Reims: Dubois, 1863-1864.

Taylor, D.M. The Oldest Manuscripts in New Zealand. Wellington: Council for Educational Research, 1955.

Telle, E.V. Le Chevalier de Berquin. Brefve Admonition de la Maniere de prier. Le Symbole des Apostres de Jesuchrist (1525). Geneva: Droz, 1979.

Thomas, A. L'Entrée d'Espagne, chanson de geste franco-italienne. 2 vols. Paris: SATF, 1913.

Thompson, E.M. Customary of the Benedictine Monasteries of Saint Augustine, Canterbury and Saint Peter, Westminster. 2 vols. London: Henry Bradshaw Society, 1902-1904.

Toja, G. Lirica cortese d'oïl sec. XII-XIII. Bologna: Riccardo, 1966.

Van den Boogaard, N.H.J. Rondeaux et refrains du XIIe au début du XIII^{e}s. Collationnement, introduction et notes. Paris: Klincksieck, 1969.

Van Emden, W. Girart de Vienne de Bertrand de Bar-sur-Aube. Paris: SATF, 1977.

Vansteenberghe, E. "Quelques écrits de Jean Gerson. Textes inédits et étude." Revue des Sciences Religieuses 13 (1933): 165-85, 393-214; 14 (1934): 191-218, 370-95; 15 (1935): 532-66; 16 (1936): 33-46.

Viard, J. Les Grandes Chroniques de France - III. Paris: Société de l'Histoire de France, 1923.

Vieillard, Françoise. Bibliotheca Bodmeriana. Catalogues II: Manuscrits français du moyen âge. Cologny: Fondation Martin Bodmer, 1975.

Vising, J. Anglo-Norman Language and Literature. London: Oxford University Press, 1923.

Wallensköld, A. Les Chansons de Thibaut de Champagne roi de Navarre. Paris: SATF, 1925.

Wels, L.E. Theologische Streifzüge durch die altfranzösische Literatur. Vechta in O: Albertus-Magnus-Verlag der Dominikaner, 1937.

Whittredge, Ruth. La Nativité et le Geu des trois roys. Two Plays from Manuscript 1131 of the Bibliothèque Sainte-Geneviève, Paris. Bryn Mawr: Byrd, 1944.

Wieck, R.S. Late Medieval and Renaissance Illuminated Manuscripts 1350-1525 in the Houghton Library. Cambridge (Mass.): Harvard College Library, 1983.

Wilshere, A.D. Mirour de seinte Eglyse (St. Edmund of Abingdon's Speculum Ecclesiae). London: Anglo-Norman Text Society, 1982.

Winternitz, E. "The Hours of Charles the Noble." Cleveland Museum of Art Bulletin 52 (1965): 84-90.

Wixom, W.D. "The Hours of Charles the Noble." Cleveland Museum of Art Bulletin 52 (1965): 50-83.

Wixom, W.D. "The Hours of Charles the Noble." Burlington Magazine 108 (1966): 370 and 373, plates 47-51.

Wormald, F. and Giles, Phyllis M. A Descriptive Catalogue of the Additional Illuminated Manuscripts in the Fitzwilliam Museum. 2 vols. Cambridge: Cambridge University Press, 1982.

Yeandle, F.G. Girart de Vienne, chanson de geste. New York: Columbia University, 1931.

Zacour, N.P. and Hirsch, R. Catalogue of Manuscripts in the Libraries of the University of Pennsylvania to 1800. Philadelphia: University of Pennsylvania Press, 1965.

ABBREVIATIONS

Acq	=	Acquisition
Anon	=	Anonymous
ANTS	=	Anglo-Norman Text Society
Apost	=	Apostolic
ASNS	=	Archiv für das Studium der Neueren Sprachen und Literaturen
Attrib	=	Attribution, Attributed
BEC	=	Bibliothèque de l'Ecole des Chartes
Bibl	=	Bibliothèque, Biblioteca
Brit	=	British
Bull. SATF	=	Bulletin de la Société des Anciens Textes Français
c	=	Century
c̲	=	Circa
Capit	=	Capitular
Cat	=	Catalogue
Corr	=	Correct, Correction
Ed	=	Edited, Edition
EETS	=	Early English Text Society
Extr	=	Extract(s)
Fac	=	Faculté
FDTMA	=	Sinclair, French Devotional Texts of the Middle Ages
Fol	=	Folio(s)
Fr	=	Français, French
Frag	=	Fragment, Fragmentary
GRLMA	=	Grundriss der Romanischen Literaturen des Mittelalters
HLF	=	Histoire Littéraire de la France
Inc	=	Incipit
Lat	=	Latin
Libr	=	Library
Liturg	=	Liturgical
Misc	=	Miscellaneous, Miscellany
MLR	=	Modern Language Review
MMBL	=	Ker, Medieval Manuscripts in British Libraries
Ms(s)	=	Manuscript(s)
Mun	=	Municipal
Nac	=	Nacional
ND	=	Nostre Dame
NM	=	Neuphilologische Mitteilungen
Not. et extr.	=	Notices et Extraits des Manuscrits

Nouv	=	Nouvelle
Npnd	=	Neither place of publication nor date
NSJC	=	Nostre Seigneur Jesu Crist
O	=	Orison
P(p)	=	Page(s)
Pag	=	Paginated, Pagination
PQ	=	_Philological Quarterly_
Ps	=	Psalm(s)
Publ	=	Public
RBPH	=	_Revue Belge de Philologie et d'Histoire_
Ref	=	Reference
Refr	=	Refrain
Rev	=	Revue, Review
RF	=	_Romanische Forschungen_
RLR	=	_Revue des Langues Romanes_
Rubr	=	Rubric
S(s)	=	Saint(s)
SAFT	=	Société des Anciens Textes Français
Str	=	Stranieri
Suppr	=	Suppress
Univ	=	University
v	=	vide
v(v)	=	line(s) of verse
Var	=	variant
ZFSL	=	_Zeitschrift für Französische Sprache und Literatur_
ZRP	=	_Zeitschrift für Romanische Philologie_

ADDITIONS AND CORRECTIONS
TO INCIPITS 2379-5372

2379. Add Ref.: Mölk and Wolfzettel, no. 860, 70.
2384. Add Ref.: Mölk and Wolfzettel, no. 888, 1.
2411. Add Ed.: Rézeau, Saints, II, pp. 162-5.
2412. Add Ref.: Mölk and Wolfzettel, no. 1491, 1.
2414. Add Ref.: Mölk and Wolfzettel, no. 852, 12.
2419. Corr. Shelf-mark: WERNIGERODE, Gräflich Stolbergische Bibl., Za
       48 > NEW YORK, New York Public Libr., Spencer 56.
2427. Corr. Shelf-mark: WERNIGERODE, Gräflich Stolbergische Bibl., Za
       48 > NEW YORK, New York Public Libr., Spencer 56.
2447. Add Ref.: Mölk and Wolfzettel, no. 149, 1.
       Add Ed.: Omont, fol. 271r° (Facsimile of Bibl. nat., fr. 837).
2453. Corr. Shelf-mark: WERNIGERODE, Gräflich Stolbergische Bibl., Za
       48 > NEW YORK, New York Public Libr., Spencer 56.
2454. Add Ref.: Mölk and Wolfzettel, no. 435, 2.
2456. Add Ed.: E.J. Dobson and F.L. Harrison, Medieval English Songs,
       London, 1979, p. 110-116, 229-40; Rosenberg and Tischler,
       p. 143-6, no. 70.
       Add Ref.: Mölk and Wolfzettel, no. 272, 9a.
2457. Add Ref.: Mölk and Wolfzettel, no. 860, 9.
2462. Add Ref.: Mölk and Wolfzettel, no. 860, 102.
2463. Add Ref.: Mölk and Wolfzettel, no. 730, 3.
2465. Add Ref.: Lângfors, p. 15.
2466. Add Ref.: Mölk and Wolfzettel, no. 535, 1.
2467. Add Ref.: Mölk and Wolfzettel, no. 217, 26.
2470. Add Ref.: Lângfors, p. 17.
2474. Add ms.: ROUEN, Bibl. mun., 1064 (Y 226a), pp. 115-17, XVIc.
       Add Ref.: Rézeau, Saints, II, p. 338 n. 2, who mentions the
       Rouen codex.
2478. Add Ref.: Mölk and Wolfzettel, no. 626, 17.
2486. Add Ref.: Mölk and Wolfzettel, no. 1181, 1.
2496. Add Ed.: Rézeau, Saints, II, pp. 16-19.
2501. Add Ref.: Lângfors, p. 34.
2517. Add Ref.: Rézeau, Saints, I, pp. 171-2.
2519. Add Ref.: Rézeau, Saints, II, p. 127.
2521. Add Ref.: Mölk and Wolfzettel, no. 1209, 73.
2523. Corr. Shelf-mark: WERNIGERODE, Gräflich Stolbergische Bibl., Za
       48 > NEW YORK, New York Public Libr., Spencer 56.
       Corr. Title: First of a large group of intercessionary prayers
       to God invoking, in particular, the prophets and
       patriarchs of the Old Testament.
       Add ms.: OPORTO, Bibl. publ. mun., 619, fol. 89r°, XVc. Inc.:
       Biaus Dex, douz rois pardurables ... (no. 3963).
       Add ms.: METZ, Bibl. mun., 600, fol. 78r°-85v°, XVc., Hours of
       Paris and Prayer-book.
       Add Ref.: Rézeau, p. 167 (Metz codex).
2525. Corr. Shelf-mark: WERNIGERODE, Gräflich Stolbergische Bibl., Za
       48 > NEW YORK, New York Public Libr., Spencer 56.
2527. Corr. Shelf-mark: WERNIGERODE, Gräflich Stolbergische Bibl., Za
       48 > NEW YORK, New York Public Libr., Spencer 56.
2539. Add Ref.: Rézeau, Saints, II, p. 511 n. 3, believes that no.
       3570 is a paragraph of this prayer. Ibid, II, p. 530, he
       relates the text to nos. 417, 420, 1911, 1994, 2176.
2541. Corr. Text: qui a heure de midi > qui a heure de minuit...
2542. Corr. Shelf-mark: WERNIGERODE, Gräflich Stolbergische Bibl., Za
       48 > NEW YORK, New York Public Libr., Spencer 56.
2557. Corr. Shelf-mark: WERNIGERODE, Gräflich Stolbergische Bibl., Za
       48 > NEW YORK, New York Public Libr., Spencer 56.
2558. Corr. Shelf-mark: WERNIGERODE, Gräflich Stolbergische Bibl., Za
       48 > NEW YORK, New York Public Libr., Spencer 56.

2559. Corr. Shelf-mark: WERNIGERODE, Gräflich Stolbergische Bibl., Za
       48 > NEW YORK, New York Public Libr., Spencer 56.
2560. Corr. Shelf-mark: WERNIGERODE, Gräflich Stolbergische Bibl., Za
       48 > NEW YORK, New York Public Libr., Spencer 56.
2561. Corr. Shelf-mark: WERNIGERODE, Gräflich Stolbergische Bibl., Za
       48 > NEW YORK, New York Public Libr., Spencer 56.
2562. Corr. Shelf-mark: WERNIGERODE, Gräflich Stolbergische Bibl., Za
       48 > NEW YORK, New York Public Libr., Spencer 56.
2565. Add ms.: LIVERPOOL, Liverpool Cathedral, Chapter Libr., 36, end
       fly-leaves 2r°-3r°, late XIV-early XVc., Hours of Sarum.
2567. Corr. Shelf-mark: WERNIGERODE, Gräflich Stolbergische Bibl., Za
       48 > NEW YORK, New York Public Libr., Spencer 56.
2571. Add Ref.: Mölk and Wolfzettel, no. 717, 1.
2575. Corr. Shelf-mark: WERNIGERODE, Gräflich Stolbergische Bibl., Za
       48 > NEW YORK, New York Public Libr., Spencer 56.
2595. Add Ref.: Mölk and Wolfzettel, no. 1163, 5.
2596. Add Ref.: Mölk and Wolfzettel, no. 901, 2.
2598. Add ms.: PARIS, Bibl. nat., fr. 13167, fol. 62v°-64r°, late
       XVc., Hours of Paris.
2599. Add ms.: BALTIMORE, Walters Art Gallery, Walters 89, fol.
       137r°-139v°, late XIVc., Hours of Isabelle de Coucy.
       Add ms.: MANCHESTER, John Rylands Univ. Libr., French 143, fol.
       89r°-90r°, commencement XVc., Hours.
2602. Add Ref.: Mölk and Wolfzettel, no. 664, 1.
2606. Add Ref.: Mölk and Wolfzettel, no. 1262, 2.
2609. Add Ref.: Mölk and Wolfzettel, no. 217, 1.
2621. Add Ref.: Mölk and Wolfzettel, no. 675, 1.
2623. Add Ref.: Mölk and Wolfzettel, no. 674, 9.
2624. Add Ref.: Mölk and Wolfzettel, no. 870, 8.
2625. Add Ref.: Mölk and Wolfzettel, no. 933, 2.
2627. Add Ref.: Mölk and Wolfzettel, no. 446, 1.
2628. Add Ref.: Mölk and Wolfzettel, no. 309, 2.
2629. Add Ref.: Mölk and Wolfzettel, no. 626, 30.
       Add Ed.: Rosenberg and Tischler, p. 141-3, no. 69.
2636. Add Ref.: Bouly de Lesdain, Manuscrits didactiques, 1966, p.
       51.
2639. Add ms.: CHICAGO, Art Institute, 15.536, p. 257-60, c. 1400,
       Psalter.
2648. Add Ed.: M. Spaziani, Antica lirica francese, Modena, 1954, pp.
       97-99; Bec, Lyrique française, II, pp. 133-4.
       Add Ref.: Mölk and Wolfzettel, no. 291, 2.
2649. Add Ed.: Rézeau, Saints, II, pp. 57-61.
2659. Add Ref.: Bouly de Lesdain, Manuscrits didactiques, 1966, p.
       56.
2661. Add Ref.: Mölk and Wolfzettel, no. 1440, 1.
2662. Add Ed.: Martineau-Genieys, Lunettes des princes, p. xxxv, n.
2665. Suppress this item and transfer the information to no. 306.
2668. Add Ref.: Mölk and Wolfzettel, no. 968, 1.
2669. Add Ref.: Långfors, pp. 111-12; Betty Hill, Notes and Queries,
       n.s. 25 (1978), p. 398; Mölk and Wolfzettel, no. 217, 35;
       Rézeau, Saints, II, p. 127.
2672. Add Ref.: Mölk and Wolfzettel, no. 227, 1.
2678. Add Ref.: Mölk and Wolfzettel, no. 901, 54.
2682. Add Ref.: Monique Santucci in Senefiance no. 10, p. 504.
2689. Add Ref.: Mölk and Wolfzettel, no. 1186, 3.
2690. Add Ref.: Mölk and Wolfzettel, no. 1079, 24.
2692. Add Ref.: Mölk and Wolfzettel, no. 860, 96.
2694. Add Ref.: Mölk and Wolfzettel, no. 1418, 1.
2697. Add ms.: BALTIMORE, Walters Art Gallery, Walters 89, fol.
       153v°-156v°, late XIVc., Hours of Isabelle de Coucy.

2699. Add Ed.: ; Cremonesi, Lirica francese, 1955, pp. 167-9;
        Toja, Lirica cortese, 1966, p. 324-5, no. 99.
        Add Ref.: Mölk and Wolfzettel, no. 626, 4.
2700. Add Ref.: Mölk and Wolfzettel, no. 647, 1.
2702. Add Ref.: Mölk and Wolfzettel, no. 1515, 1.
        Add Ed.: Rosenberg and Tischler, p. 138-9, no. 67.
2703. Add Ref.: Mölk and Wolfzettel, no. 723, 1.
2704. Add Ref.: Mölk and Wolfzettel, no. 874, 2.
2705. Add Ref.: Mölk and Wolfzettel, no. 1226, 4.
2706. Add Ed.: Tarbé, Romancero de Champagne, I, p. 67.
        Add Ref.: Mölk and Wolfzettel, no. 192, 16.
2707. Add Ed.: Tarbé, Romancero de Champagne, I, pp. 72-3.
        Add Ref.: Mölk and Wolfzettel, no. 1083, 10.
2708. Add Ref.: Mölk and Wolfzettel, no. 1255, 3.
2709. Add Ref.: Mölk and Wolfzettel, no. 130, 1.
2710. Add Ed.: Tarbé, Romancero de Champagne, I, pp. 74-5; Bec,
        Lyrique française, II, pp. 69-70.
        Add Ref.: Mölk and Wolfzettel, no. 224, 1.
2711. Corr. Shelf-mark: WERNIGERODE, Gräflich Stolbergische Bibl., Za
        48 > NEW YORK, New York Public Libr., Spencer 56.
2712. Add ms.: PARIS, Bibl. de l'Arsenal, 2467, fol. 23r⁰, XVc.
        Add Ref.: Långfors, p. 86.
2713. Add Ref.: Mölk and Wolfzettel, no. 1275, 1.
2716. Add Ref.: Mölk and Wolfzettel, no. 689, 41.
2730. Add ms.: BALTIMORE, Walters Art Gallery, Walters 89, fol.
        157r⁰-160r⁰, late XIVc., Hours of Isabelle de Coucy.
2731. Add ms.: BALTIMORE, Walters Art Gallery, Walters 89, fol. 36v⁰,
        late XIVc., Hours of Isabelle de Coucy.
2732. Add Ed.: Cremonesi, pp. 202-4; Toja, Lirica cortese, 1966, pp.
        417-19, no. 134; Rosenberg and Tischler, p. 355-60, no.
        144.
        Add Ref. L. Clédat, La Poésie lyrique et satirique en France au
        moyen âge, Paris, 1893, pp. 194-5; Mölk and Wolfzettel,
        no. 1432, 1.
2742. Corr. Shelf-mark: WERNIGERODE, Gräflich Stolbergische Bibl., Za
        48 > NEW YORK, New York Public Libr., Spencer 56.
2745. Add Ref.: Wels, p. 7, n. 17; p. 12, n. 28.
2757. Add ms.: MONTPELLIER, Bibl. Fac. Ecole de Médecine, H. 339,
        fol. 93r⁰-93v⁰, XVIc.
2761. Add. Ed.: Craig, p. 48.
2762. Add ms.: STUTTGART, Württembergische Landesbibl., Brev. 75,
        fol. 41v⁰-42r⁰, XIVc., Hours.
2765. Add Ref.: Rézeau, Saints, II, p. 127.
2770. Add Ref.: Mölk and Wolfzettel, no. 902, 18.
2771. Add Ref.: Rézeau, Saints, II, p. 13.
2772. Add Ref.: Mölk and Wolfzettel, no. 902, 85.
2784. Add Ref.: Mölk and Wolfzettel, no. 902, 28.
        Add Ed.: Rosenberg and Tischler, p. 136-8, no. 66.
2792. Add ms.: LIVERPOOL, Merseyside County Museums, Mayer 12033,
        fol. 162r⁰-162v⁰, early XVc., Hours of Rouen. This text
        added by a later hand.
2793. Add ms.: PROVIDENCE, Brown Univ. Libr., C. 28. b. 4 (H.L.
        Koopman Collection), fol. 247v⁰-248v⁰, XVc., Hours.
2802. Add ms. MALIBU, J. Paul Getty Museum, Ludwig lX 4, fol.
        135v⁰-136r⁰, early XVc., Hours for Le Mans.
2803. Add Ed.: Bec, Lyrique française, II, p. 77.
2812. Add Ed.: M. Spaziani, Antica lirica francese, Modena, 1954, pp.
        94-7.
        Add Ref.: Mölk and Wolfzettel, no 1035, 2.
2822. Add Ed.: Rézeau, Saints, II, pp. 129-30.

2823.   Add Ref.: Mölk and Wolfzettel, no. 1186, 5.
2825.   Add Ref.: Mölk and Wolfzettel, no. 936, 1.
2829.   Add Ref.: Mölk and Wolfzettel, no. 739, 1.
2833.   Add   ms.:   NORWICH,   Castle   Museum,   158.926/4   f.,   fol.
        148r°-148v°, XIVc., Hours of Sarum.
2834.   Add   ms.:   NORWICH,   Castle   Museum,   158.926/4   f.,   fol.
        145r°-145v°, XIVc., Hours of Sarum.
2835.   Add   ms.:   NORWICH,   Castle   Museum,   158.926/4   f.,   fol.
        147v°-148r°, XIVc., Hours of Sarum.
2836.   Add   ms.:   NORWICH,   Castle   Museum,   158.926/4   f.,   fol.
        146r°-146v°, XIVc., Hours of Sarum.
2837.   Add   ms.:   NORWICH,   Castle   Museum,   158.926/4   f.,   fol.
        146v°-147r°, XIVc., Hours of Sarum.
2844.   Add Ed.: Bec, Lyrique française, I, pp. 146-7; II, pp. 67-8.
2848.   Add Ref.: F. Schalk and W.D. Lange, GRLMA, VI, 2, no. 7276;
        Betty Hill, Notes and Queries, n.s. 25 (1978), p. 398.
2850.   Add Ref.: Mölk and Wolfzettel, no. 517, 1.
2853.   Add ms.: PARIS, Bibl. nat., fr. 24429, fol. 49r°-51r°, XIIIc.
        Add Ref.: Bouly de Lesdain, Manuscrits didactiques, 1966, p.
        68.
2855.   Corr. Shelfmark: HEIDELBERG, Universitäts Bibl., 362ᵃ n. 28.
        XII. Hebraic > Or. 490.
2856.   Add Ref.: Mölk and Wolfzettel, no. 825, 1.
2857.   Add Ref.: Bouly de Lesdain, Manuscrits didactiques, 1966, p.
        51.
2863.   Add ms.: STUTTGART, Württembergische Landesbibl., Brev. 75,
        fol. 52r°-53v°, XIVc., Hours. Line 2: La mer ke estes a
        Jhesu...
2866.   Add Ref.: Mölk and Wolfzettel, no. 327, 1.
2869.   Corr. Shelf-mark: WERNIGERODE, Gräflich Stolbergische Bibl., Za
        48 > NEW YORK, New York Public Libr., Spencer 56.
2870.   Add Ed.: Bec, Lyrique française, II, pp. 68-9.
        Add Ref.: Mölk and Wolfzettel, no. 215, 3.
2877.   Add Ref.: Mölk and Wolfzettel, no. 233, 1.
2880.   Add Ref.: Rézeau, Saints, II, p. 57, who considers the text to
        be a life of the saint.
2881.   Add Ref.: Mölk and Wolfzettel, no. 1274, 1.
2882.   Add Ref.: Mölk and Wolfzettel, no. 965, 1.
2896.   Add Ref.: Rézeau, Saints, II, p. 320.
2913.   Add Ed.: Cremonesi, pp. 267-8; Toja, Lirica cortese, 1966, pp.
        378-9, no. 121.
        Add Ref.: Mölk and Wolfzettel, no. 645, 1.
2916.   Add ms.: CAMBRIDGE, Harvard College Libr., Typ. 304, fol.
        7v°-9v°, c. 1470, Hours.
2917.   Add Ed.: Cremonesi, pp. 177-9; B. Woledge, Penguin Book of
        French Verse, Harmondsworth, 1961, I, pp. 139-42; Toja,
        Lirica cortese, 1966, pp. 336-8, no. 103.
        Add Ref.: Mölk and Wolfzettel, no. 300, 1.
2918.   Add ms.: PARIS, Bibl. nat., fr. 19243, fol. 174v°-175r°, XVIc.
        Add Ref.: Rézeau, Saints, II, p. 384 (who lists the Paris ms.
        and several early ed.).
2922.   Add ms.: PARIS, Bibl. nat., fr. 19243, fol. 168r°-168v°, XVIc.
        Add Early Ed.: PARIS, Bibl. Ecole Nat. Sup. des Beaux-Arts,
        Masson, impr. 29, fol. B4v°-B5r°, XVIc.
        Add Ref.: Rézeau, Saints, II, p. 302 who records the Paris
        copies of XVIc.
2931.   Add Ref.: Mölk and Wolfzettel, no. 860, 21.
2934.   Add Ed.: Rivière, pp. 63-5.
        Add Ref.: Mölk and Wolfzettel, no. 1045, 8.
2940.   Add Ed.: Craig, p. 47.

2941. Add Ref.: Mölk and Wolfzettel, no. 901, 5.
2942. Add Ed.: Rivière, pp. 67-70.
       Add Ref.: Mölk and Wolfzettel, no. 1425, 1.
2953. Corr. Shelf-mark: WERNIGERODE, Gräflich Stolbergische Bibl., Za
       48 > NEW YORK, New York Public Libr., Spencer 56.
2961. Add Ed.: Omont, fol. 244v°-246r° (Facsimile of Bibl. nat., fr.
       837).
2966. Add Ref.: Mölk and Wolfzettel, no. 535, 10.
2967. Add Ed.: Bec, Lyrique française, II, pp. 74-77.
       Add Ref.: L. Clédat, La Poésie lyrique et satirique en France
       au moyen âge, Paris, 1893, pp. 181-2; Mölk and Wolfzettel,
       no. 760, 1.
2968. Corr. Shelf-mark: HEIDELBERG, Universitäts Bibl., 362^a n. 28.
       XII. Hebraic > Or. 490.
2977. Add Ed.: Bec, Lyrique française, I, p. 144, II, pp. 80-4.
       Add Ref.: Bouly de Lesdain, Manuscrits didactiques, 1966, p.
       56; Mölk and Wolfzettel, no. 330, 2.
2978. Add Ref.: Mölk and Wolfzettel, no. 674, 6.
2981. Corr. Shelf-mark on p. 200 of FDTMA, 1979, to read: PARIS,
       Bibl. nat., fr. 13901 > 13091. At the entry for the text
       on p. 81, the shelf-mark is correct.
2992. Add ms.: PROVIDENCE, Brown Univ. Libr., C. 28. b. 4 (H.L.
       Koopman Collection), fol. 199r°-200r°, XVc., Hours.
2995. Add Ref.: Bouly de Lesdain, Manuscrits didactiques, 1966, p.
       51.
3000. Add Ref.: Långfors, p. 176.
3007. Add Ref.: Bouly de Lesdain, Manuscrits didactiques, 1964-1965,
       p. 61.
3008. Add Ref.: Långfors, p. 179.
3011. Add Ed.: Bec, Lyrique française, II, pp. 65-6.
       Add Ref.: Mölk and Wolfzettel, no. 192, 10.
3016. Add ms.: PARIS, Bibl. nat., fr. 1593, fol. 180r°-181r°, XIIIc.
       where stanzas nos xxxvi-xlii, xliv, xlvi-l, li-liii have
       been integrated into the Art d'Amours by Guiart, as his
       stanzas nos. xlvii-liii, liv, lv-lix, lxii-lxiv.
       Add Ed.: A. Långfors, Not. et extr. des mss., 39, 2 (1916), pp.
       551-2.
3023. Add Ref.: Bouly de Lesdain, Manuscrits didactiques, 1966, p.
       51.
3029. Add ms.: LEEDS, Leeds Univ. Libr., Brotherton 5, fol.
       212r°-213r°, XVc., Hours of Rome. Inc.: Je te deprye tres
       debonnaire seigneur Jhesu Crist par icelle charité...
3035. Add Ref.: Rézeau, Saints, I, p. 199.
3037. Add Ref.: Bouly de Lesdain, Manuscrits didactiques, 1966, p.
       77; Rézeau, Saints, II, p. 444.
3039. Add ms.: BALTIMORE, Walters Art Gallery, Walters 222, fol.
       96r°-97r°, c. 1470, Hours of Poitiers. The text is
       composed of heptains.
       Add Ed.: Rézeau, Saints, II, pp. 25-7.
3040. Corr. Shelf-mark: NEW YORK, Collection Clara Peck > NEW YORK,
       Pierpont Morgan Libr., Morgan 1044.
3041. Add Ref.: Rézeau, Saints, II, pp. 273-4.
3048. Corr. Shelf-mark: WERNIGERODE, Gräflich Stolbergische Bibl., Za
       48 > NEW YORK, New York Public Libr., Spencer 56.
3064. Add ms.: BALTIMORE, Walters Art Gallery, Walters 91, fol.
       16r°-16v°, c. 1300, Prayer-book.
3081. Add Ref.: Bouly de Lesdain, Manuscrits didactiques, 1966, p.
       66.
3082. Add ms.: MALIBU, J. Paul Getty Museum, Ludwig IX. 4, fol.
       135r°-135v°, XVc., Hours for Le Mans.

3092.   Add ms.: MALIBU, J. Paul Getty Museum, Ludwig IX, 4, fol.
        136v°, early XVc., Hours for Le Mans.
3096.   Add Ref.: Mölk and Wolfzettel, no. 2, 11.
3098.   Add Ref.: Bouly de Lesdain, Manuscrits didactiques, 1966, p.
        76.
3100.   Add Ref.: Mölk and Wolfzettel, no. 1052, 1.
3101.   Add Ref.: Mölk and Wolfzettel, no. 865, 9.
        Add Ed.: Rosenberg and Tischler, p. 133-5, no. 64.
3102.   Add Ref.: Bec, Lyrique française, I, p. 148; Mölk and
        Wolfzettel, no. 1087, 2.
3105.   Add Ref.: Mölk and Wolfzettel, no. 81, 2.
3109.   Add Ed.: Bec, Lyrique française, II, pp. 72-4.
        Add Ref.: Mölk and Wolfzettel, no. 381, 7; V.F. Koenig,
        Romania, 99 (1978), pp. 255-63.
3114.   Corr. Shelf-mark: WERNIGERODE, Gräflich Stolbergische Bibl., Za
        48 > NEW YORK, New York Public Libr., Spencer 56.
3118.   Add Ed.: Rézeau, Saints, II, p. 130.
3122.   Add Ref.: Mölk and Wolfzettel, no. 1034, 23.
3123.   Add Ref.: Mölk and Wolfzettel, no. 979, 5.
3125.   Add Ref.: Mölk and Wolfzettel, no. 535, 2.
3126.   Add Ed.: Gallagher, 1976, p. 112.
3129.   Add Ed.: Gallagher, 1976, p. 213.
3130.   Add Ref.: Mölk and Wolfzettel, no. 4, 18.
3136.   Corr. Shelf-mark: HEIDELBERG, Universitäts Bibl., 362^a n. 28.
        XII. Hebraic > Or. 490.
3142.   Corr. ms.: COLLECTION UNKNOWN, olim Didot, Cat. de vente, 1882,
        p. 28, no. 14 > BALTIMORE, Walters Art Gallery, Walters
        212, fol. 202v°-207v°, late XVc., Hours.
        Add Title: Adoration of parts of the Virgin's Body (in the
        order: feet, womb, heart, breasts, hands, throat, lips,
        nostrils, ears and eyes).
3145.   Add ms.: CAMBRIDGE, Fitzwilliam Museum, Fitzwilliam 41-1950,
        fol. 63v°-64r°, c. 1425, Hours of Sarum for Margaret
        Beauchamp, wife of John Talbot.
3151.   Add Ref.: Mölk and Wolfzettel, no. 2, 15.
3154.   Add Ref.: Mölk and Wolfzettel, no. 1186, 4.
        Add Ed.: Rivière, pp. 75-77.
3158.   Add ms.: STUTTGART, Württembergische Landesbibl., Brev. 75,
        fol. 53v°-54v°, XIVc., Book of Hours, Use of Sarum.
3159.   Add Ed.: Ana Dominguez Rodriguez, Libros de horas, 1979, p. 49.
3161.   Add Ref.: Mölk and Wolfzettel, no. 1045, 49.
3170.   Add Ed.: Rézeau, Saints, II, pp. 339-40.
3172.   Add Ref.: Rézeau, Saints, II, p. 128.
3174.   Corr. Shelf-mark: WERNIGERODE, Gräflich Stolbergische Bibl., Za
        48 > NEW YORK, New York Public Libr., Spencer 56.
3177.   Add Ref.: Mölk and Wolfzettel, no. 772, 2.
3178.   Add Ref.: Mölk and Wolfzettel, no. 130, 2.
3182.   Add ms. HELSINKI, Collection Kuosmanen, no shelf-mark, fol.
        108v°-109r°, early XVc., Hours.
        Add Ed.: A. Sakari, NM, 73 (1972), p. 406 (ms. Kuosmanen at
        Helsinki).
3183.   Add Ed.: Cremonesi, pp. 131-3; Toja, Lirica cortese, 1966, p.
        268-70, no. 80.
        Add Ref.: Mölk and Wolfzettel, no. 1290, 1.
3184.   Add Ed.: Rivière, pp. 79-83.
        Add Ref.: Mölk and Wolfzettel, no. 962, 2.
3189.   Add ms.: HELSINKI, Collection Kuosmanen, no shelf-mark, fol.
        109r°, early XVc., Hours.

Add Ed.: A. Sakari, NM, 73 (1972), pp. 406-7 (ms. Kuosmanen at Helsinki).

Add Ref.: Rézeau, Saints, II, p. 514-5.

3191.   Add Ref.: Mölk and Wolfzettel, no. 181, 51.

3195.   Add ms.: CHICAGO, Art Institute, 15.536, p. 256, c. 1400, Psalter.

3197.   Add ms.: HELSINKI, Collection Kuosmanen, no shelf-mark, fol. 108r°, early XVc., Hours. The text is acephalous, commencing: je voiel vivre et morir ...

Add Ed.: A. Sakari, NM, 73 (1972), p. 402 (ms. Kuosmanen at Helsinki).

3198.   Add Ref.: This text can be related to no. 1178.

3203.   Add Ref.: Martineau-Genieys, Lunettes des princes, p. xxxiv.

3210.   Add Ref.: Mölk and Wolfzettel, no. 1169, 1.

3213.   Add Ref.: Mölk and Wolfzettel, no. 673, 14.

3214.   Add Ref.: Mölk and Wolfzettel, no. 254, 1.

3216.   Add Ed.: P. Aubry, Les plus anciens monuments de la musique française, Paris, 1905, p. 7 and pl. V.

3218.   Add Ed.: Rézeau, Saints, II, pp. 397-403.

3224.   Add ms.: COLOGNY, Bibl. Bodmeriana, 147, fol. 58r°-59r°, late XIIIc.

Add ms.: PARIS, Bibl. nat., fr. 24429, fol. 49r°, XIIIc.

Add Ref.: Vielliard, Bibliotheca Bodmeriana, II, p. 49-50.

3243.   Add ms.: MONTPELLIER, Bibl. Fac. Ecole de Médecine, H. 339, fol. 20v°-21v°, XVIc.

Add Ed.: Martineau-Genieys, Lunettes des princes, pp. 32-33 (base ms. Nantes).

3255.   Add Ed.: Rivière, pp. 85-6.

3256.   Add Ed.: J.A.W. Bennett, Selections from John Gower, Oxford, 1968, p. 132-33.

Corr. line numbering: 29905-45.

3276.   Add Ed.: Craig, p. 67.

3290.   Add ms.: MONTPELLIER, Bibl. Fac. Ecole de Médecine, H. 339, fol. 20r°-20v°, XVIc.

Add Ed.: Martineau-Genieys, Lunettes des princes, p. 32 (base ms. Nantes).

3295.   Add ms.: PARIS, Bibl. nat., fr. 19243, fol. 174r°-174v°, XVIc.

Add Ref.: Rézeau, Saints, II, p. 172, who announces the Paris codex and early editions.

3296.   Add ms.: Paris, Bibl. nat., fr. 19243, fol. 162v°-163r°, XVIc.

Add Ref.: Rézeau, Saints, II, p. 529, who records the Paris ms. and gives information about early imprints.

3315.   Add Ref.: Rézeau, Saints, I, p. 100, n. 2.

3326.   Add Ed.: Rézeau, Saints, II, pp. 373-4, who draws attention to the error in the inc. and who is thereby able to restore the prayer to S. Mathie or Mastidie.

3337.   Add Ref.: Martineau-Genieys, Lunettes des princes, pp. xxxiii-iv.

3343.   Add Ref.: Längfors, p. 251.

3345.   Add Ed.: Rézeau, Saints, I, pp. 152-7.

3346.   Add Ref.: Rézeau, Saints, II, p. 117.

3356.   Suppress the item, as it repeats no. 1496.

3357.   Add Ed.: Rézeau, Saints, II, pp. 545-6.

3358.   Add Ed.: Rézeau, Saints, II, pp. 331-2.

3365.   Add Ed.: Rézeau, Saints, II, pp. 449-51.

3375.   Add Ref.: Rézeau, Saints, II, p. 117.

3378.   Add Ref.: Rézeau, Saints, II, p. 500.

3380.   Corr. Shelf-mark: WERNIGERODE, Gräflich Stolbergische Bibl., Za 48 > NEW YORK, New York Public Libr., Spencer 56.

3405.   Add Ed.: Rosenberg and Tischler, p. 131-3, no. 63.
        Add Ref.: Mölk and Wolfzettel, no. 217, 15.
3407.   Add Ed.: Rosenberg and Tischler, p. 542-4, no. 215.
        Add Ref.: Mölk and Wolfzettel, no. 1209, 31.
3420.   Add Ref.: Långfors, p. 261; Mölk and Wolfzettel, no. 156, 3.
3422.   Add Ed.: Omont, fol. 298v° (Facsimile of Bibl. nat., fr. 837).
3423.   Add Ed.: Omont, fol. 294v° (Facsimilé of Bibl. nat., fr. 837).
3428.   Suppress the entry, it repeats information already recorded at
        no. 1618.
3431.   Add Ref.: Mölk and Wolfzettel, no. 1034, 19.
3432.   Add Ref.: Martineau-Genieys, Lunettes des princes, pp.
        xxxv-xxxvii.
3438.   Add Ref.: Rézeau, Saints, II, p. 297.
3450.   Add Ref.: Mölk and Wolfzettel, no. 192, 18.
3458.   Add Ed.: Rosenberg and Tischler, p. 139-41, no. 68.
        Add Ref.: Mölk and Wolfzettel, no. 1298, 2.
3459.   Add Ref.: Bec, Lyrique française, I, p. 146; Mölk and
        Wolfzettel, no. 1431, 4; J.H. Marshall, Romania, 98
        (1977), pp. 245-9.
3462.   Corr. Shelf-mark: HEIDELBERG, Universitäts Bibl., 362^a n. 28.
        XII. Hebraic > Or. 490.
3463.   Add Ref.: Mölk and Wolfzettel, no. 776, 4.
3465.   Add Ref.: Mölk and Wolfzettel, no. 770, 1.
3468.   Add Ref.: Mölk and Wolfzettel, no. 4, 5.
3473.   Add Ref.: Mölk and Wolfzettel, no. 761, 1; Ker, MMBL, III, p.
        318.
3477.   Add Ref.: Mölk and Wolfzettel, no. 708, 1.
3478.   Add Ref.: Mölk and Wolfzettel, no. 1083, 7.
3479.   Add Ref.: Mölk and Wolfzettel, no. 1083, 8.
3482.   Add Ref.: Mölk and Wolfzettel, no. 635, 3.
3483.   Add Ref.: Mölk and Wolfzettel, no. 689, 17.
3484.   Add Ref.: It is difficult to determine, before a critical ed.
        of the text is published, which is the correct inc. Is it
        as here, or as no. 1716?
3485.   Add Ref.: Mölk and Wolfzettel, no. 673, 2.
3486.   Add Ref.: Mölk and Wolfzettel, no. 875, 1.
3487.   Add Ref.: Mölk and Wolfzettel, no. 901, 44.
3490.   Add Ed.: Rivière, pp. 71-3.
        Add Ref.: Mölk and Wolfzettel, no. 1034, 9.
3491.   Add Ref.: Mölk and Wolfzettel, no. 942, 3.
3492.   Add Ref.: Långfors, p. 303; Mölk and Wolfzettel, no. 690, 2.
3493.   Add Ref.: Mölk and Wolfzettel, no. 689, 39.
3494.   Add Ref.: Långfors, p. 303; Mölk and Wolfzettel, no. 2, 2.
3497.   Add Ref.: Mölk and Wolfzettel, no. 636, 1.
3498.   Add Ref.: Bouly de Lesdain, Manuscrits didactiques, 1966, p.
        77.
3505.   Add Ref.: Mölk and Wolfzettel, no. 1303, 4.
3506.   Add Ref.: Mölk and Wolfzettel, no. 920, 1.
3508.   Add Ref.: Mölk and Wolfzettel, no. 694, 1.
3514.   Add Ref.: Mölk and Wolfzettel, no. 979, 2.
3521.   Add Ref.: Mölk and Wolfzettel, no. 1209, 47.
3536.   Add Ed.: Rosenberg and Tischler, p. 527-9, no. 209.
        Add Ref.: Mölk and Wolfzettel, no. 1079, 35.
3537.   Add ms.: PARIS, Bibl. nat., fr. 24314, fol. 145v°, late XVc.
        Add Ed.: Champion, Histoire poétique du XV^{e}s., II, pp. 237-8
                (base ms.: Paris, Bibl. nat., fr. 24314); Chesney, Fleurs
                de Rhétorique, pp. 7-8 (Paris, Bibl. nat., fr. 24314).
3541.   Add Ed.: Rivière, pp. 87-9; Rosenberg and Tischler, p. 540-1,
                no. 214; Bec, Lyrique française, II, p. 71.
        Add Ref.: Mölk and Wolfzettel, no. 75, 5.

3549. Add Ed.: Craig, p. 48.
3550. Add Ref.: Mölk and Wolfzettel, no. 768, 1.
3558. Add Ed.: Rosenberg and Tischler, p. 135-6, no. 65; Bec, Lyrique
       française, I, p. 144 and II, pp. 79-80.
       Add Ref.: Mölk and Wolfzettel, no. 957, 9.
3562. Add Ref.: Mölk and Wolfzettel, no. 1094, 2.
3564. Add ms.: BALTIMORE, Walters Art Gallery, Walters 459, fol.
       26r°-26v°, c. 1520, Prayer-book.
       Add ms.: MANCHESTER, John Rylands Univ. Libr., Lat. 52, fol.
       257r°-257v°, 1501, Book of Hours, Use of Rouen.
       Add ms.: SAN MARINO, Huntington Library, HM 1171, fol.
       167r°-167v°, late XVc., Book of Hours, Use of Paris.
       Add ms.: WADDESDON MANOR, James A. de Rothschild Collection,
       23, fol. 21v°, early XVIc., Hours of Rome.
3570. Add Ref.: Rézeau, Saints, II, p. 511 n. 3, believes this text
       is a paragraph of no. 2539.
3571. Add Ref.: Rézeau, Saints, II, p. 244.
3572. Corr. Shelf-mark: WERNIGERODE, Gräflich Stolbergische Bibl., Za
       48 > NEW YORK, New York Public Libr., Spencer 56.
3573. Add Ref.: Rézeau, Saints, II, p. 274 note.
3575. Add Ed.: Rézeau, Saints, II, pp. 301-2.
3578. Add Ed.: Rézeau, Saints, II pp. 539-40.
3581. Add Ed.: Rézeau, Saints, II, pp. 455-8, who sees this copy as
       belonging to the long version of this orison.
3584. Add Ed.: Rézeau, Saints, II, pp. 22-3.
3585. Suppress the item; as edited by Denomy, the inc. and the ms.
       shelf-mark are incorrect. The inc. is correctly given by
       Sonet, no. 1503. Cf. Rézeau, Saints, II, pp. 91-3.
3586. Add ms.: BEAUNE, Hôtel-Dieu, Layette 123, no. 4, fol. not
       indicated, early XVIc. hand.
       Add Ed.: Rézeau, Saints, II, pp. 84-6.
3587. Add Ed.: Rézeau, Saints, II, pp. 145-6.
3593. Corr. Shelf-mark: WERNIGERODE, Gräflich Stolbergische Bibl., Za
       48 > NEW YORK, New York Public Libr., Spencer 56.
3600. Add Ref.: Rézeau, Saints, II, p. 14.
3602. Add Ed.: Omont, fol. 300r°-301v° (Facsimile of Bibl. nat., fr.
       837); Aspland, Medieval French Reader, p. 195-8, 327-8.
3603. Corr. Shelf-mark: WERNIGERODE, Gräflich Stolbergische Bibl., Za
       48 > NEW YORK, New York Public Libr., Spencer 56.
3618. Add Ref.: Monique Santucci in Senefiance no. 10, pp. 505, and
       507; Rézeau, Saints, II, pp. 1-2.
3625. Add ms.: COLOGNY, Bibl. Bodmeriana, 147, fol. 59r°, late XIIIc.
       Add Ref.: Vielliard, Bibliotheca Bodmeriana, II, p. 50.
3685. Add ms.: PARIS, Bibl. nat., fr. 13167, fol. 67v°-69v°, late
       XVc., Hours of Paris.
3687. Add ms.: PARIS, Bibl. nat., fr. 13167, fol. 69v°-70r°, late
       XVc., Hours of Paris.
3690. Add ms.: CHICAGO, Art Institute, 15.536, p. 260-3, c. 1400,
       Psalter.
3712. Add ms.: PROVIDENCE, Brown Univ. Libr., C. 28. b. 4 (H.L.
       Koopman Collection), fol. 246v°-247r°, XVc., Hours.
3729. Add ms.: STUTTGART, Württembergische Landesbibl., Brev. 75,
       fol. 59v°, XIVc., Hours.
3739. Add ms.: PARIS, Bibl. nat., fr. 13167, fol. 70r°-71v°, late
       XVc., Hours of Paris.
       Add ms.: SAN MARINO (Calif.), Huntington Libr., HM 1129, fol.
       95v°-97r°, c. 1450, Hours of Paris.
3746. Add Ref.: Rézeau, Saints, II, p. 272.
3757. Add Ref.: Mölk and Wolfzettel, no. 535, 3.
3760. Add Ref.: Mölk and Wolfzettel, no. 757, 3.

3762. Add Ref.: Mölk and Wolfzettel, no. 860, 31.
3774. Add Ref.: Mölk and Wolfzettel, no. 1302, 4.
3775. Add Ed.: Rézeau, Saints, I, pp. 193-5.
3778. Add ms.: BALTIMORE, Walters Art Gallery, Walters 191, fol.
         148v°, early XVc., Book of Hours.
         Add ms.: BRUSSELS, Bibl. royale IV. 541, fol. 159r°, 1568.
         Inc.: Ainsi comme descent en la fleur la rousee ...
         Add ms.: PARIS, Bibl. nat., Rothschild 471, fol. 146r°, XVIc.
         Add Ref.: Keller, p. 643 (Vatican ms.); Lemaire, Meschinot,
         Molinet, Villon: Témoignages inédits, 1979, pp. 69-70.
3790. Add Ed.: Rézeau, Saints, II, pp. 340-3.
3797. Add ms. MALIBU, J. Paul Getty Museum, Ludwig IX.4, fol. 135v°,
         early XVc., Hours for Le Mans.
3799. Add ms.: MALIBU, J. Paul Getty Museum, Ludwig IX.4, fol. 134v°,
         early XVc., Hours for Le Mans.
3802. Text to suppress since, through a scribal blunder, it has
         become a truncated version of no. 2222; cf. Rézeau,
         Saints, II, p. 529 n. 2.
3804. Add ms.: MALIBU, J. Paul Getty Museum, Ludwig IX.4, fol.
         136r°-136v°, early XVc., Hours for Le Mans.
3805. Add ms. MALIBU, J. Paul Getty Museum, Ludwig IX.4, fol.
         134v°-135r°, early XVc., Hours for Le Mans.
3809. Add Ed.: Rézeau, Saints, II, pp. 119-21.
3815. Add Ed.: Rézeau, Saints, II, pp. 154-6, who notes that the text
         at no. 1583 is another copy.
3819. Add Ref.: Mölk and Wolfzettel, no. 860, 8.
3821. Add Ref.: Rézeau, Saints, II, p. 128.
3830. Add Ref.: Mölk and Wolfzettel, no. 1281, 1.
3831. Add Ref.: Mölk and Wolfzettel, no. 923, 13.
3835. Add ms.: BALTIMORE, Walters Art Gallery, Walters 89, fol.
         5r°-8r°, late XIVc., Hours of Isabelle de Coucy.
         Add ms.: LILLE, Bibl. mun., Godefroy 5 (147), fol. 17v°-19r°,
         XVc., Hours.
         Add ms.: SAN MARINO (Calif.), Huntington Libr., HM 1129, fol.
         20r°-21r°, c. 1450, Book of Hours in French, Use of Paris.
3840. Add Ref.: Mölk and Wolfzettel, no. 962, 5.
3843. Add Ed.: Rézeau, Saints, II, pp. 334-5.
3844. Add Ref.: Rézeau, Saints, II, p. 126.
3845. Add Ref.: Lângfors, p. 438; Mölk and Wolfzettel, no. 850, 6.
         Add Ed.: Tarbé, Romancero de Champagne, I, pp. 76-9.
3846. Add Ed.: Omont, fol. 297r° (Facsimile of Bibl. nat., fr. 837).
3850. Add Ed.: Omont, fol. 317v°-318r° (Facsimile of Bibl. nat., fr.
         837).
3851. Add Ed.: Omont, fol. 297r° (Facsimile of Bibl. nat., fr. 837).
3852. Add Ed.: Bec, Lyrique française, II, pp. 77-9.
         Add Ref.: Mölk and Wolfzettel, no. 1048, 15.
3855. Add Ref.: Rézeau, Saints, II, p. 500.
3856. Add Ref.: Mölk and Wolfzettel, no. 860, 19.
3863. Add Ed.: Craig, p. 48.
3864. Add Ref.: One may compare with this item the nos 1943 and 5202
         about the "Trois Verités".
3877. Add Ref.: M. Bambeck in Neuphilologische Mitteilungen, 76
         (1975), pp. 372-88 (discusses the Credo content of the
         prayer).
3886. Add ms.: BALTIMORE, Walters Art Gallery, Walters 102, fol.
         2r°-2v°, c. 1300, Psalter - Book of Hours.
         Add ms.: NORWICH, Castle Museum, 158.926/4f., fol. 25r°-25v°,
         XIVc., Hours of Sarum.
         Add Ref.: McCulloch, p. 22-23.

3907. Add ms.: BALTIMORE, Walters Art Gallery, Walters 102, fol.
       80r°-80v°, c. 1300, Psalter - Book of Hours.
       Add ms.: NORWICH, Castle Museum, 158.926/4f., fol. 18v°-19r°,
       XIVc., Hours of Sarum.
       Add Ref.: McCulloch, p. 23.
3909. Add ms. BALTIMORE, Walters Art Gallery, Walters 102, fol.
       81v°-82r°, c. 1300, Psalter - Book of Hours.
       Add ms.: NORWICH, Castle Museum, 158.926/4f., fol. 20v°-21r°,
       XIVc., Hours of Sarum.
       Add Ref.: McCulloch, p. 23.
3911. Add ms.: BALTIMORE, Walters Art Gallery, Walters 102, fol.
       76r°-76v°, c. 1300, Psalter - Book of Hours.
       Add ms.: NORWICH, Castle Museum, 158.926/4 f., fol. 13v°-14r°,
       XIVc., Hours of Sarum.
       Add Ref.: McCulloch, p. 23.
3919. Add ms.: BALTIMORE, Walters Art Gallery, Walters 102, fol.
       78r°, c. 1300, Psalter - Book of Hours.
       Add ms.: NORWICH, Castle Museum, 158.926/4 f., fol. 16r°-16v°,
       XIVc., Hours of Sarum.
       Add Ref.: McCulloch, p. 23.
3924. Add ms.: BALTIMORE, Walters Art Gallery, Walters 102, fol.
       83r°-83v°, c. 1300, Psalter - Book of Hours.
       Add ms.: NORWICH, Castle Museum, 158.926/4 f., fol. 22v°-23v°,
       XIVc., Hours of Sarum.
       Add Ref.: McCulloch, p. 23.
3925. Add ms.: BALTIMORE, Walters Art Gallery, Walters 102, fol.
       74r°-74v°, c. 1300, Psalter - Book of Hours. Inc.: A
       laudes li Jeus a tere cheyent ...
       Add ms.: NORWICH, Castle Museum, 158.926/4 f., fol. 11v-12r°,
       XIVc., Hours of Sarum.
       Add Ref.: McCulloch, p. 23.
3929. Add Ed.: J. de Caluwé in Senefiance no. 10, p. 159 (using
       Mortier); Robertson-Mellor, pp. 104-5.
3934. Add Ed.: J. de Caluwé in Senefiance no. 10, p. 170 (using
       Mortier).
3936. Add ms.: METZ, Bibl. mun., 600, fol. 89v°, XVc., Hours of Paris
       and Prayer-book.
       Add Ref.: One of a large series of prayers, the first being no.
       2523; Rézeau, p. 167.
3937. Add ms.: METZ, Bibl. mun., 600, fol. 81v°, XVc., Hours of Paris
       and Prayer-book.
       Add Ref.: One of a large number of prayers, the first being no.
       2523; Rézeau, p. 167.
3940. Add Ref.: Långfors, p. 15; Bouly de Lesdain, Manuscrits
       didactiques, 1966, p. 57.
3941. Add Ref.: Mölk and Wolfzettel, no. 217, 1.
3942. Add ms.: BRUSSELS, Bibl. royale, IV. 144, fol. 11v°-12r°, XVc.
3952. Add ms.: BALTIMORE, Walters Art Gallery, Walters 89, fol.
       113v°-115v°, late XIVc., Hours of Isabelle de Coucy.
       Add ms.: SAN MARINO (Calif.), Huntington Libr., HM 1129, fol.
       68r°-69r°, c. 1450, Book of Hours in French, Use of Paris.
3962. Add ms.: METZ, Bibl. mun., 600, fol. 170r°-170v°, XVc., Hours
       of Paris and Prayer-book.
       Add Ref.: Rézeau, pp. 177-8.
3963. Add Ref.: This inc. is a variant of no. 2523.
3966. Ad Ed.: Gallagher, 1976, p. 114.
3972. Add ms.: BALTIMORE, Walters Art Gallery, Walters 89, fol.
       131v°-132v°, late XIVc., Hours of Isabelle de Coucy.
       Add ms.: SAN MARINO (Calif.), Huntington Libr., HM 1129, fol.
       76r°, c. 1450, Book of Hours in French, Use of Paris.

3981. Add ms.: METZ, Bibl. mun., 600, fol. 167v°-168r°, XVc., Hours
       of Paris and Prayer-book.
       Add Ref.: Rézeau, p. 177.
3990. Add ms.: METZ, Bibl. mun., 600, fol. 81r°-81v°, XVc., Hours of
       Paris and Prayer-book.
       Add Ref.: One of a large group of orisons, the first being no.
       2523; Rézeau, p. 167.
3993. Add Ref.: Mölk and Wolfzettel, no. 351, 1.
3997. Add ms.: METZ, Bibl. mun., 600, fol. 84v°-85r°, XVc., Hours of
       Paris and Prayer-book. The inc. omits "Biaus".
       Add Ref.: One of a series of prayers, the first being no. 2523;
       Rézeau, p. 167.
4018. Add ms.: CHICAGO, Art Institute, 15.5.36, pp. 270-2, c. 1400,
       Psalter.
4031. Add Ref.: Mölk and Wolfzettel, no. 851, 9.
4035. Add Ed.: J. de Caluwé in Senefiance no. 10, p. 160 (using
       Mortier); Robertson-Mellor, pp. 156-7.
4041. Add ms.: PARIS, Bibl. nat., fr. 15216, fol. 4v°-9r°, XVc.
4049. Add ms.: PARIS, Bibl. nat., fr. 13269, fol. 39v°-40r°, XVc.
4057. Add Ref.: Mölk and Wolfzettel, no. 1186, 5.
4059. Add Ref.: Mölk and Wolfzettel, no. 860, 106.
4060. Add Ref.: Mölk and Wolfzettel, no. 449, 3.
4097. Add ms.: NEW YORK, Pierpont Morgan Libr., Morgan 239, fol.
       121r°-123v°, XVc., Book of Hours, Use of Orleans.
       Add Ref.: This version of the "Obsecro te" is close to that
       recorded as no. 472.
4105. Add Ed.: J. de Caluwé in Senefiance no. 10, p. 172 (using
       Mortier).
4106. Add Ed.: J. de Caluwé in Senefiance no. 10, p. 165 (using
       Mortier).
4107. Add Ed.: J. de Caluwé in Senefiance no. 10, p. 169 (using
       Mortier).
4108. Add Ed.: J. de Caluwé in Senefiance no. 10, p. 162 (using
       Mortier).
4109. Add Ed.: J. de Caluwé in Senefiance no. 10, pp. 173 and 178
       (using Mortier).
4110. Add Ed.: J. de Caluwé in Senefiance no. 10, pp. 172 and 177-8
       (using Mortier).
4111. Add Ed.: J. de Caluwé in Senefiance no. 10, p. 164 (using
       Mortier).
4113. Add Ed.: J. de Caluwé in Senefiance no. 10, p. 165 (using
       Mortier).
4120. Add Ed.: J. de Caluwé in Senefiance no. 10, p. 176 (using
       Mortier).
4122. Add Ref.: Mölk and Wolfzettel, no. 1034, 29.
4129. Add Ref.: Mölk and Wolfzettel, no. 29, 1.
4130. Add Ref.: Mölk and Wolfzettel, no. 1298, 5.
4131. Add Ref.: Mölk and Wolfzettel, no. 125, 1.
4133. Add Ref.: Mölk and Wolfzettel, no. 900, 2.
4134. Add Ref.: Mölk and Wolfzettel, no. 904, 1.
4136. Add Ref.: Mölk and Wolfzettel, no. 1209, 23.
4139. Add ms.: METZ, Bibl. mun., 600, fol. 85v°, XVc., Hours of Paris
       and Prayer-book.
       Add Ref.: One of a large number, the first being no. 2523;
       Rézeau, p. 167.
4146. Add ms.: PARIS, Bibl. nat., fr. 13167, fol. 73v°-74r°, late
       XVc., Hours of Paris.
4162. Add ms.: MANCHESTER, John Rylands Univ. Libr., French 143, fol.
       88r°-89r°, early XVc., Hours.

4167.   Add ms.: BALTIMORE, Walters Art Gallery, Walters 89, fol. 66v°,
          79r°, 86v°, 103r°, late XIVc., Hours of Isabelle de Coucy.
        Add ms.: SAN MARINO (Calif.), Huntington Libr., HM 1129, fol.
          57r°, 62r°, 67r°, 72v°, 78v°, 81v, c. 1450, Book of Hours
          in French, Use of Paris.
4189.   Add Ed.: A. Roncaglia, Poesia dell'età cortese, Milan, 1961, p.
          80; Aspland, Medieval French Reader, p. 48 and 296.
4191.   Add Ed.: J. de Caluwé in Senefiance no. 10, p. 158 (using
          Mortier); Robertson-Mellor, p. 102.
4198.   Add ms.: BALTIMORE, Walters Art Gallery, Walters 89, fol.
          148r°-153v°, late XIVc., Hours of Isabelle de Coucy.
4202.   Add Ed.: J. de Caluwé in Senefiance no. 10, p. 163 (using
          Mortier).
4203.   Add Ed.: J. de Caluwé in Senefiance no. 10, p. 162 (using
          Mortier).
4204.   Add Ed.: J. de Caluwé in Senefiance no. 10, p. 169 (using
          Mortier).
4210.   Add ms.: NEW YORK, New York Public Libr., Spencer 56, fol.
          285v°, XIVc., Hours of Blanche de France, Duchess of
          Orleans.
4221.   Add Ed.: Gallagher, 1976, pp. 266-7.
4256.   Add Ed.: Craig, pp. 48-49.
4264.   Add Ref.: Huguette Legros in Senefiance no. 10, pp. 361-73.
4270.   Add ms.: METZ, Bibl. mun., 600, fol. 84v°, XVc., Hours of Paris
          and Prayer-book.
        Add Ref.: One of a group of orisons, the first being no. 2523;
          Rézeau, p. 167.
4279.   Add Ref.: Mölk and Wolfzettel, no. 1158, 1.
4304.   Add ms.: METZ, Bibl. mun., 600, fol. 50r°-51v°, XVc., Hours of
          Paris and Prayer-book.
        Add Ref.: Rézeau, p. 162.
4320.   Add Ref.: Mölk and Wolfzettel, no. 964, 1.
4321.   Add Ed.: Gallagher, 1976, p. 221.
4322.   Add Ed.: Gallagher, 1976, pp. 238-9.
4326.   Add ms.: PARIS, Bibl. nat., fr. 13167, fol. 66r°-67v°, late
          XVc., Hours of Paris.
4323.   Corr. Shelf-mark: BALTIMORE, Walters Art Gallery, 317, olim
          Ashburnham-Barrois 238 > 590.
        Add ms.: PARIS, Bibl. nat., fr. 18623, fol. 96r°, c. 1460.
        Add ms.: PARIS, Bibl. nat., fr. 19167, fol. 242v°, late XVc.
        Add ms.: PARIS, Bibl. nat., fr. 24383, fol. 48v°, late XVc.
        Add Ed.: Roach, p. 345, vv. 7136-44 (base ms.: CARPENTRAS,
          Bibl. mun., 406).
        Add Ref.: Many mss. of the Roman de Mélusine do not contain
          these lines. See also nos. 516, 672, 689, 1836, 4331 for
          other lines occurring at the end of the Roman. Roach, p.
          75 considers vv. 7021-152 of the Roman as a litany, but
          does not mention Sonet.
4331.   Corr. Shelf-mark: BALTIMORE, Walters Art Gallery, 317, olim
          Ashburnham-Barrois 238 > 590.
        Add ms.: PARIS, Bibl. nat., fr. 18623, fol. 96r°, c. 1460.
        Add ms.: PARIS, Bibl. nat., fr. 19167, fol. 242v°, late XVc.
        Add ms.: PARIS, Bibl. nat., fr. 24383, fol. 48v°, late XVc.
        Add Ed.: Roach, p. 345, vv. 7128-35 (base ms.: CARPENTRAS,
          Bibl. mun., 406).
        Add Ref.: Roach, p. 75 considers vv. 7021-152 as a litany, but
          does not mention Sonet. See also the nos. 516, 672, 689,
          1836, 4323.
4337.   Add ms.: LEEDS, Leeds Univ. Libr., Brotherton 4, fol. 202v°,
          Hours of Rome. Here the text has 10 vv.

4338. Add Ed.: Gallagher, 1976, pp. 148.
4343. Add Ed.: Gallagher, 1976, pp. 237-8.
4345. Add ms.: METZ, Bibl. mun., 600, fol. 83r°, XVc., Hours of Paris
       and Prayer-book.
       Add Ref.: One of a series of orisons, the first being no. 2523;
       Rézeau, p. 167.
4348. Add ms.: METZ, Bibl. mun., 600, fol. 79r°-81r°, XVc., Hours of
       Paris and Prayer-book.
       Add Ref.: One of a large group of prayers, the first of which
       is no. 2523; Rézeau, p. 167.
4375. Add ms.: METZ, Bibl. mun., 600, fol. 85r°, XVc., Hours of Paris
       and Prayer-book.
       Add Ref.: One of a group of orisons which commence with no.
       2523; Rézeau, p. 167.
4381. Add ms.: METZ, Bibl. mun., 600, fol. 85r°, XVc., Hours of Paris
       and Prayer-book.
       Add Ref.: One of a large group of orisons, the first being no.
       2523; Rézeau, p. 167.
4389. Add ms.: PARIS, Bibl. nat., fr. 15216, fol. 17r°-26r°, XVc.
       Inc.: E ! tres doulx Dieu, ayes mercy de moy selon ta
       grant misericorde ...
4398. Add Ed.: Rézeau, Saints, II, pp. 23-4.
4399. Add Ref.: Mölk and Wolfzettel, no. 702, 4.
4414. Add Ed.: Rézeau, Saints, II, p. 515 n. 1.
4416. Add Ref.: Perdrizet, pp. 31-2.
4419. Add Ed.: J. de Caluwé in Senefiance no. 10, pp. 170 and 175
       (using Mortier).
4423. Add Ed.: J. de Caluwé in Senefiance no. 10, pp. 173-4 (using
       Mortier).
4424. Add Ed.: J. de Caluwé in Senefiance no. 10, pp. 160-1 (using
       Mortier); Robertson-Mellor, pp. 210-212.
4426. Add Ed.: J. de Caluwé in Senefiance no. 10, pp. 179-80 (using
       Mortier).
4427. Add Ed.: J. de Caluwé in Senefiance no. 10, p. 176 (using
       Mortier).
4437. Add Ed.: J. de Caluwé in Senefiance no. 10, p. 165 (using
       Mortier).
4438. Add ms.: ROUBAIX, Archives Municipales, no shelf-mark, fol.
       131v°-132r°, XVc., Prayer-book of Jacques de Luxembourg.
4441. Add ms.: MONTPELLIER, Bibl. Fac. Ecole de Médecine, H. 339,
       fol. 10r°-10v°, XVIc.
       Add Ed.: Martineau-Genieys, Lunettes des princes, pp. 16-17
       (base ms. is Nantes).
4458. Add Ed.: Craig, p. 48.
4469. Add Ref.: Mölk and Wolfzettel, no. 941, 1.
4476. Add Ref.: Mölk and Wolfzettel, no. 985, 1.
4487. Add Ref.: S. Debenedetti in Atti della Reale Accademia delle
       Scienze di Torino, 57 (1921-1922), pp. 617-24.
4496. Add ms.: PARIS, Bibl. nat., fr. 15216, fol. 38r°-41r°, XVc.
       Inc. De parfons lieux j'ay crié a toy, Sire ...
4511. Add ms.: PROVIDENCE, Brown Univ. Libr., C. 28. b. 4 (H.L.
       Koopman Collection), fol. 233v°-234r°, XVc., Hours. Inc.:
       Je me confesse a Dieu le pere tout puissant et a la
       benoite Vierge Marie et a tous sains et a toutes sainctes
       ...
4513. Add ms.: HAGUE (THE), Koninkl. Bibl., 78. J. 49, fol.
       479r°-484r°, XVc.
4515. Add Ref.: Mölk and Wolfzettel, no. 1083, 12.
4516. Add Ref.: Mölk and Wolfzettel, no. 1233, 29.
4519. Add Ref.: Mölk and Wolfzettel, no. 1209, 51.

4539. Add ms.: PARIS, Bibl. Sainte-Geneviève, 2694, fol. lv°, XVc., this text added late XVIc.
Add ms.: PARIS, Private Collection, LF 13, fol. 170r°-171r°, early XVIc., Prayer-book.
Add Ref.: Rézeau, Saints, II, p. 437, who announces the two Paris mss. and several early printed copies. In most copies the fourth word is 'sainct'.

4557. Add Ref.: Mölk and Wolfzettel, no. 678, 1.

4577. Add Ed.: Robertson-Mellor, pp. 155-6.

4597. Add Ed.: Rosenberg and Tischler, p. 9-11, no. 6; Bec, Lyrique française, II, pp. 66-7.
Add Ref.: Mölk and Wolfzettel, no. 120, 8.

4598. Add Ref.: Mölk and Wolfzettel, no. 924, 7.

4614. Add Ref.: Mölk and Wolfzettel, no. 232, 1.

4617. Add Ed.: Gallagher, 1976, pp. 161-2.

4632. Add Ref.: Mölk and Wolfzettel, no. 1079, 55.

4646. Add Ref.: Rézeau, Saints, II, pp. 418-19.

4654. Add ms.: CAMBRIDGE, Fitzwilliam Museum, McClean 76, fol. 56v°-57v°, XIV-XVc., Hours of Paris.

4688. Add ms.: BALTIMORE, Walters Art Gallery, Walters 89, fol. 116r°-118r°, late XIVc., Hours of Isabelle de Coucy.
Add ms.: METZ, Bibl. mun., 600, fol. 34v°-35r°, XVc., Book of Hours (Use of Paris) and Prayer-book.
Add ms.: SAN MARINO (Calif.), Huntington Libr., HM 1129, fol. 69r°-69v°, c. 1450, Book of Hours in French, Use of Paris.
Add Ref.: Rézeau, p. 159 (Metz ms.).

4706. Add ms.: BALTIMORE, Walters Art Gallery, Walters 439, fol. 300r°-302v°, c. 1500, Book of Hours. Rubric: Cy s'ensieut ung bon et salutaire advertissement pour a toute heure dire a nostre seigneur et premier; inc.: Mon Dieu, j'ay pechié contre vostre bonté souveraine dont il me desplait ...

4741. Ad ms.: BALTIMORE, Walters Art Gallery, Walters 89, fol. 23r°-24v°, late XIVc., Hours of Isabelle de Coucy.
Add ms.: METZ, Bibl. mun., 600, fol. 12v°, XVc., Hours of Paris and Prayer-book. Inc.: Pere nostre qui es es cieulx ...
Add ms.: SAN MARINO (Calif.), Huntington Libr., HM 1129, fol. 26v°-27r°, c. 1450, Book of Hours in French, Use of Paris.
Add Ref.: Rézeau, p. 158 (Metz ms.).

4743. Add ms.: PROVIDENCE, Brown Univ. Libr., C. 28. b. 4 (H.L. Koopman Collection), fol. 234r°-234v°, XVc., Hours. Inc.: Nostre pere qui es es cieulx; ton nom soit sainctifié; adviegne nous ton regne ...

4778. Add ms.: PARIS, Private Collection, LF 13, fol. 168v°-170r°, XVIc., Prayer-book.
Add Ref.: Rézeau, Saints, II, p. 448, who records the Paris codex and several early editions of the text.

4789. Add Ed.: Tarbé, Romancero de Champagne, I, p. 5.

4807. Add ms.: BALTIMORE, Walters Art Gallery, Walters 89, fol. 57v°-59r°, late XIVc., Hours of Isabelle de Coucy.
Add ms.: LILLE, Bibl. mun., Godefroy 5 (147), fol. 49v°-50r°, XVc., Hours.

4812. Add ms.: METZ, Bibl. mun., 600, fol. 109v°, XVc., Hours of Paris and Prayer-book.
Add Ref.: Rézeau, p. 170.

4814. Add Ed.: Craig, p. 69.

4830. Add Ed.: Rézeau, Saints, II, pp. 150-3, who publishes the text from an early printed edition.

4876. Add ms.: METZ, Bibl. mun., 600, fol. 126r°-127v°, XVc., Hours
       of Paris and Prayer-book.
       Add Ref.: Rézeau, p. 173.
4936. Add Ref.: Mölk and Wolfzettel, no. 248, 2.
4957. Add ms.: LONDON, British Libr., Harley 4354, fol. 103r°-103v°,
       late XIIIc.
4965. Add ms.: VATICAN CITY, Bibl. apost., Reg. lat. 182, fol.
       292v°-294r°, XIVc., Breviary of Saint-Quiriace de Provins.
       This text added in XVc. Inc.: En ceste crainte de vie
       inexcusable ... (no. 5779).
       Add Early Ed.: PARIS, Bibl. nat., Rés. D. 5616 and Ye 831,
       Louenges des benoistz sainctz et sainctes de paradis, fol.
       tt 2r°-v°, Paris, Vérard; VERSAILLES, Bibl. mun., M. 129
       (Lacombe 109 quater).
       Add Ed.: Rézeau, Saints, II, pp. 392-6 (London codex not
       listed).
4970. Add Ref.: Långfors, p. 268; Champion, Histoire poétique du XVe
       siècle, I, pp. 197-215; C.S. Shapley, Studies in French
       Poetry of the Fifteenth Century, The Hague, 1970, pp.
       1-31; G. Gros in Senefiance no. 10, p. 325.
4971. Add Ref.: Molinet, Faictz et Dictz, S.A.T.F. III (1939), pp.
       1030-1.
4990. Add ms.: BALTIMORE, Walters Art Gallery, Walters 89, fol.
       139v°-144r°, late XIVc., Hours of Isabelle de Coucy.
4994. Add ms.: MANCHESTER, John Rylands Univ. Libr., French 143, fol.
       90r°-91v°, early XVc., Hours.
4995. Add ms.: BRUSSELS, Bibl. royale, IV. 144, fol. 10v°-11v°, XVc.
       Add ms.: HAGUE (THE), Koninkl. Bibl., 78. J. 49, fol.
       432v°-433r°, XVc.
       Add ms.: PARIS, Bibl. nat., fr. 24863, fol. 176r°-177v°, XVc.
       The pentasyllabic line is missing from each of the nine
       stanzas.
       Add ms.: VIENNA, Oesterreichische Nationalbibliothek, 3391,
       fol. 321v°-323v°, late XVc. Inc.: Le dieu d'amours doivent
       regracier ... (no. 4625).
       Add Ref.: P-Y. Badel in Romania, 97 (1976), p. 370, n. 3.
5004. Add Ref.: Text attributed to Gerson and also known as the
       "Complainte des ames du purgatoire"; it concludes with an
       octosyllabic quatrain, rhyming aabb. The work includes a
       prayer often rubricated separately, inc. Nostre pere qui
       es es cieulx, combien que je vostre povre creature ...
       (no. 6158).
       Add ms.: METZ, Bibl. mun., 530, fol. 92r°-94v°, XVc.
       Add ms.: METZ, Bibl. mun., 600, fol. 90r°-90v°, XVc., Hours of
       Paris and Prayer-book.
       Add ms.: PARIS, Bibl. nat., fr. 25552, fol. 25v°-29r°, XVc.
       Add ms.: ROUBAIX, Archives Municipales, no shelf-mark, fol.
       126r°-136r°, XVc., Prayer-book of Jacques de Luxembourg.
       Add Ed.: Glorieux, Gerson: Oeuvres complètes, VII, 1, pp. 363-7
       (base ms. Paris).
       Add Ref.: Rézeau, p. 167 (Metz 600).
5023. Add ms.: PARIS, Private Collection, LF 13, fol. 178r°-178v°,
       early XVIc., Prayer-book.
       Add Ref.: Rézeau, Saints, II, p. 156.
5053. Add ms.: METZ, Bibl. mun., 600, fol. 78v°, XVc., Hours of Paris
       and Prayer-book.
       Add Ref.: One of a large group of prayers, the first of which
       is recorded at no. 2523; Rézeau, p. 167.

5055.   Add ms.: GRENOBLE, Bibl. mun., 2093 (R 7853), fol. 108v°, XVc.
        Add ms.: OXFORD, Bodleian Libr., Rawlinson, e 18, fol. 78v°,
        XVc.
        Add ms.: PARIS, Bibl. nat., fr. 1370, fol. 152v°, XVc.
        Add ms.: POITIERS, Bibl. mun., 95 (350), fol. prel. vi, XVc.
        Add Ed.: Rézeau, Saints, I, p. 201, who adds the above mss. to
        the Cambridge one.
5056.   Add Ed.: Rézeau, Saints, II, pp. 175-9.
5067.   Add Ed.: Rézeau, Saints, II, pp. 80-1, who includes here
        information from no. 2306.
5074.   Add Ref.: Micheline de Combarieu in Senefiance no. 10, p. 105.
5091.   Add ms.: METZ, Bibl. mun., 600, fol. 83r°, XVc., Hours of Paris
        and Prayer-book.
        Add Ref.: One of a group of orisons, the first being no. 2523;
        Rézeau, p. 167.
5096.   Add Ref.: Mölk and Wolfzettel, no. 1102, 1.
5112.   Add Ed.: J. de Caluwé in Senefiance no. 10, p. 163 (using
        Mortier).
5117.   Add ms.: METZ, Bibl. mun., 600, fol. 83r°-83v°, XVc., Hours of
        Paris and Prayer-book.
        Add Ref.: One of a series, the first being no. 2523; Rézeau, p.
        167.
5123.   Add ms.: METZ, Bibl. mun., 600, fol. 85v°, XVc., Hours of Paris
        and Prayer-book.
        Add Ref.: One of a series of prayers, the first being no. 2523;
        Rézeau, p. 167.
5124.   Add ms.: METZ, Bibl. mun., 600, fol. 82r°-82v, XVc., Hours of
        Paris and Prayer-book.
        Add Ref.: One of a large number of prayers, the first being no.
        2523; Rézeau, p. 167.
5125.   Add ms.: METZ, Bibl. mun., 600, fol. 83v°, XVc., Hours of Paris
        and Prayer-book.
        Add Ref.: One of a series, the first of which is no. 2523;
        Rézeau, p. 167.
5127.   Add ms.: METZ, Bibl. mun., 600, fol. 84r°-84v°, XVc., Hours of
        Paris and Prayer-book.
        Add Ref.: One of a series of prayers, the first is no. 2523;
        Rézeau, p. 167.
5132.   Add ms.: METZ, Bibl. mun., 600, fol. 82v°-83r°, XVc., Hours of
        Paris and Prayer-book.
        Add Ref.: One of a series, the first being no. 2523; Rézeau, p.
        167.
5142.   Add ms.: METZ, Bibl. mun., 600, fol. 108v°-109r°, XVc., Hours
        of Paris and Prayer-book.
        Add Ref.: Rézeau, pp. 169-70.
5167.   Add ms.: METZ, Bibl. mun., 600, fol. 84r°, XVc., Hours of Paris
        and Prayer-book.
        Add Ref.: One of a series, the first orison being no. 2523;
        Rézeau, p. 167.
5173.   Add ms.: METZ, Bibl. mun., 600, fol. 108r°-108v°, XVc., Hours
        of Paris and Prayer-book.
        Add Ref.: Rézeau, p. 169.
5176.   Add ms.: METZ, Bibl. mun., 600, fol. 85v°, XVc., Hours of Paris
        and Prayer-book.
        Add Ref.: One of a large group of prayers, the first being no.
        2523; Rézeau, p. 167.
5177.   Add ms.: METZ, Bibl. mun., 60, fol. 84v°, XVc., Hours of Paris
        and Prayer-book.
        Add Ref.: One of a group of prayers, the first being no. 2523;
        Rézeau, p. 167.

5178. Add ms.: METZ, Bibl. mun., 600, fol. 85v°, XVc., Book of Hours
          and Prayer-book.
       Add Ref.: One of a group of orisons, the first of which is no.
          2523; Rézeau, p. 167.
5187. Add ms.: METZ, Bibl. mun., 600, fol. 108v°, XVc., Hours of
          Paris and Prayer-book.
       Add Ref.: Rézeau, p. 169.
5188. Add ms.: METZ, Bibl. mun., 600, fol. 85r°-85v°, XVc., Hours of
          Paris and Prayer-book.
       Add Ref.: One of a long series, the first being no. 2523;
          Rézeau, p. 167.
5194. Corr. Title: Third in order of transcription and binding, but
          Fifth in the series of Seven.
       Add ms.: PARIS, Bibl. nat., fr. 15216, fol. 26r°-38r°, XVc.
5195. Add ms.: PARIS, Bibl. nat., fr. 15216, fol. 41r°-48r°, XVc.
5196. Add ms.: METZ, Bibl. mun., 600, fol. 82v°, XVc., Hours of Paris
          and Prayer-book.
       Add Ref.: One of a series, the first being no. 2523; Rézeau, p.
          167.
5197. Add ms.: METZ, Bibl. mun., 600, fol. 84r°, XVc., Hours of Paris
          and Prayer-book.
       Add Ref.: One of a series, the first being no. 2523; Rézeau, p.
          167.
5198. Add ms.: CAMBRAI, Bibl. mun., 130 (126), fol. 77v°, XVc., Book
          of Hours.
       Add ms.: EDINBURGH, Edinburgh Univ. Libr., 309, fol. 141r°,
          late XVc., Hours of Rome.
       Add ms.: HAGUE (THE), Koninkl. Bibl., 78. J. 49, fol. 464r°,
          XVc.
       Add ms.: POITIERS, Bibl. mun., 95 (350), fol. 42r°, XVc.
       Add ms.: ROUBAIX, Archives Municipales, no shelf-mark, fol.
          5v°-6r°, XVc., Prayer-book of Jacques de Luxembourg.
       Add Ed.: Glorieux, Gerson: Oeuvres complètes, VII, 1, p. 204
          (base ms.: Paris, B.N. fr. 25551).
       Add Ref.: Before standing alone anonymously in devotional
          collections, the "Trois Verités" (prologue, three central
          sections, conclusion, resp. nos. 2372, 5202, 5198, 5199,
          5272) belonged to Jean Gerson's Miroir de l'ame alias Dix
          Commandements de la loy, inc.: Gloire soit a Dieu en qui
          pour le salut ...

5199. Add ms.: CAMBRAI, Bibl. mun., 130 (126), fol. 77v°, XVc.,
          Hours.
       Add ms.: EDINBURGH, Edinburgh Univ. Libr., 309, fol.
          141r°-142v°, late XVc., Hours of Rome.
       Add ms.: HAGUE (THE), Koninkl. Bibl., 78. J. 49, fol. 464r°,
          XVc.
       Add ms.: POITIERS, Bibl. mun., 95 (350), fol. 42r°, XVc.
       Add ms.: ROUBAIX, Archives Municipales, no shelf-mark, fol.
          6r°, XVc., Prayer-book of Jacques de Luxembourg.
       Add Ed.: Glorieux, Gerson: Oeuvres complètes, VII, 1, p. 204
          (base ms.: Paris, B.N. fr. 25551).
       Add Ref.: Before standing alone anonymously in devotional
          collections, the "Trois Verités" (prologue, three central
          sections, conclusion, resp. nos. 2372, 5202, 5198, 5199,
          5272) belonged to Jean Gerson's Miroir de l'ame alias Dix
          Commandements de la loy, inc.: Gloire soit a Dieu en qui
          pour le salut ...

5202. Add ms.: CAMBRAI, Bibl. mun., 130 (126), fol. 77v°, XVc., Book
       of Hours.
       Add ms.: EDINBURGH, Edinburgh Univ. Libr., 309, fol. 141r°,
       late XVc., Hours of Rome.
       Add ms.: HAGUE (THE), Koninkl. Bibl., 78. J. 49, fol.
       463v°-464r°, XVc.
       Add ms.: POITIERS, Bibl. mun., 95 (350), fol. 42r°, XVc.
       Add ms.: ROUBAIX, Archives Municipales, no shelf-mark, fol.
       5v°, XVc., Prayer-book of Jacques de Luxembourg.
       Add Ed.: Glorieux, Gerson: Oeuvres complètes, VII, 1, p. 204
       (base ms.: Paris, B.N. fr. 25551).
       Add Ref.: Before standing alone anonymously in devotional
       collections, the "Trois Verités" (prologue, three central
       sections, conclusion, resp. nos. 2372, 5202, 5198, 5199,
       5272) belonged to Jean Gerson's Miroir de l'ame alias Dix
       Commandements de la loy, inc.: Gloire soit a Dieu en qui
       pour le salut ...
5224. Add ms.: PARIS, Bibl. nat., fr. 15216, fol. 9r°-17r°, XVc.
       Corr. Title: First in order of transcription and binding, but
       Third in the series of Seven (Copenhagen ms.).
5225. Corr. Title: Fourth in order of transcription and binding, but
       First in the series of Seven (Copenhagen ms.).
       Add ms.: PARIS, Bibl. nat., fr. 15216, fol. 1r°-4v°, XVc.
5256. Add Ref.: Mölk and Wolfzettel, no. 1160, 2.
5260. Add Ref.: Mölk and Wolfzettel, no. 860, 46.
5272. Add ms.: CAMBRAI, Bibl. mun., 130 (126), fol. 78r°-78v°, XVc.,
       Hours.
       Add ms.: HAGUE (THE), Koninkl. Bibl., 78. J. 49, fol. 464r°,
       XVc.
       Add ms.: POITIERS, Bibl. mun., 95 (350), fol. 42v°-43v°, XVc.
       Add ms.: ROUBAIX, Archives Municipales, no shelf-mark, fol.
       6r°-7r°, XVc., Prayer-book of Jacques de Luxembourg.
       Add Ed.: Glorieux, Gerson: Oeuvres complètes, VII, 1, p. 204
       (base ms.: Paris, B.N. fr. 25551).
       Add Ref.: Before standing alone anonymously in devotional
       collections, the "Trois Verités" (prologue three central
       sections, conclusion, resp. nos. 2372, 5202, 5198, 5199,
       5272) belonged to Jean Gerson's Miroir de l'ame alias Dix
       Commandements de la loy, inc.: Gloire soit a Dieu en qui
       pour le salut ...
5299. Add Ref.: Mölk and Wolfzettel, no. 493, 5.
5302. Corr. Description: This text is not in prose, as stated after
       consulting only the London ms. It is composed of 24
       quatrains of decasyllables and a concluding distich.
       Add ms.: METZ, Bibl. mun., 600, fol. 139r°-141r°, XVc., Hours
       of Paris and Prayer-book.
       Add Ed.: Rézeau, Saints, II, pp. 476-80.
       Add Ref.: Rézeau, p. 175. No mention of the London codex.
5306. Add Ed.: J. de Caluwé in Senefiance no. 10, p. 158 (using
       Segre).
       Add Ref.: S. Debenedetti, in Atti della Reale Accademia delle
       Scienze di Torino, 57 (1921-1922), pp. 617-24.
5307. Add Ed.: J. de Caluwé in Senefiance no. 10, p. 164 (using
       Mortier).
5308. Add Ed.: J. de Caluwé in Senefiance no. 10, p. 171 (using
       Mortier).
5309. Add Ed.: J. de Caluwé in Senefiance no. 10, p. 159 (using
       Mortier); Robertson-Mellor, pp. 132-3.
5310. Add Ed.: J. de Caluwé in Senefiance no. 10, p. 158 (using
       Mortier); Robertson-Mellor, pp. 102-3.

5311.   Add Ed.: A. Roncaglia, Poesia dell'età cortese, Milan, 1961, p.
        82; Aspland, Medieval French Reader, p. 49 and 296; J. de
        Caluwé in Senefiance no. 10, p. 158 (using Segre).
        Add Ref.: S. Debenedetti, in Atti della Reale Accademia delle
        Scienze di Torino, 57 (1921-1922), pp. 617-24; P. Ariès,
        The Hour of our Death, London, 1981, p. 17.
5312.   Add Ed.: Robertson-Mellor, p. 105; J. de Caluwé in Senefiance
        no. 10, p. 159 (using Mortier).
5318.   Add ms.: LILLE, Bibl. mun., Godefroy 5 (147), fol. 54r°-54v°,
        XVc., Hours.
        Add ms.: METZ, Bibl. mun., 600, fol. 23r°-23v°, XVc., Book of
        Hours (Use of Paris) and Prayer-book.
        Add Ref.: Rézeau, pp. 158-9.
5331.   Add ms.: BALTIMORE, Walters Art Gallery, Walters 89, fol.
        129v°-130v°, late XIVc., Hours of Isabelle de Coucy.
        Add ms.: SAN MARINO (Calif.), Huntington Libr., HM 1129, fol.
        42r°-42v° and 75r°-75v°, c. 1450, Book of Hours in French,
        Use of Paris.
5333.   Add Ref.: Mölk and Wolfzettel, no. 826, 1.
5339.   Add Ed.: J. de Caluwé, in Senefiance no. 10, p. 177 (using
        Mortier).
5343.   Add Ed.: Rosenberg and Tischler, p. 7-9, no. 5.
        Add Ref.: Mölk and Wolfzettel, no. 192, 20.
5352.   Add ms.: MANCHESTER, John Rylands Univ. Libr., French 143, fol.
        91v°-93r°, early XVc., Hours.
5353.   Add ms.: BALTIMORE, Walters Art Gallery, Walters 89, fol.
        144r°-148r°, late XIVc., Hours of Isabelle de Coucy.
5369.   Add Ed.: J. de Caluwé in Senefiance no. 10, p. 177 (using
        Mortier).
5372.   Add Ed.: J. de Caluwé, in Senefiance no. 10, p. 175 (using
        Mortier).

INCIPITS 5376-6875

A

*   A ! ...

     See also the alphabetical order: Ha ! ...

5376.   A ! Deus, <u>fet il</u>, beau rey de paraÿs,
        Ky de la Virgine en Bedleem nasquis
        E en la beneyte croiz mort pur nus suffris
        E en le sepulcre fustes ensevelis ...

        Prayer to Jesus by Boeve: Boeve de Haumtone, Anglo-Norman
          version (vv. 1243-54).

        LOUVAIN, Bibl. de l'Univ., G. 170 (olim Didot, Cat. de vente,
          1878, p. 16, no. 30), XIIIc., the folio for the prayer was
          not recorded before the ms. was destroyed in World War II.
          Inc. : Hey ! <u>dist Boves</u>, roi de paraïs...

        PARIS, Bibl. nat., nouv. acq. fr., 4532, fol. 82v° (olim 28v°),
          XIVc.

        <u>Ed.</u>: Stimming, pp. 50-1 (text of both mss. given). <u>Ref.</u>: Merk,
          p. 188, n. 17; Labande, p. 78, n. 5.

5377.   A ! Dieu mon pere, ayez merchi de moy ...

        Variant of the inc.: Dieu mon pere, aies mercy de moy ... (no.
          5640).

5378.   A ! Jesu Crist, je vous mercye.
        En tous les lieux ou j'ay esté ...

        Christofle gives thanks to Jesus: Mystère de saint Christofle
          (vv. 2301-10).

        <u>Early Ed.</u>: in 4° Gothic, Paris, Veuve Jean Trepperel and Jean
          Jehannot, n.d. (<u>c</u>. 1515). <u>Ed.</u>: Runnalls, p. 72.

5379.   A ! pour Dieu, je vous pri que nul jor ne vous passe que une
foiz au mainz au vespre devant le couchier vous n'en cerchiez
en privé lieu ...

Prologue to a version of the Hours of the Cross in prose.

LONDON, British Libr., Royal 16. E. XII, fol. 306rº-308vº,
XIVc.

5380.   A ! Sire, a toy louer tous dis
Doy bien mettre mon intention ...

Orison to God by the hero: Mystère de saint Christofle (vv.
409-19).

Early Ed.: in 4º Gothic, Paris, Veuve Jean Trepperel and Jean
Jehannot, n.d. (c. 1515). Ed.: Runnalls, p. 17.

5381.   A ! toy seigneur, Jhesucrist filz de Dieu le pere ...

Variant of the inc.: Jhesucrist, filz de Dieu le pere, toy qui
es Dieu des anges ... (no. 945).

5382.   A ! tres glorieux, puissant Dieu,
Toy doy je bien regracier ...

Adam gives thanks to God: "Mystere de la Nativité" (vv.
106-11).

LONDON, British Libr., Additional 38860, fol. 2vº, XVIIIc. Copy
of a lost ms.

PARIS, Bibl. Sainte-Geneviève, 1131, Fol. 1vº, XVc.

Ed.: Whittredge, p. 99.

5383.   A ceste ymage
Je fais hommaige
Tant nette et clere
Ou nom de celle ....

Orison to the Virgin; 17 six-line stanzas rhyming aabccb.

MANCHESTER, John Rylands Univ. Libr., French 143, fol.
161rº-163vº, early XVc., Hours.

5384.   A chascune de cez heures canoniques devés avoir en vostre cuer
grant devocion et recorder celle passion ...

Epilogue to the Heures de la Croix; prose.

MANCHESTER, John Rylands Univ. Libr., French 143, fol. 87vº,
early XVc., Hours.

5385.   A complie li donnerent la sepulture et mirent son precieux
corps en sepulchre ...

Compline of the Heures de la Croix; prose.

MANCHESTER, John Rylands Univ. Libr., French 143, fol. 87r°, early XVc., Hours.

5386. A complie pensez que a cele heure fu nostre douz amis loial Jhesucrist mis u seputre, son precieus cors mult tormenté ...

Compline of the Hours of the Cross in prose; the redaction's prologue begins A ! pour Dieu ... (no. 5379).

LONDON, British Lib., Royal 16. E. XII, fol. 312v°-313r°, XIVc.

5387. A heure de complie donne au sepulchre le corps de Jhesucrist noble en esperance de vie a venir ....

Hours of the Cross: Compline, in prose, but possibly once in rhyme.

SAN MARINO (Calif.), Huntington Libr., HM 1129, fol. 83r°-83v°, c. 1450, Hours of Paris.

5388. A heure de midi fut Jhesus crucifiés et loiés entre deus larrons pendus ...

Sext of the Heures de la Croix; prose.

MANCHESTER, John Rylands Univ. Libr., French 143, fol. 84v°-85r°, early XVc., Hours.

5389. A heure de nonne li esperis le fil de Dieu criat a haulte voix: Hely ! et commandat son ame ...

Nones of the Heures de la Croix; prose.

MANCHESTER, John Rylands Univ. Libr., French 143, fol. 85v°, early XVc., Hours.

5390. A heure de nonne Nostre Seigneur Jhesus expira, 'hely ! hely !' criant. L'ame au pere commanda ....

Hours of the Cross: Nones, in prose, but possibly once in rhyme.

SAN MARINO (Calif.), Huntington Libr., HM 1129, fol. 82v°-83r°, c. 1450, Hours of Paris.

5391. A houre de prime fut Jhesus meneis a Pylate et accusez par faulz tesmongnaige ...

Prime of the Heures de la Croix; prose.

MANCHESTER, John Rylands Univ. Libr., French 143, fol. 83v°, early XVc., Hours.

5392. A heure de prime mené est Jhesus a Pilate; le menu peuple le fiert ...

Hours of the Cross: Prime, in prose, but possibly once in rhyme.

SAN MARINO (Calif.), Huntington Libr., HM 1129, fol. 82r°, c. 1450, Hours of Paris.

5393. A heure de sexte Jhesus est en la crois clavellé et avec les larrons pendant est despité ...

Hours of the Cross: Sext, in prose, but possibly once in rhyme.

SAN MARINO (Calif.), Huntington Libr., HM 1129, fol. 82v°, c. 1450, Hours of Paris.

5394. A heure de tierce il fut desvestus et batus et aprés revestus de porpre ...

Terce of the Heures de la Croix; prose.

MANCHESTER, John Rylands Univ. Libr., French 143, fol. 84r°, early XVc., Hours.

5395. A heure de vespre fut li doulz Jhesucrist despandus et mis jus de la crois et descloés ...

Vespers of the Heures de la Croix; prose.

MANCHESTER, John Rylands Univ. Libr., French 143, fol. 86r°-86v°, early XVc., Hours.

5396. A joinctes mains, devotement
De cueur entier, piteusement ...

Orison to S. Sebastian; 66 vv. rhyming in pairs.

AVIGNON, Bibl. mun., 1904, fol. 82r°-83v°, XVIc., Prayer-book.

Ed. Rézeau, Saints, II, pp. 476-8.

5397. A la povre du pain pour Dieu. Je suy la povre affamee qui suy mise entre deulx tablez; l'une est chargee des viandes du monde ...

"Oroison devisee par parties sus la quarte demande de la patenostre", in the Mendicité spirituelle by Jean Gerson.

BRUSSELS, Bibl. royale, IV. III, fol. 210v°-211v°, XVc.

LYON, Bibl. de la Ville, 1249 (1121), fol. 33r°-34v°, XVc.

PARIS, Bibl. de l'Arsenal, 2113, fol. 74v°-77v°, XVc.

PARIS, Bibl. de l'Arsenal, 2121, fol. 21v°-24r°, XVc.

VIENNA, Oesterreichische Nationalbibl., 2574, fol. 240r°-241v°, XVc.

Screening of mss. is incomplete.

Ed.: Glorieux, Gerson: Oeuvres complètes, VII, 1, pp. 245-7.

5398. A la premiere heure, c'est a dire a matines, vous devez penser
comment li benoit douz Dieu Jhesucrist, roiz de gloire,
loiaus espous des ames, se mist ...

Matins of the Hours of the Cross in prose; the prologue for
this redaction begins A ! pour Dieu ... (no. 5379).

LONDON, British Libr., Royal 16. E. XII, fol. 308v°-309r°,
XIVc.

5399. A laudes li Jeus a tere cheyent ...

Variant inc. of no. 3925: Ad laudes les Jeus tuz a terre
chairent ...

5400. A midi pensez et recordez que nostre champion qui vint du ciel
en cest monde pour nous delivrer de servage au deable ....

Sext of the Hours of the Cross in prose; the prologue of this
redaction begins A ! pour Dieu ... (no. 5379).

LONDON, British Libr., Royal 16. E. XII, fol. 311v°, XIVc.

5401. A miedi devez penser de l'anounciatioun et de la passioun ...

Variant of the inc.: Devant le midi devez penser de
l'anunciacion ... (no. 5597).

5402. A none pensez que a cele heure devia et morut nostre dous ami
loial Jhesucrist, si pensez et repensez une grant piece ...

Nones of the Hours of the Cross in prose; the redaction's
prologue begins A ! pour Dieu ... (no. 5379).

LONDON, British Libr., Royal 16. E. XII, fol. 312r°, XIVc.

5403. A prime vous devez penser et recorder comment les granz
seigneurs, les mestres de la loy, se assemblerent ...

Prime of the Hours of the Cross in prose; the inc. of the
prologue of this redaction is A ! pour Dieu ... (no. 5379).

LONDON, British Libr., Royal 16. E. XII, fol. 310r°, XIVc.

5404. A refuge vers toy, saint confesseur,
Amy de Dieu, haultain intercesseur ...

Orison to S. Claude; Ballade form of three dizains and a
five-line envoy.

Refr.: Je te requier, donne moy reconfort.

BLAIRS, Blairs College, 7, fol. 125r°-126r°, XVc., Hours of
Paris (this poem added by a XVIc. hand). Inc.: Ma priere,
Glaude, sainct confesseur ...

PARIS, Bibl. nat., Rés. D. 5616 and Ye 831, Louenges des
benoistz sainctz et sainctes de paradis, fol. vv 2r°, Paris,
Vérard.

VERSAILLES, Bibl. mun., M. 129 (Lacombe 109 quater).

Ed.: Rézeau, Saints, II, pp. 180-1, without mention of the
Blairs ms.

5405. A tierce pensez et recordez que nostre douz amis, vraiz et
loiauz espous, le benoit doz Jhesucrist, fu livrez a Pylate
...

Terce of the Hours of the Cross in prose; the inc. of this
redaction's prologue reads A ! pour Dieu ... (no. 5379).

LONDON, British Libr., Royal 16. E. XII, fol. 310v°, XIVc.

5406. A toy salut, dou saveur meire,
Vaissiaus de graice et de gloire ..

Hymn "Salve, mater Salvatoris"; 7 sizains rhyming aabccb.

METZ, Bibl. mun., 600, fol. 169v°-170r°, XVc., Hours of Paris
and Prayer-book.

Ref.: Rézeau, p. 177.

5407. A toy soit adoracion,
Louenge, veneracion ...

Praise of Jesus by Simeon: Arnoul Gréban's Mystère de la
Passion (vv. 6984-95).

CHANTILLY, Musée Condé, 614 (1691), fol. 49v°, XVc.

LE MANS, Bibl. mun., 6, fol. 79v°, XVc.

PARIS, Bibl. de l'Arsenal, 6431, fol. 42v°, XVc.

PARIS, Bibl. nat., fr. 815, fol. 55v°, 1458.

PARIS, Bibl. nat., fr. 816, fol. 49r°, 1473.

PARIS, Bibl. nat., fr. 1550, fol. 151v°, XVIc.

PARIS, Bibl. nat., fr. 15064, fol. 131v°-132r°, 1469.

PARIS, Bibl. nat., nouv. acq. fr. 14043, fol. 9v°, XVc. Only
first ten lines remain.

ROME, Accademia Nazionale dei Lincei, Bibl. Corsiniana, Rossi
412 (44. A. 7), fol. 114v°, late XVc.

Ed.: Paris-Raynaud, p. 90 (vv. 7022-33); Jodoyne, p. 96 (vv.
6984-995).

5408. A vespres pensez que en cele heure fu nostre douz ami loyal
despendu de la croiz et regardez bien et remirez ces douces
mainz ...

Vespers of the Hours of the Cross in prose; the prologue for
this redaction opens A ! pour Dieu ... (no. 5379).

LONDON, British Libr., Royal 16. E. XII, fol. 312r°-312v°, XIVc.

5409. A vous, archange sainct Michel,
Tres humblement me recommande ...

Prayer to several saints; 82 vv. grouped in eight stanzas.

PARIS, Bibl. nat., Vélins 1655, fol. A4v°-A5r°, 1525, Hours of Poitiers.

Ed.: Rézeau, Saints, I, pp. 195-8.

5410. A vous chante virge Marie
Ung chant piteux et plein de pleur ...

"Chant piteux" to the Virgin; 65 lines, in stanzas of unequal length and with varying rhyme groupings.

MANCHESTER, John Rylands Univ. Libr., French 143, fol. 164v°-166r°, early XVc., Hours.

5411. A vous, secours des desollez,
Nous venons en pelerinage ...

Orison to the Virgin by the publisher Antoine Vérard; 14 octosyllabic lines.

PARIS, Bibl. nat., Rés. D. 5616 and Ye 831, Louenges de Nostre Dame, fol. ff3r°, Paris, Vérard.

Ed.: Eugénie Droz, Romania 49 (1923), p. 58.

5412. Absoubz, sire Dieu, les ames de tes servans et servantes de tous les liens de peché en telle maniere que en la gloire ...

Orison to God, in prose.

PROVIDENCE, Brown Univ. Libr., C. 28. b. 4 (H.L. Koopman Collection), fol. 136r°-136v°, XVc., Hours.

5413. Adorable Jesus que je me represente comme si vous pendiez encore sur la croix dans les suplices inconcevables ...

"Elevation ou priere tres devote a I.C. agonisant, que chacun peut dire tous les jours pour obtenir une heureuse mort."

SAN MARINO, Huntington Libr., HM 1171, fol. 36r°-36v°, late XVc. Hours of Paris. The orison added by a XVIc. hand.

* Ai ! ...

See also the alphabetical order: Hai ! ...

5414. <u>Pues dist</u>: Ai ! saint splendor qi le monde
inlumine
Ombleté, pieté e charité divine ...

Orison to God by Roland: Entrée d'Espagne (vv. 14951-72).

VENICE, Bibl. Marciana, 257 (olim gall. XXI), fol. 287r°, XIVc.

Ed.: Thomas, II, p. 254-5.

5415.   Ai ! dist le duch, sainte Vergne Marie,
         Secorez moi, car j'ai mester d'aïe,
         Vers cist Maufer, qe ne vos ame mie,
         Car vostre fil e sa loi contralie.
                                (Complete Text)

         Orison to the Virgin by Roland: Entrée d'Espagne (vv. 3251-4).

         VENICE, Bibl. Marciana, 257 (olim gall. XXI), fol. 64v°, XIVc.

         Ed.: Thomas, I, p. 120-1.

5416.   Aï ! sire Deo qe tot li mondo formas
         Adam li primer hon de tes dos man crias
         De limon de la tere, si cun tu comandas,
         Et Eva sa muler de sa costa gitas ...

         Prayer to God by the hero: Bovo d'Antona, the Franco-Italian
         version of Beuve d'Hantone (vv. 3588-615).

         VENICE, Bibl. Marciana, 256 (olim gall. XIII), fol. 30r°, XIVc.

         Ed.: J. Reinhold, ZRP, 36 (1912), p. 9; P. Rajna, La Geste
         Francor di Venezia (codice marciano XIII della serie
         francesca). Facsimile in fototipia con un proemio, Milan and
         Rome, 1925, fol. 30r°.

5417.   Ay ! Vergne, fille do barons Johachin
         E de cil mere que les Juïf tapin ...

         Plainte to the Virgin by Charlemagne: Entrée d'Espagne (vv.
         2578-91).

         VENICE, Bibl. Marciana, 257 (olim gall. XXI), fol. 50v°, XIVc.

         Ed.: Thomas, I, p. 96-7.

5418.   Aïe ! Dieu, pere del ciel,
         Dist Lowis, li reis preisié,
         Tant par me tenc enginné ...

         Orison to God by King Louis: Gormont et Isembart (vv. 364-73).

         BRUSSELS, Bibl. royale, II. 181, fol. 3r°, XIIIc.

         Ed.: Scheler, p. 35-6; Bayot, 1906, fol. 3r°; Bartsch,
         Chrestomathie, 12 ed., p. 16; Bayot, 3 ed. CFMA, p. 24-5;
         Henry, Chrestomathie, I, p. 53 and II, p. 20.

5419.   Aïe ! pere Deu, dist il,
         Qui enz en la seinte cruiz fus mis ...

         Orison to Jesus by Isembart: Gormont et Isembart (vv. 641-50).

         BRUSSELS, Bibl. royale, II. 181, fol. 4v°, XIIIc.

Ed.: Scheler, p. 53; Bayot, 1906, fol. 4v°; Bayot, 3 ed. CFMA, p. 42-3; H. Gelzer, Altfranzösisches Lesebuch, Heidelberg, 1953, p. 11; P. Groult, V. Emond, G. Muraille, Anthologie de la littérature française du moyen âge, Gembloux, 3rd ed. 1964 and 1967, I, p. 25 and II, p. 18. Ref.: Wels, p. 9 n. 23; Perdrizet, p. 32; Koch, pp. 20-1, 96; Labande, p. 76 n. 4, p. 77 n. 3; Bélanger, p. 218; Combarieu in Senefiance no. 10, p. 99; Legros, ibid., pp. 364-5.

5420.   Aies de moy mercy, sire Dieux, puissant et misericors, et ne veilles consentir que par cestui pechié soudain, duquel je me repent de bon cueur, je soie par cestuy mescreant convainqu ne subjugué.

Orison to God by Rainouart: Bataille Loquifer in prose.

PARIS, Bibl. nat., fr. 796, fol. 293v°, early XVIc.

PARIS, Bibl. nat., fr. 1497, fol. 437r°, c. 1465.

Ed.: Castedello, p. 74 (base ms.: Paris, B.N. fr. 1497).

5421.   Aygnel de Dieu qui les pechiés
Ostez du monde qui est sechiés,
Esparne nous, si te plaist, sire,
Et donc nous refrain ton yre ...

"Agnus Dei", in rhymed couplets.

LILLE, Bibl. mun., Godefroy 5 (147), fol. 123r°-123v°, XVc., Hours.

5422.   Aignel de Dieu qui ostes le peché du monde, aies merci de nous ...

"Oroison pour dire aprés la fraction."

PROVIDENCE, Brown Univ. Libr., C. 28. b. 4 (H.L. Koopman Collection), fol. 272v°-273r°, XVc., Hours.

5423.   Aimer Dieu sus toutes choses selond que Dieu le commande est avoir bonne voulenté et ferme affection ...

"Neuf Considerations" ou "Comment on doit faire toutes euvres terriennes a la fin d'aymer Dieu", attributed to Jean Gerson.

PARIS, Bibl. nat., fr. 2452, fol. 34r°-38r°, XVc.

PARIS, Bibl. nat., fr. 24841, fol. 228r-233r°, XVc.

ROUBAIX, Archives Municipales, no shelf-mark, fol. 125r°-125v°, XVc., Prayer-book of Jacques de Luxembourg.

Ed.: Glorieux, Gerson: Oeuvres complètes, VII, 1, pp. 1-3 (base ms. Paris, B.N. fr. 24841). Ref.: E. Vansteenberghe, Revue des Sciences Religieuses, 14 (1934), pp. 191-218.

5424.   Ainsi comme descent en la fleur la rousee ...

> Variant of no. 3778: Tout ainsi que descend en la fleur la
> rosee ...

5425.   Ainsi que on trouve es fais de saint Jehan l'Evvangeliste,
Jhesus aprés l'Ascencion acorda a Marie la sainte mere ...

> Rubric introducing a verse "Ramenbrance des cinq douleurs de la
> Vierge" which begins Doulce Vierge Marie/Fontaine de pitié
> ... The rubric has similar but not identical wording as the
> rubric (no. 1913) introducing a prose version of the Cinq
> Douleurs.

> LIVERPOOL, Liverpool Public Libraries, D.435, fol. 83v°, early
> XVc. Hours of Paris.

5426.   Ainsy qu'on va seul son ennuy passant,
Ung jour alloye a tout par moy pensant
Du filz de Dieu a l'incarnation,
Qui, comme il fut filz de Dieu tout
puissant ...

> "Declamation faicte sur l'evangile de Missus est angelus
> Gabriel", by Guillaume Alexis; 42 twelve-line stanzas,
> rhyming aabaabbccdcd.

> AMIENS, Bibl. mun., 333, fol. 13r°-24v°, XVIc. This copy
> commences at line 36: Procederay par declamation.

> CAMBRIDGE (Mass.), Harvard College Libr., Typ. 321 (olim Didot,
> Cat. de vente, 1881, no. 27), fol. 15r°-25r°, early XVIc.

> PARIS, Bibl. nat., Rothschild 31 (I.5.40), fol. 15v°-29r°,
> XVIc.

> PARIS, Bibl. Sainte-Geneviève, 2734, fol. 32v°-51r°, early
> XVIc.

> ROUEN, Bibl. mun., 1064 (Y 226 a), fol. 19r°-29r°, XVIc.

> Ed.: Piaget et Picot, Oeuvres de Guillaume Alexis, II, pp.
> 25-58; Picot, Notice sur Jacques le Lieur, Rouen, 1913, p. 87
> and facsimile of fol. 19r°-29r° of Rouen ms. Ref.: Picot,
> Ibid. pp. 76 (Rothschild codex), 81 (Didot ms.), 87 (Rouen
> ms.).

*   An ...

> See the alphabetical order: En ...

5427.   Ange beneuré et esprit de bonté, qui par la grace de Dieu es
ordonné ...

> "Ci s'ensuivent oroisons aus angelz de paradis", a series of
> fourteen prayers in prose.

> AVRANCHES, Bibl. mun., 212, fol. 78r°-83v°, XVc.

<u>Ref</u>.: Rézeau, Saints, II, pp. 509-11 (extracts from each orison of the series).

5428.   Angele de Dieu, qui par la pitié divine(s) yes custode de moy ...

Orison to Guardian Angel, in prose.

BEAUNE, Bibl. mun., 59, fol. 165r°, XVc.   This text added in XVIc.

<u>Ed</u>.: Rézeau, Saints, II, p. 513.

5429.   Aouree soies (<u>ms</u>. soit) tu, saincte crois ou rechut mort Jhesus; ainsi conme che fu voirs et chou est nostre salut, si soit m'ame ...

Orison to the Cross, in prose.

CHICAGO, Newberry Libr., 52, fol. 180r°-181v°, <u>c</u>. 1470, Hours of Rheims.

5430.   Aprés ceo deis tu saver queus sunt les set prieres ...

Variant of the inc.: Aprés ço devez saver queus sunt les set prieres ... (no. 5431).

5431.   Aprés ço devez saver queus sunt les set prieres ki ostunt tuz maus e purchassent tuz biens ...

"Des set prieres de la Patenostre", in the Mirour de seinte Eglyse, a translation of the Speculum Ecclesiae by S. Edmund of Abingdon.   The texts of A and B versions are close.

CAMBRIDGE, Emmanuel College, I. 4. 31, fol. 78v°-82v°, XIVc. (A version).

CAMBRIDGE, Fitzwilliam Museum, McClean 123, fol. 7v° and a second copy on fol. 110r°, late XIIIc. (Extracts).

CAMBRIDGE, Pembroke College, 258, fol. 131r°-131v°, XIVc. (Extracts). The copy is acephalous beginning: Pater noster qui es in celis nous aprent coment nous deveoms prier ...

CAMBRIDGE, Trinity College, O. 1. 17, fol. 285r°-286v°, XIVc. (A version).

DURHAM, Durham Univ. Libr., Cosin V. V. 15, fol. 33r°-35r°, XIVc. (B version). Inc.: Aprés ce deis tu saver queus sunt les vij priers ...

LINCOLN, Chapter Libr., B. 5. 1, fol. 173r°-174r°, XIVc. (B version). Inc.: Aprés ceo deis tu savoir quels sunt les vij prieres ...

LONDON, British Libr., Arundel 288, fol. 113v°-115v°, XIIIc. (B version).

LONDON, British Libr., Harley 1121, fol. 149r°-150v°, early XIVc. (B version).

LONDON, British Libr., Royal 12. C. XII, fol. 23v°-25r°, early
XIVc. (A version).

LONDON, British Libr., Royal 20. B. XIV, fol. 59r°-60v°, early
XIVc. (A version).

MADRID, Bibl. nac., 18253, fol. 135r°-138r°, XIVc. (A version).
Inc.: Aprés ceo dois tu savoir queus sont ...

NEW HAVEN, Yale Univ. Libr., 492, fol. 92r°-94r°, early XIVc.
(A version).

OXFORD, Bodleian Libr., Digby 20, fol. 151v°-153r°, XIIIc. (B
version).

OXFORD, Bodleian Libr., Digby 98, fol. 239v°-244r°, early XIVc.
(B version).

OXFORD, Bodleian Libr., Douce 210, fol. 39r°-40r°, early XIVc.
(A version).

OXFORD, Bodleian Libr., Rawlinson, Poetry 241, pp. 177-80, late
XIIIc. (B version).

OXFORD, Bodleian Libr., Selden Supra 74, fol. 51v°-52r°, XIIIc.
(A version).

OXFORD, Corpus Christi College, 36, fol. 41r°-41v°, early XIVc.
(A version).

OXFORD, St. John's College, 190, fol. 194v°-195v°, late XIIIc.
(A version).

PARIS, Bibl. nat., fr. 13342, fol. 36r°-38r°, early XIVc. (A
version).

PARIS, Bibl. nat., nouv. acq. fr. 11200, fol. 12r°-14v°, XIIIc.
(A version). Inc.: Aprés ceo deis tu saver queus sunt ...

Ed.: Robbins, pp. 48-54 (base ms. Oxford, Digby 20); Wilshere,
pp. 46, 48, 50, 52, 54 (A version, base ms. Oxford, St.
John's College, 190); pp. 47, 49, 51, 53, 55 (B version, base
ms. London, Arundel 288). Ref.: P. Meyer, Romania, 8 (1879),
p. 326 (New Haven, Yale Univ. Libr. 492, then with J.
Techener, Paris); Bull. SATF, 6 (1880), p. 72 (Oxford, Douce
210); E. Stengel, ZFSL, 14 (1892), p. 135-6 (Oxford,
Rawlinson Poetry 241); P. Meyer, Bull. SATF, 19 (1893), p. 46
and 20 (1894), p. 66 (London, Royal 12. C. XII); Romania, 23
(1894), p. 299 (Cambridge, McClean 123, then with Quaritch,
London); Romania, 29 (1900), p. 53 (Oxford, Rawlinson Poetry
241), and 32 (1903), p. 74 (Cambridge, Trinity College, O. 1.
17); Vising, no. 156; M. Dominica Legge, MLR, 23 (1928), pp.
475-6 and 29 (1934), pp. 72-4, and her Anglo-Norman in the
Cloisters, Edinburgh, 1950, pp. 91-6, and again in MLR, 54
(1959), pp. 72-4; then in her Anglo-Norman Literature,
Oxford, 1963, pp. 211-212; Bouly de Lesdain, Manuscrits
didactiques, 1964-1965, p. 75; Helen P. Forshaw, Ephemerides
Liturgicae, 78 (1964), pp. 33-57; and in Archives d'histoire
doctrinale et littéraire du moyen âge, 38 (1971), pp. 7-33,

especially 14-15, 17; A.D. Wilshere, MLR, 71 (1976), pp. 500-12.

5432.   Au boys de dueil, a l'ombre d'ung soucy,
        Prisonnier suis, enclos en la forteresse,
        En peine, en dueil, et en tout desplaisir,
        Languissant suis en douleur et tristesse
                        ...

"Chansonnette" by a sinner in honour of Jesus; 5 stanzas each of 14 lines, on the rhyme pattern ababccdddcdddc.

Early Ed.: Plusieurs belles chansons nouvelles imprimées par Claude Nourry, Lyon, vers 1533. Ed.: Jeffery, II, PP. 112-15.

5433.   Au cuer dois avoir grant douleur
        Quant icy vois mort ton Seigneur.
        Bien dois avoir au cuer torment
        Quant vois Jhesus au monument ...

Lament before a picture of Jesus in the Sepulchre. A reference is made in the poem to "ymages que icy vees" but there is no painting. 20 rhyming couplets, each constituting a sentence.

MANCHESTER, John Rylands univ. Libr., French 143, fol. 19r°-19v°, early XVc., Hours.

5434.   Auxci verrament come Dieux fust, est et serra, e auxci verament come ce que il dist bien dist ...

Invocation, in prose.

LONDON, British Libr., Additional 36615, fol. 83v°, XIVc. This text added by another hand.

Ref.: Cook and Grillo, Revue d'histoire des textes, 8 (1978), pp. 255-6.

5435.   Ave, clere estoile de mer,
        Mere de Dieu saincte et sacree,
        Tousjours vierge sans entamer,
        Tu es du ciel porte et entree ...

"Ave maris stella", part of the Heures de Nostre Dame; 7 quatrains.

METZ, Bibl. mun., 600, fol. 33v°-34r°, 47r°-47v°, XVc., Hours of Paris and Prayer-book.

Ref.: Rézeau, p. 159, 161.

5436.   Ave Dame de tout bien plaine,
        Sur toutes autres souveraine ...

Prayer to the Virgin by S. Peter: Miracles de sainte Geneviève (vv. 396-426).

PARIS, Bibl. Sainte-Geneviève, 1131, fol. 188r°, XVc.

Ed.: Sennewaldt, p. 74.

5437.   Ave, dame du temple, Vierge bieneuree,
        Ave, li bien consute de vertu aornee ...

        Orison to the Virgin; 15 stanzas of 63 monorhymed alexandrines.

        METZ, Bibl. mun., 600, fol. 52Ar°-53r°, XVc., Hours of Paris
        and Prayer-book.

        Ref.: Rézeau, p. 163.

5438.   Ave dame saincte Marie,
        Ton glorieus fil por nous prie,
        Dame de la grasce Dieu plainne,
        Quiconques en toy ne fu vainne ...

        Orison to the Virgin; 32 lines, rhyming aabb.

        NEW YORK, Pierpont Morgan Libr., Morgan 947, fol. 74r°-75r°, c.
        1390, Hours.

5439.   Ave Deus, bea sire, ki le monde formas ...

        Variant of the inc.: Aïus Deus, bea sire, ki le monde formas
        ... (no. 60).

5440.   Ave estoile de clarté,
        Ave flour de virginité ...

        Paraphrase of the "Ave Maria".

        BARBANTANE, Collection of the Marquis de Barbantane, no
        shelf-mark, fol. 54r°-62r°, XVc.

        Ref.: F. Lecoy, Romania, 92 (1971), p. 146.

5441.   Ave estoille de mer clere
        Mere de Dieu tres digne et sainte,
        Tousjours virge necte et entere
        Porte du ciel eureuse et paignte (sic) ...

        "Ave maris stella", rhyming abab; part of the "Heures de Nostre
        Dame". This redaction is not identical with no. 3952.

        LILLE, Bibl. mun., Godefroy 5 (147), fol. 80v°-81v°, XVc.,
        Hours.

5442.   Ave glorieuse Marie Magdalene, exemplaire de penitence ...

        Prayer to S. Mary Magdalene; as prose, but containing numerous
        lines of verse.

        METZ, Bibl. mun., 600, fol. 124r°-125v°, XVc., Hours of Paris
        and Prayer-book.

        Ref.: Rézeau, p. 173; Rézeau, Saints, II, pp. 338-9.

5443. Ave gracieuse lumiere
Qui tous les desvoyés avoye ...

Variant of the inc.: Ave glorieuse lumiere ... (no. 117).

5444. Ave Jhesu, vray createur,
Vray roy de gloire, redempteur ...

"Oraison du corps de Dieu"; 46 lines rhymed in pairs; the
fourth line is missing.

NEW YORK, Pierpont Morgan Libr., Morgan 136, fol. 24r°-25v°,
XVc., Hours of Chalon-sur-Saône.

5445. Ave Maria est le plus beau salut que l'en puisse dire et qui
plus plaist alla (sic) benoite Vierge Marie, et moult plus
luy plairoit ...

Explanation of the "Ave Maria".

LONDON, Lambeth Palace, 456, fol. 216r°, XVc.

5446. Ave Maria gratia plena, Dominus tecum.   C'est a dire: A ti,
rois sovrains mon createur ...

Commentary on the Ave Maria, in prose.

METZ, Bibl. mun., 600, fol. 137v°-138r°, XVc., Hours of Paris
and Prayer-book.

Ref.: Rézeau, p. 174.

5447. Ave Marie, dou munde esperance; ave pitouse de douceur
habundance ...

Hymn "Ave mundi spes Maria", in prose, rhymed in places.

METZ, Bibl. mun., 600, fol. 49r°-49v°, XVc., Hours of Paris and
Prayer-book.

Ref.: Rézeau, p. 162.

5448. E dist suvent: Ave Marie,
Pleine de grace, Deu amie,
Damnedeu seit ensemble od te;
Ma chere dame, pens de mei !
                    (Complete text)

Paraphrase of the Ave Maria by a sacristan; Miracles de Nostre
Dame by Adgar, called Willame (vv. 11-14 of miracle no. 2,
found in one ms. only).

LONDON, British Libr., Additional 38664, fol. 4v°, c. 1240.

Ed.: J.A. Herbert, Romania, 32 (1903), p. 403. Ref.: Vising, p.
43, no. 13 (this prayer not recorded).

5449. Ave ! pour salutacion,
Je te salue d'affection ...

Paraphrase of the "Ave Maria" by Gabriel, each alternate line beginning with a Latin word of the Ave Maria: Mystère de la Passion by Arnoul Gréban (vv. 3425-36).

CHANTILLY, Musée Condé, 614 (1691), fol. 18v°, XVc.

LE MANS, Bibl. mun., 6, fol. 28r°, XVc.

PARIS, Bibl. de l'Arsenal, 6431, fol. 13v°, XVc.

PARIS, Bibl. nat., fr. 815, fol. 27r°, 1458.

PARIS, Bibl. nat., fr. 816, fol. 25v°, 1473.

PARIS, Bibl. nat., fr. 1550, fol. 66v°-67r°, XVIc.

PARIS, Bibl. nat., fr. 15064, fol. 59v°-60r°, 1469.

ROME, Accademia Nazionale dei Lincei, Bibl. Corsiniana, Rossi 412 (44. A. 7), fol. 29v°, late XVc.

Ed.: Paris-Raynaud, p. 44 (vv. 3443-53); Jodogne, p. 51 (vv. 3425-36).

5450.   Ave ! tres glorieux Baptistes,
De cui li sains evvangelistes ...

Life of S. John Baptist in prayer style; 132 vv., rhyming in pairs.

BRUSSELS, Bibl. royale, IV. 427, fol. 122r°-127v°, c. 1380. This ms. incorrectly numbered in the Sinclair ed. as IV. 227.

CARDIFF, Public Libr., 1.375, fol. 149r°-153v°, XVc., fragment from a Book of Hours.

DOLE, Bibl. mun., 45, pp. 181-9, XVc.

OXFORD, Bodleian Libr., Rawlinson, liturg. e 25, fol. 175v°-179v°, XVc., Hours of Paris.

WILLIAMSTOWN, Williams College, Museum of Art, 2, fol. 124v°-129v°, XVc.

Ed.: K.V. Sinclair, Romania, 103 (1982), pp. 529-46. Ref.: Rézeau, Saints, II, p. 282.

5451.   Ave, Vierge, du ciel roÿne,
Que es per la vertu divine
Appellee dame des aingre<s>,
Tu es celle que enlumine ...

Hymn "Ave regina celorum"; 6 sizains, Naetebus XXIX type.

METZ, Bibl. mun., 600, fol. 52r°-52v°, XVc., Hours of Paris and
   Prayer-book.

Ref.: Rézeau, p. 163.

*   Ay ...

See the alphabetical order: Ai ...

B

*   Beau(s) ....

Here are grouped the spellings: Beau ..., Beaz ..., Biau ...,
Biaul ..., Bias ..., Biaus ..., Biaux ..., Biauz ... The
alphabetical order within the group is determined by the
spelling of the second word of the incipit.

5452.   <u>Et cil respondent</u>: Biaus dolz pere Jhesu,
Sire de gloire, aorez soies tu ....

Praise of Jesus by the townsmen of Cambrai: Yon (vv. 959-63).

PARIS, Bibl. nat., fr. 1622, fol. 267r°, XIIIc.

<u>Ed</u>.: Mitchneck, p. 28.

5453.   Beau duce sire Jhesu, qi suffri passioun
En la vrai croice (<u>sic</u>) pur crestien (<u>sic</u>)
                       redempcion ...

Prayer to Jesus by Richard de Normandie: Fierabras, short
version (vv. 1351-5).

HANOVER, Niedersächsische Landesbibl., IV. 578, fol. 76v°,
early XIVc.

LONDON, British Libr., Egerton 3028, fol. 109v°, XIVc.

<u>Ed</u>.: L. Brandin, Romania, 64 (1938), p. 88.

5454.   Biaus seignors freres, vos devés savoir que, a toutes les fois
que nous departons nostre chapistre ...

Exhortation to Knights Templar to offer prayers on leaving
chapter; part of the prose "Regle du Temple".

PARIS, Bibl. nat., fr. 1977, fol. 98v° (100v°)-99r° (101r°),
early XIVc.

ROME, Accademia Nazionale dei Lincei, Bibl. Corsiniana, 44. A. 14, fol. 106rº-106vº, XIVc.

Ed.: H. de Curzon, La Règle du Temple, Paris, 1886, p. 283.

5455. Biaus seignors freres, vos devés savoir coment il est dou pardon de nostre chapistre, et qui prennent partie et qui non ...

Exhortation to confession addressed to the Knights Templar in chapter; part of the prose "Règle du Temple".

PARIS, Bibl. nat., fr. 1977, fol. 98rº (100rº)-98vº (100vº), early XIVc.

ROME, Accademia Nazionale dei Lincei, Bibl. Corsiniana, 44. A. 14, fol. 105rº-106rº, XIVc.

Ed.: H. de Curzon, La Règle du Temple, Paris, 1886, pp. 281-3.

5456. Beau sire Dieux, absollés les ames de tous les loyaulx trepassés de cest siecle de tous les lieux ...

Orison to God, in prose.

BALTIMORE, Walters Art Gallery, Walters 261, fol. 127vº, c. 1400, Hours.

5457. Biau sire Dex, dist il, aoré soies tu,
Sire, qui m'as donné u monde tel vertu ...

Prayer to God by Faradin: Gaufrey (vv. 3196-204).

MONTPELLIER, Bibl. Fac. Ecole de Médecine, H. 247, fol. 59rº, XIVc.

Ed.: Guessard and Chabaille, p. 97. Ref.: Altona, p. 34; Merk, pp. 186 n. 10, 188 n. 9 and 13.

5458. Beaz sire Deus, devant la fin,
Me faites si bon et si fin
Que je vostre pardon rechoive,
Et que je l'enemi dechoive.
                    (Complete Text)

Concluding Invocation by the author of Durmart le Galois (vv. 15991-4).

BERN, Bürgerbibl. 113, fol. 283vº, XIIIc.

Ed.: E. Stengel, Li Romans de Durmart le Galois, altfranzösisches Rittergedicht, Tübingen, 1873, p. 443; J. Gildea, Durmart le galois, roman arthurien du treizième siècle, Villanova, I, 1965, p. 418.

5459. Biaul sire Dieu en qui je croy,
A jointez mains mercy te proy
Que je meure en telle foy.
Jhesu de Nazaret, mon roy ...

Prayer to Jesus, one nine-line stanza, rhyming aaaabcbdc.

METZ, Bibl. mun., 600, fol. 7v°, XVc., Book of Hours (Use of Paris) and Prayer-book.

Ed.: Rézeau, p. 157.

5460.   Biaus sire Deus, ensi con ge por vos
        Lais le païs ou celle est cui j'ain si ...

Orison to God; one huitain in an anonymous Chanson de Croisade Por joie avoir perfite en paradis (vv. 25-32).

PARIS, Bibl. nat., fr. 20050, fol. 161r°, XIIIc.

Ed.: J. Schirmer, ASNS, 41 (1867), p. 83; P. Meyer and G. Raynaud, Le Chansonnier français de Saint-Germain-des-Prés (B.N., fr. 20050). Reproduction phototypique avec transcriptions, Paris, SATF, 1892, fol. 161r°; Bédier and Aubry, p. 284-5; B. Woledge, Penguin Book of French Verse, Harmondsworth, 1961, I, p. 115. Ref.: Koch, p. 54 and 110.

5461.   Biau sire Dieu Hely,
        Sabaoth Adonay,
        Que la mort souffry
        A jour de venredy ...

Orison to Christ on the Cross.

METZ, Bibl. mun., 600, fol. 51v°, XVc., Hours of Paris and Prayer-book.

Ref.: Rézeau, pp. 162-3.

5462.   Beaus sire Deus, je te pri que tu aies merci de tes fieus qui sunt hui mort en la bataille per la toe amor ...

Roland's prayer to God for the fallen in the Battle of Roncesvaux: Chronicle of Pseudo-Turpin in the Chronique dite saintongeaise.

ABERYSTWYTH, Nat. Libr. of Wales, 5005 B, p. 142, XIIIc.

PARIS, Bibl. nat., fr. 124, fol. 10r°, XIVc.

PARIS, Bibl. nat., fr. 5714, fol. 75v°-76r°, XIIIc.

Ed.: T.M. Auracher, ZRP, 1 (1877), p. 320 (base ms. B.N., fr. 5714, variants from B.N., fr. 124); Mandach, p. 317 (Aberystwyth codex).

5463.   Beau sire Dieu, je vous offre ce denier ou ceste chandelle, .N., en l'onneur de vous et de la benoiste vierge Marie et de tous les sains ...

"Oroison pour dire quant on offre aucune chose a l'eglise".

PROVIDENCE, Brown Univ. Libr., C. 28. b. 4 (H.L. Koopman Collection), fol. 269v°-270r°, XVc., Hours.

5464. Beaus sire Deus Jesu Criz, le fil de la beneite Virge (ma dame
       sancte Marie), toi reconois de tot mon cuer e te requier que
       (tu aies merci de moi car) tu es cil qui me remsist de mort
       durable ...

       "Oreison de Rollant" to Jesus: Chronicle of Pseudo-Turpin in
       the Chronique dite saintongeaise.

       ABERYSTWYTH, Nat. Libr. of Wales, 5005 B, p. 142, XIIIc.

       PARIS, Bibl. nat., fr. 124, fol. 10r°, XIVc.

       PARIS, Bibl. nat., fr. 5714, fol. 75v°, XIIIc.

       Ed.: T.M. Auracher, ZRP, 1 (1877), p. 319 (base ms. B.N., fr.
       5714, variants from B.N., fr. 124); Mandach, p. 316
       (Aberystwyth codex).

5465. Beaus sire Deus Jesu Criz, leiaus peres qui de la mer Rogie
       feistes deus parties e menastes lo poble Israel per mei e
       dedanz negiastes Faraon ...

       Orison to God by Charlemagne: Pseudo-Turpin Chronicle in the
       Chronique dite saintongeaise.

       ABERYSTWYTH, Nat. Libr. of Wales, 5005 B, pp. 156-7, XIIIc.

       PARIS, Bibl. nat., fr. 124, fol. 12r°, XIVc.

       PARIS, Bibl. nat., fr. 5714, fol. 83r°, XIIIc.

       Ed.: T.M. Auracher, ZRP, 1 (1877), pp. 332-3 (base ms. B.N.,
       fr. 5714, variants from B.N., fr. 124); Mandach, p. 329
       (Aberystwyth codex).

5466. Biauz Sire Deus Jesu Criz, per cui amor je laissai mon pais e
       vinc çai en iceste terre salvagie per essoucer sancte
       crestianté ...

       "Le oreison de Rollant, quant il fut pres de la mort si pria
       Deu" (B.N., fr. 124): Pseudo-Turpin Chronicle in the
       Chronique dite saintongeaise.

       ABERYSTWYTH, Nat. Libr. of Wales, 5005 B, p. 141, XIIIc.

       PARIS, Bibl. nat., fr. 124, fol. 10r°, XIVc.

       PARIS, Bibl. nat., fr. 5714, fol. 75r°-75v°, XIIIc.

       Ed.: T.M. Auracher, ZRP, 1 (1877), p. 319 (base ms. B.N., fr.
       5714, variants from B.N., fr. 124); Mandach, p. 316
       (Aberystwyth codex).

5467. Biaux sire Dieux Jhesucrist qui fesistez paiz en terre entre
       les angeles et les hommes, deffendez et delivrez .N. ....

       Orison to God in prose.

       BALTIMORE, Walters Art Gallery, Walters 103, fol. 82r°-82v°,
       late XIVc., Hours of Paris (?).

5468.   Biau sire Dieux Jhesucrist qui le derrenier jour de ta vie,
         pendant en la croix, deis .vij. saintes paroles ...

         "Sept Paroles" attributed to Bede; in prose. The Rubric begins:
         Quiconques ceste oroison ... (no. 6501).

         EDINBURGH, Edinburgh Univ. Libr., 302, fol. 182v°-185r°, XVc.,
         Hours of Paris.

5469.   Bias sire Deu Jhesucris, vos qui estes pain de vie, vuelliés me
         si de vous repaistre et soler (sic), vueuliés me si de vous
         abovrer ...

         Oraison pour la Communion, in prose.

         BALTIMORE, Walters Art Gallery, Walters 91, fol. 26r°-26v°,
         28r°-28v°, c. 1300, Prayer-book.

         METZ, Bibl. mun., 600, fol. 133r°-133v° (incomplete
         transcription) and fol. 167r° (complete text), XVc., Hours of
         Paris and Prayer-book.

         Ref.: Rézeau, pp. 174 and 176 (Metz codex).

5470.   Biau sire Diex Jhesucrist, vrai Dieu, a qui toutes les pensees
         des cuers sont apertes, qui a heure de complie deïs a tes
         deiciples (sic) ...

         Hours of the Cross in prose, compline.

         VIENNA, Oesterreichische Nationalbibl. 1969, fol. 136r°-137r°,
         XIVc., Hours.

5471.   Beau sire Dieu, mercy de nous! Doulx benoist Jhesucrist aies
         mercy de nous! Doulx benoist Jhesucrist plaise toy ...

         "La Kyrielle", en prose.

         PROVIDENCE, Brown Univ. Libr., C. 28. b. 4 (H.L. Koopman
         Collection), fol. 74v°-85r°, XVc., Book of Hours.

5472.   Beau sire Dieu, nous qui avons congneu l'incarnacion de
         Jhesucrist, ton saint filz, denoncie par l'ange, envoie en
         noz pensees ...

         Orison to God, in prose.

         PROVIDENCE, Brown Univ. Libr., C. 28. b. 4 (H.L. Koopman
         Collection), fol. 201r°, XVc., Hours.

5473.   Biaus sire Dieu omnipotent,
         Si comme je croy vraiement ...

         Variante de l'inc.: Sire Dieu roy omnipotent ... (no. 1991).

5474.   Beau sire Dieu, ouvre mes levres et ma bouche annoncera vostre
         (sic) louange. Beau sire Dieu, soiez en mon aide et de moy
         aidier te delivre ...

"Cy aprés s'ensuivent les heures du sainct Esperit en françois."

PROVIDENCE, Brown Univ. Libr., C. 28. b. 4 (H.L. Koopman Collection), fol. 94r°-97r°, XVc., Hours.

5475. Biaus sire Dieu, peirez des cielz, vuoilliez otroier per vostre tres grande courtoisie ...

"Une orison a Dieu lou peire tous poissanz."

METZ, Bibl. mun., 600, fol. 168r°-168v°, XVc., Hours of Paris and Prayer-book.

Ref.: Rézeau, p. 177.

5476. Biau sire Deus, por coi cri ge merci?
Por fol m'en tieng, recreant et honni.
Deus aidiez m'en, q'an vos me croi et fi.
                    (Complete Text)

Plainte to God by Olivier: Girart de Vienne by Bertrand de Bar-sur-Aube (vv. 5198-200).

LONDON, British Libr., Harley 1321, fol. 27v°, XIIIc.

LONDON, British Libr., Royal 20. B. XIX, fol. 30r°, XIIIc.

LONDON, British Libr., Royal 20. D. XI, fol. 57r°, XIVc.

PARIS, Bibl. nat., fr. 1374, fol. 123v°, XIIIc.

PARIS, Bibl. nat., fr. 1448, fol. 30r°, XIIIc.

Ed.: Yeandle, p. 165; Van Emden, p. 230 (both used as base ms. Royal 20. B. XIX).

5477. Beau sire Dieus, ke me deignastes a fourmer
E en la beneite croiz de tun sanc achater,
Jeo te pri, beau duz sire, de fin quer e
                                    enter
Que tu ne me lessez ci longement demurer,
Ke jeo ne sei fet pendre ou vif escorcher,
Ou tu me facez de ci toust eschaper.
                    (Complete Text)

Orison to Jesus by Boeve: Boeve de Haumtone, Anglo-Norman version (vv. 1040-5).

LOUVAIN, Bibl. de l'Univ., G. 170 (olim Didot, Cat. de vente, 1878, p. 16, no. 30), XIIIc., the folio for the prayer was not recorded before the codex was destroyed in World War II.

PARIS, Bibl. nat., nouv. acq. fr., 4532, fol. 80r° (olim 23r°) - 80v (23v°), XIVc.

Ed.: Stimming, p. 40 (text of both mss given).

5478.   Beau sire Dieu qui as establi mariage principalement pour
        engendrer lignee qui te serve, te honnoure, te loue et
        beneisse et obeisse a tes commandemens ...

        "Ceste oroison doit l'on dire pour ses enfans".

        PROVIDENCE, Brown Univ. Libr., C. 28. b. 4 (H.L. Koopman
        Collection), fol. 174v°-175r°, XVc., Book of Hours.

5479.   Beau sire Dieu qui as fait et creé et ordonné le temps et selon
        ta disposition et ton ordonnance il se mue, qui fais venter
        ...

        "Oroison devote contre la tempeste".

        PROVIDENCE, Brown Univ. Libr., C. 28. b. 4 (H.L. Koopman
        Collection), fol. 179v°-180v°, XVc., Book of Hours.

5480.   Biaus sire Dex, qui en crois fus dresciez
        Et el sepulcre refu vos cors couchiez ...

        "Plainte" to Jesus by the hero: Jourdain de Blaye (vv.
        1422-33).

        PARIS, Bibl. nat., fr. 860, fol. 118v°, XIIIc.

        Ed.: Hofmann, p. 145-6; Dembowski, p. 56.

5481.   Beau sere Dieu, dist Charles le sené,
        Qui en la Virge prin<te>s humanité ...

        Orison to Jesus by Charlemagne: Aquin (vv. 2632-66).

        PARIS, Bibl. nat., fr. 2233, fol. 47v°-48v°, XVc.

        Ed.: Joüon des Longrais, p. 101-2. Ref.: Gautier, p. 543, 545;
        Dickman, p. 195; Wels, p. 3 n. 7; Koch, p. 40-1, 102;
        Labande, p. 73 no. 2; 76 n. 4.

5482.   Beau sire Dieu qui es lumiere pardurable que nul entendement ne
        peut comprendre se ce n'est le tien tant seulement ...

        "S'ensuit une oroison contemplative pour la messe."

        PROVIDENCE, Brown Univ. Libr., C. 28. b. 4 (H.L. Koopman
        Collection), fol. 250r°-269r°, XVc., Hours.

5483.   Beau sire Dieu qui es seigneur et maistre des mors et des vifz
        de laquelle main nul ne peut eschapper car tu es partout ...

        "Oroison pour les trespassez."

        PROVIDENCE, Brown Univ. Libr., C. 28. b. 4 (H.L. Koopman
        Collection), fol. 175v°-176r°, XVc., Book of Hours.

5484.   Biaux sire Dieux qui estes commenchemenz et fin a toutes
        creatures, acroissiez le bien en luy, le sens de droiture ...

        Orison to God in prose.

BALTIMORE, Walters Art Gallery, Walters 103, fol. 82v°-83r°, late XIVc., Hours of Paris (?).

5485. Si dist: Biaus sire Diex, qui tout as a
                                    jugier,
        Qui presis char et sanc en la digne
                                    moillier,
        .ix. mos entirement; et puis, sans
                                    travellier,
        En delivra le Vierge qui te voilt alaitier
                        ...

        Orison to God by the hero: Baudouin de Sebourc (vv. 141-73 of Chant XVII).

        PARIS, Bibl. nat., fr. 12552, fol. 84v°-85r°, XIVc.

        PARIS, Bibl. nat., fr. 12553, fol. 252v°-253r°, XVc.

        Ed.: Boca, II, pp. 129-30. Ref.: Labande, pp. 74, 75, 76, 77 n. 7.

5486. Biau sire Dieux, regardez nous des yeux de vostre misericorde et entendez la douleur de noz cuers et si deffendez ...

        Orison to God in prose.

        BALTIMORE, Walters Art Gallery, Walters 103, fol. 83r°, late XIVc., Hours of Paris (?).

5487. Biau sire Dex, dist la dame vaillant,
        Si voirement con li Juif tirant ...

        Orison to Jesus by Hermanjart: Narbonnais (vv. 5104-9).

        LONDON, British Libr., Harley 1321, fol. 101r°, XIIIc.

        LONDON, British Libr., Royal 20. B. XIX, fol. 94v°, XIIIc.

        LONDON, British Libr., Royal 20. D. XI, fol. 96v°, c. 1300.

        PARIS, Bibl. nat., fr. 24369, fol. 62r°, c. 1300.

        Ed.: Suchier, I, pp. 202-3 (base ms.: London, Harley 1321).

5488. Beau sire Dieu, soies debonnaire a moy pecherresse, et soies garde de moy tous les jours de ma vie, tu qui es Dieu de Ysaac, Dieu de Jacob ...

        Prayer to God, in prose, by a woman sinner.

        PROVIDENCE, Brown Univ. Libr., C. 28. b. 4 (H.L. Koopman Collection), fol. 223v°-224v°, XVc., Hours.

5489. Biaus sire Dex, vers vous me sui guenchiz:
        Tout lais pour vous ce que je tant amoie
                        ...

Strophe of eight lines in honour of Jesus, in Thibaut de Champagne's Chanson de Croisade <u>Dame, ensi est qu'il m'en couvient aler</u> (vv. 25-32).

PARIS, Bibl. de l'Arsenal, 5198, p. 19, XIIIc.

PARIS, Bibl. nat., fr. 844, fol. 64rº, late XIIIc.

PARIS, Bibl. nat., fr. 846, fol. 34vº, late XIIIc.

PARIS, Bibl. nat., fr. 847, fol. 154vº, late XIIIc.

PARIS, Bibl. nat., fr. 12581, fol. 315rº, XIVc.

PARIS, Bibl. nat., fr. 12615, fol. 8rº, XIIIc.

PARIS, Bibl. nat., fr. 24406, fol. 75rº, XIIIc.

PARIS, Bibl. nat., nouv. acq. fr. 1050, fol. 20vº, late XIIIc.

<u>Ed.</u>: Bédier and Aubry, p. 192; Wallensköld, p. 188; J. and Louise Beck, Les Chansonniers des troubadours et des trouvères - I: Le chansonnier Cangé (Paris, Bibl. nat., fr. 846), Paris and Philadelphia, 1927, I, fol. 34vº, and II, p. 78; J. and Louise Beck, Les Chansonniers ... II: Le manuscrit du Roi, fonds français 844 de la Bibl. nat., Philadelphia, 1938, I, pl. Mt, VII, vº, no. 22.

5490. Biaux sire Dieux, voie de verité et de salut, entendez a mes proieres et si gouvernez les euvrez ...

Orison to God in prose.

BALTIMORE, Walters Art Gallery, Walters 103, fol. 81vº-82rº, late XIVc., Hours of Paris (?).

5491. Biaus sire peres, par ton commandement ...

Variant of the inc.: Glorieus Deu, par ton comandement ... (no. 5843).

5492. Biaus sire peres qui feistes le mont ...

Variant of the inc.: Glorios pere qui feïstes lo mont ... (no. 5858).

5493. Biaus Sire, rois de haute gloire,
De tot mon sens e ma memoire
E ma vertu, Sire, te ren ge
Merciz e graces e loenge ...

Thanksgiving to God by Josaphat: Roman de Barlaam et Josaphat, version anonyme en rime (vv. 449-82).

BESANCON, Bibl. mun., 552, fol. 12rº-13rº, XIIIc.

<u>Ed.</u>: J. Sonet, Le Roman de Barlaam et Josaphat: Recherches sur la tradition manuscrite latine et française, Louvain, 1949, p. 233-5.

5494.   Biaus tres doulz Jhesu Crist, en l'onneur des tres doulz loiens
        dont vous fustes loiés a l'estaque le jour du bon venredi ...

   "Chi aprés s'ensieut une moult bonne oreson qu'on doit dire
   pour lui et pour aultrui qui est alés en aucun voiage ou en
   prison ou en bataille, et doit on nonmer premierement le
   (sic) personne pour qui c'est que on le dist. Oreson."

   CHICAGO, Newberry Libr., 52, fol. 178v°-180r°, c. 1470, Hours
   of Rheims.

5495.   Biaux tres douz Jhesu Criz, teulx ovres de
                                         pitié
        Viennent de vostre grace et de vostre
                                         amitié ...

   Praise of Jesus and thanksgiving to God: Girart de Rossillon,
   Burgundian redaction (vv. 6625-34).

   BRUSSELS, Bibl. royale, 11181, fol. 112r°, XVc.

   MONTPELLIER, Bibl. Fac. Ecole de Médecine, H. 244, fol. 124v°,
   XVc.

   MONTPELLIER, Bibl. Fac. Ecole de Médecine, H. 349, fol. 90r°,
   c. 1350.

   PARIS, Bibl. nat., fr. 15103, fol. 136v°-137r°, 1417.

   Ed.: Ham, p. 298 (base ms.: Montpellier H. 349).

5496.   Beau tres doulx pere, je vous prie que vous mectez vostre
        hauberc (ms. haubere) et foy en mon doz et en vostre
        esperance en telle maniere ...

   "Derechef, quant le prestre dit l'evvangile de la messe, nous
   devons dire."

   PROVIDENCE, Brown Univ. Libr., C. 28. b. 4 (H.L. Koopman
   Collection), fol. 269r°-269v°, XVc., Hours.

*   Bias ..., Biau ..., Biaul ..., Biaus ..., Biaux ..., Biauz ...

   See the alphabetical group Beau(s) ...

5497.   Biele dame, sainte Marie,
        Qui mere iestes au digne roi ...

   "Plainte" to the Virgin by a princess about to be raped:
   Merveilles de Rigomer (vv. 4122-7).

   CHANTILLY, Musée Condé, 472 (626), fol. 14r°, XIIIc.

   Ed.: W. Förster and H. Breuer, Les Merveilles de Rigomer von
   Jehan, altfranzösischer Artusroman des XIII. Jahrhunderts,
   Dresden, I, 1908, p. 119. Ref.: Koch, p. 73, 121.

5498.   Bele tres douce dame, je vous saluerai pour icele joie que vous
        eustes quant vostre fil monta es cieux pour icele joie ...

Orison to the Virgin in prose.

NEW YORK, New York Public Libr., Spencer 56, fol. 370r°-370v°, XIVc., Hours of Blanche de France, Duchess of Orleans.

5499.   Bele tres douce dame sainte Marie, je vous saluerai en l'aneur de celle benoite joie que vous eustes quant li ange vous dit que vous feussiez ...

Orison to the Virgin in prose.

NEW YORK, New York Public Libr., Spencer 56, fol. 366v°-367r°, XIVc., Hours of Blanche de France, Duchess of Orleans.

5500.   Bele tres douce dame sainte Marie, je vous saluerai en l'aneur de cele douce pitié que votre fiuz deigna descendre en Enfer ...

Orison to the Virgin in prose.

NEW YORK, New York Public Libr., Spencer 56, fol. 370r°, XIVc., Hours of Blanche de France, Duchess of Orleans.

5501.   Bele tres douce dame sainte Marie, je vous saluerai en l'aneur de cele joie que vous aurez au jour du juïse de toutes les ames qui seront sauveez ...

Orison to the Virgin in prose.

NEW YORK, New York Public Libr., Spencer 56, fol. 371v°-372v°, XIVc., Hours of Blanche de France, Duchess of Orleans.

5502.   Bele tres douce dame sainte Marie, je vous saluerai en l'aneur de cele joie que vous eustes quant li saint ange annunça au<s> pastouriaus ...

Orison to the Virgin in prose.

NEW YORK, New York Public Libr., Spencer 56, fol. 367v°, XIVc., Hours of Blanche de France, Duchess of Orleans.

5503.   Bele tres douce dame sainte Marie, je vous saluerai en l'aneur de cele joie que vous eustes quant li .iij. roi vindrent aourer ...

Orison to the Virgin in prose.

NEW YORK, New York Public Libr., Spencer 56, fol. 368r°, XIVc., Hours of Blanche de France, Duchess of Orleans.

5504.   Bele tres douce dame sainte marie, je vous saluerai en l'aneur de cele joie que vous eustes quant Nostre Sire vous envoia ces apostres au jor ...

Orison to the Virgin in prose.

NEW YORK, New York Public Libr., Spencer 56, fol. 371r°, XIVc., Hours of Blanche de France, Duchess of Orleans.

5505.   Bele tres douce dame sainte Marie, je vous saluerai en l'aneur
        de cele joie que vos eustez quant votre biau fiuz fu
        baptiziés ou flun ...

        Orison to the Virgin in prose.

        NEW YORK, New York Public Libr., Spencer 56, fol. 368v°, XIVc.,
        Hours of Blanche de France, Duchess of Orleans.

5506.   Bele tres douce dame sainte Marie, je vous saluerai en l'aneur
        de celle joie que vous (e)eustes quant vostre douz fiuz fu né
        ...

        Orison to the Virgin in prose.

        NEW YORK, New York Public Libr., Spencer 56, fol. 366v°, XIVc.,
        Hours of Blanche de France, Duchess of Orleans.

5507.   Bele tres douce dame sainte Marie, je vous saluerai en l'aneur
        de cele joie que vous eustes quant vostre doux fiuz mua l'eve
        ...

        Orison to the Virgin in prose.

        NEW YORK, New York Public Libr., Spencer 56, fol. 368v°-369r°,
        XIVc., Hours of Blanche de France, Duchess of Orleans.

5508.   Bele tres douce dame sainte Marie, je vous saluerai en l'aneur
        de cele joie que vos eustes quant vous portastes votre fiuz
        au temple ...

        Orison to the Virgin in prose.

        NEW YORK, New York Public Libr., Spencer 56, fol. 368r°, XIVc.,
        Hours of Blanche de France, Duchess of Orleans.

5509.   Bele tres douce dame sainte Marie, je vous saluerai en l'aneur
        de cele joie que vous eustes quant vous raportates votre
        chier fil de la terre d'Egypte ...

        Orison to the Virgin in prose.

        NEW YORK, New York Public Libr., Spencer 56, fol. 368r°-368v°,
        XIVc., Hours of Blanche de France, Duchess of Orleans.

5510.   Bele tres douce dame sainte Marie, je vous saluerai en l'aneur
        de cele sainte foi et de cele sainte creance que maintenue fu
        ...

        Orison to the Virgin in prose.

        NEw YORK, New York Public Libr., Spencer 56, fol. 369v°, XIVc.,
        Hours of Blanche de France, Duchess of Orleans.

5511.   Bele tres douce dame sainte Marie, je vous saluerai en l'aneur
        de cele sainte joie que vous eustes quant saint Gabriel li
        anges vous dit ...

        Orison to the Virgin in prose.

NEW YORK, New York Public Libr., Spencer 56, fol. 367r°, XIVc., Hours of Blanche de France, Duchess of Orleans.

5512. Bele tres douce dame sainte marie, je vous saluerai en l'aneur de celle sainte joie que vous eustez quant vostre biau fiuz fu circumcis ...

Orison to the Virgin in prose.

NEW YORK, New York Public Libr., Spencer 56, fol. 367v°-368r°, XIVc., Hours of Blanche de France, Duchess of Orleans.

5513. Bele tres douce dame sainte Marie, je vous saluerai en l'aneur de cele sainte joie que vous eustes quant vous sentites Dieu ...

Orison to the Virgin in prose.

NEW YORK, New York Public Libr., Spencer 56, fol. 367r°-367v°, XIVc., Hours of Blanche de France, Duchess of Orleans.

5514. Bele tres douce dame sainte Marie, je vous saluerai en l'aneur de la virginité et de la sainte humilité ...

Orison to the Virgin in prose.

NEW YORK, New York Public Libr., Spencer 56, fol. 366r°-366v°, XIVc., Hours of Blanche de France, Duchess of Orleans.

5515. Bele tres douce dame sainte marie, je vous saluerai en non de la sainte tres glorieuse joie que vous eutes quant vous alates veoir ...

Orison to the Virgin in prose.

NEW YORK, New York Public Libr., Spencer 56, fol. 367r°, XIVc., Hours of Blanche de France, Duchess of Orleans.

5516. Bele tres douce dame sainte Marie, je vous saluerai pour cele misericorde que votre fiux deigna morir pour pecheours sauver ...

Orison to the Virgin in prose.

NEW YORK, New York Public Libr., Spencer 56, fol. 369r°-369v°, XIVc., Hours of Blanche de France, Duchess of Orleans.

5517. Benedicite. Dominus, ke dites: Esteez sus! Deu nus doint isi parler ke sauveté soit a nos almes e al confusion de l'enemi ...

Form of Absolution in Anglo-Norman, from Ramsey Benedictine Abbey.

CAMBRIDGE, Cambridge Univ. Libr., Hh. 6. 11, fol. 3r°-3v°, XIIIc.

Ref.: K.V. Sinclair, Mediaeval Studies, 42 (1980), p. 455, n. 13.

5518. Benedicite. Sire, je me confesse a Dieu et a la glorieuse
Vierge Marie et a vous ...

"Briefve maniere de confession pour jones gens", by Jean
Gerson.

DIJON, Bibl. mun., 214, fol. 77rº-78rº, XVc.

OXFORD, Bodleian Libr., Douce 252, fol. 21vº-22vº, early XVc.

PARIS, Bibl. nat., fr. 1003, fol. 10rº-11rº, XVc.

PARIS, Bibl. nat., fr. 1796, fol. 27vº-31vº, XVc.

PARIS, Bibl. nat., fr. 1861, fol. 14rº-16rº, XVc.

PARIS, Bibl. nat., fr. 13258, fol. 43rº-47rº, 1404.

PARIS, Bibl. nat., fr. 25548, fol. 104vº-105vº, XVc.

ROUBAIX, Archives Municipales, no shelf-mark, fol. 89vº-91rº,
XVc., Prayer-book of Jacques de Luxembourg.

TROYES, Bibl. mun., 1465, fol. 63rº-64rº, XVc.

Ed.: Glorieux, Gerson: Oeuvres complètes, VII, 1, pp. 408-9
(base ms. B.N. fr. 13258). Ref.: Kathleen Chesney in Studies
... presented to Mildred K. Pope, Manchester, 1939, p. 67
(mentions Oxford ms.).

*   Beneurez ..., Benurez ...

See the alphabetical order: Bieneurez ...

5519. Benois apostre sainct Symon et sainct Jude, je, qui doubte le
Jugement ...

Suffrage to SS. Simon and Jude, in prose.

NANCY, Bibl. mun., 35 (245), fol. 129vº-130rº, XVc., Hours of
Toul.

Ed.: Rézeau, Saints, II, pp. 491-2.

5520. Benoist Jesus, crucifié pour l'homme
Honteusement par le mors d'une pomme ...

Rondeau to Jesus.

MARSEILLE, Bibl. mun., 49417, fol. 39, 1545.

Ed.: A. Brun, Annales de la Faculté des Lettres d'Aix, 16
(1933-1934), pp. 181-2.

5521. Benoy saint de digne memoire,
Per vostre saincte orison ...

Prayer to several saints; 9 quatrains rhyming abab.

METZ, Bibl. mun., 600, fol. 60v°, XVc., Hours of Paris and Prayer-book.

Ed.: Rézeau, Saints, I, pp. 188-90. Ref.: Rézeau, p. 164.

5522. Benoist soit d'Israel le dieu
Yci et en tout aultre lieu,
Car son peuple il a visité
Et rachaté par charité ...

Canticle of Zechariah, in rhymed couplets, part of the "Heures de Nostre Dame".

LILLE, Bibl. mun., Godefroy 5 (147), fol. 50v°-52r°, XVc., Hours.

5523. Benoit soit le Dieu d'Israel
Qui nous vint oster le flael
Dont nous estions tous bleciés
Par nos maulx et par nos pechiés ...

Canticle of Zechariah in rhyme, forming part of an anon. Vie de S. Jean Baptiste (vv. 811-880).

PARIS, Bibl. nat., fr. 2182, fol. 15r°-16v°, 1322.

Ed.: Gieber, pp. 21-4.

5524. Beneoite soiez tu qui Deu portas,
Benoite soit ta bouche dunt tu le beisas
                    ...

Orison to the Virgin: 5 monorhymed lines, the last four each having eleven syllables. They occur in the midst of a series of Salutations to the Virgin which begin: Dex te saut sainte Marie pleine de grace ... (no. 5706).

NEW YORK, Pierpont Morgan Libr., Morgan 92, fol. 130r°, late XIIIc., Hours.

5525. Benoite Trinité, ung vray Dieu qui feiz homme et femme a ton ymage et a ta semblance et les conjoignis par mariage, assemblement ...

"Ceste oroison aprés doivent dire personnes conjoinctes par mariage."

PROVIDENCE, Brown Univ. Libr., C. 28. b. 4 (H.L. Koopman Collection), fol. 172v°-174v°, XVc., Book of Hours.

*   Benoy ...

See the alphabetical order: Benois ...

5526. Ber saint Denis(e), or m'an aidiez!
Jeo tenc de vus quite mun fies ...

Quatrain to S. Denis by King Louis: Gormont et Isembart (vv. 374-7).

BRUSSELS, Bibl. royale II. 181, fol. 3r°, XIIIc.

Ed.: Scheler, p. 36; Bayot, 1906, fol. 3r°; Bartsch, Chrestomathie, 12 ed., p. 16; Bayot, 3 ed. CFMA, p. 26-7; Henry, Chrestomathie, I, p. 53 and II, p. 20.

5527. Ber seint Richier, or m'en adiez!
Ja vus arst il vostre mustier ...

Orison to S. Richier by King Louis: Gormont et Isembart (vv. 378-83).

BRUSSELS, Bibl. royale, II, 181, fol. 3r, XIIIc.

Ed.: Scheler, p. 36; Bayot, 1906, fol. 3r°; Bartsch, Chrestomathie, 12 ed., p. 16; Bayot, 3 ed. CFMA, p. 26-7; Henry, Chrestomathie, I, p. 53 and II, p. 20.

5528. Bieneuré sont ceulx a qui Dieu a pardonné et relaissé leurs iniquités et desquels leurs pechiés sont convertis ...

Second of the Seven Penitential Psalms, in prose, but doubtless once rhymed. Not the same wording as no. 2598.

SAN MARINO (Calif.), Huntington Libr., HM 1129, fol. 85v°-87v°, c. 1450, Hours of Paris.

5529. Beneurez sont ceulx qui sont netz de cuer
Povres d'esperit qui ont paix et doulceur
                              ...

"Les huit beatitudes"; six decasyllabic lines rhyming aabbcc.

ROUBAIX, Archives Municipales, no shelf-mark, fol. 4r°, XVc., Prayer-book of Jacques de Luxembourg.

5530. Benurez seit ciel a ki ad Deu perdonez ...

Variant of the inc.: Bien eurés sont ceulx a qui Dieu a pardonnés ... (no. 229).

5531. Bieneureux est celuy qui souffre tentation, car quand il aura esté approuvé ...

"Antienne de sainct Gregoire", in prose.

PARIS, Bibl. nat., Rés. B. 9088, fol. 57r°, XVIc.

Ref.: Rézeau, Saints, II, p. 253, records other early imprints of the antiphon.

5532. Bienhureux sont ceux ausquelz leurs iniquités sont remises et desquelz les pechez sont couverts ...

Second of the Penitential Pslams, prose version: Manuel de dévotion de prêtre Pierre. Not quite the same wording as no. 4042.

NEW HAVEN, Yale Univ. Libr., 498, fol. 46r°-47v°, last quarter XVIc.

5533. Bieneureuz sont ceulx sans doubtance
       Dou pardon a leur ignorance
       Et d'iniquitez entechiez
       Desquels couvers sont leur pechiez ...

       Second of the Seven Penitential Psalms; redaction in rhymed
       couplets.

       LILLE, Bibl. mun., Godefroy 5 (147), fol. 94r°-96r°, XVc.,
       Hours.

5534. Bienviengne le roy d'Israel
       Pour son beau royaume ordonner ...

       Rondeau to Jesus: Mystère de la Passion by Arnoul Gréban (vv.
       16286-301).

       CHANTILLY, Musée Condé, 614 (1691), fol. 137v°, XVc.

       PARIS, Bibl. de l'Arsenal, 6431, fol. 115v°, XVc.

       PARIS, Bibl. nat., fr. 815, fol. 130v°, 1458.

       PARIS, Bibl. nat., fr. 816, fol. 113v°-114r°, 1473.

       PARIS, Bibl. nat., fr. 15065, fol. 131v°-132r°, 1469.

       ROME, Accademia Nazionale dei Lincei, Bibl. Corsiniana, Rossi
       412 (44. A. 7), fol. 316r°, late XVc.

       Ed.: Paris-Raynaud, p. 212 (vv. 16325-40); Jodogne, p. 217 (vv.
       16286-301).

5535. Bon Dieu, ou je me dois fïer ...

       Variant of the inc.: Doulx Dieu ou je me doy fïer ... (no.
       5741).

C

5536. Ch'est la dame de grace qui tous nous poet
                                    sauver,
       Ch'est li douche fontaine pour nous pechiés
                                    laver ...

       Praise of the Virgin by a renegade queen: Baudouin de Sebourc
         (vv. 820-7 of Chant XIV).

       PARIS, Bibl. nat., fr. 12552, fol. 68r°, XIVc.

       PARIS, Bibl. nat., fr. 12553, fol. 201r°-201v°, XVc.

       <u>Ed</u>.: Boca, II, p. 24.

5537. Ceo est la parole Jhesu Crist,
       Ke de sa boche meme dit:
       Joe sui le plus amant de tot le mu<n>d ...

       Pious utterance during a sermon in Latin; 6vv, in paired
         rhymes.

       LONDON, British Libr., Harley 505, fol. 20r°, XIVc.

       <u>Ed</u>.: P. Meyer, Romania, 35 (1906), p. 593.

5538. Ce livre en quoy nous devons ...

       Variant of the inc.: Le livre en quoy nous devons ... (no.
         6072).

5539. Ce qui est dessus escript a esté trouvé a Romme et est escript
         deriere l'autel de Saint Piere que le pape Jehan XIIe ordonna
         ...

       Explanation concerning the prayer Domine Jhesu Christe salus et
         liberatio fidelium ... See also no. 5544.

       NEW YORK, Pierpont Morgan Library, Morgan 164, fol. 48r°, XVc.,
         Hours of Dol.

5540.   Celestien citoien eternel,
        En la cité de pardurable gloire ...

        Oraison a sainct Adrien; 34 decasyllabic lines arranged in 5
        stanzas of unequal length.

        PARIS, Bibl. nat., Rés. D. 5616 and Ye 831, Louenges des
        benoictz sainctz et sainctes de paradis, fol. zz 2, Paris,
        Vérard.

        VERSAILLES, Bibl. mun., M. 129 (Lacombe 109 quater).

        Ed.: Rézeau, Saints, II, pp. 3-4.

5541.   Cellui qui vous crea de vous sa mere fist,
        Ce fut engendrement de tres grant bien
                                        eslist.
        Dame, priez celui qui dedans vous se mist,
        Pour nous tous delivrer voult grant paine
                                        soufrir ...

        Orison to the Virgin; 49 alexandrines.

        BALTIMORE, Walters Art Gallery, Walters 261, fol. 106v°-107v°,
        c. 1400, Hours.

5542.   Ces (ms. Ses) heures canoniques a grant devocion a toy saint
        Esperit a piteuse raison ...

        Epilogue, doubtless once in rhyme, to the Heures du Saint
        Esprit.

        SAN MARINO (Calif.), Huntington Libr., HM 1129, fol. 80v°, c.
        1450, Hours of Paris.

5543.   Ces (ms Ses) heures canoniques par grant devocion Jhesucrist a
        toy recognois en piteuse raison ...

        Epilogue, doubtless once in rhyme, to the Heures de la Crois.
        Wording not identical to that of no. 4053.

        SAN MARINO (Calif.), Huntington Libr., HM 1129, fol. 83v°, c.
        1450, Hours of Paris.

5544.   Cest escript a esté trouvé a Romme derriere l'autel Sainct
        Pierre. Jehan pape douziesme a donné et ottroié a tous ceulx
        et celles qui, en passant par la (sic) cimetiere ...

        Explanatory rubric preceding the antiphon: Avete omnes anime
        fideles, and the orison: Domine Jhesu Christe salus et
        liberatio fidelium ... Another version is no. 5539.

        NEW YORK, Pierpont Morgan Libr., Morgan 194, fol. 114r°-114v°,
        XVc., Hours of Paris.

5545.   Ceste oroison cy devant escripte, qui porte grant salut et qui
        tant est belle et elegant, fist monseigneur saint Augustin en
        l'onneur et reverence de la benoite vierge Marie ...

Rubric in red, postpositioned, for the prayer inc.: Salve
doulce vierge Marie ... (no. 6572).

PROVIDENCE, Brown Univ. Libr., C. 28. b. 4 (H.L. Koopman
Collection), fol. 158r°, XVc., Hours.

5546. Ceste oroison fut trouvee (var. cy soubscripte f.t./qui
s'ensuit f.t.) sur le sepulcre de Nostre Dame en valee de
Josaphat et a tant de proprietés car toute personne (var. et
est de telle vertu que quiconques) qui le dira ou le fera
dire ...

Rubric or Prologue to the prayer: Jhesucrist ,filz de Dieu le
pere ... (no. 945). There are many small variant readings in
the wording of this rubric.

BRUGES, Bibl. de la Ville, 322, fol. 1r°, XVes., Hours.

DOUAI, Bibl. mun., 184, fol. 176v., XVIes., Hours.

EPINAL, Bibl. mun., 96 (230), fol. 58v°, XVc.

NANTES, Bibl. mun., 20, p. 31, XVc., Hours.

NORWICH, Castle Museum, 149.938/1, fol. 204v°, early XVc.,
Hours of Rome.

PARIS, Bibl. Mazarine, 481, fol. 121r°, XVc., Hours of Angers.

PARIS, Bibl. nat., fr. 13269, fol. 7v°, XVc.

PARIS, Bibl. nat., nouv. acq. lat. 195, fol. 117r°, XVc.,
Hours.

PARIS, Bibl. Sainte-Geneviève, 2688, fol. 148v°, XVIc.

Ed.: A. Molinier, Cat. des mss. de la Bibl. Mazarine, Paris,
1885, t. I, p. 185. Ref.: Leroquais, Livres d'heures, t. II,
p. 238; Brayer, Livres d'heures, p. 52.

5547. Ceste oroison trouva Joseph d'Armathie sur les playes de Nostre
Seigneur Jhesu Crist du costé destre, escripte en lectre
d'or, et a telle vertu que toute personne qui la portera ...

Explanatory rubric for the prayer: Fidelium Deus omnium
conditor ...

NEW YORK, Pierpont Morgan Libr., Morgan 261, fol. 102v°-103r°,
early XVIc., Hours of Rouen.

*   Ch'est ...

See the alphabetical order: C'est ...

5548. Chante, langue, la glorieuse bataille
Et dis la triumpheuse victoire
Du grant roy des roys
Qu'il a faicte dessus la croix ...

Hymn "Pangue lingua gloriosi certaminis"; 12 stanzas each of 6 lines, rhyming aabbcc.

Early Ed.: Plusieurs belles chansons nouvelles imprimées par Claude Nourry, Lyon, vers 1533. Ed.: Jeffery, II, pp. 94-6.

5549. Chascun doibt croire ung Dieu en Trinité
       Puissant et saige, rempli de clemence ...

"Ballade" in honor of Jesus; six eight-line stanzas and one quatrain.

Refr.: Que d'aimer Dieu et ses
                        commandemenz.

BRUSSELS, Bibl. Royale, IV. 541, fol. 242v°-243v°, 1568.

Ed.: Lemaire, Meschinot, Molinet, Villon: Témoignages inédits, 1979, pp. 81, 188-19.

5550. Chief reluysant, ou tout bien est dressé,
       Saphis courtoys en beauté parfaicte ...

Orison to God by Nostre Dame to designate a pastor: Mystère des Trois Doms, by chanoine Siboud Pra de Grenoble with the assistance of Claude Chevalet de Vienne, and performed at Romans in 1509 (vv. 10620-7).

COLLECTION UNKNOWN (olim Giraud of Lyons), no shelf-mark, fol. not indicated, early XVIc.

Ed.: Giraud and Chevalier, p. 560.

*   Chil ...

See the alphabetical order: Cil ...

5551. Cy dessus est la longueur pourtraite du corps Nostre Seigneur
       par xvj fois compassé, jadis aportee en Constantinoble en une
       croix d'or. Quiconque ceste longueur voyra, en yceluy jour ne
       mourra ...

Explanatory rubric preceding the Latin orison: Benedictio Dei patris cum angelis suis ...

PARIS, Bibl. nat., lat. 1359, fol. 213v°, mid. XVc., Hours of Paris.

Ed.: Leroquais, Livres d'heures, I, p. 170.

5552. Chil Damedieu, dist il, qui maint en
                                  Orient,
       Qui tout fourma le monde et la terre
                                  ensement ...

Orison to God and Jesus by Doon de Mayence for the protection of Charlemagne: Gaufrey (vv. 8709-20).

MONTPELLIER, Bibl. Fac. Ecole de Médecine, H. 247, fol. 80v°, XIVc.

Ed.: Guessard and Chabaille, p. 262.

5553. Cil sires nos consaut qui de virge fu né,
        Et me dones la mort ans qu'il soit ajorné
                        ...

        Variant of the inc.: Damedieu sire pere qui me feïtes né ...
        (no. 5580).

5554. Clere faiçon de biaulté souveraine
        Aiez pitié de vostre chier amy ...

        Last of the "xij balades de Pasques": 13 decasyllabic lines
        rhyming abaabaabbabab, the first and second are repeated as
        the third and last respectively.

        VATICAN CITY, Bibl. apost., Reg. lat. 1728, fol. 118v°, XVc.

        Ed.: Keller, p. 620-1.

5555. Coeur de marbre, couronne d'ayemant
        Ourle de fer a la pointe acheree ...

        Fifth of the "xij balades de Pasques": 13 decasyllabic lines
        rhyming abaabaabbabab, the first and second are repeated as
        the third and last respectively.

        VATICAN CITY, Bibl. apost., Reg. lat. 1728, fol. 118r°, XVc.

        Ed.: Keller, p. 617-18.

5556. Comme il soit vray, si comme on di,
        Que noms que sont correlati ...

        Meditation on the Passion; 34 vv. Its prologue begins: O doulz
        Jhesu, per nulle voie ... (no. 6229).

        METZ, Bibl. mun., 600, fol. 177r°-177v°, XVc., Hours of Paris
        and Prayer-book.

        Ref.: Rézeau, pp. 178-9.

5557. Comme le cerf cerche les fontaines des eaux ai je crié mon ame
        aprés toy, o Dieu ! Mon ame a eu soif de toy, Seigneur Dieu
                        ...

        "Du vehement desir de l'ame a la vie eternelle de paradis":
        Manuel de dévotion de prêtre Pierre.

        NEW HAVEN, Yale Univ. Libr., 498, fol. 144r°-151r°, last
        quarter XVIc.

5558. Conseille, instruyz, conforte, chastie
        Donne, pardonne, radresse et pour tous prie
                        ...

"Les euvres de misericorde"; eight decasyllabic lines rhyming in pairs.

ROUBAIX, Archives Municipales, no shelf-mark, fol. 4r°-4v°, XVc., Prayer-book of Jacques de Luxembourg.

5559.   Crier devons a haulte alaine
De la doulour que nous sentons
Ha! roy Jhesus, toy demendons:
Dessens tost, sy nous vien hors traire!
(Complete Text)

"Plainte" to God by Daniel: "Mystere de la Nativité" (vv. 1158-61).

LONDON, British Libr., Additional 38860, fol. 24r°, XVIIIc. copy of a lost ms.

PARIS, Bibl. Sainte-Geneviève, 1131, fol. 13r°, XVc.

Ed.: Whittredge, p. 129.

5560.   Demande: Croyez vous en Dieu le pere tout puissant qui a creé le ciel et la terre? Response: Et qui d'avantaige a creé tout ce qui est contenu ...

Le Symbole des apostres (qu'on dict vulgairement le Credo) contenant les articles de la foy; par maniere de dialogue, par demande et par response. La pluspart extraict d'ung traicté de Erasme de Roterdam intitué "Devises familieres"; traduction faite par le chevalier Louis de Berquin en 1525.

Ed.: Brefve admonition de la maniere de prier selon la doctrine de Jesuchrist, avec une brefve explanation du Pater Noster, Extraict des Paraphrases de Erasme, Paris, Simon Dubois (?), 1525; Telle, pp. 47-73.

5561.   Crois, en toy voy mon pere Dieu pendre
Et moult crueusement estendre.
Croix precieusement paree
Et du corps Dieu enluminee ..

Orison to the Cross, 50 lines rhyming in 25 couplets.

MANCHESTER, John Rylands Univ. Libr., French 143, fol. 180r°-181r°, early XVc., Hours.

5562.   Crucifie! souvent criant (sic) a heure de tierce. Truffé est, vestu d'une vesture ...

Hours of the Cross: Terce, in prose, but possibly once in rhyme.

SAN MARINO (Calif.), Huntington Libr., HM 1129, fol. 82v°, c. 1450, Hours of Paris.

*   Cy ...

See the alphabetical order: Ci ...

D

5563. D'ung cueur recuyt en flamme charitable,
Tout aspergé d'amere punction ...

Ballade to S. Mary Magdalene; three stanzas each of ten lines
and an envoy of four lines.

Refr.: Place es sains cieulx, benoite
Magdalene.

CAMBRIDGE, Fitzwilliam Museum, Fitzwilliam 105, fol. 87r°-88v°,
1530, Hours of Rouen.

Ed.: Rézeau, Saints, II, pp. 354-5.

5564. Dame de grace, mere du fruict de vie,
Celle en qui toute bonté abonde,
En ceste place a joinctes mains vous prie
Que soyez de mon bien sçonde (sic) ...

Orison to the Virgin; five stanzas grouping 10, 10, 9, 9, 5
lines which are octosyllabic for the most part; each strophe
is preceded by "Ave Maria" and concludes with "Amen".

Refr.: Comme de toutes la plus digne.

NEW YORK, Pierpont Morgan Libr., Morgan 292, fol. 2r°-3r°,
early XVIc. Prayer-book.

5565. Dame des cieux, granz roïne puissanz,
Au grant besoing me soiez secorranz!
De vous amer puisse avoir droite flame!
Quant dame pert, dame me soit aidanz!

Orison to the Virgin, concluding Thibaut de Champagne's Chanson
de Croisade Dame, ensi est qu'il m'en couvient aler (vv.
41-4).

PARIS, Bibl. nat., fr. 844, fol. 64v°, late XIIIc.

PARIS, Bibl. nat., fr. 846, fol. 34v°, late XIIIc.

PARIS, Bibl. nat., fr. 12615, fol. 8r°, XIIIc.

PARIS, Bibl. nat., nouv. acq. fr. 1050, fol. 20v°, late XIIIc.

Ed.: Bédier and Aubry, p. 194; Wallensköld, p. 189; J. and Louise Beck, Les Chansonniers des troubadours et des trouvères - I: Le chansonnier Cangé (Paris, Bibl. nat., fr. 846), Paris and Philadelphia, 1927, I, fol. 34v°, and II, p. 78; J. and Louise Beck, Les Chansonniers ... II: Le Manuscrit du Roi, fonds français 844 de la Bibl. nat., Philadelphia, 1938, I, pl. Mt, VII, v°, no. 22. Ref.: L. Clédat, La Poésie lyrique et satirique en France au moyen âge, Paris, 1893, p. 192.

5566. Dame, donnés moy heure et temps
       De venir en vostre service.
       A vostre mercy je me rens.
       Estre vueilliés moy propice ...

       "Oraison a Nostre Dame"; one eight-line stanza, rhyming ababbcbc.

       NEW YORK, Pierpont Morgan Libr., Morgan 161, fol. 22r°, late XVc., Hours for Le Mans.

5567. Dame, je sai certennement que vos devenistes meire de Deu por les pecheours ne j'ai seste digniteit ...

       Prayer to the Virgin, in prose.

       BALTIMORE, Walters Art Gallery, Walters 91, fol. 28v°, 27r°-27v°, 29r°, c. 1300, Prayer-book.

5568. Dame, metez le en voz coffre
       Et ly priez, Vierge pucelle ...

       Orison to the Virgin by Melchior: "Geu des trois roys" (vv. 724-33).

       PARIS, Bibl. Sainte-Geneviève, 1131, fol. 28r°-28v°, XVc.

       Ed.: Whittredge, pp. 174-5.

5569. Dame, qui mes Sire tant prise
       Qu'i ne puet plus, prenez cest offre ...

       Orison to Virgin by Balthazar: "Geu des trois roys" (vv. 682-91).

       PARIS, Bibl. Sainte-Geneviève, 1131, fol. 28r°, XVc.

       Ed.: Whittredge, pp. 173-4.

5570. Dame saincte Anne glorieuse,
       Digne, vaillant et vertueuse ...

       Prayer to S. Anne; 50 lines rhyming in pairs.

PARIS, Bibl. nat., Rés. D. 5616 and Ye 831, Louenges des benoictz sainctz et sainctes de paradis, fol. yy 4v°, Paris, Vérard.

VERSAILLES, Bibl. mun., M. 129 (Lacombe 109 quater).

Ed.: Rézeau, Saints, II, pp. 32-33.

5571.   Dame soverainne et antiere,
        Dieu, ou panra je la maniere ...

        "O intemerata", 99 vv., lacking one, 50 paired rhymes.

        METZ, Bibl. mun., 600, fol. 179r°-180v°, XVc., Hours of Paris and Prayer-book.

        Ref.: Rézeau, p. 179.

*   Damedieu ...

        Here are grouped the spellings: Damedex ..., Damedieu ..., Damedieus ..., Damediex ..., Dameldé ..., Dameldieu ..., Dammedé ... The alphabetical order within the group is determined by the spelling of the next word that is not underlined.

5572.   Dameldé, reclama, le pere esperital,
        El ventre del pisson garistes saint Jonas
                                    ...

        Orison to God and the Virgin by Galopin: Elie de Saint-Gille (vv. 1961-5).

        PARIS, Bibl. nat., fr. 25516, fol. 89v°, XIIIc.

        Ed.: Förster, p. 375; Raynaud, p. 65. Ref.: Merk, p. 9 n. 4 and 8; 28 n. 10 etc.

5573.   Dameldé, dist il, pere, par ton digne
                                    commant,
        Mar furent nostre cors, li preu et li
                                    vaillant ...

        Plainte to God by Guillaume d'Orange: Elie de Saint-Gille (vv. 285-9).

        PARIS, Bibl. nat., fr. 25516, fol. 78r°, XIIIc.

        Ed.: Förster, p. 327; Raynaud, p. 10. Ref.: Merk, p. 235, n. 1.

5574.   Dameldieu, fist il, pere, qui me fesistes
                                    né,
        Je ne mangai de pain bien a .iij. jors
                                    passé,
        Puis a je tant maint cop recheu et doné:
        Vous me donés hui home qui me doinst a
                                    disner.
                        (Complete Text)

        Orison to God by the hero: Elie de Saint-Gille (vv. 1049-52).

PARIS, Bibl. nat., fr. 25516, fol. 83r°, XIIIc.

Ed.: Foerster, p. 349; Raynaud, p. 35. Ref.: Merk, p. 298 n.

5575. Damedieu pere, dist Guiberz li menbrez,
Qui por nos futes an sainte croiz penez
Par itel gent dom n'estiez amez,
Por vostre pueple qui toz estoit dampnez

...

Orison to Jesus by Guibert before being crucified: Narbonnais
(vv. 5035-70).

LONDON, British Libr., Harley 1321, fol. 100v°-101r°, XIIIc.

LONDON, British Libr., Royal 20. B. XIX, fol. 94r°, XIIIc.

Ed.: Suchier, I, pp. 200-1. Ref.: Merk, pp. 15 n. 3, 19 n. 8,
20 n. 1, 21 n. 13, 187 n. 1, 188 n. 17 etc.; Dickman, p. 195;
Scheludko, ZFSL, 58 (1934), pp. 79 and 179; Wels, p. 3 n. 4
and 7; Koch, pp. 77 and 125; Labande, pp. 72 n. 9, 73 n. 9,
76 n. 7; Saly, p. 51.

5576. Damediex, peres soverains
Qui as tote cose en tes mains,
Home fesis a ta sanlance,
Aprés li donas habondance ...

Prayer to God by Floire, about to enter the lion's den: Floire
et Blancheflor (vv. 919-32).

PARIS, Bibl. nat., fr. 375, fol. 249v°, late XIIIc.

PARIS, Bibl. nat., fr. 12562, fol. 74v°, XVc.

Ed.: E. du Méril, Floire et Blanceflor, poèmes du XIIIe siècle,
Paris, 1856, p. 233; Wilhelmina Wirtz, Flore et Blancheflor
nach der Pariser Handschrift 375 (A), Frankfurt, 1937, p. 37;
Felicitas Krüger, Li Romanz de Floire et Blanchflor in
beiden   Fassungen   nach   allen   Handschriften   ...   neu
herausgegeben, Berlin, 1938, pp. 40-1; Margaret M. Pelan,
Floire et Blancheflor, édition du ms. 1447 du fonds fr. avec
notes, variantes et glossaire, Paris, 1956, p. 104; J.L.
Leclanche, Le Conte de Floire et Blancheflor, Paris, 1980, p.
42. Ref.: Koch, pp. 49 and 108.

5577. Dammedé, ce dist Charlez le ber,
Qui descendis du ciel le monde saulver ...

Orison to Jesus by Charlemagne: Aquin (vv. 1922-80).

PARIS, Bibl. nat., fr. 2233, fol. 34v°-35v°, XVc.

Ed.: Joüon des Longrais, p. 75-7. Ref.: Gautier, p. 543; Merk,
p. 21 n. 13; p. 186 n. 1; p. 188 n. 17; Dickman, p. 195; D.
Scheludko, ZFSL, 58 (1934), p. 82, 178; Koch, p. 37-9, 102;
Labande, p. 73, 74 n. 1, 75, 76 n. 7, 77 n. 1, 6, 7, 8.

5578.   Damedex sire pere, qui an croiz fu penez,
        Et an la sainte Virge preïs humelité,
        Tu me desfant, beauz sire, par ta sainte
                                    bonté,
        Que ne puisse mon pere occire ne afoler!
                    (Complete Text)

        Orison to Jesus by Hugues de Vauvenice: Parise la duchesse (vv.
           2170-3).

        PARIS, Bibl. nat., fr. 1374, fol. 15r, XIIIc.

        Ed.: Guessard and Larchey, p. 65.

5579.   Damedex sire peres, qui formastes Adan
        Et Evain sa mollier par vo conmandement,
        An paradis terrestre meïs chacun vivant,
        De toz les frus des abres dont il ot ilec
                                    tant ...

        Orison to God by Countess Aceline de Beauvais, about to be
           burnt at the stake: Orson de Beauvais (vv. 2071-82).

        PARIS, Bibl. nat., nouv. acq. fr. 16600 (olim Phillipps 222),
           fol. 33r°, XIIIc.

        Ed.: Paris, p. 69. Ref.: Merk, p. 186, n. 4; 187, n. 1; 188, n.
           18; Koch, p. 61, 116; Labande, p. 62, n. 3; 71, n. 2.

5580.   Damedieu sire pere, qui me feïtes né,
        Car me donez la mort einz que soit avespré,
        Ou tel home m'envoies par la teue bonté
        Que de ceanz me giet ennuit a sauveté.
                    (Complete Text)

        Orison to God by Beuves de Commarchis: Siège de Barbastre (vv.
           573-6).

        LONDON, British Libr., Harley 1321, fol. 125r°, late XIIIc.

        LONDON, British Libr., Royal 20. B. XIX, fol. 114r°, mid XIIIc.

        LONDON, British Libr., Royal 20. D. XI, fol. 217v°-218r°, XIVc.

        PARIS, Bibl. nat., fr. 1448, fol. 113v°, mid. XIIIc. First two
           lines have a variant inc.: Cil sires nos consaut qui de virge
           fu né, Et me dones la mort ans qu'il soit ajorné ...

        PARIS, Bibl. nat., fr. 24369, fol. 119v°, XIVc.

        Ed.: Perrier, p. 19 (base ms. London, Royal 20. B. XIX).

*   Dameldé ..., Dameldieu ..., Dammedé ...

        See the alphabetical order: Damedieu ...

5581.   De celle sainte beneichon soies tu huy beneis .N. dont Dieu
           beneÿ les trois roys que Herode vouloit ochire ...

        Orison to the Trinity.

CHICAGO, Newberry Libr., 52, fol. 181v°-183r°, <u>c</u>. 1470, Hours of Rheims.

5582.   De cueur et de bouche je vous recongnois et confesse, vostre subgect et homme, creature et serviteur. Mon tres cher Sire et benoist, je vous mercye ...

La tierce leçon (du salut eternel); for the first two, see the inc.: La premier leçon du salut eternel ...; and Mon benoist Dieu, ainsy comment ...

CAMBRIDGE, Harvard College Libr., Lat. 251, fol. 75r°-76v°, late XVc., Hours of Rome.

5583.   De grant parfondetei, Dieux, crien en ta
                                    haultesse.
Ressoi ma voix en grei si m'aide et
                              adresse.
Encline moi t'orelle si me fais tel pardon
Que m'ame ne soit dempnee (<u>sic</u>) ne voit a
                              perdicion ...

Sixth of the Penitential Psalms; dodecasyllabic lines; not identical with no. 2697.

MANCHESTER, John Rylands Univ. Libr., French 143, fol. 94v°-96r°, early XVc., Hours.

5584.   De grant parfundesce (<u>sic</u>)
Te cri a ta hautesce.
Reçoif ma voiz a gré
Si me aÿe e adresce ...

Sixth of the Penitential Psalms; a rhymed version.

STUTTGART, Württembergische Landesbibl., Brev. 75, fol. 74r°-75r°, XIVc., Hours of Sarum.

5585.   De grant travail et de petit esploit
Voi le siecle charchié et encombré,
Que tant sonmes plain de malëurté
Que nus ne pense a fere ce qu'il doit ...

"Chanson à la Vierge" on the subject of the wickedness of the world; five stanzas of nine decasyllabic lines, rhyming abbabccbc, and a three line envoy. Attributed to Thibaut de Champagne, roi de Navarre.

PARIS, Bibl. de l'Arsenal, 5198, p. 29, XIIIc.

PARIS, Bibl. nat., fr. 846, fol. 35r°, late IIIc.

PARIS, Bibl. nat., fr. 12581, fol. 318r°, XIVc.

PARIS, Bibl. nat., fr. 12615, fol. 14r°, XIIIc.

PARIS, Bibl. nat., fr. 24406, fol. 15r°, XIIIc.

PARIS, Bibl. nat., nouv. acq. fr. 1050, fol. 27r°, late XIIIc.

Ed.: P. Tarbé, Chansons de Thibault IV, comte de Champagne et
de Brie, Reims, 1851, p. 117; A. Jeanroy and P. Aubry, Le
Chansonnier de l'Arsenal ... Reproduction phototypique du ms.
5198 de la Bibl. de l'Arsenal, Paris, 1912, p. 29; A.
Wallensköld, Les Chansons de Thibaut de Champagne, Paris,
1925, p. 21, no. LX; Järnström and Längfors, pp. 8, 50-3; J.
and Louise Beck, Les Chansonniers des troubadours et des
trouvères. - I: Le chansonnier Cangé (Paris, Bibl. nat., fr.
846), Paris and Philadelphia, 1927, I, fol. 35r°. Ref.:
Spanke, no. 1843.

5586.   De la crois est deposé a heure de vespres; force est chassee en
pensee divine ...

Hours of the Cross: Vespers, in prose, but possibly once in
rhyme.

SAN MARINO (Calif.), Huntington Libr., HM 1129, fol. 83r°, c.
1450, Hours of Paris.

5587.   De la passion e de pentecoste devez penser devaunt tierce
coment ...

Variant of the inc.: Devant tierce devez penser de la passion
et de la pentecoste ... (no. 5612).

5588.   De parfons lieux j'ay crié a toy,
Sire! Sire, exaulche ma voix ...

Variant of the inc.: J'ay crié a toy, Sire ... (no. 4496).

5589.   De toutes les orisons qui onques furent faites et establies en
terre et en sainte Eglize, si est la plus haute et la plus
digne la patenostre ...

"Exposicion de la patenostre en françois"; the prayer itself
precedes and begins: Pater noster qui es in celis ...
(no. 6543).

BRUSSELS, Bibl. royale, 10574-85, fol. 116r°-118v°, XIIIc.

5590.   Debonnaire mere de pitié, soies pour nous advocas et aies
pitiés des meschans devant le throne ...

"Antene de Nostre Dame: Ante thronum trinitatis".

MANCHESTER, John Rylands Univ. Libr., French 143, fol. 18r°,
early XVc., Hours.

5591.   Deduict d'amours, nourry en doulx espoir,
Out mon cuer mis en noble seignourie ...

Ninth of the "xij balades de Pasques": 13 decasyllabic lines
rhyming abaabaabbabab, the first and second are repeated as
the third and last respectively.

VATICAN CITY, Bibl. apost., Reg. lat. 1728, fol. 118v°, XVc.

Ed.: Keller, p. 619.

5592. Delivre moy de mes ennemis, Seigneur. J'ay prins mon refuge a
      toy. Enseigne moy a fere ta voulonté car tu es mon Dieu ...

      "Oraison contre les tentations du diable": Manuel de dévotion
      de prêtre Pierre.

      NEW HAVEN, Yale Univ. Libr., 498, fol. 134v°-135v°, last
      quarter XVIc.

5593. Demostenes, eloquent orateur,
      Ne pourroit bien, celeste implorateur ...

      Orison to S. Nicolas; 110 vv. grouped in various ways.

      ROUEN, Bibl. mun., 1064 (Y 226a), pp. 118-123, XVIc.

      Ed.: Rézeau, Saints, II, pp. 405-9.

5594. Desormais Dieu en pais me laisse,
      Que mi eul ont veu ta face.
      Des yeuz as fais et biaulz et gens
      Pour lumiere estre en toute gens.
                    (Complete Text)

      "Nunc dimittis" in Compline of the Heures de Nostre Dame.

      MANCHESTER, John Rylands Univ. Libr., French 143, fol. 81r°,
      early XVc., Hours.

*   Deu ..., Deus ...

      See the alphabetical order: Dieu ...

5595. Devant complie deis tu penser coment Joseph et Nichodemus ...

      Variant of the inc.: Devant complie devez penser coment Josep e
      Nichomede ... (no. 5596).

5596. Devant complie devez penser coment Josep e Nichomede
      envoluperent le cors Jhesu en beus lincheus ...

      Meditation for Compline of the Hours of the Cross, in the
      Miror de seinte Eglyse, a translation of the Speculum
      Ecclesiae by S. Edmund of Abingdon. The texts of A and B
      versions are close.

      CAMBRIDGE, Emmanuel College, I. 4. 31, fol. 99v°, XIVc. (A
      version). Inc.: Devaunt complie deis tu penser coment Joseph
      ...

      DURHAM, Durham Univ. Libr., Cosin V.V. 15, fol. 40r°-40v°,
      XIVc. (B version). Inc.: Devant complie deis tu penser coment
      Josep ...

      LINCOLN, Chapter Libr., B. 5. 1, fol. 176v°, XIVc. (B version).
      Inc.: Devant complie deis tu penser coment Joseph ...

      LONDON, British Libr., Arundel 288, fol. 119v°, XIIIc. (B
      version).

LONDON, British Libr., Harley 1121, fol 153v°, early XIVc. (B version).

LONDON, British Libr., Royal 12. C. XII, fol. 28r°, early XIVc. (A version).

LONDON, British Libr., Royal 20. B. XIV, fol. 63r°-63v°, early XIVc. (A version).

MADRID, Bibl. nac., 18253, fol. 142r°-142v°, XIVc., (A version).

NEW HAVEN, Yale Univ. Libr., 492, fol. 96v°, early XIVc. (A version).

OXFORD, Bodleian Libr., Digby 20, fol. 155v°, XIIIc. (B version). Inc.: Devant complie dois tu penser coment Joseph ...

OXFORD, Bodleian Libr., Digby 98, fol. 250v°-251r°, early XIVc. (B version).

OXFORD, Bodleian Libr., Douce 210, fol. 41v°-42r°, early XIVc. (A version).

OXFORD, Bodleian Libr., Rawlinson Poetry 241, p. 185, late XIIIc. (B version). Inc.: Devant comp(e)lie doys tu penser ...

OXFORD, Bodleian Libr., Selden Supra 74, fol. 56v°, XIIIc. (A version).

OXFORD, Corpus Christi College, 36, fol. 43r°-43v°, early XIVc. (A version).

OXFORD, St. John's College, 190, fol. 197v°, late XIIIc. (A version).

PARIS, Bibl. nat., fr. 13342, fol. 42r°, early XIVc. (A version). Inc.: Devant complie doiz tu penser coment Joseph ...

PARIS, Bibl. nat., nouv. acq. fr. 11200, fol. 19r°, XIIIc. (A version). Inc.: Devant complie deis tu penser coment ...

Ed.: Robbins, p. 67 (base ms. Oxford, Digby 20); Wilshere, p. 72 (A version, base ms. Oxford, St. John's College, 190); p. 73 (B version, base ms. London, Arundel 288). Ref.: Same as the Ref. section of the inc.: Aprés ço devez saver queus sunt les set prieres ... (no. 5431).

5597. Devant le midi devez penser de l'anunciacion e de la passion. De l'annunciation devez penser de la misericorde Nostre Seyngnur ...

Meditation for Sext of the Hours of the Cross, in the Mirour de seinte Eglyse, a translation of the Speculum Ecclesiae by S. Edmund of Abingdon. The texts of A and B versions are close.

CAMBRIDGE, Emmanuel College, I. 4. 31, fol. 96v°-98r°, XIVc. (A version). Inc.: Devant midi deis tu penser de la misericorde Nostre Seignur Jhesu Crist pur quei il voleit ...

CAMBRIDGE, Pembroke College, 258, fol. 128v°, XIVc. (Extracts). Inc.: Devaunt midy deis tu penser de l'annunciacioun et de la passioun ...

DURHAM, Durham Univ. Libr., Cosin V.V. 15, fol. 38r°-39r°, XIVc. (B version). Inc.: Devant midi deis tu penser de l'anunciacion e de la passion ...

LINCOLN, Chapter Libr., B. 5. 1, fol. 175v°-176r°, XIVc. (B version). Inc.: Devant mydi deis tu penser de l'anunciacion et de la passion ...

LONDON, British Libr., Arundel 288, fol. 117v°-118v°, XIIIc. (B version).

LONDON, British Libr., Harley 1121, fol. 152v°-153r°, early XIVc. (B version). Inc.: A miedi devez penser de l'anounciatioun et de la passioun ...

LONDON, British Libr., Royal 12. C. XII, fol. 26v°-27r°, early XIVc. (A version).

LONDON, British Libr., Royal 20. B. XIV, fol. 62r°-62v°, early XIVc. (A version).

MADRID, Bibl. nac., 18253, fol. 141r°, XIVc. (A version). Acephalous copy commencing near the end: -nere de pité Nou goth sunne under ...

NEW HAVEN, Yale Univ. Libr., 492, fol. 95v°-96r°, early XIVc. (A version).

OXFORD, Bodleian Libr., Digby 20, fol. 154v°-155r°, XIIIc. (B version). Inc.: Devant midi deis tu penser de l'annunciacion e de la passion ...

OXFORD, Bodleian Libr., Digby 98, fol. 248r°-249r°, early XIVc. (B version).

OXFORD, Bodleian Libr., Douce 210, fol. 41r°-41v°, early XIVc. (A version).

OXFORD, Bodleian Libr., Rawlinson Poetry 241, pp. 183-4, late XIIIc. (B version). Inc.: Devant midy doys tu penser de l'anunciation ...

OXFORD, Bodleian Libr., Selden Supra 23, fol. 2v°, XIVc. (Fragments).

OXFORD, Bodleian Libr., Selden Supra 74, fol. 55r°-55v°, XIIIc. (A version).

OXFORD, Corpus Christi College, 36, fol. 42v°, early XIVc. (A version).

OXFORD, St. John's College, 190, fol. 196v°-197r°, late XIIIc. (A version).

PARIS, Bibl. nat., fr. 13342, fol. 40v°-41r°, early XIVc. (A version). Inc.: Devant mydi dois tu penser de l'anunciacion ...

PARIS, Bibl. nat., nouv. acq. fr. 11200, fol. 17v°-18r°, XIIIc. (A version). Inc.: Devant midi deis tu penser de l'anunciation ...

Ed.: Robbins, pp. 61-4 (base ms. Oxford, Digby 20); Wilshere, pp. 64, 66, 68 (A version, base ms. Oxford St. John's College 190); pp. 65, 67, 69 (B version, base ms. London, Arundel 288). Ref.: Same as the Ref. section of the inc.: Aprés ço devez saver queus sunt les set prieres ... (no. 5431).

5598. Devant matines/matins deis tu penser ententivement le tens e le lu e le hure ...

Variant of the inc.: Devant matines/matins devez penser de la nativeté primes ... (no. 5600).

5599. Devaunt matines devet (= devez) penser de ce(s) ij (choses) especiaument. La primere chose est ke a tel houre fu Jhesu pris et lié ...

Matins of the Hours of the Cross, part of the "Meditationes de dulci passione Jhesucristi".

LONDON, British Libr., Additional 11579, fol. 32v°, XIVc.

5600. Devant matines/matins devez penser de la nativeté primes, e pus de la passion. De la nativité devez penser ententivement le tens e le lu ...

Meditation for Matins of the Hours of the Cross, in the Mirour de seynte Eglyse, a translation of the Speculum Ecclesiae by S. Edmund of Abingdon. The texts of A and B versions are close.

CAMBRIDGE, Emmanuel College, I. 4. 31, fol. 94r°-94v°, XIVc. (A version). Inc.: Devaunt matins deis tu penser ententivement le temps et le liu et le houre ...

CAMBRIDGE, Pembroke College, 258, fol. 127v°, XIVc. (Extracts). Inc.: Devaunt matyns deis tu penser ententivement le temps et le lu et le houre ...

CAMBRIDGE, Trinity College, O. 1. 17, fol. 287r°-287v°, XIVc. (A version). Inc.: Devant matin devez vous pensir ententivement del temps del lu e de l'hure ...

DURHAM, Durham Univ. Libr., Cosin V.V. 15, fol. 36r°-36v°, XIVc. (B version). Devant matines deis tu penser ententivement le tens e le lou e le hure ...

LINCOLN, Chapter Libr., B. 5. 1, fol. 174v°-175r°, XIVc. (B version). Inc.: Devant matins deis tu penser ententivement le tens le leu e l'ure ...

LONDON, British Libr., Arundel 288, fol. 116r°-116v°, XIIIc. (B version).

LONDON, British Libr., Harley 1121, fol. 151v°, early XIVc. (B version).

LONDON, British Libr., Royal 12. C. XII, fol. 25v°-26r°, early XIVc. (A version).

LONDON, British Libr., Royal 20. B. XIV, fol. 61r°, early XIVc. (A version).

MADRID, Bibl. nac., 18253, fol. 139r°-140r°, XIVc. (A version).

NEW HAVEN, Yale Univ. Libr., 492, fol. 94r°-94v°, early XIVc.

OXFORD, Bodleian Libr., Digby 20, fol. 153r°, XIIIc. (B version).

OXFORD, Bodleian Libr., Digby 98, fol. 245r°-246r°, early XIVc. (B version).

OXFORD, Bodleian Libr., Douce 210, fol. 40r°-40v°, early XIVc. (A version).

OXFORD, Bodleian Libr., Rawlinson Poetry 241, p. 181, late XIIIc. (B version). Inc.: Devant matyns doys tu penser ententivement le temps, le leu et la houre ...

OXFORD, Bodleian Libr., Selden Supra 74, fol. 54r°, XIIIc. (A version).

OXFORD, Corpus Christi College, 36, fol. 41v°-42r°, early XIVc. (A version).

OXFORD, St. John's College, 190, fol. 196r°, late XIIIc. (A version).

PARIS, Bibl. nat., fr. 13342, fol. 39r°-39v°, early XIVc. (A version). Inc.: Devant matins pensez ententivement du temps, du lu et de l'houre ...

PARIS, Bibl. nat., nouv. acq. fr. 11200, fol. 15v°-16r°, XIIIc. (A version). Inc.: Devant matines deis tu penser de la nativité primes e puis de la passion ...

Ed.: Robbins, pp. 56-7 (base ms. Oxford Digby 20); Wilshere, pp. 58, 60 (A version, base ms. Oxford, St. John's College, 190); p. 59, 61 (B version, base ms. London, Arundel 288). Ref.: Same as the Ref. section of the inc. Aprés ço devez saver queus sunt les set prieres ... (no. 5431).

5601. Devant matines devez (vous) penser ententivement del temps, du lu e de l'hure ...

Variant of the inc.: Devant matines/matins devez penser de la nativeté primes ... (no. 5600).

5602. Devaunt midy deis tu penser de l'annunciacioun et de la passioun ...

Variant of the inc.: Devant le midi devez penser de l'anunciacion ... (no. 5597).

5603. Devant midi deis tu penser de la misericorde Nostre Seignur ...

Variant of the inc.: Devant le midi devez penser de l'anunciacion e de la passion ... (no. 5597).

5604. Devant noune deis tu penser de la passion e de l'assencioun ...

Variant of the inc.: Devant nune devez penser de la passion e de l'assencion ... (no. 5605).

5605. Devant nune devez penser de la passion e de l'assencion. De la passion devez penser ke a tele hure del jur murut ...

Meditation for Nones of the Hours of the Cross, in the Mirour de seinte Eglyse, a translation of the Speculum Ecclesiae of S. Edmund of Abingdon. The texts of A and B versions are close.

CAMBRIDGE, Emmanuel College, I. 4. 31, fol. 98r⁰-98v⁰, XIVc. (A version). Inc.: Devaunt noune deis tu penser de la passion e de l'asscencion ...

CAMBRIDGE, Pembroke College, 258, fol. 128v⁰-129r⁰, XIVc. (Extracts).

DURHAM, Durham Univ. Libr., Cosin V.V. 15, fol. 39r⁰-39v⁰, XIVc. (B version). Inc.: Devant noun deis (tu) penser de la passion ...

LINCOLN, Chapter Libr., B. 5. 1, fol. 176r⁰, XIVc. (B version). Inc.: Devant noune deis tu penser de la passion ...

LONDON, British Libr., Arundel 288, fol. 118v⁰-119r⁰, XIIIc. (B version).

LONDON, British Libr., Harley 1121, fol. 153r⁰-153v⁰, early XIVc. (B version).

LONDON, British Libr., Royal 12. C. XII, fol. 27r⁰-27v⁰, early XIVc. (A version).

LONDON, British Libr., Royal 20. B. XIV, fol. 62v⁰-63r⁰, early XIVc. (A version).

MADRID, Bibl. nac., 18253, fol. 141r⁰-141v⁰, XIVc. (A version).

NEW HAVEN, Yale Univ. Libr., 492, fol. 96r⁰, early XIVc. (A version).

OXFORD, Bodleian Libr., Digby 20, fol. 155r⁰-155v⁰, XIIIc. (B version). Inc.: Devant none dois tu penser de la passion ...

OXFORD, Bodleian Libr., Digby 98, fol. 249r⁰-250r⁰, early XIVc. (B version).

OXFORD, Bodleian Libr., Douce 210, fol. 41v°, early XIVc. (A version).

OXFORD, Bodleian Libr., Rawlinson Poetry 241, pp. 184-5, late XIIIc. (B version). Inc.: Devant noune doys tu penser de la passion ...

OXFORD, Bodleian Libr., Selden Supra 74, fol. 55v°-56r°, XIIIc. (A version).

OXFORD, Corpus Christi College, 36, fol. 42v°-43r°, early XIVc. (A version).

OXFORD, St. John's College, 190, fol. 197r°, late XIIIc. (A version).

PARIS, Bibl. nat., fr. 13342, fol. 41r°-41v°, early XIVc. (A version). Inc.: Devant noune doiz tu penser de la passion ...

PARIS, Bibl. nat., nouv. acq. fr. 11200, fol. 18r°-18v°, XIIIc. (A version).

Ed.: Robbins, pp. 64-5 (base ms. Oxford, Digby 20); Wilshere, pp. 68, 70 (A version, base ms. Oxford, St. John's College, 190); pp. 69, 71 (B version, base ms. London, Arundel 288). Ref.: Same as the Ref. section of the inc. Aprés ço devez saver queus sunt les set prieres ... (no. 5431).

5606. Devant prime deis tu penser de la passion et de la resurrection ...

Variant of the inc.: Devant prime devez penser de la passion e de la resurreccion ... (no. 5608).

5607. Devant prime devez penser coment les Jeus le menent/menerent en leur concil/courtil ...

Variant of the inc.: Devant prime devez penser de la passion e de la resurreccion ... (no. 5608).

5608. Devant prime devez penser de la passion e de la resurreccion. De la passion devez penser coment les Gieus le menerent en lur consil e porterent faus testmoynes ...

Meditation for Prime of the Hours of the Cross, in the Mirour de seinte Eglyse, a translation of the Speculum Ecclesiae by S. Edmund of Abingdon. The texts of A and B versions are very close.

CAMBRIDGE, Emmanuel College, I. 4. 31, fol. 94v°-96v°, XIVc. (A version). Inc.: Devaunt prime deis tu penser de la passion et de la resurrection. De la passion deis tu penser coment les Jeus le menerent en cortil ...

CAMBRIDGE, Pembroke College, 258, fol. 127v°-128r°, XIVc. (Extracts).

DURHAM, Durham Univ. Libr., Cosin V.V. 15, fol. 36v⁰-37v⁰, XIVc. (B version). Inc.: Devant prime deis tu penser de la passion et de la resurrection. De la passion deis tu penser coment les Juis le menerent en curtile ...

LINCOLN, Chapter Libr., B. 5. 1, fol. 175r⁰, XIVc. (B version). Inc.: Devant prime deis tu penser de la passion ...

LONDON, British Libr., Arundel 288, fol. 116v⁰-117v⁰, XIIIc. (B version). Inc.: Devaunt prime devez penser coment les Jeus le menent en leur concil ...

LONDON, British Libr., Harley 1121, fol. 151v⁰-152r⁰, early XIVc. (B version). Devant prime devez penser coment les Juis l'amenerent en lur courtil ...

LONDON, British Libr., Royal 12. C. XII, fol. 26r⁰-26v⁰, early XIVc. (A version).

LONDON, British Libr., Royal 20. B. XIV, fol. 61r⁰-61v⁰, early XIVc. (A version).

MADRID, Bibl. nac., 18253, fol. 140r⁰-140v⁰, XIVc. (A version).

NEW HAVEN, Yale Univ. Libr., 492, fol. 94v⁰-95r⁰, early XIVc. (A version).

OXFORD, Bodleian Libr., Digby 20, fol. 153v⁰-154r⁰, XIIIc. (B version).

OXFORD, Bodleian Libr., Digby 98, fol. 246r⁰-247r⁰, early XIVc. (B version).

OXFORD, Bodleian Libr., Douce 210, fol. 40v⁰, early XIVc. (A version).

OXFORD, Bodleian Libr., Rawlinson Poetry 241, pp. 181-2, late XIIIc. (B version). Inc.: Devant prime deys tu penser de la passion ...

OXFORD, Bodleian Libr., Selden Supra 74, fol. 54r⁰-55r⁰, XIIIc. (A version).

OXFORD, Corpus Christi College, 36, fol. 42r⁰, early XIVc. (A version).

OXFORD, St. John's College, 190, fol. 196r⁰-196v⁰, late XIIIc. (A version).

PARIS, Bibl. nat., fr. 13342, fol. 39v⁰-40r⁰, early XIVc. (A version). Inc.: Devant prime doiz tu penser de la passion ...

PARIS, Bibl. nat., nouv. acq. fr. 11200, fol. 16r⁰-17r⁰, XIIIc. (A version). Inc.: Devant prime deis tu penser de la passion ...

Ed.: Robbins, pp. 58-60 (base ms. Oxford, Digby 20); Wilshere, pp. 60, 62 (A version, base ms. Oxford, St. John's College, 190); pp. 61, 63 (B version, base ms. London, Arundel 288).

Ref.: Same as the Ref. section of the inc. Aprés ço devez saver queus sunt les set prieres ... (no. 5431).

5609.   Devaunt prime devet (= devez) penser principaument de ce(s) deus choses. La primere chose est ke a tel houre fu Jhesu amené devaunt Pilate por estre jugé ...

Prime of the Hours of the Cross, part of the "Meditationes de dulci passione Jhesucristi".

LONDON, British Libr., Additional 11579, fol. 32v°-33v°, XIVc.

5610.   Devant terce deis tu penser de la passion ...

Variant of the inc.: Devant tierce devez penser de la passion e de la pentecoste ... (no. 5612).

5611.   Devant terce deis tu penser de sa flagellacioun e de la pentecuste ...

Variant of the inc.: Devant tierce devez penser de la passion et de la pentecoste ... (no. 5612).

5612.   Devant tierce devez penser de la passion e de la pentecoste. De la passion devez penser coment nostre duz seynur estoit a icele hore ...

Meditation for Terce of the Hours of the Cross, in the Mirour de seinte Eglyse, a translation of the Speculum Ecclesiae by S. Edmund of Abingdon. The texts of A and B versions are close.

CAMBRIDGE, Emmanuel College, I. 4. 31, fol. 96r°-96v°, XIVc. (A version). Inc.: Devant tierce deis tu penser de la passion coment Nostre Sire estoit ...

CAMBRIDGE, Pembroke College, 258, fol. 128r°-128v°, XIVc. (Extracts). Inc.: Devaunt terce deis tu penser de sa flagellacioun e de la pentecuste ...

DURHAM, Durham Univ. Libr., Cosin V.V. 15, fol. 37v°-38r°, XIVc. (B version). Inc.: Devant terce deis tu penser de la passion coment Nostre Sire esteit ...

LINCOLN, Chapter Libr., B. 5. 1, fol. 175v°, XIVc. (B version). Inc.: Devant tierce deis tu penser de la passion et de la pentecost ...

LONDON, British Libr., Arundel 288, fol. 117v°, XIIIc. (B version).

LONDON, British Libr., Harley 1121, fol. 152r°-152v°, early XIVc. (B version).

LONDON, British Libr., Royal 12. C. XII, fol. 26v°, early XIVc. (A version).

LONDON, British Libr., Royal 20. B. XIV, fol. 61v°-62r°, early XIVc. (A version).

NEW HAVEN, Yale Univ. Libr., 492, fol. 95r°-95v°, early XIVc. (A version).

OXFORD, Bodleian Libr., Digby 20, fol. 154r°-154v°, XIIIc. (B version). Inc.: Devant terce deis tu penser de la passion et de la pentecoste ...

OXFORD, Bodleian Libr., Digby 98, fol. 247v°-248r°, early XIVc. (B version).

OXFORD, Bodleian Libr., Douce 210, fol. 40v°-41r°, early XIVc. (A version).

OXFORD, Bodleian Libr., Rawlinson Poetry 241, pp. 182-3, late XIIIc. (B version). Inc.: Devant terce doys tu penser de la passion ...

OXFORD, Bodleian Libr., Selden Supra 74, fol. 55r°, XIIIc. (A version). Inc.: De la passion e de pentecoste devez penser devaunt tierce coment ...

OXFORD, Corpus Christi College, 36, fol. 42r°-42v°, early XIVc. (A version).

OXFORD, St. John's College, 190, fol. 196v°, late XIIIc. (A version).

PARIS, Bibl. nat., fr. 13342, fol. 40r°-40v°, early XIVc. (A version). Inc.: Devant tierce doiz tu penser de la passion ...

PARIS, Bibl. nat., nouv. acq. fr. 11200, fol. 17r°-17v°, XIIIc. (A version). Inc.: Devant tierce deis tu penser de la passion ...

Ed.: Robbins, pp. 60-1 (base ms. Oxford, Digby 20); Wilshere, pp. 62, 64 (A version, base ms. Oxford, St. John's College, 190); pp. 63, 65 (B version, base ms. London, Arundel 288). Ref.: Same as the Ref. section of the inc. Aprés ço devez saver queus sunt les set prieres ... (no. 5431).

5613. Devaunt   terce   devez   vos   penser   de   ce(s)   ij   choses principaument. La primer(e) chose est ke a tel houre fu Jhesu fläelé ...

Terce of the Hours of the Cross, part of the "Mediationes de dulci passione Jhesucristi".

LONDON, British Libr., Additional 11579, fol. 33r°-34r°, XIVc. The copy is incomplete.

5614. Devant vespres deis tu penser de la cene e de la passion ...

Variant of the inc.: Devant vespres devez penser de la cene e de la passion ... (no. 5615).

5615. Devant vespres devez penser de la cene e de la passion. De la passion devez penser coment Josep de Arimathie purchasa le cors ...

Meditation for Vespers of the Hours of the Cross, in the Mirour de seinte Eglyse, a translation of the Speculum Ecclesiae by S. Edmund of Abingdon. The texts of A and B versions are close.

CAMBRIDGE, Emmanuel College, I. 4. 31, fol. 98v°-99r°, XIVc. (A version). Inc.: Devaunt vespres deis tu penser de la cene et de la passion ...

CAMBRIDGE, Pembroke College, 258, fol. 129r°, XIVc. (Extracts). Inc.: Devant vespres deis tu penser de la cene e de la deposicioun ...

DURHAM, Durham Univ. Libr., Cosin V.V. 15, fol. 39v°-40r°, XIVc. (B version). Inc.: Devant vespres deis tu penser de la cene ...

LINCOLN, Chapter Libr., B. 5. 1, fol. 176r°-176v°, XIVc. (B version). Inc.: Devant vespres deis tu penser de la cene ...

LONDON, British Libr., Arundel 288, fol. 119r°-119v°, XIIIc. (B version).

LONDON, British Libr., Harley 1121, fol. 153v°, early XIVc. (B version).

LONDON, British Libr., Royal 12. C. XII, fol. 27v°-28r°, early XIVc. (A version).

LONDON, British Libr., Royal 20. B. XIV, fol. 63r°, early XIVc. (A version).

MADRID, bibl. nac., 18253, fol. 141v°-142r°, XIVc. (A version).

NEW HAVEN, Yale Univ. Libr., 492, fol. 96r°-96v°, early XIVc. (A version).

OXFORD, Bodleian Libr., Digby 20, fol. 155v°, XIIIc. (B version). Inc. Devant vespres dois tu penser de la cene ...

OXFORD, Bodleian Libr., Digby 98, fol. 250r°-250v°, early XIVc. (B version).

OXFORD, Bodleian Libr., Douce 210, fol. 41v°, early XIVc. (A version).

OXFORD, Bodleian Libr., Rawlinson Poetry 241, p. 185, late XIIIc. (B version). Inc.: Devant vespres doys tu penser de la cene ...

OXFORD, Bodleian Libr., Selden Supra 23, fol. 11v°, XIVc. (Fragments).

OXFORD, Bodleian Libr., Selden Supra 74, fol. 56r°-56v°, XIIIc. (A version).

OXFORD, Corpus Christi College, 36, fol. 43r°, early XIVc. (A version).

OXFORD, St. John's College, 190, fol. 197r°, late XIIIc. (A version).

PARIS, Bibl. nat., fr. 13342, fol. 41v°-42r°, early XIVc. (A version). Inc.: Devant vespres doiz tu penser de la cene ...

PARIS, Bibl. nat., nouv. acq. fr. 11200, fol. 18v°-19r°, XIIIc. (A version).

Ed.: Robbins, pp. 66-7 (base ms. Oxford, Digby 20); Wilshere, pp. 70, 72 (A version, base ms. Oxford, St. John's College, 190); pp. 71, 73 (B version, base ms. London, Arundel 288). Ref.: Same as the Ref. section of the inc. Aprés ço devez saver queus sunt les set prieres ... (no. 5431).

5616. Devotement te vien prier,
       Amy de Dieu, vray chevalier ...

       Prayer to S. Sebastian; 139 vv. rhyming in pairs.

       AVIGNON, Bibl. mun., 1904, fol. 77r°-80r°, XVIc., Prayer-book.

       Ed.: Rézeau, Saints, II, pp. 478-83.

5617. Di aux benois angelz des cieulx ...

       Variant of the inc.: Benois angelz des cieulx ... (no. 241).

5618. Dÿamant cler, rubi trop enflammé,
       Jaspe luisant, en vertu reclamé ...

       Prayer to S. Lawrence; 3 dizains rhyming aabaabbcbc.

       PARIS, Bibl. nat., Rés. D. 5616 and Ye 831, Louenges des benoistz sainctz et sainctes de paradis, fol. yy5v°, Paris, Vérard.

       VERSAILLES, Bibl. mun., M. 129 (Lacombe 109 quater).

       Ed.: Rézeau, Saints, II, pp. 303-4.

*   Dieu ...

       Here are grouped the spellings: Deu ..., Deus ..., Dex ..., Dieu ..., Dieus ..., Dieux ..., Diex ... The alphabetical order within the group is determined by the spelling of the next word that is not underlined.

5619. Deus, a la moye aÿe entendez!
       Sire, a moy ayder wus hastez!

       Hours of the Virgin in French, with an alternate wording for the parts of the Hours: Deus, entendez a ma aÿe ... (no. 5627).

       STUTTGART, Württembergische Landesbibl., Brev. 75, fol. 7r°-60v°, XIVc. Hours of Sarum. Opens abruptly in ps. 94: en psaumes a lui façom ...

5620.   Dieus ait l'ame des trespassés!
         Car des biens qu'il ont amassés
         Dont il n'orent oncques assés
         Ont il toute leur part eüe ...

    "Le codicille" or "Le petit codicille" or "Le derrenier
    testament", each attributed to Jehan de Meun; another title
    is "Epitaphe des trespassez". 88 octosyllabic lines.

    ABERYSTWYTH, Nat. Libr. of Wales, 5016 D, fol. 136r°-136v°,
       XIVc.

    BESANCON, Bibl. mun., 553, fol. 142r°-143r°, late XIVc.

    BRUSSELS, Bibl. royale, 10394-414, fol. 111r°-111v°, XVc.

    BRUSSELS, Bibl. royale, 11000-3, fol. 189r°-189v°, XVc.

    BRUSSELS, Bibl. royale, 11244-51, fol. 98r°-98v°, XVc.

    DIJON, Bibl. mun., 525, fol. 162r°-162v°, XIVc.

    LENINGRAD, Publichnaya Bibl., Fr. Q. v. XIV. 2, fol. 29r°-29v°,
       XVc.

    LONDON, British Libr., Additional 42133, fol. 143v°-144r°,
       XIVc.

    LONDON, British Libr., Royal 19. B. XII, fol. 193v°-194v°, XVc.

    LONDON, British Libr., Royal 19. C. VII, fol. 165r°-167r°, XVc.

    LONDON, Gray's Inn Libr., 10, fol. 160v°-161r°, late XIVc.

    LYON, Bibl. de la Ville, 764 (678), fol. 153v°-154v°, XVc.

    MADRID, Bibl. nac., Res. 4a, 14, fol. 183r°-183v°, XIVc.

    MONTPELLIER, Bibl. Fac. Ecole de Médecine, H. 245, fol.
       131r°-131v°, XIVc.

    NEW YORK, Pierpont Morgan Libr., Morgan 48, fol. 179v°-180r°,
       XVc.

    NEW YORK, Pierpont Morgan Libr., Morgan 185, fol. 106v°-107r°,
       XIVc.

    NEW YORK, Pierpont Morgan Libr., Morgan 324, fol. 171v°-172r°,
       XIVc.

    PARIS, Bibl. de l'Arsenal, 3339, fol. 186r°-186v°, XVc.

    PARIS, Bibl. Mazarine, 3872, fol. 153r°-153v°, XIVc.

    PARIS, Bibl. nat., fr. 380, fol. 159v°-160r°, XIVc.

    PARIS, Bibl. nat., fr. 804, fol. 164r°-165r°, XVc.

    PARIS, Bibl. nat., fr. 806, fol. 173r°-173v°, XVc.

PARIS, Bibl. nat., fr. 814, fol. 132r°-132v°, XIVc.; incomplete at the end.

PARIS, Bibl. nat., fr. 1103, fol. 63r°-64r°, XVc.

PARIS, Bibl. nat., fr. 1551, fol. 38r°-40r°, XVc.

PARIS, Bibl. nat., fr. 1556, fol. 78r°-78v°, XVc.

PARIS, Bibl. nat., fr. 1557, fol. 42r°-42v°, XVc.

PARIS, Bibl. nat., fr. 1563, fol. 174r°-175r°, XVc.

PARIS, Bibl. nat., fr. 2192, fol. 81r°-81v°, XVc.

PARIS, Bibl. nat., fr. 9345, fol. 71r°-71v°, XVc.

PARIS, Bibl. nat., fr. 12593, fol. 158v°, XIVc., only contains 64 vv.

PARIS, Bibl. nat., fr. 12595, fol. 200r°-200v°, XVc.

PARIS, Bibl. nat., fr. 12596, fol. 205r°-205v°, XVc.

PARIS, Bibl. nat., fr. 22551, fol. 79r°, 1428.

PARIS, Bibl. nat., fr. 24392, fol. 207r°-207v°, XVc.

PARIS, Bibl. nat., lat. 8654 B, fol. 83r°-83v°, early XIVc.

PARIS, Bibl. nat., nouv. acq. fr. 4237, fol. 76r°-77v°, XVc.

PARIS, Bibl. nat., nouv. acq. fr. 10042, fol. 38r°-38v°, XVc.

PHILADELPHIA, Philadelphia Museum of Art, 45.65.3, fol. 200v°-201v°, 1450.

PRINCETON, Princeton Univ. Libr., Garrett 126, fol. 182r°-183r°, late XIVc.

STOCKHOLM, Kungl. Bibl., Vu 39, fol. 191v°-193r°, XVc.

TURIN, Bibl. naz. univ., L. III. 14, fol. 141r°-141v°, XVc.

VATICAN CITY, Bibl. apost., Reg. lat. 1492, fol. 179r°-179v° and second copy 227r°-227v°, XVc.

VATICAN CITY, Bibl. apost., Reg. lat. 1518, fol. 117v°-119r°, XVc.

VATICAN CITY, Bibl. apost., Reg. lat. 1709, fol. 116v°-117r°, XVc.

VIENNA, Oesterreichische Nationalbibl., 2568, fol. 203r°-203v°, c. 1420.

VIENNA, Oesterreichische Nationalbibl., 2592, fol. 147r°-147v°, c. 1370.

Screening of mss. is incomplete.

Ed.: Keller, pp. 328-331. Ref.: P. Paris in HLF, XXVIII, pp. 427-9; G. Paris, Bull SATF, I (1875), p. 48; E. Langlois, Manuscrits français de Rome, 1889, p. 162, 164, 182-3, 222-3; Naetebus, no. XXIII, 1; E. Langlois, Recueil des arts de seconde rhétorique, Paris, 1902, p. xix; Omont, BEC, 64 (1903), p. 227; M. Schiff, Bibliothèque du marquis de Santillane, Paris, 1905, p. 369; P. Meyer, Romania, 36 (1907), p. 3; E. Langlois, Manuscrits du Roman de la Rose, Paris, 1911, passim; A. Långfors, Romania, 45 (1918-1919), p. 63; W. Söderhjelm, in Bok och Biblioteks-historiske Studier tillägnade Isak Collijn, Uppsala, 1925, p. 79; Borodina and Mal'kevic, p. 112; Anon. in GRLMA, VI, 2, no. 2233.

5621. Deus, dist Berniers, biaus pere roiamant,
Mauvés servise ai fait an mon vivant ...

Orison to God by Berniers: Yon (vv. 5908-12).

PARIS, Bibl. nat., fr. 1622, fol. 308v°, XIIIc.

Ed.: Meyer and Longnon, Raoul de Cambrai, p. 307; Mitchneck, p. 167-8.

5622. Dieu des vertus duquel est ce qui est tres bon, plante en noz coeurs l'amour de ton nom ...

"Dimence vj^e, oraison".

NEW YORK, Pierpont Morgan Libr., Morgan 78, fol. 35r°, XVc., Hours of Rome. Text added in XVIc.

5623. Dieu donneur de pardon et amateur d'umain salut, nous deprions ta pitié et clemence que les freres et seurs, parens et amis ...

Orison to God: "Deus venie largior".

PROVIDENCE, Brown Univ. Libr., C. 28. b. 4 (H.L. Koopman Collection), fol. 104r°-104v°, XVc., Hours.

5624. Dieu, duquel tous les biens procedent, donne a tes suppliant (sic), toy inspirant, de penser les choses droictes et, toy gouvernant, icelles faire.
(Complete Text)

"Oraison, le ve dimence de Pasques".

NEW YORK, Pierpont Morgan Libr., Morgan 78, fol. 105r°, XVc., Hours of Rome. Prayer in a XVIc. hand.

5625. E dist: Deu en qui je crei,
Ore eez merci de mei ...

Prayer to God by Alisandrine before being killed: Vie de saint Georges by Simund de Freine (vv. 1343-8).

PARIS, Bibl. nat., fr. 902, fol. 115v°, XIIIc.

Ed.: Matzke, p. 105. Réf.: Vising, p. 43, no. 16 (no mention of the prayer).

5626. Dieu, enten en mon adjutoire;
De moi aidier aiez memoire ...

Hours of the Virgin, in rhyme; inc. for Matins and Nones. Not the same inc. as no. 390 which announces the Hours of the Cross.

BALTIMORE, Walters Art Gallery, Walters 89, fol. 4v° and 94r°, late XIVc., Hours of Isabelle de Coucy.

METZ, Bibl. mun., 600, fol. 8r°-39v°, XVc., Hours of Paris and Prayer-book.

Ref.: Rézeau, pp. 157-8.

5627. Deus, entendez a ma aÿe!
Sire, a moy ayder ne targez mie!

Alternate beginning for parts of the Hours of the Virgin in French, herein recorded at the inc.: Deus, a la moye aÿe entendez ... (no. 5619).

5628. Dieus essauce men pri ça jus!
A ti mes cris viegne la sus!
                    (Complete Text)

Orison to God; one octosyllabic couplet copied as prose, repeated after each of the Heures de la Croix which begin: En l'eure de ...

NEW YORK, New York Public Libr., 28, fol. 127v°, 129r°, 131r°, 132v°, 134r°, 135v°, 137v°, XVc., Book of Hours.

5629. Dieu eternel, formateur de nature,
Roy supernel, qui tout tiens soubz ta cure
                    ...

Prayer to God by Nostre Dame: Mystère des Trois Doms, by chanoine Siboud Pra de Grenoble with the aid of Claude Chevalet de Vienne, and performed at Romans in 1509 (vv. 8944-55).

COLLECTION UNKNOWN (olim Giraud of Lyons), no shelf-mark, no fol. indicated, early XVIc.

Ed.: Giraud and Chevalier, pp. 473-4.

5630. Dieu faiseur et racheteur de tous, donne remission de tous pechez aux armes (sic) de tes serviteurs ...

Orison to God: "Fidelium deus omnium".

PROVIDENCE, Brown Univ. Libr., C. 28. b. 4 (H.L. Koopman Collection), fol. 104v°-105r°, XVc., Hours.

5631. Dieu, glorification des fideles et vie des justes, qui par ton
       serviteur Moyse nous a apris en la modulation du dittier
       sacré ...

       "(La veille de pentecouste, iij^e) oraison".

       NEW YORK, Pierpont Morgan Libr., Morgan 78, fol. 121v°, XVc.,
       Hours of Rome. This text by a XVIc. hand.

5632. Dieus, dist elle, glorious rois,
       Qui donastes totes les lois,
       Le ciel et la terre feïstes
       Et tot le monde beneïstes ...

       Orison to God by Blancheflor: Floire et Blancheflor (second
       version), vv. 773-846.

       PARIS, Bibl. nat., fr. 19152, fol. 195v°-196r°, late XIIIc.

       Ed.: E. du Méril, Floire et Blanceflor, poèmes du XIIIe siècle,
       Paris, 1856, pp. 147-9; E. Faral, Le manuscrit 19152 du fonds
       français de la Bibl. nat. Reproduction phototypique, Paris,
       1934; Felicitas Krüger, Li Romanz de Floire et Blancheflor in
       beiden   Fassungen   nach   allen   Handschriften ... neu
       herausgegeben, Berlin, 1938, pp. 165-7; Margaret A. Pelan,
       Floire et Blancheflor, seconde version, Paris, 1975, pp.
       44-6. Ref.: Wels, p. 7 n. 20, p. 31 n. 91.

5633. Deu, fait il, le rei celestre,
       Qui hom pur nus deignas nestre;
       Deu, tut poissant sanz dotance
       Qui par vertu e poissance ...

       Orison to God by S. Georges: Vie, by Simund de Freine (vv.
       1298-1315).

       PARIS, Bibl. nat., fr. 902, fol. 115v°, XIIIc.

       Ed.: Matzke, pp. 103-4. Réf.: Vising, p. 43, no. 16 (no mention
       of the prayer).

5634. Deu, fait il, le rei de glorie,
       Desur tuz avez victorie ...

       Prayer to God by S. Georges: Vie, by Simund de Freine (vv.
       1640-5).

       PARIS, Bibl. nat., fr. 902, fol. 117r°, XIIIc.

       Ed.: Matzke, p. 115. Ref.: Vising, p. 43, no. 16 (no reference
       to the orison).

5635. Dieu, ma bouche euvre et je dira (sic)
       Ta loenge et aniuncera.
       Biau Dieu, entens a mon aÿe
       Haste toy, Dieu, et sy m'aÿe.

       "Ce sont les heures en romant"; also found at the beginning of
       the Heures de la Croix.

MANCHESTER, John Rylands Univ. Libr., French 143, fol.
56r°-82r°, and fol. 82v°-87v°, early XVc., Hours.

5636. Diex, moie corpe, <u>dist Guibert li senez,</u>
De mes pechiez don ge sui anconbrez.
N'en ai prevoire a qui soient contez:
Entandez les, Jesu de maietez!
                    (Complete Text)

Confession by Guibert: Narbonnais (vv. 5071-4).

LONDON, British Libr., Harley 1321, fol. 101r°, XIIIc.

LONDON, British Libr., Royal 20. B. XIX, fol. 94r°, XIIIc.

<u>Ed.</u>: Suchier, I, p. 201 (base ms.: Harley 1321). <u>Ref.</u>: Merk, p.
188 n. 6; Dickman, p. 195; Koch, pp. 77, 125.

5637. Dieu mon bon pere, aies mercy de moy ...

Variant of the inc.: Dieu mon pere, aies mercy de moy ... (no.
5640).

5638. Dieu mon bon pere, je commande mon esperit ...

Variant of the inc.: Dieu mon pere, aies mercy de moy ... (no.
5640).

5639. Dieu, mon createur, je te donne
Et presente d'entente pure
Cest aigneau masle sans soullure,
Comme ton povre serviteur ...

Abel's prayer to God: Mystère de la Passion by Arnoul Gréban
(vv. 818-35).

PARIS, Bibl. nat., fr. 815, fol. 7v°, 1458.

PARIS, Bibl. nat., fr. 816, fol. 9v°, 1473.

PARIS, Bibl. nat., fr. 1550, fol. 16v°-17r°, XVIc.

PARIS, Bibl. nat., fr. 15064, fol. 16r°-16v°, 1469.

<u>Ed.</u>: Paris-Raynaud, p. 16 (vv. 1040-57); Jodogne, p. 22
(818-35).

5640. Dieu mon pere, aies mercy de moy. Dieu mon bon pere, je
commande mon esperit en vos mains ...

"Briefves oroisons" in the third part of the Medecine de l'ame
<u>alias</u> Science de bien mourir, by Gerson.

BRUSSELS, Bibl. royale, 10394-414, fol. 122v°, XVc. Inc.: Dieu
mon bon pere, aies mercy de moy ...

HAGUE (THE), Koninkl. Bibl., 78. J. 49, fol. 476r°-476v°, XVc.

LONDON, British Libr., Additional 29279, fol. 48r°-48v°, XVc.
Inc.: Dieu mon bon pere, je commande mon esperit ...

LONDON, British Libr., Harley 1310, fol. 87r°-87v°, XVc.

LYON, Bibl. de la Ville, 1249 (1121), fol. 49v°, XVc. Inc.: A!
Dieu mon pere, ayez merchi de moy ...

PARIS, Bibl. Mazarine, 966, fol. 121r°, XVc.

ROUBAIX, Archives Municipales, no shelf-mark, fol. 77v°-78r°,
XVc., Prayer-book of Jacques de Luxembourg. Inc.: Dieu mon
bon pere, je commande mon esperit ...

VIENNA, Oesterreichische Nationalbibl., 3391, fol. 435v°, XVc.

Screening of mss. is incomplete.

Ed.: Glorieux, Gerson: Oeuvres complètes, VII, 1, p. 406. Ref.:
Anne-Louise Masson, Jean Gerson, sa vie, son temps, ses
oeuvres, Lyon, 1894, p. 143.

5641. Dieu, nostre refuge, nostre vertu soyes aux prieres de ton
eglise et donne ce que demandons fidellement le obte(n)ir
efficasement.
                    (Complete Text)

"Dimence xxe, oraison".

NEW YORK, Pierpont Morgan Libr., Morgan 78, fol. 65r°, XVc.,
Hours of Rome. This text added in XVIc.

5642. Deu nus doint isi parler ke sauveté soit a nos almes ...

Possible variant of the inc.: Benedicite. Dominus, ke dites ...
(no. 5517).

5643. Deus oy ma oreisun
Et la reçoif en gré(e),
Si (me) mustrez pardun
Sulum ta verité ...

Seventh of the Penitential Psalms; a rhymed version.

STUTTGART, Württembergische Landesbibl., Brev. 75, fol.
75r°-77v°, XIVc., Hours of Sarum.

5644. Dieus, oye m'orison et entens ma clamour,
Escoute mon sermon et entent ma douleur.
Ne m'aie en des aing, ma(i)s donne moy
                              medicine
Des malz dont je me plains, et t'oreille
                              m'encline ...

Fifth of the Penitential Psalms; dodecasyllabic lines copied as
prose.

MANCHESTER, John Rylands Univ. Libr., French 143, fol.
93r°-93v°, early XVc., Hours.

5645. Diex, oies m'orison et la ressoit (sic) en
                                    grei
       Sy m'ottroye pardon selon ta volentei;
       Quant venrat au juïse ne met on (sic) lez
                                    fault
       Car selon ta justice nulz ne serat sauls
                          ...

       Last of the Seven Penitential Psalms, twelve-syllable lines;
          not identical with no. 4197.

       MANCHESTER, John Rylands Univ. Libr., French 143, fol.
          96r°-97r°, early XVc., Hours.

5646. Deus, oyez ma oreysun
       Si entendez ma clamur
       Escotez ma reisun
       Si me mustrez t'amur ...

       Fifth Penitential Psalm, in rhyme abab; part of the Heures de
          Nostre Dame.

       STUTTGART, Württemburgische Landesbibl., Brev. 75, fol.
          69v°-74r°, XIVc., Hours of Sarum.

5647. Dieu omnipotent, nous prions, donne a ceulx qui ont solennisé
          les festes pasquales toy largiteur le nous (sic) et fais
          tenir par vie et bonnes meurs.
                     (Complete Text)

       "Le premier dimence de Pasque, oraison".

       NEW YORK, Pierpont Morgan Libr., Morgan 78, fol. 93r°, XVc.,
          Hours of Rome. This text added in XVIc.

5648. Dieu omnipotent, nous prions que nous qui creons nostre
          redempteur estre monté au ciel ...

       "Le jour de l'Ascension, oraison".

       NEW YORK, Pierpont Morgan Libr., Morgan 78, fol. 105r°, XVc.,
          Hours of Rome. This text added by a XVIc. hand.

5649. Dieu omnipotent, nous prions, regarde les veulx des humbles et
          pour nostre deffence estens la dextre de ta maiesté. Amen.
                     (Complete Text)

       "Le troisime dimence de quaremme, (oraison)".

       NEW YORK, Pierpont Morgan Libr., Morgan 78, fol. 92v°, XVc.,
          Hours of Rome. This prayer added in XVIc.

5650. Dieu omnipotent, nous te prions, accorde que la nouvelle
          nativité de ton filz unicque selonc la char ...

       "Le jour du Noel, (oraison)".

       NEW YORK, Pierpont Morgan Libr., Morgan 78, fol. 75r°, XVc.,
          Hours of Rome. This prayer is by a XVIc. hand.

5651.   Dieu omnipotent, nous te prions que nous qui somes par nos
        merites affligiés que soions allegiés par consolation de ta
        grace.
                        (Complete Text)

        "Dimence quatrisme (de quaremme), oraison".

        NEW YORK, Pierpont Morgan Libr., Morgan 78, fol. 92v°, XVc.,
        Hours of Rome. This text added in XVIc.

5652.   Deu, fait il, omnipotent,
        Pere sanz cumencement,
        Pere e Fiz e seint Esprit,
        Deu poissant senz cuntredit ...

        Prayer to God by S. Georges to ressuscitate the Dead: Vie, by
        Simund de Freine (vv. 1397-1434).

        PARIS, Bibl. nat., fr. 902, fol. 116r°, XIIIc.

        Ed.: Matzke, pp. 107-8. Ref.: Vising, p. 43, no. 16 (no mention
        of the prayer).

5653.   Dex, dit elle, par ta bonté
        Tien moi en senz et en creance!
        Dont revient ceste mescheance
        Dont n'ai a nulli rienz forfait ...

        Plainte to God by a hapless mother: Roman du comte d'Anjou by
        Jean Maillart (vv. 3824-40).

        PARIS, Bibl. nat., fr. 765, fol. 21r°, XVc.

        PARIS, Bibl. nat., nouv. acq. fr. 4531, fol. 32v°, early XIVc.

        Ed.: Roques, p. 117.

5654.   Dex, dist Guillelmes, par ton saintisme
                                non,
        Glorīeus pere, qui formas Lazaron
        Et en la Virge preīs anoncīon,
        Jonas garis el ventre del poisson ...

        Orison to God by Guillaume: Prise d'Orange (AB redaction), vv.
        804-17.

        LONDON, British Libr., Royal 20. D. XI, fol. 120v°, early XIVc.

        MILAN, Bibl. Trivulziana, 1025, fol. 52v°, XIIIc.

        PARIS, Bibl. nat., fr. 368, fol. 169v°, XIVc.

        PARIS, Bibl. nat., fr. 774, fol. 46v°, XIIIc.

        PARIS, Bibl. nat., fr. 1449, fol. 52v°-53r°, XIIIc.

        Ed.: Katz, pp. 22-3 (base ms.: Paris, B.N. fr. 774); Régnier,
        1966, p. 128 and Régnier, 1970, p. 76 (base ms. on both
        occasions: Paris, B.N. fr. 774). Ref.: Merk, pp. 9 n. 4 and
        7; 186 n. 1 and 11; 187 n. 1; 188 n. 18; Dickman, p. 196;

Labande, Credo, pp. 63 n. 2; 75 n. 1, 78; Marguerite Rossi in Senefiance no. 10, pp. 464 and 472.

5655. Dex, <u>dist Amiles</u>, par ton saintisme non,
Meïs saint Pierre au chief de Pré Noiron
...

Orison to God by Amile: Ami et Amile (vv. 1177-88).

PARIS, Bibl. nat., fr. 860, fol. 99r°, XIIIc.

<u>Ed.</u>: Hofmann, p. 34-5; Dembowski, p. 38-9. <u>Ref.</u>: Altona, p. 13 n. 1; Merk, p. 9 n. 4, 7, 9; p. 188 n. 18; D. Scheludko, ZFSL, 55 (1931), p. 452, 457 and ZFSL, 58 (1934), p. 190; Wels, p. 12 n. 28; Labande, p. 72 n. 4; p. 78 n. 2.

5656. Diex, <u>dist li enfes</u>, par ton saintisme non,
Qui mer feïs, eve douce et pisson
Et en la Virge preïs anoncïon,
Jonas salvas el ventre del poisson ...

Prayer to God by Guielin: Prise d'Orange (CE redaction), vv. 770-8.

BOULOGNE-SUR-MER, Bibl. mun., 192, fol. 52v°, 1295.

<u>Ed.</u>: Régnier, 1966, p. 200. <u>Ref.</u>: Frappier, Cycle de Guillaume d'Orange, II, p. 299, n. 2.

5657. Diex, <u>dist li enfes</u>, par ton saintisme non,
Qui mer feïstes, ewe douce et poisson,
Adam formastes de terre, de limon;
Puis fu .c. ans, si com lisant trovon ...

Prayer to God by Guielin: Prise d'Orange (CE redaction), vv. 1245-82.

BOULOGNE-SUR-MER, Bibl. mun., 192, fol. 55v°, 1295.

<u>Ed.</u>: Régnier, 1966, pp. 214-15. <u>Ref.</u>: Frappier, Cycle de Guillaume d'Orange, II, pp. 280 n. 1; 306 n. 3.

5658. Dieu pardurable, tout puissant,
Qui, par ta digneté tres grant ...

"Memoire de saint Julian", one ten-line poem, paired rhymes.

OXFORD, Keble College, 15, fol. 92v°, XIVc.

<u>Ed.</u>: Rézeau, Saints, II, pp. 297-8.

5659. Dieu, <u>dist il</u>, pere! par la vostre mercy,
Deffendez moy d'Aiquin mon anemy;
Que mon royaulme ne soit par luy febly
Ne saint baptesme emperé ne ledy!
                    (Complete Text)

Orison to God by Charlemagne: Aquin (vv. 585-8).

PARIS, Bibl. nat., fr. 2233, fol. 11r°, XVc.

Ed.: Joüon des Longrais, p. 24. Ref.: Merk, p. 186 n. 3.

5660.   Dex, dist il, peres, par ton saintisme non,
Saint Pierre mis el chief de Pré Noiron ...

Prayer by Ami to God: Ami et Amile (vv. 1762-74).

PARIS, Bibl. nat., fr. 860, fol. 102r°, XIIIc.

Ed.: Hofmann, p. 51; Dembowski, p. 57. Ref.: Gautier, p. 542,
543; Merk, p. 9 n. 4, 7, 9; Wels, p. 12 n. 28.

5661.   Dex, dist il, peres qui en la crois fus mis
Et en la Virge et char et sanc preïz
Quant tu fuz nés, touz li mons s'esjoïst
...

"Plainte" to Jesus by Renier: Jourdain de Blaye (vv. 493-500).

PARIS, Bibl. nat., fr. 860, fol. 113v°, XIIIc.

Ed.: Hofmann, p. 119; Dembowski, p. 29. Ref.: Merk, p. 13 n. 2;
72 n. 11; 73 n. 20.

5662.   Dex, dist il, peres qui en la crois fus mis
Et en la Virge et char et sanc preïs,
Randez moi, sire, ma moillier, la gentil
Otiabel, cui je quier et desir.
(Complete Text)

Orison to Jesus by the hero: Jourdain de Blaye (vv. 2458-61).

PARIS, Bibl. nat., fr. 860, fol. 124r°, XIIIc.

Ed.: Hofmann, p. 175; Dembowski, p. 86. Ref.: Merk, p. 72 n.
11, 73 n. 20, 188 n. 18.

5663.   Dex, dist il, peres qui formas tout le
mont,
Meïs saint Pierre el chief de Pré Noiron
...

Orison to God by Ami: Ami et Amile (vv. 1667-74).

PARIS, Bibl. nat., fr. 860, fol. 101v°, XIIIc.

Ed.: Hofmann, p. 48-9; Dembowski, p. 54; Ref.: Marguerite Rossi
in Senefiance no. 10, pp. 452, 453, 468.

5664.   Dex, fait il, pere qui formas tout lou
mont,
Qui an la Virge preïs anoncïon
Et dan saint Piere meïs en Pré Noiron
Et convertis saint Pol son compaignon ...

Orison to God by Guielin: Prise d'Orange (D redaction), vv.
658-71.

PARIS, Bibl. nat., fr. 1448, fol. 103v°, late XIIIc.

Ed.: Régnier, 1966, pp. 280-1.

5665. Dex, _fait il_, peres qui formastez le mont,
La Mazelainne feistez le pardon ...

"Plainte" to God by the hero: Jourdain de Blaye (vv. 1290-5).

PARIS, Bibl. nat., fr. 860, fol. 117v°, XIIIc.

Ed.: Hofmann, p. 142; Dembowski, p. 52.

5666. Dex, _fait il_, peres, rois glorioz,
                              puissans,
Qui en la Virge preïs harbergemant ...

Orison to God by the hero: Jourdain de Blaye (vv. 2449-54).

PARIS, Bibl. nat., fr. 860, fol. 124r°, XIIIc.

Ed.: Hofmann, p. 175; Dembowskï, p. 86. Ref.: Merk, p. 188 n.
18; D. Scheludko, ZFSL, 55 (1931), p. 457.

5667. Dieu pere tout puissant et pardurable sans fin a toy commant
huy l'ame de moy et ma vie et toutes mes angoisses ...

"Orison a Nostre Seigneur tres devote a dire".

NEW YORK, Pierpont Morgan Libr., Morgan 221, fol. 269v°-270v°,
_c_. 1455, Diurnal.

5668. Dieu peire tous possanz, pleinz et ramply de misericorde, qui
nulle creature ne vuelz perdre ...

Orison to God, in prose.

METZ, Bibl. mun., 600, fol. 94r°-95v°, XVc., Hours of Paris and
Prayer-book.

Ref.: Rézeau, pp. 167-8.

5669. Dex, _dist Gavains_, plains de pooir,
Done me cel baron veoir
Qui tant est fiers et oltrageus,
Et desreés et orgillex ...

Orison to God by Gauvain: Merveilles de Rigomer (vv. 11129-38).

CHANTILLY, Musée Condé, 472 (626), fol. 36r°, XIIIc.

Ed.: W. Förster and H. Breuer, Les Merveilles de Rigomer von
Jehan, altfranzösischer Artusroman des XIII. Jahrhunderts,
Dresden, I, 1908, p. 329. Ref.: Koch, p. 73, 121.

5670. Dieu qui a tes apostres as donné le sainct Esprit, concede a ta
famille l'effet de ta protection ...

"Le lundy de la pentecouste, oraison".

NEW YORK, Pierpont Morgan Libr., Morgan 78, fol. 148v°, XVc., Hours of Rome. This prayer in a XVIc. hand.

5671. Dieu qui a⟨s⟩ aujourd'huy enseigné de la lumiere du sainct Esprit les coeurs fideles, donne nous en icelluy esprit ...

"Le jour de la Pentecoustes, (oraison)".

NEW YORK, Pierpont Morgan Libr., Morgan 78, fol. 147r°, XVc., Hours of Rome. The prayer in a XVIc. hand.

5672. Dieu qui a(s) preparé a ceulx quy t'aiment biens invisibles respirans en noz coeurs ...

"Dimence v^e, oraison".

NEW YORK, Pierpont Morgan Libr., Morgan 78, fol. 35r°, XVc., Hours of Rome. Prayer by a XVIc. hand.

5673. Dieu qui as revelé le monde couchié par humilité de ton filz a tes fideles, accorde leesse perpetuelle ...

"Oraison, le second dimence aprés Pasques".

NEW YORK, Pierpont Morgan Libr., Morgan 78, fol. 104v°, XVc., Hours of Rome. This prayer by a XVIc. hand.

5674. Dieu qui a(s) volus que pour nous ton filz se soit submis au gibet de la croix affin de expulser de nous ...

"Memoire de la Croix".

NEW YORK, Pierpont Morgan Libr., Morgan 78, fol. 93r°, XVc., Hours of Rome. This orison by a XVIc. hand.

5675. Dieu qui aujourd'huy ton filz unicque aux gentilz as rendu, conduis de l'estoille, accorde et soie a nous ...

"Le jour des Roys, oraison".

NEW YORK, Pierpont Morgan Libr., Morgan 78, fol. 79v°-80r°, XVc., Hours of Rome. This prayer added in XVIc.

5676. Dieu, qui aux trois enfans adoucis les flammes de feu a nous propice ...

"La nuyct de la Trinité, vij^e oraison".

NEW YORK, Pierpont Morgan Libr., Morgan 78, fol. 151r°, XVc., Hours of Rome. Prayer by a XVIc. hand.

5677. Dieu, qui crees noz esperis, noz pensees ne metz en oubly; ampliz de grace souveraine ceulx ...

"Veni creator spiritus," in prose.

PROVIDENCE, Brown Univ. Libr., C. 28. b. 4 (H.L. Koopman Collection), fol. 32r°-32v°, again 37r°-37v° and 41v°-42r°, XVc., Hours.

5678.   Dieu qui demonstre aux errans la lumiere de verité affin qu'il
        retournent en la voie de justice ...

        "Le troisime dimence (aprés Pasques), oraison."

        NEW YORK, Pierpont Morgan Libr., Morgan 78, fol. 104v°, XVc.,
        Hours of Rome. This text copied by a XVIc. hand.

5679.   Dieu, qui des corps as fors formeres (sic)
        Et ses ames as rachetees,
        Tu leur donne biau sire Dieu
        Tousjours parmenable repoz
        Per Nostre Signour Jhesu Crist
        Qu'adés avec ton fil regne et vist.
                        (Complete Text)

        "Orison pour lez mors", a version of the "Fidelium deus omnium"
        in the Vigiles des Morts in rhyme.

        MANCHESTER, John Rylands Univ. Libr., French 143, fol.
        120r°-120v°, early XVc., Hours.

5680.   Dieu qui du ventre de la bieneuree vierge Marie par l'ange
        nunciant de Crist ton fil ...

        Orison to God in prose, as part of Lauds in the Heures de
        Nostre Dame.

        CAMBRIDGE, Fitzwilliam Museum, McClean 76, fol. 33v°, XIV-XVc.,
        Hours of Paris.

5681.   Dieu qui en l'operation de ton serviteur Abraham a monstré au
        monde exemple d'obedience ...

        "La veille de Pentecouste, oraison."

        NEW YORK, Pierpont Morgan Libr., Morgan 78, fol. 105r°, XVc.,
        Hours of Roma. This text by a XVIc. hand.

5682.   Dieu qui en temps de peris nous congnois, constitues et sces
        pour nostre humaine fragilité ...

        "Le troisime dimence aprés le (jour des) Roys, oraison."

        NEW YORK, Pierpont Morgan Libr., Morgan 78, fol. 80r°, XVc.,
        Hours of Rome. This text added in XVIc.

5683.   Deus, dist Girberz, qui feïstes le vin
        De l'eve as noces de saint Archeteclin ...

        Prayer to Jesus by Gerbert: Yon (vv. 2222-8).

        PARIS, Bibl. nat., fr. 1622, fol. 277v°, XIIIc.

        Ed.: Mitchneck, p. 64.

5684.   Dieu qui le benoist glorieux
        Saint Jehan apostre piteux ...

Prayer to S. John the Evangelist; 18 octosyllabic lines, rhyming in pairs.

OXFORD, Keble College, 15, fol. 93v°, late XIVc., Hours of Rome.

Ed.: Rézeau, Saints, II, p. 273 note.

5685. Dieux! fait elle, qui le revel
En l'umain lignage meÿs,
Quant char et sanc ou corps preïs
De la vierge pucelle sage ...

Orison to God by a prioress: Galeran de Bretagne, attributed by critics to both a certain Renaut and to Jean Renart (vv. 1880-902).

PARIS, Bibl. nat., fr. 24042, fol. 43v°-44r°, XVc.

Ed.: A Boucherie, Le Roman de Galerent, comte de Bretagne, par le trouvère Renaut, Montpellier, 1888, p. 51-2; L. Foulet, Jean Renart, Galeran de Bretagne, roman du XIIIe siècle, Paris, 1925, p. 58. Ref.: Koch, p. 75, 122.

5686. Dieu, qui les ames des fidelles fais estre d'une volunté, donne a ton poeuple aimer ce que tu commande ...

"Dimence quatrime (aprés Pasques), oraison."

NEW YORK, Pierpont Morgan Libr., Morgan 78, fol. 104v°, XVc., Hours of Rome. This prayer added in XVIc.

5687. Dieu, qui muastes l'iaue en vin
Es nopces chiez Archedeclin ...

Orison to Jesus by the heroine: Miracles de Sainte Geneviève (vv. 2343-50).

PARIS, Bibl. Sainte-Geneviève, 1131, fol. 208v°, XVc.

Ed.: Sennewaldt, p. 137.

5688. Dieu qui nous a(s) soubz le sacrement merveilleux delaissé memoire de ta passion ...

"Le jour du sainct sacrement oraison."

NEW YORK, Pierpont Morgan Libr., Morgan 78, fol. 28r°, XVc., Hours of Rome. This text in XVIc. hand.

5689. Dieu qui nous regarde(s) destitués de toutes vertus dedens et dehors nous garde ...

"Dimence second (de quaresme, oraison)."

NEW YORK, Pierpont Morgan Libr., Morgan 78, fol. 85r°, XVc., Hours of Rome. This prayer by a XVIc. hand.

5690. Dieu, qui par l'anuelle expectation de nostre redemption nous resjouy, preste que ainsy que joieulz rechevons ...

"La nuyct du Noel, oraison."

NEW YORK, Pierpont Morgan Libr., Morgan 78, fol. 75r°, XVc.,
   Hours of Rome. This text added in XVIc.

5691. Dieu, qui par laquelle providence en la disposition de soy ne
   poeult estre dechupt devotement nous prions ...

"Dimence vij^e, oraison."

NEW YORK, Pierpont Morgan Libr., Morgan 78, fol. 35r°, XVc.,
   Hours of Rome. Prayer added in XVIc.

5692. Dieu qui par les bouches des prophetes nous a(s) commandé de
   relenquir les choses temporelles et se hater ...

"(La veille de pentecouste), oraison v^e."

NEW YORK, Pierpont Morgan Libr., Morgan 78, fol. 122r°, XVc.,
   Hours of Rome. This text by a XVIc. hand.

5693. Dieu qui par lumiere du Nouviau Testament as ouvers le(s)
   miracles fais es temps anchiens et que la mer Rouge ...

"La veille de pentecouste, ij^e oraison."

NEW YORK, Pierpont Morgan Libr., Morgan 78, fol. 121v°, XVc.,
   Hours of Rome. This prayer added in XVIc.

5694. Diex, <u>dist li rois</u>, qui par tout fais
                              vertus,
   Ja a passé .XXV. ans ou plus
   Que je pardi mes honmes et mes drus
   Par Guenelon qui nous ot touz vendus ...

Lament to God by Charlemagne: Narbonnais, text of the prayer is
   a variant version of vv. 2963-77 whose inc. is: E ! Dex, <u>fet
   il</u>, qui le mont as formé ... (no. 5768).

LONDON, British Libr., Royal 20. D. XI, fol. 91v°, <u>c</u>. 1300.

PARIS, Bibl. nat., fr. 24369, fol. 53r°, <u>c</u>. 1300.

<u>Ed</u>.: Suchier, II, p. 16 (base ms.: London codex).

5695. Dieu qui parmis le fruit a la bieneuree Marie de virginité
   ramplie a l'umain lignage donnas le loier ...

Orison to God in prose, in Vespers of the Heures de Nostre
   Dame, prose version (no. 3658).

CAMBRIDGE, Fitzwilliam Museum, McClean 76, fol. 57v°-58v°,
   XIV-XVc., Hours of Paris.

PROVIDENCE, Brown Univ. Libr., C. 28. b. 4 (H.L. Koopman
   Collection), fol. 53v°, XVc., Hours.

5696.   Dieu qui, pour la medicine des ames, as comandé chatier le
         corpz par devotion de junes ...

         "(La nuyct de la Trinité), iiij^e oraison."

         NEW YORK, Pierpont Morgan Libr., Morgan 78, fol. 151r°, XVc.,
         Hours of Rome. This prayer added in XVIc.

5697.   Dieu qui purifie(s) ton eglise par annuelle observance
         cadragesimale preste a ta famille ...

         "Dimence premier de quaresme, (oraison)."

         NEW YORK, Pierpont Morgan Libr., Morgan 78, fol. 85r°, XVc.,
         Hours of Rome. This prayer by a XVIc. hand.

5698.   Dieu qui regarde que nulle oeuvre que faisons ne nous confions
         concede a proufit ...

         "Le dimence de la sexag(es)isme, oraison."

         NEW YORK, Pierpont Morgan Libr., Morgan 78, fol. 85r°, XVc.,
         Hours of Rome. Prayer by a XVIc. hand.

5699.   Dieux qui sur touz as la puissance,
         Secours nous, Sire, sy te plaist! ...

         Prayer to God by Isaiah: "Mystere de la Nativité" (vv. 565-75).

         LONDON, British Libr., Additional 38860, fol. 9v° and 12v°,
         XVIIIc. copy of a lost ms.

         PARIS, Bibl. Sainte-Geneviève, 1131, fol. 7r°, XVc.

         Ed.: Whittredge, pp. 112-13.

5700.   Dex! dist Jordains a la chiere membree,
         Sainte Marie, roïne coronee,
         Sauvez ma gent que j'ai ci amenee,
         Qu'elle ne soit ocise n'afolee.
                        (Complete Text)

         Orison to God by the hero: Jourdain de Blaye (vv. 3955-8).

         PARIS, Bibl. nat., fr. 860, fol. 131v°, XIIIc.

         Ed.: Hofmann, p. 218; Dembowski, p. 130.

5701.   Dieu sempiternel, Dieu fais nous a toy tousjours avoir devote
         volunté et a ta saincte majesté de pur coeur servir.
                        (Complete Text)

         "Le dimence aprés (l'Ascension), oraison."

         NEW YORK, Pierpont Morgan Libr., Morgan 78, fol. 105r°, XVc.,
         Hours of Rome. This text by a XVIc. hand.

5702.   Dex sire, pere royamant,
         Quer veilliez mon enfant secourre

Et de si laide mort rescourre!
Encor ne puet pechierres estre ...

Orison to God by a distraught mother: Roman du comte d'Anjou by
Jean Maillart (vv. 4060-72).

PARIS, Bibl. nat., fr. 765, fol. 22v°, XVc.

PARIS, Bibl. nat., nouv. acq. fr. 4531, fol. 34r°, early XIVc.

Ed.: Roques, p. 124.

5703.   Dex, <u>dist il</u>, sire pere, ton saint non
                                glorifi,
         Toi aor, toi depri et vers toi m'humili,
         Qui m'as par tant de foiz de traïson gari.
                        (Complete Text)

Richard I, Duke of Normandy gives thanks to God: Wace, Roman de
Rou (vv. 3638-40).

PARIS, Bibl. nat., Duchesne 79, fol. 26v°, XVIIc., copy of a
lost ms. of late XIIIc. or early XIVc.

Ed.: A.J. Holden, Le Roman de Rou de Wace, Paris, SATF, I,
1970, p. 133.

5704.   Dieu souverain et tout puissant,
         Tout gouvernant et nourrissant ...

Orison to God by S. Andrew: Arnoul Gréban's Mystère de la
Passion (vv. 33509-20).

PARIS, Bibl. de l'Arsenal, 6431, fol. 256v°-257r°, XVc.

PARIS, Bibl. nat., fr. 815, fol. 270v°, 1458.

PARIS, Bibl. nat., fr. 816, fol. 232r°, 1473.

ROME, Accademia Nazionale dei Lincei, Bibl. Corsiniana, Rossi
412 (44. A. 7), fol. 659v°-660r°, late XVc.

Ed.: Paris-Raynaud, p. 440 (vv. 33656-667); Jodogne, p. 445
(vv. 33509-20).

5705.   Dieu te sault, estoille de mer,
         Sainte mere Dieu a amer,
         Tousjours vierge que on peut reclamer,
         Porte du ciel sans mesnommer ...

Paraphrase in rhyme of the "Ave maris stella," copied as prose,
but 24 vv. Part of the Heures de Nostre Dame (no. 3658). Not
the same as no. 424.

CAMBRIDGE, Fitzwilliam Museum, McClean 76, fol. 55v°-56r°,
XIV-XVc., Hours of Paris.

PROVIDENCE, Brown Univ. Libr., C. 28. b. 4 (H.L. Koopman
Collection), fol. 51r°-52r°, XVc., Hours.

5706.   Dex te saut, sainte Marie pleine de grace, tu ies benoite sur
        toutez fenmes e li fruiz de ton ventre est benois. Dex te
        saut bele dame sainte Marie, tu aletaz ...

        Salutations to the Virgin, not everywhere identical with no.
        427; only 6 "saluts" among which occur a five-line poem:
        Beneoite soiez tu qui Deu portas ... (no. 5524), and at the
        end is the prayer: Si voirement cum je croi sanz dotance ...
        (no. 6597).

        NEW YORK, Pierpont Morgan Libr., Morgan 92, fol. 130r°, late
        XIIIc., Book of Hours.

5707.   Dieu te sault! sang precieux decourant du dextre costé de
        Jhesucrist; efface noz pechez et nous donne la vie pardurable
        ...

        "On doit dire ces parolles quant on lieve le calice."

        PROVIDENCE, Brown Univ. Libr., C. 28. b. 4 (H.L. Koopman
        Collection), fol. 191v°, XVc., Book of Hours.

5708.   Dieu te sault, tres saincte char de Dieu, laquelle la Vierge
        tres chaste a enfanté, deffens nous de mort soudaine!
                    (Complete Text)

        "On doit dire ces parolles quant on lieve Dieu."

        PROVIDENCE, Brown Univ. Libr., C. 28. b. 4 (H.L. Koopman
        Collection), fol. 191r°-191v°, XVc., Book of Hours.

5709.   Dieu tout puissant ait mercy de toy et te pardoint tous tes
        pechez; il te delivre de tout mal ...

        "Quant le prestre a dit son confiteor, dis cecy."

        PROVIDENCE, Brown Univ. Libr., C. 28. b. 4 (H.L. Koopman
        Collection), fol. 249v°-250r°, XVc., Hours.

5710.   Dieu tout puissant, donez moy lermes
        Affin que puisse fort plourer
        Gettant regretz et piteux termes
        Pour vostre douleur savourer ...

        "Devote oraison a Nostre Seigneur Jhesucrist"; 16 stanzas of
        varying length and rhyme patterns.

        LONDON, British Libr., Additional 17446, fol. 38r°-41v°, XVc.

5711.   Dieu tout puyssant et eternel, qui pour conserver l'homme a
        toy, n'as pardonné a ton propre filz ...

        "Oraison pour dire le dimenche": Manuel de dévotion de prêtre
        Pierre.

        NEW HAVEN, Yale Univ. Libr., 498, fol. 107v°-108v°, last
        quarter XVIc.

5712.   Dieu tout puissant et pardurable, qui en confession de vraie
        foy as donné a tes serviteurs congnoissance ...

"La premiere oroison," first of three prayers to the Trinity,
in prose.

PROVIDENCE, Brown Univ. Libr., C. 28. b. 4 (H.L. Koopman
Collection), fol. 237v°-238r°, XVc., Hours.

5713. Dieu tout puissant, la vraye reception de ton corps et sang me
vienne non pas a jugement et a damnation, mais me soit ...

Orison after the Communion.

CHICAGO, Newberry Libr., 43, fol. 159v°-160r°, XVIc., Hours of
Rouen.

5714. Dieu tout puissant, nous te requeron qu'il te plaise nous
ottrier que l'intercession de la benoiste virge Marie ...

Orison for All Hallows (on feast-day).

PARIS, Bibl. de l'Arsenal, 2162, fol. 169v°-170r°, XVc., Hours
of Paris.

5715. Dieu tous poissanz, peire misericors, de cui doulçour est
dessus toutez aultrez ...

Orison to God, in prose.

METZ, Bibl. mun., 600, fol. 114r°-115v°, XVc., Hours of Paris
and Prayer-book.

Ref.: Rézeau, p. 170.

5716. Dieu tout puissant, seigneur sempiterne qui ordonnas le corps
tant sollempnel de la tres saincte et dame glorieuse ...

Orison to God, in prose.

NEW YORK, New York Public Libr., 149, fol. 111r°-111v°, XVc.,
Book of Hours. This text added by a XVIc. hand.

5717. Dex, dist la damme, voirs glorioz dou ciel,
Tant me soloient ces grans nuis anuier ...

"Plainte" to God by Eremborc: Jourdain de Blaye (vv. 669-77).

PARIS, Bibl. nat., fr. 860, fol. 114v°, XIIIc.

Ed.: Hofmann, p. 124; Dembowski, p. 34.

5718. Diex, vostre aide par charité!
Je ne sens qu'engoisse et meschief ...

"Plainte" to God by a dropsical patient: Miracles de sainte
Geneviève (vv. 2629-46).

PARIS, Bibl. Sainte-Geneviève, 1131, fol. 212v°, XVc.

Ed.: Sennewaldt, p. 150-1.

5719. Deu, vos rent jo grez e merciz
       Que or(e) m'avez fait bonté pleniere;
       La bonté est en tel(e) maniere
       Que mon fiz ai; de çoe e de el ...

       Yder's father gives thanks to God: Yder (vv. 4833-43).

       CAMBRIDGE, Cambridge Univ. Libr., Ee. 4. 26, fol. 38v°-39r°,
       late XIIIc.

       Ed.: Gelzer, p. 138-9.

5720. Dispose toy! il te convient mourir,
       Laisser tes biens et en terre pourrir ...

       "De la mort et du jugement"; six decasyllabic lines rhyming
       aabbcc.

       ROUBAIX, Archives Municipales, no shelf-mark, fol. 4v°, XVc.,
       Prayer-book of Jacques de Luxembourg.

5721. Dist la Vierge debonnaire:
       Je voy mon enfant ...

       Chanson de la Vierge Marie: 5 quatrains plus one huitain and
       three nine-line stanzas.

       Refr.: Veulliés l'en requerir.

       BRUSSELS, Bibl. royale, IV. 541, fol. 172r°-173v°, 1568.

       Ref.: Lemaire, Meschinot, Molinet, Villon: Témoignages inédits,
       1979, p. 72.

5722. Dites vos patenostres pour toute sainte
                              Eglise,
       Car elle est acouchiee, et si ne scet ou
                              gist ...

       Dit des Patenostres, by Giefroy, identified as Gefroi des Nés,
       or de Paris, a well-known chronicler. 37 six-line stanzas.

       PARIS, Bibl. nat., fr. 24432, fol. 148v°-152r°, XIVc.

       Ed.: A. Jubinal, Nouveau Recueil de contes, dits, fabliaux et
       autres pièces inédites, Paris, 1845, II, pp. 238-49; A. Mary,
       Fleurs de la poésie française, Paris, 1951, pp. 471-3
       (extracts). Ref.: Naetebus, XV, 1; Långfors, p. 100; C.V.
       Langlois in H.L.F., XXXV, 1921, pp. 338-40.

5723. Domine labia mea
       Aperi, car volenté a
       Mon cuer d'annoncier par la boiche
       La louenge qui pres luy toiche ...

       "Heures de la Virge Marie en françoys ..."; a version similar
       to that in no. 452.

       METZ, Bibl. mun., 600, fol. 8r°-39v°, XVc., Hours of Paris and
       Prayer-book.

Ref.: Rézeau, p. 157.

5724. Donne, je prie, a ton poeuple (ms. poeupleu) eviter dangiers contagieux et toy seul Dieu ...

"Dimence xve, oraison."

NEW YORK, Pierpont Morgan Libr., Morgan 78, fol. 53r°, XVc., Hours of Rome. This text added in XVIc.

5725. Donne moy, Seigneur, que mon coeur te puysse louer si longuement que je seray en ce corps fragille ...

"Seconde oraison a la saincte Trinité": Manuel de dévotion de prêtre Pierre.

NEW HAVEN, Yale Univ. Libr., 498, fol. 15v°-17r°, last quarter XVIc.

5726. Donne nous, Sire, que ce cours du monde par ton ordre soit mené pacifiquement ...

"Dimence iiij, oraison."

NEW YORK, Pierpont Morgan Libr., Morgan 78, fol. 34v°-35r°, XVc., Hours of Rome. Prayer in a XVIc. hand.

5727. Donne, sire Dieu, ensieuvre ce que ramembrons affin que nous aprendons d'aimer nos ennemys ...

"Au sainct Estienne, oraison."

NEW YORK, Pierpont Morgan Libr., Morgan 78, fol. 79v°, XVc., Hours of Rome. This text is by a XVIc. hand.

*   Dou ...

See the alphabetical order: Du ...

5728. Douce dame de misericorde, mere de pitié, fontaine de tous biens, qui portastes Jhesucrist neuf mois en voz precieux flans ...

"Orison a Nostre Dame," in prose; not the same text as nos. 458 or 4273.

PROVIDENCE, Brown Univ. Libr., C. 28. b. 4 (H.L. Koopman Collection), fol. 163v°-164v°, XVc., Hours.

5729. Doulce dame qui Dieu portas
Et Dieu nourris et alaitas
Et a Dieu veis paine souffrir
Et en la Croiz pour nous mourir ...

Prayer to the Virgin; one huitain, aabb.

BALTIMORE, Walters Art Gallery, Walters 261, fol. 106r°, c. 1400, Hours.

5730. Douce dame, roïne coronee,
       Prïez pour nos, Virge bien ëuree!
       Et puis aprés ne nos puet meschëoir.

       Orison to the Virgin, closing Thibaut de Champagne's Chanson de
          Croisade Seigneurs, sachiez: qui or ne s'en ira (vv. 36-8).

       PARIS, Bibl. de l'Arsenal, 5198, p. 1, XIIIc.

       PARIS, Bibl. nat., fr. 844, fol. 13v°, late XIIIc.

       PARIS, Bibl. nat., fr. 845, fol. 1v°, XIIIc.

       PARIS, Bibl. nat., fr. 846, fol. 127v°, late XIIIc.

       PARIS, Bibl. nat., fr. 12581, fol. 316r°, XIVc.

       PARIS, Bibl. nat., fr. 12615, fol. 2v°, XIIIc.

       PARIS, Bibl. nat., fr. 24406, fol. 2v°, XIIIc.

       PARIS, Bibl. nat., nouv. acq. fr. 1050, fol. 8v°, late XIIIc.

       Ed.: A. Leroux de Lincy, Recueil de chants historiques
          français, Paris, 1841, I, p. 127; P. Meyer, Recueil d'anciens
          textes, Paris, 1874, p. 372; K. Bartsch and A. Horning, La
          Langue et la littérature française depuis le IXe siècle
          jusqu'au XIVe siècle, Paris, 1887, col. 386; Bédier and
          Aubry, p. 173; Wallensköld, p. 185; J. and Louise Beck, Les
          Chansonniers des troubadours et des trouvères - I: Le
          Chansonnier Cangé (Paris, Bibl. nat., fr. 846), Paris and
          Philadelphia, 1927, I, fol. 127v°, and II, p. 295; J. and
          Louise Beck, Les Chansonniers ... II: Le manuscrit du Roi,
          fonds français 844 de la Bibl. nat., Philadelphia, 1938, I,
          pl. Mt, I, v°, no. 2; A. Mary, Fleurs de la poésie française,
          Paris, 1951, p. 311; F. Gennrich, Altfranzösischer Lieder -
          I, Halle, 1953, p. 12; F. Igly, Troubadours et trouvères,
          Paris, 1960, p. 210; R.L. Wagner, Textes d'étude, Paris,
          1961, p. 80-2.

5731. Dulce dame sainte Marie,
       Defendez nus de mal, d'envie,
       E donez nus force e vertu
       Ke de nus seit malfé vencu.

       Prayer to the Virgin: Miracles de Nostre Dame by Adgar called
          Willame (no. XX, vv. 89-92).

       LONDON, British Libr., Egerton 612, fol. 37v°, c. 1300.

       Ed.: Neuhaus, p. 129. Ref.: Vising, p. 43, no. 13 (orison not
          mentioned).

5732. Duce dame seynt(e) Marie, ostez cete prureture (sic) de mun
       quer par quei je su desturbe(e) de sentir la verité et priez
       vostre fiz ...

       Orison to the Virgin at the close of an Anglo-Norman Epistle to
          a Nun on the Sufferings of Jesus.

LONDON, British Libr., Egerton 613, fol. 5v°-6r°, XIIIc.

Ed.: Betty Hill, Notes and Queries, n.s. 25 (1978), p. 500.

5733.   Douce dame saincte Marie qui portates le
                                                roy
        Qui devint mortel homme pour acomplir la
                                                loy ...

        Orison to the Virgin; 7 lines mainly alexandrine, aaaaabb.

        LIVERPOOL, Merseyside County Museums, Mayer 12033, fol. 162v°,
           early XVc., Hours of Rouen. The poem added by a late XVc.
           hand.

5734.   Doulce dame vierge Marie, tres humblement je te prye, qui es
           dame de pitié et de misericorde et d'amitié, fille du
           souverain roy ...

        Orison to the Virgin, in prose.

        SAN MARINO (Calif.), Huntington Libr., HM 1129, fol.
           138r°-142v°, c. 1450, Hours of Paris.

5735.   Doulce Vierge Marie,
        Fontaine de pitié,
        Jhesus mere et amie,
        Qui pour moy fus pené ...

        "En ramembrance des .V. douleurs" in 44 hexasyllables, rhyming
           abab. For the rubric, see the inc.: Ainsi que on trouve es
           faits ... (no. 5425).

        LIVERPOOL, Liverpool Public Libr., D. 435, fol. 83v°-86r°,
           early XVc., Hours of Paris.

5736.   Ains disoit toute nuit: Douche Vierge
                                              Marie,
        Qui portas en tes flans le digne fruit de
                                              vie,
        Je te prie et requier, douche Vierge
                                              saintie,
        Que me voelliez garder que n'aie villonnie
                                              ...

        Prayer to the Virgin by Eliénor: Baudouin de Sebourc (vv. 8-23
           of Chant III).

        PARIS, Bibl. nat., fr. 12552, fol. 11r°, XIVc.

        PARIS, Bibl. nat., fr. 12553, fol. 31r°, XVc.

        Ed.: Boca, I, p. 63.

5737.   Doulce Vierge meire pucelle
        Que de vous (sic) doulcez mamellez ...

        Variant of the inc.: Glorieuse vierge pucelle/Qui de ta tres
           douce mamelle ... (no. 690).

*   Doux ...

Here are grouped the spellings: Doulx ..., Doulz ..., Dous ...,
Doux ..., Douz ... The order within the group is determined
by the next word of the incipit.

5738. Doulx amoureux Dieu, manifeste
       Cy endroit ta haulte puissance ...

Orison to God by the hero: Mystère de saint Christofle (vv.
1896-1905).

Early Ed.: in 4° Gothic, Paris, Veuve Jean Trepperel and Jean
Jehannot, n.d. (c. 1515). Ed.: Runnalls, p. 60.

5739. Doulx Dieu, ayes de moy mercy.
       Pour ce te viens saluer cy
       Selon ta grand misericorde
       Les cordons de pechié descorde ...

Fourth of the Seven Penitential Psalms; redaction in rhymed
couplets.

LILLE, Bibl. mun., Godefroy 5 (147), fol. 100r°-103r°, XVc.,
Hours.

5740. Doux Diex debonnaires Jhesucrist, esperance ferme de ceuz qui
       croient en toi, a heure de midi fuz levez en la crois et
       pendus honteusement en guise de larron ...

Hours of the Cross in prose, sext. The version is very close to
that in no. 503.

VIENNA, Oesterreichische Nationalbibl. 1969, fol. 133r°-134r°,
XIVc., Hours.

5741. Doulx Dieu, ou je me doy fīer,
       Conforte moy par ta mercy!
       Doulx Dieu, quel nouvelle esse cy?
       Iray je ou se je demourray? ...

Plainte to God by the Virgin: Arnoul Gréban's Mystère de la
Passion (vv. 24131-62).

CHANTILLY, Musée Condé, 614 (1691), fol. 205r°-205v°, XVc.

PARIS, Bibl. de l'Arsenal, 6431, fol. 180v°, XVc.

PARIS, Bibl. nat., fr. 815, fol. 195v°, 1458.

PARIS, Bibl. nat., fr. 816, fol. 170r°-170v°, 1473. Inc.: Bon
Dieu ou je me dois fīer ...

ROME, Accademia Nazionale dei Lincei, Bibl. Corsiniana, Rossi
412 (44. A. 7), fol. 468v°, late XVc.

Ed.: Paris-Raynaud, p. 317 (vv. 24172-203); Jodogne, pp. 323-4
(vv. 24131-62).

5742. Doulx Dieux, pere misericorps,
       Je vous requiers par bon remors ...

       Orison to God by the hero: Mystère de saint Christofle (vv.
          2245-79).

       Early Ed.: in 4° Gothic, Paris, Veuve Jean Trepperel and Jean
          Jehannot, n.d. (c. 1515). Ed.: Runnalls, p. 70-1.

5743. Doulx Dieu pere tout puissant, a qui est propre chose avoir
       pitié et mercy de ta creature et la espargner ...

       Orison to God in prose, after the Litany.

       PROVIDENCE, Brown Univ. Libr., C. 28. b. 4 (H.L. Koopman
          Collection), fol. 85r°-86v°, XVc., Hours.

5744. Doulz Dieu, qui es nostre salut et sauveur, veulles oÿr et
       exaucier nos oreisons affin que nous esjoïsson de la
       festivité ...

       Orison for S. Lucy (on feast-day).

       PARIS, Bibl. de l'Arsenal, 2162, fol. 161v°-162r°, XVc., Hours
          of Paris.

5745. Doulz Dieu, qui est ce haultain son
       Que je oz si tres hault ressonner? ...

       Rondeau in honor of the Holy Spirit: Mystère de la Passion by
          Arnoul Gréban (vv. 33679-94).

       PARIS, Bibl. de l'Arsenal, 6431, fol. 258r°, XVc.

       PARIS, Bibl. nat., fr. 815, fol. 272r°, 1458.

       PARIS, Bibl. nat., fr. 816, fol. 233r°, 1473.

       ROME, Accademia Nazionale dei Lincei, Bibl. Corsiniana, Rossi
          412 (44. A. 7), fol. 663r°, late XVc.

       Ed.: Paris-Raynaud, p. 443 (vv. 33826-41); Jodogne, p. 447 (vv.
          33679-94).

5746. Doulx Dieu qui me creastes
       Par vostre bonté naturelle ...

       Variant of the inc. O bon Jhesu doulx et piteux/Par vostre
          bonté naturelle ... (no. 1293).

5747. Doulz Dieu, qui par grant amistié
       Et par pitié tres charitable ...

       Orison to God by the heroine: Miracles de sainte Geneviève (vv.
          2564-80).

       PARIS, Bibl. Sainte-Geneviève, 1131, fol. 211v°, XVc.

       Ed.: Sennewaldt, p. 148.

5748.   Doulx Dieu, veullies (sic) estre debonnaire et bening a tes
serviteurs (in) indignes par les merites glorieuses du
benoist confesseur saint Maturin ...

Orison for S. Mathurin (on feast-day).

PARIS, Bibl. de l'Arsenal, 2162, fol. 146r°-146v°, XVc., Hours
of Paris.

5749.   Doulx Dieu, veulles nous ottrier que ainsi comme ton peuple
cristien se esjoïst en Dieu de la solennité temporele ...

Orison for S. Christopher (on feast-day).

PARIS, Bibl. de l'Arsenal, 2162, fol. 138r°-138v°, XVc., Hours
of Paris.

5750.   Douz Jhesucrist, cueur Fauvel seure,
Car il gaste tout et deveure ...

Orison to Jesus, part of Chaillou de Pesstain's interpolation
(vv. 1785-98) in the Roman de Fauvel by Gervais du Bus.

PARIS, Bibl. nat., fr. 146, fol. 44v°, XIVc.

Ed.: Aubry, Fauvel, fol. 44v°; Långfors, Fauvel, p. 195.

5751.   Doulz Jhesucrist, espous et pere
Dez vierges, volentiers alasse ...

Orison to Jesus by the heroine: Miracles de sainte Geneviève
(vv. 177-86).

PARIS, Bibl. Sainte-Geneviève, 1131, fol. 185r°, XVc.

Ed.: Sennewaldt, p. 66.

5752.   Doulz Jhesucrist, filz Dieu le pere,
Qui de pur let de vierge mere ...

Orison to Jesus; one sizain, aabaab.

BALTIMORE, Walters Art Gallery, Walters 261, fol. 108r°, c.
1400, Hours.

5753.   Doulz Jhesucrist, le cuer me part
Du dueil qu'a ceste bonne dame ...

Orison to Jesus by the heroine: Miracles de sainte Geneviève
(vv. 1666-92).

PARIS, Bibl. Sainte-Geneviève, 1131, fol. 200v°, XVc.

Ed.: Sennewaldt, p. 110-11.

5754.   Doulz Jhesucrist, par ta passion et par ta croix et par ta
mort, maine moy ton ame en ta gloire ...

Orison to Jesus, after each of the Heures de la Croix.

MANCHESTER, John Rylands Univ. Libr., French 143, fol. 83r, early XVc., Hours.

5755. Doulx Jesu Crist, qui a la saine
Repeustes de gens a foison ...

Thanks given to Jesus by Avicene: Mystère de saint Christofle (vv. 1620-9).

Early Ed.: in 4° Gothic, Paris, Veuve Jean Trepperel and Jean Jehannot, n.d. (c. 1515). Ed.: Runnalls, p. 52.

5756. Doulz Jhesucrist, qui de penance
M'avez ostee et de douleur ...

Thanksgiving to Jesus by the mother of S. Geneviève: Miracles de sainte Geneviève (vv. 25-32).

PARIS, Bibl. Sainte-Geneviève, 1131, fol. 183r°, XVc.

Ed.: Sennewaldt, p. 61.

5757. Et dist: Dous Jhesucris, qui pour nous mort
souffri,
Car ne consentés ja que mes corpz muire
chi;
Si soie baptisie en .j. fons benëi
Et voie Esmeret, le damoisel nouri ...

Orison to Jesus by Eliénor: Baudouin de Sebourc (vv. 542-550 of Chant II).

PARIS, Bibl. nat., fr. 12552, fol. 9r°, XIVc.

PARIS, Bibl. nat., fr. 12553, fol. 24v°, XVc.

Ed.: Boca, I, p. 48.

5758. Doulz Jhesu, qui du ciel venistes
En terre, et homme devenistes ...

Orison to Jesus by the heroine: Miracles de sainte Geneviève (vv. 1927-36).

PARIS, Bibl. Sainte-Geneviève, 1131, fol. 204r°, XVc.

Ed.: Sennewaldt, p. 121.

5759. Doulz Jhesu, qui me dignaiz racheter de ton preciouz sanc et volz soffrir c'on te meist en la croix ...

Prayer to Jesus, in prose.

METZ, Bibl. mun., 600, fol. 109v°, XVc., Hours of Paris and Prayer-book.

Ref.: Rézeau, p. 170.

5760. Doulx Jhesus, qui tous cueurs pourvoyes
De vraye consolacion,

Quel bien, quel retribucion
Te ferons nous pour les biensfaiz ...

Praise of Jesus by Jeremiah: Arnoul Gréban's Mystère de la Passion (vv. 32671-84).

PARIS, Bibl. de l'Arsenal, 6431, fol. 250rº, XVc.

PARIS, Bibl. nat., fr. 815, fol. 264rº, 1458.

ROME, Accademia Nazionale dei Lincei, Bibl. Corsiniana, Rossi 412 (44. A. 7), fol. 642vº-643rº, late XVc.

Ed.: Paris-Raynaud, p. 430 (vv. 32822-35); Jodogne, p. 435 (vv. 32671-84).

5761. Doulx roy de paradis,
Qui ce monde formastes ...

Prayer to the Evangelists; 12 quatrains rhyming abab.

SENS, Bibl. mun., 39, rouleau, XVc., lines 1179-1208.

Ed.: Tarbé, Romancero de Champagne, I, pp. 85-6; Rézeau, Saints, I, pp. 209-11.

5762. Doulx sire Jhesucrist, qui a heure de nonne que tenebres estoient sur terre, quant vous doulcement eustes prié ...

Nones of the Hours of the Cross; prose.

PROVIDENCE, Brown Univ. Libr., C. 28. b. 4 (H.L. Koopman Collection), fol. 91rº-92rº, XVc., Hours.

5763. Doulx sire Jhesucrist, qui a heure de tierce, aprés ce que vous feustes condampné a mort, vous feustes vestu de robe de pourpre ...

Terce of the Hours of the Cross; prose.

PROVIDENCE, Brown Univ. Libr., C. 28. b. 4 (H.L. Koopman Collection), fol. 88vº-89vº, XVc., Hours.

5764. Du profont de mon coeur remply d'angoisses et amertumes a cause de mes pechés et de ton yre, je crie a toy, o Seigneur ...

Sixth of the Penitential Psalms, prose version: Manuel de dévotion de prêtre Pierre.

NEW HAVEN, Yale Univ. Libr., 498, fol. 56rº-57vº, last quarter XVIc.

5765. Dou Salvor meire debonnaire,
En qui toute graice repaire ...

Hymn "Salvatoris mater pia"; 6 sizains rhyming aabccb.

METZ, Bibl. mun., 600, fol. 60r°, XVc., Hours of Paris and Prayer-book.

Ref.: Rézeau, p. 164.

5766.   Dueil ou plaisir me fault avoir sans cesse
        Dueil quant je voy et jour plain de rudesse
                         ...

"Devost Rondeau sur le crucifix."

LONDON, British Libr., Additional 17446, fol. 11v°-12r°, XVc.

E

5767. E! Diex, <u>dist il</u>, par la vostre pieté,
Si voiremant com par le Adam peché ...

Orison to Jesus by Estout de Langres, about to engage Ferragu:
  Entrée d'Espagne (vv. 1396-407).

VENICE, Bibl. Marciana, 257 (olim gall. XXI), fol. 27v°, XIVc.

<u>Ed</u>.: Thomas, I, p. 54-55.

5768. E! Dex, <u>fet il</u>, qui le mont as formé,
Tant par ai ore a perdre acostumé!
N'a oncor pas .xxv. ans passé
Que je refui an estrange regné ...

Lament to God by Charlemagne: Narbonnais (vv. 2963-77). For a
  variant version, see Diex, <u>dist li rois</u>, qui par tout fais
  vertus ... (no. 5694).

LONDON, British Libr., Harley 1321, fol. 87v°, XIIIc.

LONDON, British Libr., Royal 20. B. XIX, fol. 82v°, XIIIc.

<u>Ed</u>.: Suchier, I, p. 111 (base ms.: Harley 1321).

5769. E! Dieu, <u>ce dist Huon</u>, sainte Verge prisie,
Puisque si noble grace m'est de vous
                                     otroiie,
Je vous pri et requier que me fachiez aÿe,
Par coy on tiengne men honneur a emploiie
Qui par ceste roïne m'a esté otroiie.

Prayer to God by the hero: Hugues Capet (vv. 3353-7).

PARIS, Bibl. de l'Arsenal, 3145, fol. 62r°, XVc.

<u>Ed</u>.: La Grange, p. 144.

5770. E! Diex sans començaile, e ja non dois
                                    finir,
       Qe non volis orgoil en ton reigne sofrir
                        ...

       Orison to God by Roland: Entrée d'Espagne (vv. 11717-63).

       VENICE, Bibl. Marciana, 257 (olim gall. XXI), fol. 228v°-229r°,
         XIVc.

       Ed.: Thomas, II, p. 134-6.

5771. E! Dix, <u>dist il</u>, vrais roys de paradis,
       Puis que perdi ma dame Bïatris ...

       "Plainte" to God by prince Baudris: Hervis de Mez (vv.
         3374-81).

       PARIS, Bibl. de l'Arsenal, 3143, fol. 12v°, XIVc.

       PARIS, Bibl. nat., fr. 19160, fol. 29r°, XIIIc.

       TURIN, Bibl. naz. univ., L. II. 14, fol. 124v°-125r°, XIVc.

       Ed.: Stengel, p. 136-7.

5772. E! douce dame glorieuse,
       Dame de Dieu corex espouse,
       Marie, mere tres mielee
       Amie, corelment amee ...

       Variant of the inc.: Douce dame tres gloriouse ... (no. 478).
         Other variants at nos. 2134, 2136, 2818.

5773. E! tres douce sainte Gertrux
       Ancelle et amie de Jhesus ...

       Orison to S. Gertrude; 37 octosyllabic lines without stanzas.

       MANCHESTER, John Rylands Univ. Libr., French 143, fol.
         157v°-158v°, early XVc., Hours.

5774. E! tres doulx Dieu, ayes mercy de moy selon ta grant
         misericorde ...

       Variant of the inc.: Et tres doulx Dieu, ayes mercy de moy ...
         (no. 4389).

5775. E! tres doulx sire Jhesucrist que du (<u>ms.</u> su) saing de Dieu le
         pere tout puissant es transmis au monde ...

       Prayer to Jesus, the introduction to which opens: Se aucuns ha
         tribulation ou maladie ... (no. 6578). Other redactions of
         the orison are nos. 1561 and 1562.

       MANCHESTER, Chetham's Libr., 8007 (Mun. A. 2. 161), fol.
         115v°-118v°, XVc., Hours of Besançon.

*   E(= Et) ...

See the alphabetical order: Et ...

5776. El ne pourra trouver aide, secours et misericorde ...

Variant inc. for no. 5804.

5777. En ce doulx temps que raverdit la pree,
       Que cilz arbre flourissent de nouvel ...

"First of the "xij balades de Pasques": 13 decasyllabic lines
rhyming abaabaabbabab, the first and second are repeated as
the third and last respectively."

VATICAN CITY, Bibl. apost., Reg. lat. 1728, fol. 117v°, XVc.

Ed.: Keller, p. 616.

5778. En cez parollez ci ait contenut iij chosez:
       La premiere est moult digne et moult tres preciouse ...

"Ung Sermon que saint Jehan apostre fist," 14 quatrains of
alexandrines.

METZ, Bibl. mun., 600, fol. 96v°-97r°, XVc., Hours of Paris and
Prayer-book.

Ref.: Rézeau, p. 168.

5779. En ceste crainte de vie inexcusable ...

Variant of the inc.: Ou c'est crainte de vie inexcusable ...
(no. 4965).

5780. An Diex, que pourray devenir?
       Diex, de quelle heure fu je né ...

"Plainte" of a hunchback to God: Miracles de sainte Geneviève
(vv. 2647-74).

PARIS, Bibl. Sainte-Geneviève, 1131, fol. 212v°, XVc.

Ed.: Sennewaldt, p. 151.

5781. En Jhesu roy soveraign,
       You Lady fare and fre,
       En fine amour certain,
       Als reson telleth me ...

Orison to the Virgin; a macaronic poem of nine quatrains
rhyming abab.

OXFORD, Bodleian Libr., Douce 95, fol. 6r°, XVc.

5782. En l'(e)ure de matines Dieus no meffait
                                    compere,
       La verité divine, patience dou pere,
       Quant de Judas vendus et des siens
                                    relenquis,

Prins assis fu de ceulx qui a mort l'ont
                                    enquis.
          (Complete Text)

     Heures de la Croix; matins; in twelve-syllable quatrains, this
        one rhyming aabb. For the refrain, see the inc.: Fieus de
        Dieu le vif ... (no. 5818).

     NEW YORK, New York Public Libr., 28, fol. 127v°, XVc., Hours.

5783. En l'eure de mydi fu en crois estendus,
       Dedans fu afiquiés entre larons pendus;
       Le buvrage fieleus a son soif ont livré
       A l'engniel debonnaire qui nous a delivrés.
                 (Complete Text)

     Heures de la Croix; sext; in twelve-syllable quatrains, this
        one rhyming aabb. For the refrain, see the inc.: Fieus de
        Dieu le vif ... (no. 5818).

     NEW YORK, New York Public Libr., 28, fol. 132v°, XVc., Hours.

5784. En l'eure de prime quant solaus fu levés,
       Au soleil de justice fu blasmés, eslevés
       Par faus tesmoins, devant Pylate amenés,
       Lors raquies (?) fu laidement sourmenés.
                 (Complete Text)

     Heures de la Croix; prime; a twelve-syllable monorhymed
        quatrain. For the refrain, see the inc.: Fieus de Dieu le vif
        ... (no. 5818).

     NEW YORK, New York Public Libr., 28, fol. 129r°, XVc., Hours.

5785. En l'eure de vespres jus de le crois fu
                                    mis.
       Joseph d'Arimatie qui de çou s'entremist,
       Medecine de vie tellement amortist
       Con le couronne de glore ensi souvine gist.
                 (Complete Text)

     Heures de la Croix; vespers; a twelve-syllable monorhymed
        quatrain. For the refrain, see the inc.: Fieus de Dieu le vif
        ... (no. 5818).

     NEW YORK, New York Public Libr., 28, vol. 135v°, XVc., Hours.

5786. En l'eure dou jour tierce en criant Juys
                                    dirent:
       "C'on le crucefīast!" en pourpre le
                                    couvrirent,
       La couronne d'espines sur son chief li
                                    assirent
       Et le crois a porter sur ses espaules
                                    mirent.
                 (Complete Text)

Heures de la Croix; terce; a twelve-syllable monorhymed quatrain. For the refrain, see the inc.: Fieus de Dieu le vif ... (no. 5818).

NEW YORK, New York Public Libr., 28, fol. 131r°, XVc., Hours.

5787. En l'eure noefvisine morut en crois
                              pendant,
Criant: "Ely! (Ely)" et lui a Dieu
                              recommandant.
Uns chevalier le lance, ou costé li branla;
Li solaus obscurci et li terre en crola.
           (Complete Text)

Heures de la Croix; nones; in twelve-syllable quatrains, this one rhyming aabb. For the refrain, see the inc.: Fieus de Dieu le vif ... (no. 5818).

NEW YORK, New York Public Libr., 28, fol. 134r°, XVc., Hours.

5788. En l'onneur de nostre doulx sauveur Jhesus et de sa tres bienamee Marie Magdalayne, je, povre creature pecheresse ...

Prologue to the seven Prayers that constitute the "Heures de la benoite et glorieuse dame, saincte Marie Magdalayne."

ROUBAIX, Archives Municipales, no shelf-mark, fol. 9r°, XVc., Prayer-book of Jacques de Luxembourg.

5789. En le honurance de Deu e de ma dame seynte Marie, la tres gloriuse virgine, mere e pucele, e de tuz les vertuz du cel e nomeement ...

Orison to God, in prose.

NORWICH, Castle Museum, 158.926/4 f., fol. 153v°-154r°, XIVc., Hours of Sarum.

5790. En le noun de le Pere et de le Fis
E de le seintz Espyritz
A cui honour e gloire apent
Sauntz fyn e sauntz comencement
Si come est, fust e serra
En le siecle qe tous jours durra.
           (Complete Text)

Invocation; one six-line stanza, rhyming aabbcc.

LONDON, Brit. Libr., Harley 2253, fol. 118r°, XIVc.

Ed.: N.R. Ker, Facsimile of British Museum ms. Harley 2253, London, 1965 (EETS o.s. 255). Ref.: Långfors, p. 127.

5791. En sepucre fu mis en l'eure de complie
Li dous cors Jhesucrist esperance de vie
La jut enbaussumés, le fiertre en fu
                              emplie.
Li memore m'en soit ens ou cuer asegie!
           (Complete Text)

Heures de la Croix; compline; a twelve-syllable monorhymed
quatrain. For the refrain, see the inc.: Fieus de Dieu le vif
... (no. 5818).

NEW YORK, New York Public Libr., 28, fol. 137r°, XVc., Hours.

5792. En simplesse de sçavoir
Te rendons hommaige ...

Rondeau to Jesus: Mystère de la Passion by Arnoul Gréban (vv.
5558-70). The piece is also termed a fatras.

CHANTILLY, Musée Condé, 614 (1691), fol. 37r°, XVc.

LE MANS, Bibl. mun., 6, fol. 58v°, XVc.

PARIS, Bibl. de l'Arsenal, 6431, fol. 30r°, XVc.

PARIS, Bibl. nat., fr. 815, fol. 44r°, 1458.

PARIS, Bibl. nat., fr. 816, fol. 39r°, 1473.

PARIS, Bibl. nat., fr. 1550, fol. 115r°-115v°, XVIc.

PARIS, Bibl. nat., fr. 15064, fol. 102v°, 1469.

ROME, Accademia Nazionale dei Lincei, Bibl. Corsiniana, Rossi
412 (44. A. 7), fol. 79r°, late XVc.

Ed.: Paris-Raynaud, p. 71 (vv. 5581-93); L.C. Porter, La
Fatrasie et le fatras, Geneva, 1960, pp. 166-7; Jodogne, p.
77 (vv. 5558-70).

5793. En une isle de mer avironnee
Say une tour qui est de grant noblesse ...

Tenth of the "xij balades de Pasques": 13 decasyllabic lines
rhyming abaabaabbabab, the first and second are repeated as
the third and last respectively.

VATICAN CITY, Bibl. apost., Reg. lat. 1728, fol. 118v°, XVc.

Ed.: Keller, p. 619-20.

5794. Encline, Dieu, a nos prieres
De tes oreilles qui sont chieres.
Nous prions ta misericorde
Que digne repoz et concorde
Celluy qu'est de vie passeis
Que compains soit de ces priveis.
(Complete Text)

Prayer "Inclina domine" as part of the Vigiles des Morts in
rhyme.

MANCHESTER, John Rylands Univ. Libr., French 143, fol. 120r°,
early XVc., Hours.

5795. Endebtee suy grandement, et vient a ceste debte des folz
       marchiez que j'ay fait avec l'ennemi en la foire ...

       "Oroison ou meditacion sus la quinte demande de la patenostre,"
       in the Mendicité spirituelle by Jean Gerson.

       BRUSSELS, Bibl. royale, IV. III, fol. 211v°, XVc.

       LYON, Bibl. de la Ville, 1249 (1121), fol. 34v°, XVc.

       PARIS, Bibl. de l'Arsenal, 2113, fol. 77v°-78v°, XVc.

       PARIS, Bibl. de l'Arsenal, 2121, fol. 24r°-24v°, XVc.

       VIENNA, Oesterreichische Nationalbibl., 2574, fol. 241v°-242r°,
       XVc.

       Screening of mss. is incomplete.

       Ed.: Glorieux, Gerson: Oeuvres complètes, VII, 1, pp. 247-8.

5796. Enfant de haulte noblesse
       Bien soies tu né! ...

       Rondeau to Jesus: Mystère de la Passion by Arnoul Gréban (vv.
       5545-57). The piece is also termed a fatras.

       CHANTILLY, Musée Condé, 614 (1691), fol. 37r°, XVc.

       LE MANS, Bibl. mun., 6, fol. 58r°, XVc.

       PARIS, Bibl. de l'Arsenal, 6431, fol. 30r°, XVc.

       PARIS, Bibl. nat., fr. 815, fol. 43v°-44r°, 1458.

       PARIS, Bibl. nat., fr. 816, fol. 39r°, 1473.

       PARIS, Bibl. nat., fr. 1550, fol. 115r°, XVIc.

       PARIS, Bibl. nat., fr. 15064, fol. 102r°-102v°, 1469.

       ROME, Accademia Nazionale dei Lincei, Bibl. Corsiniana, Rossi
       412 (44. A. 7), fol. 78v°-79r°, late XVc.

       Ed.: Paris-Raynaud, p. 71 (vv. 5568-80); L.C. Porter, La
       Fatrasie et le fatras, Geneva, 1960, p. 166; Jodogne, p. 77
       (vv. 5545-57).

5797. Enlumine mez yeulz, mon Dieu,
       Affin que en pechié je ne dorme ...

       "Lez vers saint Bernard," 7 quatrains.

       METZ, Bibl. mun., 600, fol. 132v°, XVc., Hours of Paris and
       Prayer-book.

       Ref.: Rézeau, p. 174.

5798.   Entans (a) moy Jhesucris, pere espiritable
        Qui es en paradiz en grant joie perdurable
                              ...

        Orison to Jesus, one monorhymed quatrain.

        METZ, Bibl. mun., 600, fol. 7v°, XVc., Book of Hours (Use of
          Paris) and Prayer-book.

        Ed.: Rézeau, p. 157.

5799.   Entour hore de noune leva Nostre Seygnur Jhesu Crist un grant
          cri et dist en ebreu ...

        "Meditatiun devant none," part of an anon. redaction in prose.
          Legge believes this version is related to the one contained
          in the Mirour de seinte Eglyse, a translation of S. Edmund of
          Abingdon's Speculum Ecclesiae.

        LONDON, Lambeth Palace, 522, fol. 56v°-58r°, late XIII - early
          XIVc.

        Ref.: M. Dominica Legge, MLR, 29 (1934), pp. 72-4.

5800.   Estoille de mer clere
        Dieu te sault, fille et mere,
        Et tout adés vierge es,
        Dame, porte du saint cielz ...

        Hymn "Ave maris stella" in Vespers of the Heures de Nostre
          Dame.

        MANCHESTER, John Rylands Univ. Libr., French 143, fol.
          77v°-78r°, early XVc., Hours.

5801.   Et Dex, biau sire, biau dolz pere,
        Sainte Marie, dolce mere ...

        Prayer to God and All Saints to preserve the author from Hell:
          Livre des manières by Etienne de Fougères; 9 quatrains
          monorhyming, vv. 1309-44.

        ANGERS, Bibl. mun., 304 (295), fol. 150r°, XIIIc.

        Ed.: R.A. Lodge, Etienne de Fougères, Le Livre des manières,
          Geneva, 1979, p. 104.

5802.   E Deu nus doinst eschapement
        De l'horrible, enfernel turment;
        Par cele dame aium defense,
        Ki les soens encuntre tuz tense.
                        (Complete Text)

        Concluding Invocation: Miracles de Nostre Dame by Adgar called
          Willame (no. XXXV, vv. 61-4).

        LONDON, British Libr., Egerton 612, fol. 66r°, c. 1300.

        Ed. Neuhaus, p. 212. Ref.: Vising, p. 43, no. 13 (prayer not
          mentioned).

5803.   Et Deus! _dit Charles,_ voir rois de
                                majesté,
         Qui ce vosites, par la vostre bonté ...

         Orison to God by Charlemagne: Girart de Vienne by Bertrand de
         Bar-sur-Aube (vv. 6859-64).

         LONDON, British Libr., Harley 1321, fol. 38r°, XIIIc.

         LONDON, British Libr., Royal 20. B. XIX, fol. 39r°, XIIIc.

         LONDON, British Libr., Royal 20. D. XI, fol. 62v°, XIVc. Inc.:
         Hé! Deus, _dit Charles,_ vrais rois de majesté ...

         PARIS, Bibl. nat., fr. 1374, fol. 132v°, XIIIc.

         PARIS, Bibl. nat., fr. 1448, fol. 40r°, XIIIc.

         _Ed._: Yeandle, p. 215; Van Emden, p. 302-3 (both use as base ms.
         Royal 20. B. XIX).

5804.   Et ne pourra trouver ayde, secours et misericorde ceste povre
         ame miserable envers tant de princes, riches et puissans ...

         "Oroison a tous les sains ensamble," part of the Mendicité
         spirituelle by Jean Gerson.

         BRUSSELS, Bibl. royale, IV. III, fol. 213r°-217r°, XVc.

         LYON, Bibl. de la Ville, 1249 (1121), fol. 36v°-41r°, XVc.

         PARIS, Bibl. de l'Arsenal, 2113, fol. 83r°-95v°, XVc.

         PARIS, Bibl. de l'Arsenal, 2121, fol. 28r°-36v°, XVc.

         ROUBAIX, Archives Municipales, no shelf-mark, fol. Er°-Fv°,
         XVc., Prayer-book of Jacques de Luxembourg.   Inc.:   El ne
         pourra trouver aide ...

         VIENNA, Oesterreichische Nationalbibl., 2574, fol. 244r°-249v°,
         XVc.

         Screening of mss. is incomplete.

         _Ed._: Glorieux, Gerson: Oeuvres complètes, VII, 1, pp. 252-60.

5805.   Et se je suy tele et tant pardue et degettee que par moy je ne
         doy ou puisse aumosne empetrer par mon pourchas ...

         "Oroison pour les autres vifz et mors sus ce mot Orate pro
         invicem ut salvemini, in the Mendicité spirituelle by Jean
         Gerson.

         BRUSSELS, Bibl. royale, IV. III, fol. 217r°-217v°, XVc.

         LYON, Bibl. de la Ville, 1249 (1121), fol. 41r°-41v°, XVc.

         PARIS, Bibl. de l'Arsenal, 2113, fol. 95v°-96r°, XVc.

PARIS, Bibl. de l'Arsenal, 2121, fol. 37r°-38r°, XVc.

VIENNA, Oesterreichische Nationalbibl., 2574, fol. 249v°-250r°, XVc.

Screening of mss. is incomplete.

Ed.: Glorieux, Gerson: Oeuvres complètes, VII, 1, pp. 260-1.

5806. Et ta grace, Sire, te requerons en noz pensees en telle maniere que nous qui aions congneu par l'ange ...

Orison "Gratiam tuam quesumus domine" in prose, as part of Compline in the Heures de Nostre Dame en françois (no. 3658).

PROVIDENCE, Brown Univ. Libr., C. 28. b. 4 (H.L. Koopman Collection), fol. 59r°, XVc., Hours.

5807. Et te plaise par ta tres grant misericorde moy octroier .N. pour quoy en especial je te fais offrir ce saint sacrifice ...

"Et se tu fais en especial dire la messe, dis ce qui s'ensuit aprés."

PROVIDENCE, Brown Univ. Libr., C. 28. b. 4 (H.L. Koopman Collection), fol. 248v°-249v°, XVc., Hours.

5808. Et toy mon bon angel glorieux, l'un des nobles princes de la cité de Paradis, a qui par la divine bonté et ordonnance piteuse ...

Orison to one's Guardian Angel, incorporated into the prayer to the Angels, ninth of the Hierarchical Order. The wording is almost identical to the version included by Jean Gerson in his Mendicité spirituelle.

ROUBAIX, Archives Municipales, no shelf-mark, fol. Cv°-Er°, XVc., Prayer-book of Jacques de Luxembourg.

Ed.: Glorieux, Gerson: Oeuvres complètes, VII, 1, pp. 249-50.

5809. Et tu, mesires saint Jaques, se ce est veritez que tu t'apareusses a moi, proie a Nostre Seigneur que il me laist ceste cité prendre.
                    (Complete Text)

Orison to S. James the Great by Charlemagne: Pseudo-Turpin Chronicle in the Grandes Chroniques de France.

PARIS, Bibl. Saint-Geneviève, 782, fol. 142r°, c. 1275.

Screening of mss. incomplete.

Ed.: Viard, III, p.205; Mortier, III, p. 7.

5810. Et vous requier, Vierge Marie,
        En qui Jhesu prist char humaine ...

Orison to the Virgin; 12 vv. rhyming abab.

METZ, Bibl. mun., 600, fol. 104v°, XVc., Hours of Paris and Prayer-book.

Ref.: Rézeau, p. 169.

5811.   Et vous sainct Michel, qui estes garde et prince de l'Eglise, qui vainquistes le dragon, c'est assavoir l'ennemy ...

Orison to S. Michael, incorporated into the Prayer to the Archangels, eighth of the Hierarchical Order. The wording is almost identical to the verson included by Jean Gerson in his Mendicité spirituelle.

ROUBAIX, Archives Municipales, no shelf-mark, fol. Bv°-Cr°, XVc., Prayer-book of Jacques de Luxembourg.

Ed.: Glorieux, Gerson: Oeuvres complètes, VII, 1, p. 251.

5812.   Exauce et conserve moy, mon Dieu, de tout scandale, de tout mal, voire de tout peché mortel afin que toutes mes actions te soyent consacrees ...

"Oraison pour tous les matins recomander a Dieu toutes les actions de la journee": Manuel de dévotion de prêtre Pierre.

NEW HAVEN, Yale Univ. Libr., 498, fol. 20v°-22r°, last quarter XVIc.

5813.   Excite, sire Dieu, ta puissance et viens affin que ceulx qui en ta pitié se confient soient plus tost de toute adversité delivrez.
                    (Complete Text)

"Le vendredi (des quatre temps), oraison."

NEW YORK, Pierpont Morgan Libr., Morgan 78, fol. 75r°, XVc., Hours of Rome. This text added in XVIc.

5814.   Exemplayre de chasteté, glorieux confesseur et amy de Dieu, monseigneur saint Fiacre ...

Orison to s. Fiacre, in prose.

PARIS, Bibl. Ecole Nat. Sup. des Beaux-Arts, Masson, impr. 29, fol. D4v°-D5r°, XVIc.

PARIS, Bibl. nat., fr. 19243, fol. 179v°-180r°, XVIc.

Ref.: Rézeau, Saints, II, p. 212.

5815.   Exupere, torne ta face,
        Pleysir n'est que joye me face ...

Orison to S. Exupere: Mystère des Trois Doms, by chanoine Siboud Pra de Grenoble with the aid of Claude Chevalet de Vienne, and performed at Romans in 1509 (vv. 11226-37).

COLLECTION UNKNOWN (olim Giraud of Lyons), no shelf-mark, fol.
  not indicated, early XVIc.

Ed.: Giraud and Chevalier, p. 588.

F

5816. Fiacre, tu partis d'Ibernie,
      Renonçant aux biens temporelz ...

   Orison to S. Fiacre, ballade form with three eight-line stanzas
      and a final envoy of four lines.

   Refr.: Soiez moy au besoing secourable.

   PARIS, Bibl. nat., Rés. D. 5616 and Ye 831, Louenges des
      benoistz sainctz et sainctes de paradis, fol. yy5v°-yy6r°,
      Paris, Vérard.

   VERSAILLES, Bibl. mun., M. 129 (Lacombe 109 quater).

   Ed.: Rézeau, Saints, II, p. 212-4.

5817. Filz de Dieu hault et precïeulx,
      Paix soit ou vous, honneur et gloire! ...

   Rondeau to Jesus: Mystère de la Passion by Arnoul Gréban (vv.
      13180-92).

   CHANTILLY, Musée Condé, 614 (1691), fol. 108v°, XVc.

   PARIS, Bibl. nat., fr. 815, fol. 106r°, 1458.

   PARIS, Bibl. nat., fr. 816, fol. 92r°, 1473.

   PARIS, Bibl. nat., fr. 15065, fol. 67v°-68r°, 1469.

   ROME, Accademia Nazionale dei Lincei, Bibl. Corsiniana, Rossi
      412 (44. A. 7), fol. 259v°-260r°, late XVc.

   Ed.: Paris-Raynaud, p. 172 (vv. 13221-233); Jodogne, pp. 177-8
      (vv. 13180-92).

5818. Fieus de Dieu le vif Jhesu(crist) sire,
      Met te soufrance et ten martire
      De mort et ton definement
      Entre m'ame et ten jugement

Tant qu'en men cors m'ame sera
Jusqu'en fin qu'elle en istera.
                (Complete Text)

Orison to Jesus; one six-syllable stanza, rhyming aabbcc, repeated as a refrain after each of the Heures de la Croix which begin En l'eure de ...

NEW YORK, New York Public Libr., 28, fol. 128r°, 129v°, 131r°, 132v°, 134r°, 135v°, 137v°, XVc., Hours.

5819. Filz de la Vierge, qui es cieulx
Montastes a l'ascention,
En ceste amere passion
Me secourés.
                (Complete Text)

Prayer to Jesus by the hero: Mystère de saint Christofle (vv. 2064-7).

Early Ed.: in 4° Gothic, Paris, Veuve Jean Trepperel and Jean Jehannot, n.d. (c. 1515). Ed.: Runnalls, p. 65.

5820. Flour de lis per virginité
Rose vermelle per martyre ...

Orison to S. Peter the Martyr of Verona; 7 huitains and one ten-line stanza.

METZ, Bibl. mun., 600, fol. 141r°-142r°, XVc., Hours of Paris and Prayer-book.

Ed.: Rézeau, Saints, II, pp. 432-5. Ref.: Rézeau, p. 175.

5821. Fois, loaulteis, solais et cortoixie
Voi, se m'est vis, en mainte gens fineir,
Deloaultés est sovent essaucie.
Le siecle voi durement triboleir ...

"Chanson" to the Virgin attributed to Aubertin d'Araines; five seven-line stanzas rhyming ababbab, and a three-line envoy: bab.

BERN, Bürgerbibl., 389, fol. 82r°, XIIIc.

Ed.: A. Dinaux, Trouvères, jongleurs et ménestrels ... t. IV, Les trouvères brabançons ... Paris, 1863, p. 48; J. Brakelmann, ASNS, 42 (1868), p. 309; Järnström, pp. 94-6, no. XXXVII; A. Jeanroy and A. Långfors, Chansons satiriques et bachiques, Paris, 1921, pp. 5-6, 89-90. Ref.: Spanke, no. 1119.

5822. Franche pucele reïne,
De refui forte fermine ...

Oraison a Nostre Dame, inserted by Grosseteste into his Château d'amour (vv. 789-820).

BRUSSELS, Bibl. royale, 9030-9037, fol. 261v°, XVc. This version retains only vv. 817-20.

BRUSSELS, Bibl. royale, 10747, fol. 234r°, XIIIc. (This text copied in XVc.).

CAMBRIDGE, Fitzwilliam Museum, McClean 123, fol. 7v°, late XIIIc.

LONDON, British Libr., Egerton 846 B, fol. 6r°-6v°, XIVc.

LONDON, British Libr., Harley 1121, fol. 161v°, XIVc.

LONDON, British Libr., Harley 3860, fol. 54r°, XIVc.

LONDON, British Libr., Royal 20. B. XIV, fol. 91r°, XIVc.

LONDON, Lambeth Palace, 522, fol. 22v°-23v°, late XIII-early XIVc.

METZ, Bibl. mun., 1238, fol. not recorded before the destruction of the codex in World War II, XIIIc.

OXFORD, Bodleian Libr., Bodley 399, fol. 109v°-110r°, c. 1300.

OXFORD, Bodleian Libr., Bodley 652, fol. 57v°, XIIIc.

OXFORD, Bodleian Libr., Douce 132, fol. 27v°, XIIIc.

OXFORD, Bodleian Libr., Hatton 99, fol. 166r°-166v°, XVc.

OXFORD, Bodleian Libr., Laud Misc. 471, fol. 100r°-100v°, XIVc.

OXFORD, Corpus Christi College, 232, fol. 16v°-17r°, XIIIc.

PARIS, Bibl. nat., fr. 902, fol. 103r°-103v°, XIVc.

Ed.: M. Cooke, Robert Grosseteste Carmina Anglo-Normannica, London, 1852, pp. 29-30 (base mss. London, Harley 1121 and Oxford, Corpus Christi College 232); J. Murray, Le Château d'amour de Robert Grosseteste, évêque de Lincoln, Paris, 1918, p. 111. Ref.: E. Stengel, Codicem manuscriptum Digby 86, Halle, 1871, pp. 49-52 (corrections to the Cooke edition and more mss.); Vising, p. 56, no. 153 (prayer not identified); A. Långfors, Not. et extr. des mss., 42 (1932), pp. 206-8 (more mss. than in Murray's list); S.H. Thomson, The Writings of Robert Grosseteste, Bishop of Lincoln 1235-1253, Cambridge, 1940, pp. 152-4 (prayer not mentioned); M. Dominica Legge, Anglo-Norman in the Cloisters, Edinburgh, 1950, pp. 98-101; Anglo-Norman Literature, pp. 223-4.

5823. Fruit precieux de vignes d'Engerdi,
Laurier flairant, qui en tous temps verdoye
· · ·

"Louenge de la venue de saint Florent," Ballade form with three stanzas of eight and an envoy of four lines.

PARIS, Bibl. nat., lat. 17313, fol. 156r°-156v°, XVc., Missal.

Ed.: Rézeau, Saints, II, pp. 218-220.

G

5824. Garis lo, Sire, par la toe vertu;
       N'oi mes tel dote de paien mescrëu
       Come j'ai hui del felon roi Baudu.
       Que mon filluel n'ocie!
                     (Complete Text)

    Aymeri de Narbonne prays to Jesus to protect his godson
      Aymerïet: Guibert d'Andrenas (vv. 845-8 Melander, vv. 831-4
      Crosland).

    LONDON, British Libr., Harley 1321, fol. 181v°, mid XIIIc.

    LONDON, British Libr., Royal 20. B. XIX, fol. 156v°, mid XIIIc.

    LONDON, British Libr., Royal 20. D. XI, fol. 242v°, XIVc. Inc.:
      Glorieux peres, par la toe vertu ...

    PARIS, Bibl. nat., fr. 24369, fol. 162v°, XIVc. Inc.: Glorieus
      peres, par la toe vertu ...

    PARIS, Bibl. nat., nouv. acq. fr. 6298, fol. 25v°, XIIIc.

    Ed.: Melander, p. 34 and Crosland, p. 28 (both use as base ms.
      London, Royal 20. B. XIX).

*   Ge ...

    See the alphabetical order: Je ...

5825. Gloire en ait Dieu le peire et le sien
                                    digne filz,
       Jhesu nostre saverz et le saint Esprilz
                          ...

    Prayer for the Quick and the Dead; 8 vv.

METZ, Bibl. mun., 600, fol. 56v°, XVc., Hours of Paris and Prayer-book.

Ref.: Rézeau, p. 164.

5826. Gloire, loenge et enneur soient rendues en (humble) reverence et ententives devocion a Dieu ...

Praise of S. Louis IX, King of France, at the head of the prologue to the Vie by Guillaume de Saint-Pathus.

PARIS, Bibl. nat., fr. 4976, fol. 1r°, c. 1300.

PARIS, Bibl. nat., fr. 5716, p. 1, XIVc.

PARIS, Bibl. nat., fr. 5722, fol. 1r°, c. 1320.

Ed.: F. Delaborde, Vie de saint Louis par Guillaume de Saint-Pathus, confesseur de la reine Marguerite, Paris, 1899, p. 1-2.

5827. Gloire soit au hault lieu donnee,
A Dieu qui toute chose ordonne!
Et en terre paix ordonnee
Aux hommes de voulenté bonne!
                    (Complete Text)

Hymn "Gloria in excelsis": Mystère de la Passion by Arnoul Gréban (vv. 5185-8).

CHANTILLY, Musée Condé, 614 (1691), fol. 33v°, XVc.

LE MANS, Bibl. mun., 6, fol. 53r°, XVc.

PARIS, Bibl. de l'Arsenal, 6431, fol. 26v°, XVc.

PARIS, Bibl. nat., fr. 815, fol. 40v°, 1458.

PARIS, Bibl. nat., fr. 816, fol. 36v°, 1473.

PARIS, Bibl. nat., fr. 1550, fol. 106r°, XVIc.

PARIS, Bibl. nat., fr. 15064, fol. 95r°, 1469.

ROME, Accademia Nazionale dei Lincei, Bibl. Corsiniana, Rossi 412 (44. A. 7), fol. 65v°, late XVc.

Ed.: Paris-Raynaud, p. 67 (vv. 5208-11); Jodogne, pp. 72-3 (vv. 5185-8).

*   Glorieuse ...

Sometimes copyists added 'O' before this epithet, so it is necessary to consult also the alphabetical order: O glorieuse ...

5828. Gloriuse dame, mere Dieu, ke Jesu Crist
                              portastes,
Marie, le tres haut roy des angeles
                              aleitastes ...

"O gloriosa dei genitrix," as part of the Heures de Nostre
Dame; eight fourteen-syllable lines, rhyming aaaabbcc.

STUTTGART, Württembergische Landesbibl., Brev. 75, fol.
33v°-34r°, XIVc., Hours of Sarum.

5829. Glorieuse saincte dame
Sanz nul blasme
Vers vous je vuel recourir
Pour sauver corpz et ame ...

"Salutacion" to the Virgin; five douzains of which lines 2, 5,
8, 11 are three syllables and the remaining lines are
heptasyllabic. An octosyllabic quatrain concludes the
composition.

METZ, Bibl. mun., 600, fol. 14r°-14v°, XVc., Hours of Paris and
Prayer-book.

Ref.: Rézeau, p. 158.

5830. Glorieuse vierge, je vous prie que en l'honneur de celle doleur
veulliés estre mon advocate et impetrer de vostre filx vraie
repentance ...

Orison to the Virgin on the Seven Dolours.

BALTIMORE, Walters Art Gallery, Walters 218, fol. 2r°-4v°,
early XVc., Prayer-book. Orison added in a later XVc. hand.

5831. Glorieuse vierge Marie
En qui le digne fruit de vie
Fut nouris glorieusement
Et de vous nasquist sanz haschie ...

Prayer to the Virgin, 12 vv. octosyllabic.

METZ, Bibl. mun., 600, fol. 46r°, XVc., Hours of Paris and
Prayer-book.

Ref.: Rézeau, p. 161.

5832. Glorieuse vierge Marie, mere de nostre seigneur Jhesucrist,
plene de tous biens, come ainsy soit que le benoist filz ...

Orison to the Virgin, in prose.

SAN MARINO, Huntington Library, HM 1172, fol. 71r°-71v°, early
XVIc., Hours of Amiens.

5833. Glorieuse vierge Marie,
Qui de l'angele fustes siervie,
Et de toute grace raemplie,
Desfem (sic) moy, presieuse amie,
De l'anemit (sic), plain de bifame,
Et si reçoif a le mort m'arme.
                    (Complete Text)

"Orison a nostre dame qui tient son enfant ou droit bras et est pour les heures." The poem may be incomplete; it has lines or ideas in common with no. 4412.

CHICAGO, Newberry Libr., 52, fol. 29r°, c. 1470, Hours of Rheims.

5834. Glorieuse virge Marie
Qui portastes le fruit de vie,
Qui pour nous cruel mort soufri
Quan (ms. quai) Longins son costé fendi ...

Orison to the Virgin, in rhyming couplets.

WADDESDON MANOR, James A. de Rothschild Collection, 4, fol. 115r°-115v°, c. 1425-1430, Book of Hours of Guillebert de Lannoy, Use of Tournai.

5835. Glorieuse vierge, mere de Dieu, par la vertu de humilité par laquelle vous avés attraict le filz de Dieu du ciel en terre ...

Orison to the Virgin, in prose.

NEW YORK, New York Public Libr., 57, fol. 29r°-29v°, first quarter XVIc., Book of Hours for a certain Yolène, perhaps of the Héricourt family.

5836. Glorieuse Verge, mere de Jhesucrist, le vray Dieu tout puissant, royne tres piteuse, je te recommande et mes du tout en ta garde ...

Variant of no. 680.

5837. Gloriouse Vierge senz taiche, dame du monde, roÿne des aingez, espouse de Jhesucrist, temple de Nostre Signour ...

"O intemerate," in prose.

METZ, Bibl. mun., 600, fol. 98r°-99v°, XVc., Hours of Paris and Prayer-book.

Ref.: Rézeau, p. 168.

5838. Glorieuse Virge, si vraiement que tu sormontas l'ardour et le mauveistié de cest siecle et eus ton corage ...

Orison to the Virgin.

NEW YORK, Pierpont Morgan Libr., Morgan 92, fol. 129v°, late XIIIc., Hours.

*   Glorieux ...

Sometimes scribes added "O" before this epithet, so it is necessary to consult also the alphabetical order: O glorieux.

5839. Glorieulx angle, l'un de nobles princes de la cité de paradis, a qui par la divine bonté et piteuse ordonnance ...

"Oroison a son ange et a tous les autres par son moyen," in the Mendicité spirituelle by Jean Gerson.

BRUSSELS, Bibl. royale, IV. 111, fol. 212r°-213r°, XVc.

LYON, Bibl. de la Ville, 1249 (1121), fol. 35r°-36v°, XVc.

PARIS, Bibl. de l'Arsenal, 2113, fol. 79v°-83r°, XVc.

PARIS, Bibl. de l'Arsenal, 2121, fol. 25v°-28r°, XVc. Inc.: Mon glorieux angle l'un des nobles ...

VIENNA, Oesterreichische Nationalbibl., 2574, fol. 242v°-244r°, XVc.

Screening of mss. is incomplete.

Ed.: Glorieux, Gerson: Oeuvres complètes, VII, 1, pp. 249-51.

5840. Glorieux confesseur et amy de Dieu, monseigneur saint Anthoine, qui par les dyables ...

"Oraison du benoist hermite saint Anthoine/Qui est d'humilité exemple a tout vray moine"; in prose.

PARIS, Bibl. Ecole Nat. Sup. des Beaux-Arts, Masson, impr. 29, fol. C2v°-C3r°, XVIc.

PARIS, Bibl. nat., fr. 19243, fol. 172v°-173r°, XVIc.

Ref.: Rézeau, Saints, II, p. 44.

5841. Glorieux confesseur saint Françoys, qui pour l'amour de povreté ...

"Oroyson devote de monseigneur saint Francoys," in prose.

LOCHES, Bibl. mun., 17, fol. 137v°-139r°, XVc., Prayer-book.

VIENNA, Oesterreichische Nationalbibliothek, 1910, fol. 161r°-163r°, XVc. This copy lacks its opening.

Ref.: Rézeau, Saints, II, p. 220.

5842. Glorieus Deu, par la teue merci,
       Plet ai vëu, onques mes tel ne vi ...

Plainte to God by Charlemagne: Girart de Vienne by Bertrand de Bar-sur-Aube (vv. 5974-81).

LONDON, British Libr., Harley 1321, fol. 32v°, XIIIc. Inc.: Pere puissant, par la teue merci ...

LONDON, British Libr., Royal 20. B. XIX, fol. 34r°, XIIIc.

LONDON, British Libr., Royal 20. D. XI, fol. 59v°, XIVc. Inc.: Pere puissant per la toie merci ...

PARIS, Bibl. nat., fr. 1374, fol. 127v°, XIIIc. Inc.: Pere puissanz, par la tue marci ...

PARIS, Bibl. nat., fr. 1448, fol. 37r°, XIIIc. Le premier vers manque.

Ed.: Yeandle, p. 189; Van Emden, p. 264-5 (both used as base ms. Royal 20. B. XIX).

5843.   Glorieus Deu, par ton comandement,
Garis mon cors, Sire, d'afolement;
Bataille ai quise, si l'aurai voirement,
.V. m'en vienent requerre.
                    (Complete Text)

Orison to God by Aymeri de Narbonne: Guibert d'Andrenas (vv. 1828-31 Melander, vv. 1783-6 Crosland).

LONDON, British Libr., Harley 1321, fol. 187v°, mid XIIIc. Inc.: Gloriex pere, par ton digne conment,/Garis moi, Sire de mort et de torment ...

LONDON, British Libr., Royal 20. B. XIX, fol. 162v°, mid XIIIc.

LONDON, British Libr., Royal 20. D. XI, fol. 245v°, XIVc. Inc.: Biaus sire peres, par ton commandement,/Garissies moi de mort et de torment ...

PARIS, Bibl. nat., fr. 24369, fol. 167v°-168r°, XIVc. There is a variant reading for v. 2: Garissiez moi de mort et de torment.

Ed.: Melander, p. 74 and Crosland, pp. 59-60.

5844.   Glorieus Deus, par vos seintime nom,
Qui estorates terre, mer et poison
Et le seint ciel, par vostre eleccion ...

Orison to God by Aude: Girart de Vienne by Bertrand de Bar-sur-Aube (vv. 5683-722).

LONDON, British Libr., Harley 1321, fol. 30v°-31r°, XIIIc.

LONDON, British Libr., Royal 20. B. XIX, fol. 32v°, XIIIc.

LONDON, British Libr., Royal 20. D. XI, fol. 58v°-59r°, XIVc.

PARIS, Bibl. nat., fr. 1448, fol. 33r°-33v°, XIIIc.

Ed.: Yeandle, p. 180-1; Van Emden, p. 252-3 (both used as base ms. Royal 20. B. XIX). Ref.: Merk, p. 186 n. 6 and 11, p. 188 n. 12, 14, 17, 18; Dickman, p. 195; Wels, p. 3 n. 4; Koch, p. 56 and 115; Labande, p. 66 n. ; 73 n. 2; 77 n. 5; Marguerite Rossi, in Senefiance no. 10, p. 464.

5845.   Glorieus Deu, prengne vos en pitié
Des ii barons ou tote est m'amistié.
Que il n'i soient honni ne vergongnié!
                    (Complete Text)

Orison to God by Aude: Girart de Vienne by Bertrand de Bar-sur-Aube (vv. 5292-4).

LONDON, British Libr., Harley 1321, fol. 28r°, XIIIc.

LONDON, British Libr., Royal 20. B. XIX, fol. 30v°, XIIIc.

LONDON, British Libr., Royal 20. D. XI, fol. 57v°, XIVc.

PARIS, Bibl. nat., fr. 1374, fol. 124r°, XIIIc.

PARIS, Bibl. nat., fr. 1448, fol. 31r°, XIIIc.

Ed.: Yeandle, p. 168; Van Emden, p. 235 (both used as base ms. Royal 20. B. XIX). Ref.: Micheline de Combarieu, in Senefiance no. 10, p. 97.

5846. Gloriex Diex, puissant et fin,
       Sanz commancement et sanz fin ...

       Orison to God by Seth: "Mystere de la Nativité" (vv. 449-63).

       LONDON, British Libr., Additional 38860, fol. 10r°-10v°, XVIIIc. copy of a lost ms.

       PARIS, Bibl. Sainte-Geneviève, 1131, fol. 6r°, XVc.

       Ed.: Whittredge, p. 109.

5847. Glorieus Deu, ce dit la damoisele,
       Qui descendites en la Virge pucele ...

       Orison to God by Aude: Girart de Vienne by Bertrand de Bar-sur-Aube (vv. 5281-6).

       LONDON, British Libr., Harley 1321, fol. 28r°, XIIIc.

       LONDON, British Libr., Royal 20. B. XIX, fol. 30r°, XIIIc.

       LONDON, British Libr., Royal 20. D. XI, fol. 57v°, XIVc.

       PARIS, Bibl. nat., fr. 1374, fol. 124r°, XIIIc.

       PARIS, Bibl. nat., fr. 1448, fol. 30v°-31r°, XIIIc.

       Ed.: Yeandle, p. 168; Van Emden, p. 234 (both used as base ms. Royal. 20. B. XIX). Ref.: Dickman, p. 195; Koch, pp. 55, 115.

5848. Gloriex Dex qui en la croix fus mis ...

       Variant of the inc.: Gloriex pere qui onques ne mentis ... (no. 5861).

5849. Glorieux Dieux qui es roys et sires de tout le monde et qui nous feis et formas a ton ymage et te laissas mettre en croiz ...

       Orison of the Virgin to God, in prose.

       BALTIMORE, Walters Art Gallery, Walters 261, fol. 126r°-127r°, c. 1400, Hours.

5850. Glorieux Dieu, vous avés tant daigné amer l'umain lignage que
       vous avez voulu vostre filz par l'operation du saint Esperit
       ...

       Prayer to God, in the "Considérations sur saint Joseph" by Jean
       Gerson.

       PARIS, Bibl. nat., fr. 24841, fol. 117r°, XVc.

       Ed.: Glorieux, Gerson: Oeuvres complètes, VII, 1, p. 63.

5851. Glorios piere, de qui toz bien comance,
       Je prant ceste hovre en nom de penetançe
                                  ...

       Orison to God by Roland, in the course of the combat with
         Ferragu: Entrée d'Espagne (vv. 2196-203).

       VENICE, Bibl. Marciana, 257 (olim gall. XXI), fol. 43r°, XIVc.

       Ed.: Thomas, I, p. 83.

5852. Glorios Piere, do legnaje Davi
       De part ta mere, qe vergene parturi ...

       Orison to Jesus by Roland in the course of his combat with
         Ferragu: Entrée d'Espagne (vv. 3504-19).

       VENICE, Bibl. Marciana, 257 (olim gall. XXI), fol. 67v°, XIVc.

       Ed.: Thomas, I, p. 130.

5853. Gloriox pere, par la toe vertu,
       Aies pitié de ton home chanu,
       Que mes fillex n'i soit morz ne perdu,
       Pris ne noiez n'en l'eue retenu!
                     (Complete Text)

       Aymeri de Narbonne prays to God to protect his godson Aymeriet:
         Guibert d'Andrenas (vv. 835-8 Melander, vv. 822-5 Crosland).

       LONDON, British Libr., Harley 1321, fol. 181r°, mid XIIIc.

       LONDON, British Libr., Royal 20. B. XIX, fol. 156v°, mid XIIIc.

       LONDON, British Libr., Royal 20. D. XI, fol. 242v°, XIVc.

       PARIS, Bibl. nat., fr. 24369, fol. 162v°, XIVc.

       PARIS, Bibl. nat., nouv. acq. fr., 6298, fol. 25v°, XIIIc.

       Ed.: Melander, pp. 33-4 and Crosland, pp. 27-8 (both use as
         base ms. London, Royal 20. B. XIX). Ref.: Dickman, p. 141, n.
         1 and p. 196.

5854. Glorieus peres, par la toe vertu,
       N'oi mes tel dote de paien mescrëu ...

       Variant of the inc.: Garis lo, Sire, par la toe vertu ... (no.
         5824).

5855.   Gloriex pere, par ton digne comment ...

Variant of the inc.: Glorieus Deu, par ton comandement ... (no. 5843).

5856.   Gloriex pere qui es et fus todis ...

Variant of the inc.: Gloriex pere qui onques ne mentis ... (no. 5861).

5857.   Glorïeus peres qui feïs tote gent
        Et de la Virge nasquis en Bethleem ...

Variant of the inc.: Glorieus Sire qui formas tote gent/Et de la Virge fus nez en Belleant ... (no. 5878).

5858.   Glorios pere, qui feïstes lo mont,
        Et en la Virje preïs anoncion,
        Nestre deingas por raenbre lo mont,
        Lo ber saint Pere meïs en pré Noiron ...

Orison to God by the hero: Mort Aymeri de Narbonne (vv. 1444-77).

LONDON, British Libr., Harley 1321, fol. 200r°-200v°, late XIIIc.

LONDON, British Libr., Royal 20. B. XIX, fol. 175r°, mid. XIIIc. Omits first three lines.

LONDON, British Libr., Royal 20. D. XI, fol. 252r°, XIVc. Inc.: Biax sire peres qui feistes le mont ...

PARIS, Bibl. nat., fr. 24370, fol. 15r°-15v°, XIVc. Inc.: Biaus sire peres qui feistes le mont ...

Ed.: Couraye du Parc, 1884, pp. 63-4 (base ms. London, Royal 20. B. XIX). Ref.: Merk, pp. 9, 186, 188; Dickman, p. 194; Wels, p. 12 n. 28; Koch, pp. 74, 121; Labande, pp. 63, 66, 71, 72 n. 5, 74, 78 n. 2.

5859.   Glorïeus peres, qui formas Lazaron,
        Et en la Virge preïs anoncïon,
        Garis mon cors de mort et de prison,
        Ne nos ocïent cist Sarrazin felon.
                    (Complete Text)

Orison to Jesus by Guillaume: Prise d'Orange (AB redaction), vv. 541-4.

LONDON, British Libr., Royal 20. D. XI, fol. 119v°, early XIVc.

MILAN, Bibl. Trivulziana, 1025, fol. 50v°, XIIIc.

PARIS, Bibl. nat., fr. 368, fol. 168v°, XIVc.

PARIS, Bibl. nat., fr. 774, fol. 45r°, XIIIc.

PARIS, Bibl. nat., fr. 1449, fol. 51r°, XIIIc.

PARIS, Bibl. nat., fr. 24369, fol. 104v°, early XIVc.

Ed.: Katz, p. 15 (base ms.: Paris, B.N. fr. 774); Régnier,
1966, p. 117 and Régnier, 1970, p. 65 (base ms. on each
occasion: Paris, B.N. fr. 774). Ref.: Dickman, p. 196;
Frappier, Cycle de Guillaume d'Orange, II, p. 290 n. 1;
Marguerite Rossi in Senefiance no. 10, pp. 464 and 472.

5860.   Glorieus pere qui formastes Adan,
Garissiez hui moi et tote ma gent,
Qu'il ne soient veincu ne recreant!

Orison to God by Aimeri de Narbonne: Enfances Guillaume (vv.
410, 413, 414; variante de: Damedeu peire, ki formaistes
Adan).

PARIS, Bibl. nat., fr. 774, fol. 2r°-2v°, XIIIc.

Ed.: Patrice Henry, p. 20.

5861.   Gloriex pere qui onques ne mentis,
Garis mon cors que il n'i soit ocis
Ne de paiens afolé ne malmis,
Que vers moi voi venir si ademis.
                    (Complete Text)

Orison to God by Romanz: Narbonnais (vv. 4831-4).

LONDON, British Libr., Harley 1321, fol. 99v°, XIIIc.

LONDON, British Libr., Royal 20. B. XIX, fol. 93r°, XIIIc.
Inc.: Gloriex Dex qui en la croix fus mis ...

LONDON, British Libr., Royal 20. D. XI, fol. 95v°, c. 1300.
Inc.: Gloriex pere qui es et fus todis ...

PARIS, Bibl. nat., fr. 24369, fol. 60v°, c. 1300.

Ed.: Suchier, I, p. 191 (base ms.: London, Harley 1321).

5862.   Glorieus pere qui sofris passion
Et sucitas de mort seint Lazaron,
La Mazelainne feïs verai pardon ...

Prayer by the hero to God the Father and God the Son: Girart de
Vienne by Bertrand de Bar-sur-Aube (vv. 5264-71).

LONDON, British Libr., Harley 1321, fol. 28r°, XIIIc.

LONDON, British Libr., Royal 20. B. XIX, fol. 30r°, XIIIc.

LONDON, British Libr., Royal 20. D. XI, fol. 57v°, XIVc.

PARIS, Bibl. nat., fr. 1374, fol. 124r°, XIIIc. Lines 3-5 are
wanting.

PARIS, Bibl. nat., fr. 1448, fol. 30v°, XIIIc.

Ed.: Yeandle, pp. 167-8; Van Emden, p. 233 (both used as base ms. Royal 20. B. XIX). Ref.: Merk, p. 9 n. 4, 186 n. 1; Dickman, p. 195; Scheludko, ZFSL, 55 (1931), p. 452, 457; Wels; p. 3 n. 6; Koch, p. 55, 115; Labande, p. 62 n. 4, p. 72 n. 5.

5863. Gloriouz peres, qui souffris passion,
Lai moi vengier de cel cuivert larron,
Qui m'a mené par si grant traïson
Et m'a gieté de ceste region.
(Complete Text)

Orison to Jesus by the hero: Jourdain de Blaye (vv. 3678-81).

PARIS, Bibl. nat., fr. 860, fol. 130r°, XIIIc.

Ed.: Hofmann, p. 210; Dembowski, p. 122.

5864. Glorious pere, qui tot as a sauver,
En sante crois laissas ton cors pener ...

Variant of the inc.: Gloriouz Deus qui tout as a sauver ... (no. 4419).

5865. Glorïeus peres, qui tot as a sauver
Et en la Vierge te deignas aonbrer
Tot por le pueple que tu vosis sauver,
Lessas ton cors traveillier et pener ...

Orison to Jesus by Guillaume: Prise d'Orange (AB redaction), vv. 783-90.

LONDON, British Libr., Royal 20. D. XI, fol. 120v°, early XIVc.

MILAN, Bibl. Trivulziana, 1025, fol. 52r°-52v°, XIIIc.

PARIS, Bibl. nat., fr. 368, fol. 169v°, XIVc.

PARIS, Bibl. nat., fr. 774, fol. 46v°, XIIIc.

PARIS, Bibl. nat., fr. 1449, fol. 52v°, XIIIc.

Ed.: Katz, p. 22 (base ms.: Paris, B.N. fr. 774); Régnier, 1966, p. 127 and Régnier, 1970, p. 75 (base ms. on both occasions: Paris, B.N. fr. 774). Ref.: Merk, pp. 186 n. 11; 187 n. 1; 188 n. 18; Dickman, p. 196; Frappier, Cycle de Guillaume d'Orange, II, p. 299; Marguerite Rossi in Senefiance no. 10, pp. 464 and 472.

5866. Glorieux roy des cieulz la sus, en la benoite naissance duquel au jour d'uy fut faicte ceste belle parçon ...

Orison to Jesus by Jean Gerson in his Sermon pour le jour de Noel: Gloria in excelsis.

BRUSSELS, Bibl. royale, 11065-73, fol. 62r°-62v°, XVc.

CHANTILLY, Musée Condé, 145 (869), fol. 118v°, XVc.

LONDON, British Libr., Additional 12215, fol. 221r°-221v°, XVc.

PARIS, Bibl. nat., fr. 936, fol. 81r°, XVc.

PARIS, Bibl. nat., fr. 974, fol. 88r°, XVc.

PARIS, Bibl. nat., fr. 1029, fol. 68r°, XVc.

PARIS, Bibl. nat., fr. 13318, fol. 85r°, XVc.

PARIS, Bibl. nat., fr. 24839, fol. 105r°, XVc.

TOURS, Bibl. mun., 385, fol. 170r°, XVc.

TOURS, Bibl. mun., 386, fol. 125v°, XVc.

TROYES, Bibl. mun., 2292, fol. 12v°, XVc.

Ed.: Mourin, Six Sermons, 1946, p. 314; Glorieux, Gerson:
Oeuvres complètes, VII, 2, p. 650.

5867. Gloriex roys du firmament,
Ne me pourroie plus tenir
Que ne disisse mon plaisir
A vous, Sire, qui couchiez estes ...

Prayer to the Infant Jesus by Jaspar: "Geu des trois roys" (vv.
740-58).

PARIS, Bibl. Sainte-Geneviève, 1131, fol. 28v°, XVc.

Ed.: Whittredge, p. 175.

5868. Glorieux saint Anthoine, qui au jour d'hui aprez continuelle et
longue penitence avez receup bien eureuse ...

Orison to S. Anthony: Sermon pour la fête de saint Antoine, by
Jean Gerson.

PARIS, Bibl. nat., fr. 974, fol. 135v°-136r°, XVc.

PARIS, Bibl. nat., fr. 1029, fol. 99r°-99v°, XVc.

TROYES, Bibl. mun., 2292, fol. 82r°-82v°, XVc.

Ed.: Glorieux, Gerson: Oeuvres complètes, VII, 2, pp. 947-8.

5869. Glorieux sainct de Dieu amis,
Blaise martyr, a toy commis ...

"Oraison a sainct Blaise"; 36 octosyllabic lines, rhyming in
pairs.

PARIS, Bibl. nat., Rés. D. 5616 and Ye 831, Louenges des
benoistz sainctz et sainctes de paradis, fol. 226v°-227r°,
Paris, Vérard.

VERSAILLES, Bibl. mun., M. 129 (Lacombe 109 quater).

Ed.: Rézeau, Saints, II, pp. 123-4.

5870.   Glorieux saint ou saincte, N., j'ay eu fiance ...

    Variant of the inc.: O glorieux sains ou sainte, N. ... (no.
    6259).

5871.   Glorĭeux, <u>ce redist pour l'amour Dé</u>,
    Sere, delivre ceste crestĭenté!
    Et moy mesmez, se il vous vient a gré,
    Que <ge> ne saye noyé ne tourmenté.

    Orison to God by an archbishop: Aquin (vv. 2701-4).

    PARIS, Bibl. nat., fr. 2233, fol. 50r°, XVc.

    <u>Ed</u>.: Joüon des Longrais, p. 103-4.

5872.   Gloriex sire Dex, mon pere n'oblier ...

    Variant of the inc.: Sire Dieus, <u>dit Girart</u>, mon pere n'oublier
    ... (no. 6612).

5873.   Glorios Sires peres, par tes saintes
                           mercis,
    Moult par fu grant la joie le jor que tu
                          naquis ...

    Orison to Jesus by the heroine: Parise la duchesse (vv.
    806-21).

    PARIS, Bibl. nat., fr. 1374, fol. 6r, XIIIc.

    <u>Ed</u>.: Guessard and Larchey, p. 25. <u>Ref</u>.: Merk, p. 21 n. 13;
    Scheludko, ZFSL, 58 (1934), pp. 80, 179; Koch, pp. 76, 125;
    Labande, p. 75 n. 4, p. 77 n. 2; Colliot, 1970, I, p. 123.

5874.   Glorieuz sire pere, par vos saintes bontés,
    Qui de la sainte Virge fus an Bethleem nez
                     ...

    Orison to Jesus by Count Doon de Clermont: Orson de Beauvais
    (vv. 2681-5).

    PARIS, Bibl. nat., nouv. acq. fr. 16600 (olim Phillipps 222),
    fol. 42v°, XIIIc.

    <u>Ed</u>.: Paris, p. 89.

5875.   Glorios Sire pere, qui an crois fu penez,
    Les rois an Belleam feïtes vos aler ...

    Orison to Jesus by the young Hugues de Vauvenice: Parise la
    duchesse (vv. 1383-93).

    PARIS, Bibl. nat., fr. 1374, fol. 10r, XIIIc.

    <u>Ed</u>.: Guessard and Larchey, p. 42. <u>Ref</u>.: Gautier, p. 543; Merk,
    p. 186 n. 11, 187 n. 1, 188 n. 1 and n. 18; Scheludko, ZFSL,
    55 (1931), p. 456; ZFSL, 58 (1934), p. 180; Wels, p. 7 n. 20

and p. 9 n. 23; Koch, pp. 76, 125; Labande, p. 66 n. and p. 68 n. 2.

5876. Glorios Sire pere, qui maint an Trinité,
        Secorrés moi, beauz sire, par le vostre
                                    bonté!
        Au droit que je i ai, isi me secorrez!
                    (Complete Text)

        Orison to God by the heroine: Parise la duchesse (vv. 567-9).

        PARIS, Bibl. nat., fr. 1374, fol. 4v, XIIIc.

        Ed.: Guessard and Larchey, p. 18. Ref.: Altona, p. 37.

5877. Glorios sire pere, qui te laissas pener,
        Et fesistes la lune et le solail lever ...

        Prayer to God by Rosamunde, a convert to Christianity: Elie de
        Saint-Gille (vv. 2388-94).

        PARIS, Bibl. nat., fr. 25516, fol. 92v°, XIIIc.

        Ed.: Förster, p. 387; Raynaud, p. 79. Ref.: Merk, p. 186 n. 7;
        188 n. 12; Koch, pp. 69 and 119.

5878. Glorïeus Sire qui formas tote gent
        Et de la Virge fus nez en Belleant
        Quant li troi roi vos aloient querant,
        Et en la croiz vos penerent tirant ...

        Orison to Jesus by Guillaume: Prise d'Orange (AB redaction),
        vv. 499-509.

        LONDON, British Libr., Royal 20. D. XI, fol. 119v°, early XIVc.
        Inc.: Glorieus peres qui feïs tote gent/Et de la Virge
        nasquis en Bethleem ...

        MILAN, Bibl. Trivulziana, 1025, fol. 50v°, XIIIc.

        PARIS, Bibl. nat., fr. 368, fol. 168v°, XIVc.

        PARIS, Bibl. nat., fr. 774, fol. 44v°, XIIIc.

        PARIS, Bibl. nat., fr. 1449, fol. 51r°, XIIIc.

        PARIS, Bibl. nat., fr. 24369, fol. 102v°, early XIVc.

        Ed.: Katz, p. 14 (base ms.: Paris, B.N., fr. 774); Régnier,
        1966, p. 115 and Régnier, 1970, p. 63 (base ms. on both
        occasions: Paris, B.N. fr. 774). Ref.: Merk, pp. 21 n. 13;
        186 n. 5; 187 n. 1; 188 n. 18; Dickman, p. 196; Scheludko,
        ZFSL, 58 (1934), p. 80; Frappier, Cycle de Guillaume
        d'Orange, II, p. 290, n. 1; Garel, pp. 311-18; Marguerite
        Rossi in Senefiance no. 10, pp. 464 and 472.

5879. Graces vous rend, sire Jhesu Crist, qi moy en cest nuyt avez
        gardé, defendu et visité ...

Thanksgiving Prayer, a rendering of "Gratias tibi ago domine
Jhesu Christe qui me miserum peccatorem in hac nocte" ... It
is part of the Mirour de Seinte Eglyse, a translation of the
Speculum Ecclesiae by S. Edmund of Abingdon. The Anglo-Norman
prayer is found in only one ms. of the B version. It occurs
in one ms. of the A version but with a different inc.: Jeo
vus reng graces ... (no. 6007).

LONDON, British Libr., Harley 1121, fol. 143r°, early XIVc.

Ed.: Robbins, p. 10 from Harley 1121; not in Wilshere, whose
base ms. of the B version does not contain the vernacular
prayer. Ref.: Same as the Ref. section of the inc. Aprés ço
devez saver queus sunt les set prieres ... (no. 5431).

H

*   Ha! ...

      See also the alphabetical order: A! ...

5880.   Ha! Deus, <u>dist il</u>, verai pere Jhesu,
        Commant puet estre? Qui a ce esmëu ...

      "Plainte" to Jesus by Gerbert: Yon (vv. 2232-40).

      PARIS, Bibl. nat., fr. 1622, fol. 278r°, XIIIc.

      <u>Ed.</u>: Mitchneck, p. 64-5.

5881.   Ha! douz peres du firmament,
        Qui tout feistes certainement
        Le ciel et la terre et la mer
        Vous doy je servir et amer ...

      Prayer to God by the Virgin: "Mystere de la Nativité" (vv. 1601-30).

      LONDON, British Libr., Additional 38860, fol. 33r°-33v°, XVIIIc. copy of a lost ms.

      PARIS, Bibl. Sainte-Geneviève, 1131, fol. 17v°, XVc.

      <u>Ed.</u>: Whittredge, pp. 141-2.

5882.   Ha! fille, voys que je seuffre pour toy ...

      Variant of no. 727.

5883.   Ha! gloriuse rëyne ...

      Variant of the inc.: Ha! tres gloriuse reïne ... (no.5898).

5884.   Ha! Jhesu, vroy pere tout puissant,
        Que nous soiez en aide et secourant!
        Traïz nous ont les payens soudement!

        Orison to Jesus by Christian combattants: Aquin (vv. 1556-8).

        PARIS, Bibl. nat., fr. 2233, fol. 28r°, XVc.

        Ed.: Joüon des Longrais, p. 61.

5885.   Ha! Jhesu Crist, beau tres doulx sire,
        Qui pour nous souffrit passïon,
        Envoye moy consolatïon
        En ce martire, s'il te plaist.
                        (Complete Text)

        Prayer to Jesus by Avicene: Mystère de saint Christofle (vv.
        1518-21).

        Early Ed.: in 4° Gothic, Paris, Veuve Jean Trepperel and Jean
        Jehannot, n.d. (c. 1515). Ed.: Runnalls, p. 49.

5886.   Haa! Jhesucrist tres bon, bien soiés vous venu! Je croy de tout
        mon cuer et certainement gehis que dessoubs celle blancheur
        ...

        Orison at the Elevation.

        LONDON, British libr., Harley 2952, fol. 57r°-57v°, XVc.,
        Hours.

5887.   Ha! mon Seigneur, ha! mon doulz filz,
        Ha! doulz Jhesus, plus doulz que miel ...

        Orison to Jesus by the Virgin: Miracles de sainte Geneviève
        (vv. 701-14).

        PARIS, Bibl. Sainte-Geneviève, 1131, fol. 190v°, XVc.

        Ed.: Sennewaldt, p. 81.

5888.   Ha! Nostre Dame de Monfort,
        Je tremble dent a dent, hareu! ...

        "Plainte" to the Virgin and to God by a fever patient: Miracles
        de sainte Geneviève (vv. 2675-714).

        PARIS, Bibl. Sainte-Geneviève, 1131, fol. 212v°-213r°, XVc.

        Ed.: Sennewaldt, p. 151-2.

5889.   Haa! Nostre dame, royne des cieulx et mere de misericorde ...

        Variant of the inc.: Royne des cieulx et mere de misericorde
        ... (no. 6512).

5890.   Ha! rois de paradis, vuilles ovrir tes
                                    portes,
        Les ames des crestiens reçoy en ta grant
                                    sale

Dont li corps sont ci mors tuit roit, tuit
                         froit, tuit pale.
          (Complete Text)

Plainte to God by the hero: Girart de Rossillon, Burgundian
    redaction (vv. 4082-4).

BRUSSELS, Bibl. royale, 11181, fol. 69v°, XVc.

MONTPELLIER, Bibl. Fac. Ecole de Médecine, H. 244, fol. 77v°,
    XVc.

MONTPELLIER, Bibl. Fac. Ecole de Médecine, H. 349, fol. 56r°,
    c. 1350.

PARIS, Bibl. nat., fr. 15103, fol. 84r°, 1417.

Ed.: Ham, p. 226 (base ms.: Montpellier H. 349).

5891. Ha! dit el, saint Jehan Baptiste,
        Seray je tousjours mais si triste ...

        "Plainte" by a woman to the Saint: anon. Vie de S. Jean
            Baptiste (vv. 6385-90).

        PARIS, Bibl. nat., fr. 2182, fol. 113r°, 1322.

        PARIS, Bibl. nat., nouv. acq. fr. 7515, fol. 105v°-106r°, XIVc.

        Ed.: Gieber, p. 183 (base ms. fr. 2182).

5892. Ha! saint Jehan, tres chier amy,
        Tres doulz prophete entent a my ...

        Orison by a woman to the Saint: anon. Vie de S. Jean Baptiste
            (vv. 6307-29).

        PARIS, Bibl. nat., fr. 2182, fol. 111v°-112r°, 1322.

        PARIS, Bibl. nat., nouv. acq. fr. 7515, 104r°-104v°, XIVc.

        Ed.: Gieber, pp. 180-1 (base ms. fr. 2182).

5893. Ha! saint Jehan tres debonnaire,
        Aies de cest chetif pitié ...

        A contrait prays to the Head of S. John the Baptist for
            recovery of his health: anon. Vie (vv. 7547-556).

        PARIS, Bibl. nat., fr. 2182, fol. 134r°, 1322.

        PARIS, Bibl. nat., nouv. acq. fr. 7515, fol. 131v°, XIVc.

        Ed.: Gieber, p. 216 (base ms. fr. 2182).

5894. Ha! sire Dieu, amoureux Dieux,
        De cueur humblement te mercy ...

        Christofle gives thanks to God: Mystère de saint Christofle
            (vv. 1946-51).

Early Ed.: in 4° Gothic, Paris, Veuve Jean Trepperel and Jean
Jehannot, n.d. (c. 1515). Ed.: Runnalls, p. 61.

5895. Ha! tres douce Marye ...

Variant of the inc.: Ha! tres gloriuse reïne ... (no. 5898).

5896. Ha! tres doulce vierge Marie pucelle ...

Variant of the inc.: Hé! tres doulce vierge pucelle, Marie ...
(no. 755).

5897. Ha! tres doulx benoit Jhesucrist, ainsi vraiement comme je croy
que vous nasquistes de la benoite vierge Marie a tres grant
joie ...

"Ceste oroison doit dire femme qui traveille."

PROVIDENCE, Brown Univ. Libr., C. 28. b. 4 (H.L. Koopman
Collection), fol. 179r°-179v°, XVc., Book of Hours.

5898. Ha! tres gloriuse reïne,
Marie, mere e virgine ...

Oraison a Nostre Dame, inserted by Grosseteste into his Château
d'amour (vv. 1173-1200).

BRUSSELS, Bibl. royale, 9030-9037, fol. 265r°, XVc. Inc.: Ha!
glorieuse roÿne ...

BRUSSELS, Bibl. royale, 10747, fol. 236r°-236v°, XIIIc. (This
text copied in XVc.). Inc.: Ha! gloriouse roÿ<ne> ...

LONDON, British Libr., Egerton 846 B, fol. 8v°, XIVc. Inc.: Ha!
tres douce Marye ...

LONDON, British Libr., Harley 1121, fol. 164r°, XIVc.

LONDON, British Libr., Harley 3860, fol. 57r°, XIVc.

LONDON, Lambeth Palace, 522, fol. 33r°-34r°, late XIII - early
XIVc. Inc.: Ha! gloriuse reÿne ...

METZ, Bibl. mun., 1238, fol. not recorded before the
destruction of the codex in World War II.

OXFORD, Bodleian Libr., Bodley 399, fol. 112r°, c. 1300. Inc.:
A! tres gloriose reÿne ...

OXFORD, Bodleian Libr., Bodley 652, fol. 60r°, XIIIc. Inc.: A!
tres glorieuse reïne ...

OXFORD, Bodleian Libr., Douce 132, fol. 30r°-30v°, XIIIc.

OXFORD, Bodleian Libr., Hatton 99, fol. 172r°-172v°, XVc.

OXFORD, Bodleian Libr., Laud Misc. 471, fol. 103r°, XIVc. Inc.:
A! tres gloriuse reïne ...

OXFORD, Corpus Christi College, 232, fol. 23v°-24r°, XIIIc.
Inc.: Ha! gloriuse reïne/Mere Deu, pucele fine ...

PARIS, Bibl. nat., fr. 902, fol. 105r°-105v°, XIVc. Inc.: La
tres gloriuse reïne ...

Ed.: M. Cooke, Robert Grosseteste Carmina Anglo-Normannica,
London, 1852, pp. 42-3 (base mss. London, Harley 1121 and
Oxford, Corpus Christi College 232); J. Murray, Le Château
d'amour de Robert Grosseteste, évêque de Lincoln, Paris,
1918, pp. 121-2. Ref.: E. Stengel, Codicem manuscriptum Digby
86, Halle, 1871, pp. 49-52 (corrections to the Cooke edition
and more mss.); Vising, p. 56, no. 153 (prayer not
identified); A. Långfors, Not. et extr. des mss., 42 (1932),
pp. 206-8 (more mss. than in Murray's list); S.H. Thomson,
The Writings of Robert Grosseteste, Bishop of Lincoln
1235-1253, Cambridge, 1940, pp. 152-4 (prayer not mentioned);
M. Dominica Legge, Anglo-Norman in the Cloisters, Edinburgh,
1950, pp. 98-101; Anglo-Norman Literature, pp. 223-4.

5899.   Ha! vrais Jhesus et vrais Sires,
         Par t'amoreuse amistié ...

         "Plainte" to Jesus by Isaiah: "Mystère de la Nativité" (vv.
         586-93).

         LONDON, British Libr., Additional 38860, fol. 13r°, XVIIIc.
         copy of a lost codex.

         PARIS, Bibl. Sainte-Geneviève, 1131, fol. 7v°, XVc.

         Ed.: Whittredge, p. 113.

*   Hai! ...

         See the alphabetical order: Hé! ...

5900.   Haulte prefference
         Et magnificence ...

         Rondeau to Jesus: Mystère de la Passion by Arnoul Gréban (vv.
         33063-83).

         PARIS, Bibl. de l'Arsenal, 6431, fol. 253r°-253v°, XVc.

         PARIS, Bibl. nat., fr. 815, fol. 267r°, 1458.

         PARIS, Bibl. nat., fr. 816, fol. 229r°, 1473.

         ROME, Accademia Nazionale dei Lincei, Bibl. Corsiniana, Rossi
         412 (44. A. 7), fol. 650r°-650v°, late XVc.

         Ed.: Paris-Raynaud, p. 435 (vv. 33210-30); Jodogne, p. 439 (vv.
         33063-83).

5901.   Haulte roine, mere du roy,
         Qui suz tous roys et princes regne ...

Prayer to the Virgin by S. Paul: Miracles de sainte Geneviève (vv. 427-74).

PARIS, Bibl. Sainte-Geneviève, 1131, fol. 188r°-188v°, XVc.

Ed.: Sennewaldt, p. 75-6.

5902.   Haute sur les esteilles, gloriuse pucele, celui ke te crea
        <a>leitas de ta mamele ...

        "O gloriosa domina," in prose, perhaps once in rhyme; part of
        the Heures de Nostre Dame.

        STUTTGART, Württembergische Landesbibl., Brev. 75, fol.
        31r°-32r°, XIVc., Hours of Sarum.

5903.   Haulte Trinité,
        Parfaicte unité,
        Singuliere essence,
        A ta magesté ...

        Praise of the Trinity: Mystère de la Passion by Arnoul Gréban
        (vv. 33755-66).

        PARIS, Bibl. de l'Arsenal, 6431, fol. 258v°, XVc.

        PARIS, Bibl. nat., fr. 815, fol. 272v°, 1458.

        PARIS, Bibl. nat., fr. 816, fol. 233v°, 1473.

        ROME, Accademia Nazionale dei Lincei, Bibl. Corsiniana, Rossi
        412 (44. A. 7), fol. 664v°, late XVc.

        Ed.: Paris-Raynaud, p. 443 (vv. 33902-13); Jodogne, p. 448 (vv.
        33755-66).

*   Hé! ...

        Here are grouped the spellings: Hai! ..., Hé! ..., Hee! ...

5904.   Hee! dame du ciel esmeree,
        De sains et de saintes honoree ...

        Orison to the Virgin, part of Chaillou de Pesstain's
        interpolation (vv. 1653-60) in the Roman de Fauvel by Gervais
        du Bus.

        PARIS, Bibl. nat., fr. 146, fol. 42v°, XIVc.

        Ed.: Aubry, Fauvel, fol. 42v°; Långfors, Fauvel, p. 191.

5905.   Hai! Dieux de paradis, qe pur nus fustez né
        De la gloriouse Virgine qe Marie est nomé
                            ...

        Charlemagne prays to God: Fierabras, short version (vv.
        281-92).

        HANOVER, Niedersächsische Landesbibl., IV. 578, fol. 39r°,
        early XIVc.

LONDON, British Libr., Egerton 3028, fol. 88v°-89r°, XIVc.

Ed.: L. Brandin, Romania, 64 (1938), p. 62.

5906. Hé! Diex, hé! Diex, que j'ay grant joye!
Et comment, doulz Diex, me tendroye ...

Praise of God and the Virgin by a mother: Miracles de sainte
Geneviève (vv. 1841-60).

PARIS, Bibl. Sainte-Geneviève, 1131, fol. 202v°-203r°, XVc.

Ed.: Sennewaldt, p. 118.

5907. Hé! Deus, dist il, par la toie merci,
Done moi vie, je te requier et pri,
Que vangier puisse Fromondin mon ami,
Qui a esté a si grant tort murtri.
                    (Complete Text)

Orison to God by Doon le Gris de Boulogne: Yon (vv. 312-15).

PARIS, Bibl. nat., fr. 1622, fol. 261v°-262r°, XIIIc.

Ed.: Mitchneck, p. 10.

5908. Hé! Deus, dist il, par ton saintisme non,
Salvez le pueple que la voi environ ...

Orison to God by Hernaut: Yon (vv. 2454-60).

PARIS, Bibl. nat., fr. 1622, fol. 279v°, XIIIc.

Ed.: Mitchneck, p. 71.

5909. Hé! Deus, dist il, peres de majesté,
Tant sommes or chaitif et esgaré ...

"Plainte" to Jesus by Huedon de Flandres: Yon (vv. 5273-9).

PARIS, Bibl. nat., fr. 1622, fol. 303v°, XIIIc.

Ed.: Mitchneck, p. 150.

5910. Hé! Dieu, que j'ay tant remancier
En mes grans doleurs maintefoiz,
Plaise vous, tres doulx roy des roiz,
Conforter vostre povre encelle ...

Orison to God by Nathalie: Mystère de saint Adrien (vv.
5399-420).

CHANTILLY, Musée Condé, 620 (1603), fol. 108r°-108v°, 1485.

Ed.: Picot, p. 105.

5911. Hé! Dieux, que penses tu, qui tel duel m'as
                              or fait?

Je croi tout de certaim qu'anvers toi ai
                              forfait ...

Plainte to God by King Charles le Chauve: Girart de Rossillon,
   Burgundian redaction (vv. 5287-94).

BRUSSELS, Bibl. royale, 11181, fol. 89v°-90r°, XVc.

MONTPELLIER, Bibl. Fac. Ecole de Médecine, H. 244, fol. 99v°,
   XVc.

MONTPELLIER, Bibl. Fac. Ecole de Médecine, H. 349, fol. 72r°,
   c. 1350.

PARIS, Bibl. nat., fr. 15103, fol. 107v°, 1417.

Ed.: Ham, p. 260 (base ms.: Montpellier H. 349).

5912. Hé! Dex, dist elle, qui formas toute jant
        Et conmandas au baron Abrahant ...

        "Plainte" to God by Charlemagne's wife: Ami et Amile (vv.
        1278-321).

        PARIS, Bibl. nat., fr. 860, fol. 99v°, XIIIc.

        Ed.: Hofmann, p. 37-9; Dembowski, p. 41-3; Ref.: Gautier, p.
           542; Merk, p. 21 n. 13; p. 188 n. 17; D. Scheludko, ZFSL, 58
           (1934), p. 81; Wels, p. 3 n. 7; Dickman, p. 195; Labande, p.
           71 n. 4; p. 74 n. 2; p. 75; p. 76 n. 3; p. 77 n. 3 and 10;
           Saly, p. 50.

5913. Hé! Dex, dist elle, qui fuz nés de la Virge
        Et le pain d'orge menjastez a la ceinne ...

        "Plainte" to Jesus by Charlemagne's wife: Ami et Amile (vv.
        1333-9).

        PARIS, Bibl. nat., fr. 860, fol. 99v°, XIIIc.

        Ed.: Hofmann, p. 39; Dembowski, p. 43; Ref.: Marguerite Rossi
           in Senefiance no. 10, pp. 452, 453, 468.

5914. Hé! Dieus, ce dist ly rois, trez dignez
                              perez vrais,
        Je te pri et requier que cez bacellers lais
        Aller en sauveté, car ne vy onquez mais
        Faire sy hardy fait, si m'ait saint
                              Nicollais.

        Orison to God by King Drogon: Hugues Capet (vv. 2617-20).

        PARIS, Bibl. de l'Arsenal, 3145, fol. 50r°, XVc.

        Ed.: La Grange, p. 116.

5915. Hé! Deus, dit Charles, vrais vois de majesté ...

        Variant of the inc.: Et Deus! dit Charles, voir rois de majesté
           ... (no. 5803).

5916. Hé! Dix, <u>dist il</u>, vrais rois de maïsté,
      Qui de la Virge en Belleem fu nés ...

      Orison to Jesus by the hero: Hervis de Mez (vv. 8106-10).

      PARIS, Bibl. de l'Arsenal, 3143, fol. 30v°, XIVc.

      PARIS, Bibl. nat., fr. 19160, fol. 68v°, XIIIc.

      TURIN, Bibl. naz. univ., L. II. 14, fol. 154r°, XIVc.

      <u>Ed.</u>: Stengel, p. 328.

5917. Hé! doulz Jhesucrist, que ma mere
      Trait de paine et d'angoisse amere ...

      "Plainte" to Jesus by the heroine: Miracles de sainte Geneviève
         (vv. 212-19).

      PARIS, Bibl. Sainte-Geneviève, 1131, fol. 185v°, XVc.

      <u>Ed.</u>: Sennewaldt, p. 67.

5918. Hé! hault Sire du firmament
      Qui toutez chosez composas ...

      Prayer to God by Seth: "Mystère de la Nativité" (vv. 516-29).

      LONDON, British Libr., Additional 38860, fol. 8v°-9r°, XVIIIc.
      copy of a lost ms.

      PARIS, Bibl. Sainte-Geneviève, 1131, fol. 5r°-5v°, XVc.

      <u>Ed.</u>: Whittredge, p. 111.

5919. Hé! mesires sains Nicaises, qui estes appellés vrais hastieux
         pour la grant bonté de vostre digne corps ...

      Orison to S. Nicaise.

      CHICAGO, Newberry Libr., 52, fol. 173r°-173v°, <u>c</u>. 1470, Hours
      of Rheims.

5920. Hé! mesire saint Nicaise, vrai ami especial a Dieu, je vous
         prie et appelle conme men seigneur ...

      Orison to S. Nicaise.

      CHICAGO, Newberry Libr., 52, fol. 172v°-173r°, <u>c</u>. 1470, Hours
      of Rheims.

5921. Hé! mesire saint Nicaise, vrai martyr a qui Dieu donna grace de
         souffrir tel martire ...

      "De saint Nicaise un⟨e⟩ boin⟨e⟩ orison."

      CHICAGO, Newberry Libr., 52, fol. 172v°, <u>c</u>. 1470, Hours of
      Rheims.

5922. Hee! plaine de grace devine ...

Variant of the inc.: O plaine de grace divine ... (no. 1472).

5923. Hey! dist Boves, roi de paraïs ...

Variant of the Inc.: A! Deus, fet il, beau rey de paraÿs ...
(no. 5376).

5924. Hé! Sire Dieus, doulces graces vous rens ...

Prayer at Mass, in prose.

LIVERPOOL, Liverpool Public Libr. D. 435, fol. 74rº, early
XVc., Hours of Paris.

5925. Hé! sire Dieu, qui tous biens donne,
Je te gracie de ce martire ...

Orison to God by the hero: Mystère de saint Christofle (vv.
998-1005).

Early Ed.: in 4º Gothic, Paris, Veuve Jean Trepperel and Jean
Jehannot, n.d. (c. 1515). Ed.: Runnalls, p. 33.

5926. Hee! sire Deu, fet il, roy benuré,
Ke pur nostre sauvacioun
Suffrites si forte passioun,
Tu, Sire, ke vois e entens ...

"Plainte" to Jesus by Amilun: Amis e Amilun (Anglo-Norman
version); 28 lines.

KARLSRUHE, Badische Landesbibliothek, Karlsruhe 345 (olim
Durlac. 38), fol. 61vº, XIVc.

Ed.: E. Kölbing, Amis and Amiloun, zugleich mit der
altfranzösischen Quelle, Heilbronn, 1884, p. 154-55 (lines
numbered 38-65 in the variant passage).

5927. Hé! sire saint Michel, archangele de paradis, conduisseur des
ames, et ma dame saincte Eutrope ...

Orison to SS. Michael and Eutrope.

CHICAGO, Newberry Libr., 52, fol. 175rº, c. 1470, Hours of
Rheims.

5928. Hé! sire saint Nicaise, je vous prie que quant m'ame se partira
de mon corps et de ce siecle et je ne pourrai plus ...

Orison to S. Nicaise.

CHICAGO, Newberry Libr., 52, fol. 174vº, c. 1470, Hours of
Rheims.

5929. Hé! sire saint Nicaise, je vous reclame pour toutes les
besongnes dont j'ay besoing d'estre aidiés et dont li doulx
Jhesu Crist ...

Orison to S. Nicaise.

CHICAGO, Newberry Libr., 52, fol. 173v°-174r°, <u>c</u>. 1470, Hours of Rheims.

5930. Hé! sire saint Nicaise, vous a celle priere soiés aparilliés pour aidier et desfendre m'ame ...

Orison to S. Nicaise.

CHICAGO, Newberry Libr., 52, fol. 174v°, <u>c</u>. 1470, Hours of Rheims.

5931. Hé! sire saint Nicaise, vueillés prier pour tous chieux et pour toutes celles pour qui je sui tenu de prier ...

Orison to S. Nicaise.

CHICAGO, Newberry Libr., 52, fol. 174r°, <u>c</u>. 1470, Hours of Rheims.

5932. Hé! Sire, tres bien puissiés vous estre tenus ...

"Orison de la Messe," in prose.

LIVERPOOL, Liverpool Public Libr. D. 435, fol. 73r°-74v°, early XVc., Hours of Paris.

5933. Hé! tres doulce vierge Marie,
Mere de Dieu mon createur ...

Orison to the Virgin by a martyr: Mystère de saint Adrien (vv. 4201-6).

CHANTILLY, Musée Condé, 620 (1603), fol. 84v°-85r°, 1485.

<u>Ed.</u>: Picot, p. 82.

5934. Hé! tres doulce vierge pucelle, mere Jhesucrist, roÿne glorieuse, donnes consolacion et confort a tous desconfortés ...

Variant or different redaction of the inc.: Hé! tres doulce vierge pucelle, Marie ... (no. 755).

5935. Hé! tres doulx Jhesus, qui es vray Dieu du sein du pere Dieu tout puissant, es envoié au monde pardonner les pechez ...

Orison to Jesus, in prose.

PROVIDENCE, Brown Univ. Libr., C. 28. b. 4 (H.L. Koopman Collection), fol. 219r°-223v°, XVc., Hours.

5936. Hé! tres doulz roys du firmamant,
De tout mon cuer servir vous vueil,
Amer, doubter plus que ne suel,
Car je voy tout pour certain ...

Orison to the Infant Jesus by Melchior: "Geu des trois roys" (vv. 708-23).

PARIS, Bibl. Sainte-Geneviève, 1131, fol. 28r°, XVc.

Ed.: Whittredge, p. 174.

5937.   Crioient hautement: Hé! Vierge trezoriere,
Car nous sauvez Gaufroit, drois est c'on
                                    t'en requiere ...

Orison to the Virgin by Mendicants to save Gaufroit: Baudouin
   de Sebourc (vv. 893-7 of Chant I).

PARIS, Bibl. nat., fr. 12552, fol. 5r°, XIVc.

PARIS, Bibl. nat., fr. 12553, fol. 14v°, XVc. Inc.: Crioient
   hautement: Roine tresoriere ...

Ed.: Boca, I, p. 26.

5938.   Hé! vray roy Jhesucrist, tres puissant tres debonnaire, tres
   doulx, tres souef ...

Orison to Jesus in prose.

CHANTILLY, Musée Condé, 127 (628), fol. 9r°-10r°, XVc.

*   Hee! ...

See the alphabetical order: Hé!

5939.   Helais! ce dit coins Doz, com par sui
                                    malbalis.
Damedex sire peres, qui onques ne mantis,
Si com jel fis por bien, me puisiez vous
                                    garir
Que je vilment ne soe afolez ne malmis!

Lament to God by Count Doon de Clermont, captured in battle:
   Orson de Beauvais (vv. 2301-4).

PARIS, Bibl. nat., nouv. acq. fr. 16600 (olim Phillipps 222),
   fol. 36v°, XIIIc.

Ed.: Paris, p. 76.

5940.   Helas! mon doulz sauveur Jhesus,
Que feray ne que deviendray?
Benoit Jhesus, tu scez que j'ay
Journee prinse pour respondre ...

"Plainte" to Jesus by Nathalie: Mystère de saint Adrien (vv.
   8926-53).

CHANTILLY, Musée Condé, 620 (1603), fol. 178r°-178v°, 1485.

Ed.: Picot, p. 174-5.

5941.   Helas! mon doulx sauveur, quant tu vivoies, homme mortel, en ce
   present monde, a ceulx qui te vouloient croire ...

Orison to Jesus, in prose.

PROVIDENCE, Brown Univ. Libr., C. 28. b. 4 (H.L. Koopman Collection), fol. 274r°-274v°, XVc., Hours.

5942. Helais! que ne travelle tu, chaitive creature, que es endormie et obliee en tes iniquitez ...

Meditation on the Passion, in prose; an adaptation of Anselm's Meditatio XI.

METZ, Bibl. mun., 600, fol. 57r°-59r°, XVc., Hours of Paris and Prayer-book.

Ref.: Rézeau, p. 164.

5943. Honors de virges, dame de gens, roine des angles, fonteine des vergiers, pardon de pechiez ...

"Oroisons a Deu et Nostre Dame."

NEW YORK, Pierpont Morgan Libr., Morgan 92, fol. 137r°-138r°, late XIIIc., Hours.

5944. Honneur, puissance et reverence
Soit a vous, Dieu et createur! ...

Praise of God by the Seraphim: Mystère de la Passion by Arnoul Gréban (vv. 98-113). Rondeau.

PARIS, Bibl. nat., fr. 815, fol. 1v°, 1458.

PARIS, Bibl. nat., fr. 816, fol. 4v°, 1473.

PARIS, Bibl. nat., fr. 1550, fol. 2v°, XVIc.

PARIS, Bibl. nat., fr. 15064, fol. 2v°-3r°, 1469.

Ed.: Paris-Raynaud, p. 7 (vv. 320-335); Jodogne, p. 14 (vv. 98-113).

I

5945. Il est certain que la mere de Dieu
Estoit present et prochaine du lieu
Ou son enfant fut tout nud estendu
Et hault en croix ataché et pendu ...

"La tres devote oraison de Stabat mater dolorosa en françois en
risme"; 82 lines as one hexasyllabic stanza and nineteen
quatrains.

LONDON, British Libr., Additional 17446, fol. 35rº-37rº, XVc.

5946. Il fault mourir a ce coup cy,
Puisque le grant sainct est sonné.
N'avez vous point ouÿ le cry?
Quant a moy, je suis estonné ...

"Chanson piteuse," anonymous, but often ascribed to Olivier
Maillard; twelve eight-line stanzas, rhyming ababbcbc.

VIENNA, Oesterreichische Nationalbibl., 3391, fol. 506rº-506vº,
520rº-520vº, late XVc.

Early Eds.: Le Routier de la mer jusques au fleuve de Jourdain,
Rouen for Jacques le Forestier, c. 1502-1510, reproduced in
D.W. Waters, The Rutters of the Sea, New Haven (Conn.), 1967,
pp. 166-8. See also the text of another Gothic ed. reproduced
in A. de Montaiglon, Recueil de poésies françoises des XVe et
XVIe siècles, Paris, 1857, VII, pp. 148-52. Ref.: A de La
Borderie, Oeuvres françaises d'Olivier Maillard, Nantes,
1877, p. 77 ss.; A. Piaget, Annales du Midi, 5 (1893), pp.
315-25 (with bibliography for editions).

5947. Illuminez, seigneur Dieu, createur des cieux et de la terre et
       de tous les anymaulx qui sont en icelle ...

       "Oraison du matin aprés le resveil": Manuel de dévotion de
       prêtre Pierre.

       NEW HAVEN, Yale Univ. Libr., 498, fol. 18v°-20v°, last quarter
       XVIc.

J

5948. J'ay aymé pour ce que Nostre Seigneur orra la voix de mon oroison, car il a encliné son oreille a moy et je l'appellay ...

"Vigile des morts."

PROVIDENCE, Brown Univ. Libr., C. 28. b. 4 (H.L. Koopman Collection), fol. 97v°-136v°, XVc., Hours.

5949. J'ay amé que je de voir say
Que Dieu mon orison orray (<u>sic</u>);
S'oreille a moi (<u>ms</u>. mois) enclinee at
Et en mes jours m'apellerat ...

"Vigiles des morts," in rhyme.

MANCHESTER, John Rylands Univ. Libr., French 143, fol. 102r°-120v°, early XVc., Hours.

5950. J'aime celui Jhesu qui souffri passion ...

Variant of the inc.: Je creing et ain celui qui sofri pasion ... (no. 5954).

*   Je ...

Here are grouped the spellings: Ge ..., Je .., Jeo ..., Jou ...

5951. Jë aim et croi celui qui sofri passion ...

Variant of the inc.: Je creing et ain celui qui sofri pasion ... (no. 5954).

5952. Je beneiz mes enfans, tel et tel, que Dieu m'a donné en mon mariage et tous les autres qu'il luy plaira ...

"Benediction que le pere peut faire et donner a ses enfans."

ROUBAIX, Archives Municipales, no shelf-mark, fol. 132r°, XVc.,
Prayer-book of Jacques de Luxembourg.

5953.   Je confesse, o benin et misericordieux Seigneur, que j'ai
griefvement peché et que ma conscience a merité la damnation
...

"Oraison afin que Jesus Christ ayt pitié de nous quant il
viendra juger le monde": Manuel de dévotion de prêtre Pierre.

NEW HAVEN, Yale Univ. Libr., 498, fol. 138r°-140v°, last
quarter XVIc.

5954.   Je crieng et ain celui qui sofri pasion
Conme en croiz le penerent li mal Juïf
                          felon,
Et de mort au cart jor sucita Lazaron,
Et gueri seint Jonas el ventre del poison.
              (Complete Text)

Credo by a renegade pagan leader, Clarion de Vaudune: Siège de
Barbastre (vv. 1028-31).

LONDON, British Libr., Harley 1321, fol. 128r°, late XIIIc.
Inc.: Jë aim et croi celui qui sofri pasion ...

LONDON, British Libr., Royal 20. B. XIX, fol. 116v°, mid XIIIc.

LONDON, British Libr., Royal 20. D. XI, fol. 219r°, XIVc. Inc.:
J'aime celui Jhesu qui souffri passion ... This copy lacks v.
2.

PARIS, Bibl. nat., fr. 1448, fol. 116v°, mid XIIIc. Inc.: Jë
ain ⟨et croi⟩ celui qui soffri passion ... This copy lacks v.
2.

PARIS, Bibl. nat., fr. 24369, fol. 122r°, XIVc. Inc.: J'aime
celui Jhesu qui souffri passion ... This copy lacks v. 2.

Ed.: Perrier, p. 33 (base ms. London, Royal 20. B. XIX). Ref.:
Koch, p. 53.

5955.   Je croy en Dieu le pere tout puissant, createur du ciel et de
la terre et en Jesu Christ son filz unicque ...

Credo in prose by Guillaume Farel, 1524. The text is not
identical with no. 794.

Ed.: Le Pater noster et le Credo en françoys avec une tresbelle
et tresutile exposition et declaration sur chascun, Bâle, A.
Cratander, 1524; Higman, p. 48.

5956.   Je croy en Dieu le pere tout puissant, createur du ciel et de
la terre et en Jhesucrist son filz ung seul nostre Seigneur
...

"Le Credo contient douze articles de la foy selon les douze
apostres": ABC des simples gens, by Jean Gerson.

HAGUE (THE), Koninkl. Bibl., 78. J. 49, fol. 485v°, XVc.

LONDON, British Libr., Additional 29279, fol. 50r°-50v°, XVc.

PARIS, Bibl. de l'Arsenal, 3386, fol. 52v°-53r°, XVc.

PARIS, Bibl. Mazarine, 966, fol. 130r°, XVc.

PARIS, Bibl. Sainte-Geneviève, 2440, fol. 43v°, XVc.

Screening of mss. is incomplete.

Ed.: Glorieux, Gerson: Oeuvres complètes, VII, 1, p. 155.

5957. Je croy en la puissance du saint Esperit qui est saincte eglise
        catholique, en la communion des sains, en la remission des
        pechez, en la resurrection de char et en la vie pardurable.
        Ainsi soit il.
                    (Complete Text)

        "Le petit Credo," in prose.

        PROVIDENCE, Brown Univ. Libr., C. 28. b. 4 (H.L. Koopman
        Collection), fol. 235r°-235v°, XVc., Hours.

5958. Ge croy en ung Dieu fermement
        Vroy pere et filx et saint Esprit
        Seul createur du firmament
        De tout corps et de tout esprit ...

        "Les douze articles de la foy en franczois"; 13 quatrains,
        rhyming abab.

        GLASGOW, Glasgow Museums and Art Galleries, Burrell 2, fol.
        73r°-75r°, XVc., Hours.

5959. Je croy et confesse que tu es vray Jesus Christ, filz de Dieu
        vivant, qui es venu en ce monde pour sa<u>ver les pecheurs
        ...

        Prayer before receiving the Holy Sacrament: Manuel de dévotion
        de prêtre Pierre.

        NEW HAVEN, Yale Univ. Libr., 498, fol. 79r°-79v°, last quarter
        XVIc.

5960. Je croi la sainte Trinité
        Et si sai bien de verité
        Que Deus nasqui virginelment
        Et prist baptesme disnement ...

        Profession of Faith by Queen Fenise: Durmart le Galois (vv.
        14347-70).

        BERN, Bürgerbibl., 113, fol. 279r°, XIIIc.

        Ed.: E. Stengel, Li Romans de Durmart le Galois,
        Altfranzösisches Rittergedicht, Tübingen, 1873, p. 398; J.
        Gildea, Durmart le Galois, roman arthurien du treizième
        siècle, Villanova, I, 1965, p. 375-6. Ref.: Koch, p. 90-1,
        129.

5961. Je croi la saincte Trinité,
      La souveraine maiesté,
      Diex est peres et si est fils
      Diex est aussi sains Esperis ...

      Credo in rhyme, part of an anonymous rhymed version of Cato.

      NEW YORK, Pierpont Morgan Libr., Morgan 947, fol. 70rº-72vº, c.
      1390, Hours.

5962. Je dis en la moitié de mes jours: je iré aus portes d'enfer; je
      demanderé le residu de mes ans ...

      Canticle of Hezekiah, in prose; similar but not quite identical
      with no. 2997.

      CHICAGO, Art Institute, 15.536, p. 254-6, c. 1400, Psalter.

5963. Je me confesse a Dieu le pere tout puissant et a la benoite
      vierge Marie et a tous sains et a toutes sainctes ...

      Variant of the inc.: Je me confesse a Dieu et a la virge Marie
      et a touz sains et a toutes saintes ... (no. 4511).

5964. Je me leve au nom de Nostre Seigneur Jesus Christ qui a esté
      crucifié pour moy. Celluy me veulhe benir ...

      "Oraison quant on se leve": Manuel de dévotion de prêtre
      Pierre.

      NEW HAVEN, Yale Univ. Libr., 498, fol. 20vº, last quarter XVIc.

5965. Je, miserable pecheur,
      Ayant peur
      De la mort cruelle et fiere ...

      Prayer to S. Sebastian by Jean de Cerisy; 13 douzains of
      complex rhyme.

      PARIS, Bibl. nat., Rés. D. 5616 and Ye 831, Louenge des
      benoistz sainctz et sainctes de paradis, fol. vv 2vº-vv 3vº,
      Paris, Vérard.

      VERSAILLES, Bibl. mun., M. 129 (Lacombe 109 quater).

      Ed.: Rézeau, Saints, II, pp. 470-5.

5966. Je .N. donne et rens moy, et les biens que j'ay apportez avec
      moy, a l'ostel et maladerie de ceans, et renunce a toute
      proprieté ...

      Reception of a leper in the leper-house at Meaux.

      MELUN, Archives départ. de Seine-et-Marne, Archives
      hospitalières, Meaux, II. A. 3, fol. 32vº, XIVc.

      Ed.: Le Grand, p. 189.

5967.   Jou, N., fai profession et promech obedience a Diu et a me dame
        sainte Marie et a vous maistres ...

        Profession of a novice at the Hôtel-Dieu de Lille.

        LILLE, Bibl. mun., 176 (750), fol. 34v°-35r°, XIVc.

        LILLE, Bibl. mun., God. 185 (70), fol. 43v°-44r°, XIIIc.

        Ed.: Le Grand, pp. 84-5.

5968.   Ge, seror N. fais profession selonc le ordre saint Augustin en
        tele maniere: ge voeu et promet a Dieu et a Nostre Dame
        sainte Marie ...

        Profession of a novice in Les Constitutions le roi de France
        lesquels l'an doit garder en la Meson Dieu de Vernon.

        PARIS, Bibl. nat., nouv. acq. fr. 4171, fol. 6r°-6v°, late
        XIIIc.

        Ed.: Le Grand, p. 158.

5969.   Je suis pecheur horrible et detestable,
        Vray redempteur, de ce me rens coupable ...

        Orison to S. Louis IX, King of France by Jean Panier; eleven
        douzains.

        PARIS, Bibl. nat., Rés. D. 5616 and Ye 831, Louenges des
        benoistz sainctz et sainctes de paradis, fol. xx 2r°-xx 3v°,
        Paris, Vérard.

        VERSAILLES, Bibl. mun., M. 129 (Lacombe 109 quater).

        Ed.: Rézeau, Saints, II, pp. 309-13. Ref.: Eugénie Droz,
        Romania, 49 (1923), p. 59.

5970.   Je t'adore, je te fais hommage so<lo>nnel comme je puys et
        selon que je say, mon Dieu, mon sauveur, qui par ta bonté
        infinie ...

        "Autre a mesmes fins" = Oraison a l'elevation du corps de
        Nostre Seigneur: Manuel de dévotion de prêtre Pierre.

        NEW HAVEN, Yale Univ. Libr., 498, fol. 88v°-89r°, last quarter
        XVIc.

5971.   Je t'ay requis de deux choses, Seigneur, mon Dieu et mon pere;
        ne me les denie devant que je meure. Fay que de moy vanité
        soit esloignee ...

        "Oraison pour subvenir aux necessitez quotidiennes": Manuel de
        dévotion de prêtre Pierre.

        NEW HAVEN, Yale Univ. Libr., 498, fol. 115v°-116r°, last
        quarter XVIc.

5972. Je te adore, corps precieux, et sang de Nostre Seigneur
Jhesucrist qui icy es sacriffié. Que tu soyes piteux et
misericors ...

Orison at the Elevation, in prose.

SAN MARINO (Calif.), Huntington Libr., HM 1129, fol.
143v°-144r°, c. 1450, Hours of Paris.

5973. Je te adore, mon tres doulx sauveur et redempteur Jhesucrist,
vray Dieu eternel et mon bon juge ...

"S'ensuit tres devote protestation a dire chascun jour de
cuer."

ROUBAIX, Archives Municipales, no shelf-mark, fol. 91v°-92v°,
XVc., Prayer-book of Jacques de Luxembourg.

5974. Je te commande a Dieu le roy ...

Variant of the inc.: Je te command .N. a Dieu le pere, le roy
puissant ... (no. 837).

5975. Je te deprye, tres debonnaire seigneur Jhesu Crist, par icelle
charité ...

Variant of the inc.: Je te pri tres debonnaire sire Jhesucrist
... (no. 3029).

5976. Je te prie, doulx Jhesucrist, qu'il te plaise a nous esjouir de
santé perpetuelle de nostre corps ...

Orison to Jesus, in prose.

PROVIDENCE, Brown Univ. Libr., C. 28. b. 4 (H.L. Koopman
Collection), fol. 197v°, XVc., Hours.

5977. Je te regracie, tres vraiz Sire,
Tout puissant Dieu glorieux ...

Eve gives thanks to God: "Mystère de la Nativité" (vv. 136-43).

LONDON, British Libr., Additional 38860, fol. 3r°, XVIIIc. copy
of a lost ms.

PARIS, Bibl. Sainte-Geneviève, 1131, fol. 2r°, XVc.

Ed.: Whittredge, pp. 100-1.

5978. Je te salue char precieuse hostie sacrefice en l'abre de la
crois pour nostre redempcion ...

"Oroison pour saluer le corps nostre seigneur Jhesus," in
prose.

NEW YORK, New York Public Libr., 52, fol. 200v°, XVc., Hours of
Paris.

5979. Je te salue, corps Jesu Crist, plaisant vaisiaus de la deitet;
je te salue, sainte iaue (ms. wau) de fontaine ...

Orison at the Elevation, in prose.

BALTIMORE, Walters Art Gallery, Walters 269, fol. 3v°, c. 1440,
Hours.

5980.   Je te salue dame honnouree,
Car le roy tu as enfanté
Qui ciel et terre, mer et gelee,
Gouvernes en perpetuité ...

"Cy commence la messe de Nostre Dame."

PROVIDENCE, Brown Univ. Libr., C. 28. b. 4 (H.L. Koopman
Collection), fol. 196v°-202v°, XVc., Hours.

5981.   Je te salue, Dieu du ciel glorïeux,
Dieu immortel, Dieu sur tous vertueux,
Vray filz de Dieu qui creas ciel et terre.
Je te salue, roy pardessus les cieulx ...

Ballade to Jesus by the Three Kings: Arnoul Gréban's Mystère de
la Passion (vv. 6634-72).

Refr.: Present te fais d'or, de mirre et
d'encens,
Toy demonstrant Dieu, roy et mortel
homme.

CHANTILLY, Musée Condé, 614 (1691), fol. 46v°-47r°, XVc.

LE MANS, Bibl. mun., 6, fol. 74v°-75r°, XVc.

PARIS, Bibl. de l'Arsenal, 6431, fol. 39r°-39v°, XVc.

PARIS, Bibl. nat., fr. 815, fol. 52v°-53r°, 1458.

PARIS, Bibl. nat., fr. 816, fol. 46v°, 1473.

PARIS, Bibl. nat., fr. 1550, fol. 143r°-143v°, XVIc.

PARIS, Bibl. nat., fr. 15064, fol. 125r°-125v°, 1469.

PARIS, Bibl. nat., nouv. acq. fr. 14043, fol. 6r°-6v°, XVc.

ROME, Accademia Nazionale dei Lincei, Bibl. Corsiniana, Rossi
412 (44. A. 7), fol. 107r°-107v°, late XVc.

Ed.: Paris-Raynaud, p. 86 (vv. 6670-6708); Jodogne, p. 92 (vv.
6634-72).

5982.   Je te salue, estoille maritime,
De tous pechés remede et medicine,
Port de salut, radressant a la voie
Le pauvre humain qui par peché desvoie ...

"Salutation a la vierge Marie," a rendering of the Salve Regina
in 30 quatrains, rhyming aabb.

NEW YORK, Pierpont Morgan Libr., Morgan 78, fol. 11v°-14v°, XVc., Hours of Rome.

5983.   Je te salue gloriouse
        Virge, maire et espouse,
        Devotement te vult loer
        Et tez grans joies <recorder> ...

"Les .XII. joie an roman"; 2 sizains, 11 quatrains and 1 huitain, most lines rhyming in pairs.

METZ, Bibl. mun., 600, fol. 4r°-4v°, XVc., Hours of Paris and Prayer-book.

Ref.: Rézeau, p. 156.

5984.   Je te salue, Jhesucrist, roy des roys, parolle ...

Variant of no. 875: Je te salue, Jhesucrist, parole du pere, filz de Vierge ...

5985.   Je te salue, Marie, pleine de grace; Dieu est avec toy. Escoute, filhe de David et d'Abraham et encline ton oreilhe a nos prieres ...

Oraison a la Vierge Marie: Manuel de dévotion de prêtre Pierre.

NEW HAVEN, Yale Univ. Libr., 498, fol. 93r°-94r°, last quarter XVIc.

5986.   Je te salue Marie, plaine de grace, Dieux nostre sires soit avec toy, dame! Benoit soit le fruit de ton ventre! Ainsi soit il!
                    (Complete Text)

Ave Marie in prose, not identical with no. 881. It occurs in the Heures de Nostre Dame.

CAMBRIDGE, Fitzwilliam Museum, McClean 76, fol. 13v°, XIV-XVc., Hours of Paris.

5987.   Je te salue, Marie, plainne de grace, le Seigneur est avec toy; tu es benoite entre les femmes et le fruit de ton ventre benoist, Jhesus, Amen.
                    (Complete Text)

Ave Maria, part of the ABC des simples gens, by Jean Gerson.

HAGUE (THE), Koninkl. Bibl., 78. J. 49, fol. 485r°, XVc.

LONDON, British Libr., Additional 29279, fol. 50r°, XVc.

PARIS, Bibl. de l'Arsenal, 3386, fol. 52v°, XVc.

PARIS, Bibl. Mazarine, 966, fol. 129v°, XVc.

PARIS, Bibl. Sainte-Geneviève, 2440, fol. 43r°, XVc.

Screening of mss. is incomplete.

Ed.: Glorieux, Gerson, Oeuvres complètes, VII, 1, p. 155.

5988.   Je te salue Marie,
        Plaine de grace sans envie ...

        "Ave Maria" in paired rhymes; part of the "Heures de Nostre
          Dame."

        LILLE, Bibl. mun., Godefroy 5 (147), fol. 27v°-28r°, XVc.,
          Hours.

5989.   Je te salue, Marie,
        Qui de grace es remplie;
        Avecquez toy est le Seigneur
        Qui sur tous te donne honneur.
                        (Complete Text)

        Ave Maria in rhyme, at the head of the Sermon pour
          l'Annonciation, by Gerson; found in isolation in the Metz
          codex.

        CAMBRAI, Bibl. mun., 578, fol. 1r°, XVc.

        METZ, Bibl. mun., 600, fol. 166r°, XVc., Hours of Paris and
          Prayer-book.

        PARIS, Bibl. nat., fr. 974, fol. 40v°, XVc.

        PARIS, Bibl. nat., fr. 1029, fol. 35r°, XVc.

        PARIS, Bibl. nat., fr. 24841, fol. 64v°, XVc.

        PARIS, Bibl. nat., lat. 14974, fol. 350r°, XVc.

        Ed.: Anne-Louise Masson, Jean Gerson, sa vie, son temps, ses
          oeuvres, Lyon, 1894, p. 197 (Paris, B.N. fr. 974); L. Mourin,
          Scriptorium, 2 (1948), p. 239; Glorieux, Gerson: Oeuvres
          complètes, VII, 2, p. 538; Rézeau, p. 176 (Metz ms.). Ref.:
          L. Mourin, RBPH, 27 (1949), pp. 561-98 (plan and style of the
          Sermon).

5990.   Je te salue, Marie, tres saincte mere de Dieu, roîne du ciel,
          porte de paradis, dame du monde, tu es vierge pure ...

        "Oraison tres devote a la glorieuse Vierge, mere de Dieu."

        CAMBRIDGE, Trinity College, O. 10a. 27, fol. 87v°, XVc., Hours
          of Coutances. This prayer added in XVIc.

5991.   Je te salue, o benoit et digne sainct sacrement, parolle du
          pere, saincte hostie, vraye chair et sang ...

        "Oraison a l'elevation du corps de Nostre Seigneur": Manuel de
          dévotion de pretre Pierre.

        NEW HAVEN, Yale Univ. Libr., 498, fol. 87v°-88r°, last quarter
          XVIc.

5992. Je te salue (ms. salus), roÿne des cielz, mere dez anges, o
       Marie, la flours des vierges ...

       "Antene de Nostre Dame: Ave regina celorum mater regis."

       MANCHESTER, John Rylands Univ. Libr., French 143, fol. 18v°,
       early XVc., Hours.

5993. Je te salue, sainct ange de Dieu, garde de mon ame et de mon
       corps ...

       Prayer to Guardian Angel, in prose.

       OXFORD, Bodleian Libr., Rawlinson, liturg. f. 33, fol. 118r°,
       1566.

       Ref.: Rézeau, Saints, II, p. 515.

5994. Je te salue, tres noble sang qui as decolé du cousté precieux
       de mon seigneur Jesu Christ, qui nettoyes les taches ...

       "Oraison a l'elevation d<u> calice": Manuel de dévotion de
       prêtre Pierre.

       NEW HAVEN, Yale Univ. Libr., 498, fol. 89r°-89v°, last quarter
       XVIc.

5995. Je te salue, tres saintisme et tres precieulx corps de
       Jhesucrist qui fut posé en l'arbre de la crois pour le
       sauvement du monde ...

       Orison at the Elevation, in prose.

       SAN MARINO (Calif.), Huntington Libr., HM 1129, fol.
       144r°-144v°, c. 1450, Hours of Paris.

5996. Je te salue, Vierge pucelle,
       De celle joye que tu receupt
       Quant a toy vint l'angle Gabriel
       Et t'apourtat ce doulx salut ...

       "Ung ditiez notable selonc les hystoires du mistere de nostre
       redemption. Et premier de l'anunciation Gabriel."

       METZ, Bibl. mun., 675, fol. 122r°-128r°, XVc.

5997. Je te salue, Vierge pure
       Qui le doulx Jhesus enfantas ...

       Orison to the Virgin; one eight-line stanza rhyming ababbcbc.

       BALTIMORE, Walters Art Gallery, Walters 255, fol. 119v°-120r°,
       c. 1480, Hours.

5998. Je te supplie, esprit angelicq<ue> auqel(z) moy, povre vermine
       de terre ...

       Prayer to Guardian Angel, in prose; an adaptation of the
       Obsecro te, angelice spiritus ...

AMIENS, Bibl. mun., 202, fol. 53r°-54r°, XVIc., Prayer-book.

Ref.: Rézeau, Saints, II, p. 514.

5999. Je te supplie, o esprit angelique a qui je suis donné en charge
        ...

        Orison to Guardian Angel, in prose; an adaptation of the
        Obsecro te, angelice spiritus ...

        PARIS, Bibl. nat., lat. 18035, fol. 41v°-42v°, XVIc.,
        Prayer-book.

        Ref.: Rézeau, Saints, II, p. 513.

6000. Je viens a toy, o mere de Dieu, congnoissant la multitude de
        mes pechez. Visite mon ame qui est malade et demande a ton
        filz ...

        Oraison a la Vierge Marie: Manuel de dévotion de prêtre Pierre.

        NEW HAVEN, Yale Univ. Libr., 498, fol. 93r°, last quarter XVIc.

6001. Je viens a toy, tres benigne,
        Face encline,
        Dolant et desconforté,
        Non pas que j'en soie digne ...

        "Oraison a Nostre Dame," by Jean Cerisy.

        PARIS, Bibl. nat., Rés. D. 5616 and Ye 831, Louenges de Nostre
        Dame, fol. oo4v°, Paris, Vérard.

        Ref.: Eugénie Droz, Romania, 49 (1923), p. 54.

6002. Je vous aoure, gloriouse Vierge Marie et trezoriere de ce saint
        sacrement et especialment dez benoiz ainglez ...

        Prayer to the Virgin, in prose.

        METZ, Bibl. mun., 600, fol. 109r°-109v°, XVc., Hours of Paris
        and Prayer-book.

        Ref.: Rézeau, p. 170.

6003. Je vous aoure singulerement, soverainement, Trinitey, peire et
        filz et saint Esperit a cui cleire cognoissance ...

        Orison to the Trinity, in prose.

        METZ, Bibl. mun., 600, fol. 109r°, XVc., Hours of Paris and
        Prayer-book.

        Ref.: Rézeau, p. 170.

6004. Je vous conmans a Dieu, le roy tout puissant, par ycelle meisme
        grasce que Dieu conmanda sa benoite mere a monseigneur saint
        Jehan evvangeliste ...

Orison to God; similar but not identical in wording to nos. 837, 919 and 3033.

CHICAGO, Newberry Libr., 52, fol. 16r⁰-17r⁰, c. 1470, Hours of Rheims.

6005. Je vous commant huy .N. a Dieu le tout puissant par ycelle meisme grace que il conmanda son esperit a son pere ...

Orison to God; not the same textual wording as 919 or 3033.

BALTIMORE, Walters Art Gallery, Walters 103, fol. 80r⁰-81v⁰, late XIVc., Hours of Paris (?).

6006. Je vous recommande l'estat de sainte Esglise, en chief et en membres ...

Closing section, an epitome of the Prone Prayers, in the "Sermon Poenitemini: Contre la gourmandise" by Jean Gerson.

PARIS, Bibl. nat., fr. 24842, fol. 12r⁰, XVc.

Ed.: Glorieux, Gerson: Oeuvres complètes, VII, 2, p. 800-1; K.V. Sinclair, Annuale Mediaevale, XXI (1981), pp. 134-8.

6007. Jeo vus reng graces, pere saint, Deu tut pussant, ky mei peccheresse avez en cete nuit gardé (sic) par vostre misericorde ...

Thanksgiving Prayer, a rendering for female worshipper of Gratias tibi ago domine sancte patre omnipotens qui me peccatorem dignatus es in hac nocte ... It is part of the Mirour de seinte Eglyse, a translation of the Speculum Ecclesiae by S. Edmund of Abingdon. The Anglo-Norman prayer is found in one ms. of the A version. It occurs also in one codex of the B version but with a different inc.: Graces vous rend, sire Jhesu Crist ... (no. 5879).

LONDON, British Libr. Royal 20. B. XIV, fol. 55r⁰, early XIVc.

Ed.: Robbins, p. 10, note to line 247; not in Wilshere, whose base ms. of the A version does not contain the vernacular prayer. Ref.: Same as for the Ref. section of the inc. Aprés ço devez saver queus sunt les set prieres ... (no. 5431).

6008. Je vous salue, glorieuse lumiere,
Resplendissant en la joye pleniere,
A tousjours mais sans jamais prendre fin.
Aprés Marie, qui de Jesus fut mere ...

Orison to S. Barbara, by Jean Barsuire. Complex stanzaic patterns.

PARIS, Bibl. nat., Rés. D. 5616 and Ye 831, Louenges des benoistz sainctz et sainctes de paradis, fol. xx6v⁰-yy2r⁰, Paris, Vérard.

VERSAILLES, Bibl. mun., M. 129 (Lacombe, 109 quater).

Ed.: Rézeau, Saints, II, pp. 97-102.

6009. Je vous salue, glorieuse mere de Dieu et royne du ciel, ma
        singuliere advocate, et aujourd'huy je reconmande a vostre
        maternelle bonté ...

        "A la saincte Vierge, mere de Dieu."

        CHICAGO, Newberry Libr., 43, fol. 161r°-161v°, XVIc., Hours of
        Rouen.

6010. Je vous salue, noble pastur saint Geray, avec de Toul,
        bieneurou ...

        Suffrage to S. Gérard, Bishop of Toul, in prose.

        METZ, Bibl. mun., 600, fol. 142v°, XVc., Hours of Paris and
        Prayer-book.

        Ref.: Rézeau, p. 175; Rézeau, Saints, II, p. 246.

6011. Je vous supplie, esprit angelique, gardien et defenseur fidele,
        qu'e⟨n⟩ vostre conduite je sois aujourd'huy dressé et mis ...

        "Au sainct ange gardien."

        CHICAGO, Newberry Libr., 43, fol. 161v°, XVIc., Hours of Rouen.

6012. Jhesucriz biau doz (sic) sires plains de pitié, je vous requier
        que vous me regardez en pitié et en la remanbrance et en
        l'amour ...

        Orison to Jesus in prose.

        NEW YORK, New York Public Libr., Spencer 56, fol. 286v°-287r°,
        XIVc., Hours of Blanche de France, Duchess of Orleans.

6013. Jhesucriz biaus sire Dieu, fil Dieu, je vous requier que vous
        me regardés en vraie pitié et en vrai conseil ...

        Orison to Jesus in prose.

        NEW YORK, New York Public Libr., Spencer 56, fol. 286r°, XIVc.,
        Hours of Blanche de France, Duchess of Orleans.

6014. Jhesucriz biau sire doux glorieus fiuz douz debonairez, je vous
        pri et requier que vous me regardés en pitié ...

        Orison to Jesus, in prose.

        NEW YORK, New York Public Libr., Spencer 56, fol. 286r°, XIVc.,
        Hours of Blanche de France, Duchess of Orleans.

6015. Jhesucriz biau sire, je vous requier par votre sainte
        misericorde que vous me regardez en pitié et me faciez pardon
        de mes pechiez ...

        Orison to Jesus, in prose.

NEW YORK, New York Public Libr., Spencer 56, fol. 287r°-287v°, XIVc., Hours of Blanche de France, Duchess of Orleans.

6016.   Jhesucris, en tant que de my, je ne sui point digne de vous rechevoir ne que vous descendés (ms. descendeus) en my ...

Orison to Jesus, in prose.

LONDON, St. Paul's Chapter Libr., 19, fol. 67v°-68r° (another copy on fol. 74v°-75r°), XVc., Hours.

6017.   Jhesucriz fil de Dieu le vif, aiez de moi merci selon ta debonaire misericorde ...

Orison to Jesus in prose.

NEW YORK, New York Public Libr., Spencer 56, fol. 285v°-286r°, XIVc., Hours of Blanche de France, Duchess of Orleans.

6018.   Jhesucrist fiuz Dieu le pere vif qui a heure de prime resucitas du saint sepulchre de mort a vie, et a icele heure ...

Prime of Hours of the Cross in prose; the version is close to no. 947.

VIENNA, Oesterreichische Nationalbibl., 1969, fol. 131v°-132r°, XIVc., Hours.

6019.   Jhesucrist nos doint si ouvrer
Que nos a bien puissons finer ...

Concluding Invocation: Vie des Peres, no. XLIII De l'ermite qui sala son pain (vv. 307-14).

BERKELEY, Univ. of California Libr., 106 (olim Phillipps 3643), fol. 67r°, XIIIc.

BERN, Collection Steiger Mai, no shelf-mark, fol. 80r°, XVc.

BRUSSELS, Bibl. royale, 9229-9230, fol. 152r°, XIVc.

CAMBRIDGE, Fitzwilliam Museum, McClean 178, fol. 122v°, XVc.

CHANTILLY, Musée Condé, 475 (1578), fol. 101v°, XIVc.

HAGUE (THE), Koninkl. Bibl., 71. A. 24, fol. 150v°, XIVc.

PARIS, Bibl. de l'Arsenal, 3641, fol. 125v°, XIIIc.

PARIS, Bibl. de l'Arsenal, 5204, fol. 176r°, XIVc.

PARIS, Bibl. nat., fr. 1039, fol. 164v°, XIIIc.

PARIS, Bibl. nat., fr. 1546, fol. 101v°, XIIIc.

PARIS, Bibl. nat., fr. 2094, fol. 53v°, late XIIIc.

PARIS, Bibl. nat., fr. 12483, fol. 266r°, XIVc.

PARIS, Bibl. nat., fr. 15110, fol. 46v°, XIIIc. Inc.: Or nos
doint Dex si bien ouvrer ...

PARIS, Bibl. nat., fr. 23111, fol. 107v°, late XIIIc.

Ed.: Bornäs, p. 102 (base ms. Paris, Bibl. nat., fr. 23111).

6020. Jhesucrist, vray Dieu pardurable,
Jhesus tre⟨s⟩ misericordable,
Jhesus doulx pere de pitié,
De indulgence et d'amitié ...

"Oracio Jhesu Cristi"; 107 lines, aabb.

BALTIMORE, Walters Art Gallery, Walters 261, fol. 131v°-134r°,
c. 1400, Hours.

6021. Jhesu, abisme de profunde misericorde, je te prye par la
profundité de tes playes ...

Eleventh of the prayers of S. Bridget.

MANCHESTER, Chetham's Libr., 8007 (Mun. A. 2. 161), fol. 109v°,
XVc., Hours of Besançon.

6022. Jhesu, commencement et finement de toutes choses vivant et
vertus en tous moyens ...

Tenth of the fifteen prayers of S. Bridget.

MANCHESTER, Chetham's Libr., 8007 (Mun. A. 2. 161), fol.
109r°-109v°, XVc., Hours of Besançon.

6023. Jhesu, doulceur de tes vrays amateurs et excessive suavitey de
toutes nettes pensees, je te prie ...

Eighth of the fifteen orisons of S. Bridget.

MANCHESTER, Chetham's Libr., 8007 (Mun. A. 2. 161), fol.
108r°-108v°, XVc., Hours of Besançon.

6024. Jesus en croix, filz de Dieu le pere omnipotens, toy quy es
Dieu des anges, filz de la vierge Marie ...

Orison to the Virgin in prose.

MANCHESTER, John Rylands Univ. Libr., Lat. 136, fol. 413r°,
XVc., Breviary. This prayer added in XVIc.

6025. Jesus, eternel filz de pere sans mere et filz temporel de mere
sans pere, seul filz de vierge et mere par la filiale charité
...

Fourth of the Orisons 'selon les sept paroles de Jesus en
croix.'

PARIS, Bibl. nat., fr. 13269, fol. 4r°-5r°, XVc.

6026. Jhesu, eternelle doulceur, joye de tes vrays amateurs,
surmontant toute joye, desirable sur tous desirs ...

First of the fifteen prayers of S. Bridget.

MANCHESTER, Chetham's Libr., 8007 (Mun. A. 2. 161), fol. 104r°-105v°, XVc., Hours of Besançon.

6027.   Jhesu, facteur du monde qui tiens la terre et toutes choses en ton poing ...

Third of the fifteen orisons of S. Bridget.

MANCHESTER, Chetham's Libr., 8007 (Mun. A. 2. 161), fol. 106r°, XVc., Hours of Besançon.

6028.   Jhesu, filz de Dieu le pere, splendeur eternelle, souviengne toy de celle humble recommendation quant tu ...

Fourteenth orison of S. Bridget.

MANCHESTER, Chetham's Libr., 8007 (Mun. A. 2. 161), fol. 110v°-111r°, XVc., Hours of Besançon.

6029.   Jesus, fontaine d'eau salutaire, bevee (<u>ms.</u> bevue) de vie, torrent de volupté, floave enrosant paradis celeste ...

Fifth of the Orisons 'selon les sept paroles de Jesus en croix.'

PARIS, Bibl. nat., fr. 13269, fol. 5r°-5v°, XVc.

6030.   Jhesu, fontaine de pitié qui ne se peult espusier que par grant dilection, haz dis en la croix ...

Seventh orison of S. Bridget.

MANCHESTER, Chetham's Libr., 8007 (Mun. A. 2. 161), fol. 108r°, XVc., Hours of Besançon.

6031.   Jesus, justice parfaicte, consumacion de toustes (<u>sic</u>) vertuz, couroune de tous preux chevaliers bataillans, qui avez dit ...

Sixth of the Orisons 'selon les sept paroles de Jesus en croix.'

PARIS, Bibl. nat., fr. 13269, fol. 5v°-6r°, XVc.

6032.   Jhesu le fiz Marie, ky verays Deux verais hom <est>, si veraiment come vous deignastes char prendre de la gloriuse dame ...

Orison to Jesus, in prose.

NORWICH, Castle Museum, 158.926/4f., fol. 152v°-153v°, XIVc., Hours of Sarum.

6033.   Jhesu, medicim (<u>sic</u>) celeste, souviengne toy des langueurs et douleurs que tu portoye ...

Fourth orison of S. Bridget.

MANCHESTER, Chetham's Libr., 8007 (Mun. A. 2. 161), fol. 106v°-107r°, XVc., Hours of Besançon.

6034.   Jhesu, mireur de eternelle clarter (<u>sic</u>), souviengne toy de la grant douleur que tu heuz quant tu regardis (<u>sic</u>) ou mireur ...

Fifth of the fifteen orisons of S. Bridget.

MANCHESTER, Chetham's Libr., 8007 (Mun. A. 2. 161), fol. 107r°-107v°, XVc., Hours of Besançon.

6035.   Jhesus, nous vous remercĩons
Des biens haultement aprestez ...

Rondeau to Jesus: Mystère de la Passion by Arnoul Gréban (vv. 12954-69).

CHANTILLY, Musée Condé, 614 (1691), fol. 106v°, XVc.

PARIS, Bibl. de l'Arsenal, 6431, fol. 89r°-89v°, XVc.

PARIS, Bibl. nat., fr. 815, fol. 104r°, 1458.

PARIS, Bibl. nat., fr. 816, fol. 90v°, 1473.

PARIS, Bibl. nat., fr. 15065, fol. 62v°-63r°, 1469.

ROME, Accademia Nazionale dei Lincei, Bibl. Corsiniana, Rossi 412 (44. A. 7), fol. 255r°-255v°, late XVc.

<u>Ed</u>.: Paris-Raynaud, p. 169 (vv. 12993-13008); Jodogne, pp. 174-5 (vv. 12954-69).

6036.   Jhesus, quant ta chair benoite ...

Variant of no. 973: Jhesu quant vostre benoite char precieuse ...

6037.   Jhesus qui avez soif de nostre salut ...

Variant of the inc.: Vous, doncques, Jhesus, qui avez soif de nostre salut ... (no. 6837).

6038.   Jhesu, qui es la vraye vigne plainne de fecunditey, haye souvenance de la tres grande habundance ...

Fifteenth of the orisons of S. Bridget.

MANCHESTER, Chetham's Libr., 8007 (Mun. A. 2. 161), fol. 111r°-112r°, XVc., Hours of Besançon.

6039.   Jhesus, qui pour la maleiçon
Oster d'original pechié ...

Benediction by S. Remi: Miracles de sainte Geneviève (vv. 84-9).

PARIS, Bibl. Sainte-Geneviève, 1131, fol. 183v°-184r°, XVc.

Ed.: Sennewaldt, p. 62.

6040. Jhesu, regale vertus et jubilation de noz ames, souviengne toy
des angoisses et douleurs que tu soubtenoye ...

Ninth orison of S. Bridget.

MANCHESTER, Chetham's Libr., 8007 (Mun. A. 2. 161), fol.
108v°-109r°, XVc., Hours of Besançon.

6041. Jhesu, roy amyable et de tous desirable, souviengne toy de la
douleur et affliction que tu heuz ...

Sixth of the fifteen prayers of S. Bridget.

MANCHESTER, Chetham's Libr., 8007 (Mun. A. 2. 161), fol.
107v°-108r°, XVc., Hours of Besançon.

6042. Jhesu, seigneur de unitey, loyal de charitey, souvyengne toy
des innumerables playes ...

Twelfth of the fifteen prayers of S. Bridget.

MANCHESTER, Chetham's Libr., 8007 (Mun. A. 2. 161), fol.
109v°-110r°, XVc., Hours of Besançon.

6043. Jesus, souverene deité, tresor de sapience et science, sans
vostre povoir et ordonnance ne peult riens estre faict ou
ciel ...

Third of the Orisons 'selon les sept paroles de Jesus en
croix.'

PARIS, Bibl. nat., fr. 13269, fol. 3v°-4r°, XVc.

6044. Jesus, souveraine plenitude de tous biens, inexplicable
liberalité, magnificence nonpareille, qui avez inspiré le bon
larron ...

Second of the Orisons 'selon les sept paroles de Jesus en
croix.'

PARIS, Bibl. nat., fr. 13269, fol. 3r°-3v°, XVc.

6045. Jesus tout puissant a qui Dieu le pere par eternelle
originacion a donné sa deité et a mis toutes creatures ...

Seventh of the Orisons 'selon les sept paroles de Jesus en
croix.'

PARIS, Bibl. nat., fr. 13269, fol. 6r°-7r°, XVc.

6046. Jhesu, tres puissant roy victorieux et immortel, souviengne toy
de la douleur que souffroye ...

Thirteenth orison of S. Bridget.

MANCHESTER, Chetham's Libr., 8007 (Mun. A. 2. 161), fol.
110r°-110v°, XVc., Hours of Besançon.

6047.   Jhesu, tu soy begny mil millionz de foy
Que tant az souffriz por moy en la croy ...

Orison to Jesus; one quatrain aabb.

METZ, Bibl. mun., 600, fol. 183v°, XVc., Hours of Paris and
Prayer-book.

Ref.: Rézeau, p. 179.

6048.   Jhesus, vrai pasteur, lequel nous avons tant de fois ...

Variant of the inc.: O Jhesus, vrai pasteur ... (See later
Supplement).

6049.   Jhesus, vray predicateur,
Aprés toy plourons ...

Rondeau to Jesus: Mystère de la Passion by Arnoul Gréban (vv.
24002-14). The piece is also termed a fatras.

CHANTILLY, Musée Condé, 614 (1691), fol. 204r°, XVc.

PARIS, Bibl. de l'Arsenal, 6431, fol. 179v°, XVc.

PARIS, Bibl. nat., fr. 815, fol. 194v°, 1458.

PARIS, Bibl. nat., fr. 816, fol. 169v°, 1473.

ROME, Accademia Nazionale dei Lincei, Bibl. Corsiniana, Rossi
412 (44. A. 7), fol. 466v°, late XVc.

Ed.: Paris-Raynaud, p. 315 (vv. 24043-55); L.C. Porter, La
Fatrasie et le fatras, Geneva, 1960, pp. 167-8; Jodogne, p.
322 (vv. 24002-14).

6050.   Jhesu, vraye libertey des anges de paradis et de tous delices,
souviengne toy de l'orreur ...

Second of the fifteen prayers of S. Bridget.

MANCHESTER, Chetham's Libr., 8007 (Mun. A. 2. 161), fol. 105v°,
XVc., Hours of Besançon.

*   Jou ...

See the alphabetical order: Je ...

K

*   Ky ...

See the alphabetical order: Qui ...

6051.   Kyrieleyson, Christe eleyson; Crist nus oyez; pere de cel,
        Deus, aiez merci de nus. Deus ki es le seint Espirit ...

Litany, in prose.

STUTTGART, Württembergische Landesbibl., Brev. 75, fol.
77v°-84r°, XIVc., Hours for Use of Sarum.

6052.   Kyrieleyson! Christeleyson! Kyrieleyson! Dieu sire, ayes merci
        de nous; Jhesucrist oyes nous ...

Litany, in prose.

SAN MARINO (Calif.), Huntington Libr., HM 1129, fol.
97v°-101r°, c. 1450, Hours of Paris.

6053.   Kyrieleison, Dieu sire, ayez merci de nous. Jhesucrist, oyez
        nous. Pere des cieulx, ayez merci de nous ...

Litany, in prose.

PARIS, Bibl. nat., fr. 13167, fol. 71v°-73v°, late XVc., Hours
of Paris.

L

6054. L'ame de moi magnifie
Dieu le pere, mon seigneur,
Et si s'est mout esjoï
Mon esprit en Dieu mon sauveur ...

Hyme "Magnificat," in rhyme.

PARIS, Bibl. nat., nouv. acq. fr. 4600, fol. 253r°-254r°, XIVc.

Ref.: Rézeau, p. 159.

6055. L'ange du seigneur ha annoncé a Marie et a conceu du sainct
Esprit: Je vous salue, Marie, pleine de grace etc. Voicy la
servante ...

"Au son de la salutation angelique."

CHICAGO, Newberry Libr., 43, fol. 162r°, XVIc., Hours of Rouen.

6056. L'eternel, qui crea toutes choses de rien, benisse par sa bonté
et sanctifie les biens ...

"Priere avant le repas," in prose.

SAN MARINO, Huntington Libr., HM 1170, fol. 99v°, late XVc.,
Book of Hours, Use of Rome. This orison added in 1561.

6057. La deïté qu'en troi part est sevree
Et en un seul stablie et ordonee ...

Explanation of the Trinity by Roland to Ferragu: Entrée
d'Espagne (vv. 3699-725).

VENICE, Bibl. Marciana, 257 (olim gall. XXI), fol. 71r°, XIVc.

Ed.: Thomas, I. p. 136-7.

6058.   La divine majesté et deïté une (<u>sic</u>), pere et filz et sainct
       Esprit, nous delivre de tout mortel peché et scandale ...

       "Pour obtenir la benediction celeste."

       CHICAGO, Newberry Libr., 43, fol. 161v°-162r, XVIc., Hours of
       Rouen.

6059.   La gloire soit a Dieu lassus et en terre paix aux hommes de
       bonne voulenté! Roy des cieulx, nous te louons ...

       "La gloria in excelsis deo," in prose.

       PROVIDENCE, Brown Univ. Libr., C. 28. b. 4 (H.L. Koopman
       Collection), fol. 197r°-197v°, XVc., Hours.

6060.   La grace du sainct Esprit nous vueille assister; nostre ayde
       soit au non de Dieu qui a faict le ciel et la terre ...

       "Exercice pour bien et heureusement commencer la journee: vous
       direz le matin quand il se fault lever du lict."

       CHICAGO, Newberry Libr., 43, fol. 160r°, XVIc., Hours of Rouen.

6061.   La jolie marionnette
       Qui nourrist de sa mammelette ...

       "Chanson de la Vierge Marie"; 6 quatrains, plus 1 tercet and a
       final quatrain.

       Refr.: Qu'il ne nous maiche en oubly.

       BRUSSELS, Bibl. royale, IV. 541, fol. 171v°-172r°, 1568.

       <u>Ref</u>.: Lemaire, Meschinot, Molinet, Villon: Témoignages inédits,
       1979, p. 72.

6062.   La premiere est a sa nature quant Diex devint hom pour nous.
       Ceste pensee aquiert humilité. La seconde ...

       "On doit penser a Jhesucrist en iiij manieres": section of the
       Beghine text Règle des fins amants.

       BERLIN, Deutsche Staatsbibl., Gall. oct. 28, fol. 89r°-89v°,
       early XIVc., Prayer-book (destroyed).

       <u>Ed</u>.: Christ, p. 202.

6063.   La premiere joie est qu'eles sont amies especiax Jhesucrist; et
       qui est plus grant joie qu'estre amie Jhesucrist, le biau
       dous rois de gloire ...

       "Les .xij. joies que Diex doune a ses amis": section of the
       Beghine work Règle des fins amants.

       BERLIN, Deutsche Staatsbibl., Gall. oct. 28, fol. 86v°-87r°,
       early XIVc., Prayer-book (destroyed).

       <u>Ed</u>.: Christ, pp. 194-5.

6064. La premiere leçon du salut eternel: faire le signe de la croix
       et dire la credo jusques a la fin.
       (Complete Text)

   Three "leçons du salut eternel"; for the other two, see the
   inc.: Mon benoist Dieu, ainsy comment ...; and De cueur et de
   bouche je vous recongnois ...

   CAMBRIDGE, Harvard College Libr., Lat. 251, fol. 75r°, late
   XVc., Hours of Rome.

6065. La reception du corps et du sanc de Nostre Seigneur Jhesucrist
       que moy, indigne, ay faicte ne me soit point en jugement ...

   Orison after the Communion, in prose.

   BARNARD CASTLE, Bowes Museum, 091/MED/8, fol. 86r°, 1471, Hours
   for the use of Marguerite de La Chaussee, nun in the
   Dominican Convent at Poissy.

6066. La reception du sainct corps de Jesu Christ me soit profitable
       et propice a la vie eternelle.
       (Complete Text)

   Orison after the Communion.

   CHICAGO, Newberry Libr., 43, fol. 159v°, XVIc., Hours of Rouen.

6067. La sainte ame dit en son livre
       J'a fait un faxelet de mierre ...

   Meditation on the Canticum Canticorum I, 12; 22 vv. grouped in
   2 sizains and one dizain.

   METZ, Bibl. mun., 600, fol. 187v°, XVc., Hours of Paris and
   Prayer-book.

   Ref.: Rézeau, p. 180.

6068. La tres gloriuse reïne ...

   Variant of the inc.: Ha! tres gloriuse reïne ... (no. 5898).

6069. Lasse! chetive, et que feray?
       Et comment me confesseray ...

   "Plainte" to God by a nun: Miracles de sainte Geneviève (vv.
   1364-402).

   PARIS, Bibl. Sainte-Geneviève, 1131, fol. 197r°, XVc.

   Ed.: Sennewaldt, p. 101.

6070. Le don d'amours qui tous les cuers attraict
       Nous met et tient en amoureux servage ...

   Fourth of the "xij balades de Pasques": 13 decasyllabic lines
   rhyming abaabaabbabab, the first and second are repeated as
   the third and last respectively.

VATICAN CITY, Bibl. apost., Reg. lat. 1728, fol. 118r°, XVc.

Ed.: Keller, p. 617.

6071.   Le glorieux Dieu debonnaire,
Qui pour nous voult souffrir tourment ...

Orison to Jesus by Avicene: Mystère de saint Christofle (vv. 1644-57).

Early Ed.: in 4° Gothic, Paris, Veuve Jean Trepperel and Jean Jehannot, n.d. (c. 1515). Ed.: Runnalls, p. 53.

6072.   Le livre en quoy nous devons especialment lire sans nul entrelaissement ...

"Les Lamentations saint Bernard," in prose.

CHANTILLY, Musée Condé, 127 (628), fol. 2v°-9r°, XVc. Inc.: Ce livre en quoy nous debvons estudier espiciallement et lire ...

LYON, Bibl. de la Ville, 1234 (1106), fol. 3r°-12v°, XVc.

PARIS, Bibl. nat., fr. 434, fol. 1r°-24r°, XVc. Inc.: Ce livre en quoy ...

PARIS, Bibl. nat., fr. 916, fol. 1r°-13r°, 1474. Inc.: Ly livres en quoy ...

PARIS, Bibl. nat., fr. 918, fol. 1r°-13r°, XVc.

PARIS, Bibl. nat., fr. 966, fol. 95, XVc.

PARIS, Bibl. nat., nouv. acq. fr. 10059, fol. 172r°-175r°, XVc.

PARIS, Bibl. nat., nouv. acq. fr. 21632, pp. 5-22, XVc.

Screening of mss. is incomplete.

Ref.: J. Morawski, Diz des Sages, p. xiv; C.E. Pickford, Medieval Miscellany presented to Eugene Vinaver, Manchester, 1965, p. 251.

6073.   Le mariage pur virginel
De sainct Joseph et de Marie ...

"Devote commemoration du sainct sacré et virginal mariage ...";
ten octosyllabic lines rhyming in pairs.

ROUBAIX, Archives Municipales, no shelf-mark, fol. 131v°, XVc., Prayer-book of Jacques de Luxembourg.

6074.   Le pauvre pecheur ayant desir de son salut doibt retourner sauvent soy ...

"Remede pour recepvoir la grace de Jesus."

STUTTGART, Württembergische Landesbibl., Brev. 31, fol. 184r°, XVc., Book of Hours for a diocese in Brittany. This text added in XVIc.

6075.   Le premier aide ou remede pour obtenir remission de noz pechez et recouvrer la grace de Dieu est <u>afflictio cordis et corporis</u> ...

"S'ensuivent neuf aides ou remedes ... pour nous convertir de noz pechez ..."

ROUBAIX, Archives Municipales, no shelf-mark, fol. 93r°-104r°, XVc., Prayer-book of Jacques de Luxembourg.

6076.   Le roy des roys, le hault Dieu glorieux,
Par fol orgueil d'aucuns angles mauvais ...

"Ballade" on the Fall of Man, attributed to René d'Anjou; three ten-line stanzas rhyming ababbccdcd, with refrain.

Refr.: Dont leur lignage ont assez fait doloir.

LENINGRAD, Publichnaia Bibl., Fr. F. v. III. 2, fol. 1r°, XVc.

<u>Ed</u>.: Sismarev, p. 174. <u>Ref</u>.: Laborde, p. 45.

6077.   Le roy du ciel qui nous crea,
Qui en la crois nous recrea ...

Prayer to God by the heroine: Miracles de sainte Geneviève (vv. 226-36).

PARIS, Bibl. Sainte-Geneviève, 1131, fol. 185v°, XVc.

<u>Ed</u>.: Sennewaldt, p. 67-8.

6078.   Le sang de Nostre Seigneur Jhesucrist nous soit salut et vie et remission de tous noz pechez. Ainsi soit il.
(Complete Text)

"Quant on lieve le sang de Nostre Seigneur, on doit dire Sanguis domini nostri Jhesu Christi qui ci aprés s'ensuit en françois."

PROVIDENCE, Brown Univ. Libr., C. 28. b. 4 (H.L. Koopman Collection), fol. 272v°, XVc., Hours.

6079.   Le vray Dieu eternel, nostre pere celeste, aprés que par son infinie bonté et misericorde il nous eust declairé par plusieurs ambassadeurs, patriarches et prophetes ...

Brefve admonition de la maniere de prier by the chevalier Louis de Berquin in 1525.

<u>Ed</u>.: Brefve admonition de la maniere de prier selon la doctrine de Jesuchrist, avec une brefve explanation du Pater Noster, Extraict des Paraphrases de Erasme, Paris, Simon Dubois (?), 1525; Telle, pp. 9-22.

6080. Les .vij. heures chi faites par grant
                                      devotion
       Jhesucrist te ramenbre par tel condition
       Qu'ensi que t'as soufiert en penance, en
                                      grevance
       Parçongnier de te glore me fay par
                                      penitance.
                    (Complete Text)

       Heures de la Croix; concluding stanza, a twelve-syllable
         quatrain rhyming aabb. For the refrain, see the inc.: Fieus
         de Dieu le vif ... (no. 5818).

       NEW YORK, New York Public Libr., 28, fol. 137v°-137v°, XVc.,
         Book of Hours.

6081. Les tenebres ont esté faictes par toute la terre lorsque Jesus
         Christ devoit mourir en la croix et envyron neuf heures ...

       "Oraison en souvenance de la mort de Nostre Seigneur": Manuel
         de dévotion de prêtre Pierre.

       NEW HAVEN, Yale Univ. Libr., 498, fol. 37v°-38v°, last quarter
         XVIc.

6082. Li (Ly) livres en quoy nous devons ...

       Variant of the inc.: Le livre en quoy ... (no. 6072).

6083. Lois naturex premiers qui est de tel afaire
       Qui fait autrui tout ce que l'en vuet a lui
                                      faire ...

       "Pour les mors prier, huit causes ...": Girart de Rossillon,
         Burgundian redaction (vv. 4205-44).

       BRUSSELS, Bibl. royale, 11181, fol. 71v°-72r°, XVc.

       MONTPELLIER, Bibl. Fac. Ecole de Médecine, H. 244, fol.
         79v°-80v°, XVc.

       MONTPELLIER, Bibl. Fac. Ecole de Médecine, H. 349, fol.
         57v°-58r°, c. 1350.

       PARIS, Bibl. nat., fr. 15103, fol. 86r°-86v°, 1417.

       Ed.: Ham, p. 229-30 (base ms.: Montpellier H. 349).

6084. Lorsque tu vas dormir, tu rendras (ms. rerendras) graces a Dieu
         que par sa grande misericorde il t'a preservé ceste journee
         ...

       "Meditation avant le someil": Manuel de dévotion de prêtre
         Pierre.

       NEW HAVEN, Yale Univ. Libr., 498, fol. 28r°-28v°, last quarter
         XVIc.

6085. Loué soit Dieu d'umble vouloir
       Qu'i nous a octroyé l'espace ...

Rondeau to God: Mystère de la Passion by Arnoul Gréban (vv. 10279-96).

CHANTILLY, Musée Condé, 614 (1691), fol. 78v°, XVc.

PARIS, Bibl. de l'Arsenal, 6431, fol. 69v°, XVc.

PARIS, Bibl. nat., fr. 815, fol. 82v°, 1458.

PARIS, Bibl. nat., fr. 816, fol. 72r°, 1473.

PARIS, Bibl. nat., fr. 15065, fol. 7r°-7v°, 1469.

ROME, Accademia Nazionale dei Lincei, Bibl. Corsiniana, Rossi 412 (44. A. 7), fol. 195v°-196r°, late XVc.

Ed.: Paris-Raynaud, p. 135 (vv. 10313-330); Jodogne, p. 139 (vv. 10279-96).

6086. Loué soit Dieu, Nostre Seigneur,
De tous les biens qu'il nous envoye ...

Praise of God: Mystère de la Passion by Arnoul Gréban (vv. 4571-81). Rondeau.

CHANTILLY, Musée Condé, 614 (1691), fol. 28v°, XVc.

LE MANS, Bibl. mun., 6, fol. 44v°, XVc.

PARIS, Bibl. de l'Arsenal, 6431, fol. 22v°, XVc.

PARIS, Bibl. nat., fr. 815, fol. 36r°, 1458.

PARIS, Bibl. nat. fr. 816, fol. 32v°, 1473.

PARIS, Bibl. nat., fr. 1550, fol. 91v°, XVIc.

PARIS, Bibl. nat., fr. 15064, fol. 82v°-83r°, 1469.

PARIS, Bibl. nat., nouv. acq. fr. 12908, fol. 5r°-5v°, XVIc.

ROME, Accademia Nazionale dei Lincei, Bibl. Corsiniana, Rossi 412 (44. A. 7), fol. 52v°-53r°, late XVc.

Ed.: Paris-Raynaud, p. 59 (vv. 4589-99); Jodogne, p. 65 (vv. 4571-81).

M

6087. M'ame fait Nostre Signour grant
Et je m'esjoy a Dieu puissant
Car Nostre Sire ait regardé
Sa chambreriere en humilitei ...

Hymn "Magnificat" in Vespers of the Heures de Nostre Dame and
in the Vigiles des Morts.

MANCHESTER, John Rylands Univ. Libr., French 143, fol.
78r°-78v° and 103v°-104r°, early XVc., Hours.

6088. M'ame loe Nostre Seigneur et mon esperit c'est esjoÿ en Dieu
qui est mon salut car il a regardé la humilité de moy ...

Hymn "Magnificat" in prose, as part of a French version of the
Vigiles des morts. Not the same wording as no. 1077.

SAN MARINO (Calif.), Huntington Libr., HM 1129, fol.
106v°-107v°, c. 1450, Hours of Paris.

6089. Ma dame sainte Katherine,
Fille de roy et de roÿne ...

"Memoire de sainte Katherine"; 18 octosyllabic lines, rhyming
in pairs.

OXFORD, Keble College, 15, fol. 93r°, late XIVc., Hours of
Rome.

Ed.: Rézeau, Saints, II, p. 128.

6090. Ma doulce dame et gracïeuse,
Ceste meschante douloureuse
Vueilliez aidier et secourir ...

Prayer to S. Geneviève by a mother at the drowning of her son:
Miracles de sainte Geneviève (vv. 1587-93).

PARIS, Bibl. Sainte-Geneviève, 1131, fol. 200r°, XVc.

Ed.: Sennewaldt, p. 108.

6091. Ma priere, Glaude (sic), sainct confesseur,
       Amy de Dieu, haultain intercesseur ...

       Variant of the inc.: A refuge vers toy, saint confesseur ...
          (no. 5404).

6092. Magdeleine, glorieuse dame,
       Chastellaine de corps et de ame ...

       Prayer to S. Mary Magdalene; 174 vv. in paired rhymes.

       PARIS, Bibl. nat., Rés. D. 5616 and Ye 831, Louenges des
          benoistz sainctz et sainctes de paradis, fol. xx5r°-xx6v°,
          Paris, Vérard.

       VERSAILLES, Bibl. mun., M. 129 (Lacombe 109 quater).

       Ed.: Rézeau, Saints, II, pp. 348-54.

6093. Maintenant, Sire, tu laisses ton serviteur selon ta parolle en
          paix, car mes yeulx ont veu ...

       Canticle of Simeon, prose version as part of Compline in the
          Heures de Nostre Dame en françois (no. 3658).

       PROVIDENCE, Brown Univ. Libr., C. 28. b. 4 (H.L. Koopman
          Collection), fol. 58v°, XVc., Book of Hours.

6094. Marchiez du pié legierement
       L'herbe du joly pré regiault (ms. regnant)
                                   ...

       Seventh of the "xij balades de Pasques": 13 octosyllabic lines
          rhyming abaabaabbabab, the first and second are repeated as
          the third and last respectively.

       VATICAN CITY, Bibl. apost., Reg. lat. 1728, fol. 118r°-118v°,
          XVc.

       Ed.: Keller, p. 618.

6095. Marguerite, de Dieu ancelle,
       Doulce vierge, sainte pucelle ...

       Prayer to S. Margaret; one sizain in rhymed couplets.

       BESANCON, Bibl. mun., 121, fol. 95r°, late XIVc., this text
          added XVIc.

       Ed.: Rézeau, Saints, II, pp. 333-4.

6096. Marie, escoutés vostre mere
       Anne a qui je fay (ms. foy) ma priere ...

       Orison to the Virgin, at the conclusion of a prayer to S. Anne
          (inc. no. 3039). One huitain, aabbccdd.

BALTIMORE, Walters Art Gallery, Walters 222, fol. 97v°, c.
1470, Hours.

6097.   Marie humblement
        En l'advenement ...

        Lamentation de la passion Jesuchrist; 130 six-line stanzas.

        BRUSSELS, Bibl. royale, IV. 541, fol. 147r°-156v°, 1568.

        Ref.: Lemaire, Meschinot, Molinet, Villon: Témoignages inédits,
           1979, p. 69.

6098.   Marie, mere de concorde,
        Fontaine de misericorde ...

        Orison to the Virgin; one six-line stanza rhyming aabbcc. Text
           is not a variant of no. 1100.

        SAN MARINO, Huntington Libr., HM 1148, fol. 136v°, c. 1500,
        Hours of Rome.

6099.   Marie, tu es la plus amee,
        Quar en Dieu as grant grace trouvee.
        Je dis premierement en ma chansonnette
        Que toutes seurmonte Marion neste ...

        "Chansonnette" in honour of the Immaculate Conception by Simon
           de Plumetot; text in Latin and French, in verse and prose.

        PARIS, Bibl. nat., lat. 14970, fol. 69v°, XVc.

        Ref.: G. Ouy, in Miscellanea codicologica F. Masai dicata
           MCMLXXIX, Ghent, 1979, II, pp. 360-1.

6100.   Marthe de Dieu honnouree
        Couronnee,
        En paradis haultement ...

        Orison to S. Martha; 228 vv.

        AVIGNON, Bibl. mun., 1904, fol. 60r°-65r°, XVIc., Prayer-book.

        Ed.: Rézeau, Saints, II, pp. 360-8.

6101.   Mathĭas, amy, preu vous face
        Se benefice gracĭeulx ...

        Rondeau to S. Mathias: Mystère de la Passion by Arnoul Gréban
           (vv. 33589-604).

        PARIS, Bibl. de l'Arsenal, 6431, fol. 257v°, XVc.

        PARIS, Bibl. nat., fr. 815, fol. 271r°, 1458.

        PARIS, Bibl. nat., fr. 816, fol. 232v°, 1473.

        ROME, Accademia Nazionale dei Lincei, Bibl. Corsiniana, Rossi
           412 (44. A. 7), fol. 661r°-661v°, late XVc.

Ed.: Paris-Raynaud, pp. 441-2 (vv. 33736-51); Jodogne, p. 446 (vv. 33589-604).

6102. Mauvez arbres ne puet florir,
        Ainz seche toz et va crolant;
        Et hom qui n'aime, sanz mentir,
        Ne porte fruit, ainz va morant ...

        "Chanson" expressing a spiritual longing for the Fruit de vie, by Thibaut de Champagne, roi de Navarre; five eleven-line stanzas and two four-line envoys.

        BERN, Bürgerbibl., 231, fol. 4v°-5r°, XIVc.

        PARIS, Bibl. de l'Arsenal, 5198, p. 27-8, XIIIc.

        PARIS, Bibl. nat., fr. 844, fol. 75v°, late XIIIc.

        PARIS, Bibl. nat., fr. 846, fol. 81r°-81v°, late XIIIc.

        PARIS, Bibl. nat., fr. 1591, fol. 76v°-77r°, and 183v°-184v°, XIVc.

        PARIS, Bibl. nat., fr. 12581, fol. 375r°-375v°, XIVc.

        PARIS, Bibl. nat., fr. 12615, fol. 13r°, XIIIc.

        PARIS, Bibl. nat., fr. 24406, fol. 14v°-15r°, XIIIc.

        PARIS, Bibl. nat., nouv. acq. fr. 1050, fol. 25v°-26v°, late XIIIc.

        Ed.: P. Tarbé, Chansons de Thibault IV, comte de Champagne et de Brie, Reims, 1851, pp. 122-4; A. Rochat, Jahrbuch für romanische und englische Literatur, 10 (1869), p. 92; A. Jeanroy and P. Aubry, Le Chansonnier de l'Arsenal ... Reproduction phototypique du ms. 5198 de la Bibl. de l'Arsenal, Paris, 1912, pp. 27-8; A. Wallensköld, Les Chansons de Thibaut de Champagne, Paris, 1925, pp. 203-8; Järnström and Långfors, p. 45-8; Rosenberg and Tischler, pp. 368-71. Ref.: Spanke, no. 1410; Mölk and Wolfzettel, Répertoire, no. 1090, 6.

6103. Mercy, sire Dieux, glorieux pere tout puissant, fet il, veilles moy adrecier tellement que je puisse de cellui ...

        Anseïs d'Auvergne prays to God: Moniage Guillaume en prose.

        PARIS, Bibl. nat., fr. 796, fol. 352v°, XVc.

        PARIS, Bibl. nat., fr. 1497, fol. 534v°, XVc.

        Ed.: G. Schläger and W. Cloetta, ASNS, 97 (1896), p. 258.

6104. Mere de Dieu, ne vous deplaise,
        Se je vien a vous a refuge ...

        Orison to the Virgin by S. Denis: Miracles de sainte Geneviève (vv. 475-528).

PARIS, Bibl. Sainte-Geneviève, 1131, fol. 188v°-189r°, XVc.

Ed.: Sennewaldt, p. 76-7.

6105.   Et a dit: Mere Dieu, dame de paradis,
         Tant d'onneur ai eut et de vairs et de
                                          gris,
         De robes et des joiaus, et de destriés de
                                          pris,
         Biaus bores, biaus maingniers, tant de
                                 carnés delis ...

         Prayer to the Virgin by Baudouin: Baudouin de Sebourc (vv.
            123-35 of Chant XII).

         PARIS, Bibl. nat., fr. 12552, fol. 55v°, XIVc.

         PARIS, Bibl. nat., fr. 12553, fol. 162v°, XVc.

         Ed.: Boca, I, pp. 332-3.

6106.   Mere Deu et virge pucele,
         M'ounor, mon cors, m'ame et ma vie ...

         Orison to the Virgin by the hero's wife, unjustly accused of
            adultery: Roman du Comte de Poitiers (vv. 544-550).

         PARIS, Bibl. de l'Arsenal, 3527, fol. 173r°, early XIVc.

         Ed.: Koenig, p. 15-16; Malmberg, p. 119-20. Ref.: Koch, p. 51
            and 109.

6107.   Si a dit: Mere Dieu, je te lo et gracie
         Que j'ai donnet m'amour et mon corpz et ma
                                          vie ...

         Praise to the Virgin by Blanche: Baudouin de Sebourc (vv.
            798-805 of Chant III).

         PARIS, Bibl. nat., fr. 12552, fol. 15r°, XIVc.

         PARIS, Bibl. nat., fr. 12553, fol. 42v°, XVc.

         Ed.: Boca, I. p. 86.

6108.   Et a dit: Mere Dieu, royne courronnee,
         Dame, si vraiement que vous fuistez craee
         Et saintie a une eure enchois que fuissiez
                                          nee,
         Et que la prophesie fu sus toi contournee
                                 ...

         Prayer to the Virgin by Rose: Baudouin de Sebourc (vv. 134-63
            of Chant V).

         PARIS, Bibl. nat., fr. 12552, fol. 21v°, XIVc.

         PARIS, Bibl. nat., fr. 12553, fol. 61v°, XVc. This copy has
            only six lines of the prayer.

Ed.: Boca, I, p. 127; Labande, p. 69. Ref.: Labande, p. 72 n. 6
and p. 76.

6109. Met ta grace, Sire, ce te requerons nous, en nos pensees en
telle manere que nous qui avons cogneu ...

Orison to God in prose, as part of Compline in the Heures de
Nostre Dame.

CAMBRIDGE, Fitzwilliam Museum, McClean 76, fol. 63r°-63v°, XIV
- XVc., Hours of Paris.

6110. Misericordieux Dieu, nous requerons, donne a ton eglise que,
congregie par toy et en ton sainct Esprit ...

"La nuyct de la Trinité, <oraison>."

NEW YORK, Pierpont Morgan Libr., Morgan 78, fol. 149r°, XVc.,
Hours of Rome. This text added in XVIc.

6111. Misericorz Dieu, otroie a moy ce qu'il te plaist ardamment
desirer, sagement encerchier ...

Prayer to God, in prose.

METZ, Bibl. mun., 600, fol. 104r°-104v°, XVc., Hours of Paris
and Prayer-book.

Ref.: Rézeau, p. 169.

6112. Mon ame ayant recongnoissance
Des graces, faveurs et bienfaictz
Venuz de la divine puyssance
A elle departiz et faictz ...

Hymn "Magnificat", by Charles Senin; ten huitains rhyming
ababbcbc.

PARIS, Bibl. nat., fr. 2206, fol. 256r°-257r°, XVIc.

Ref.: Rézeau, p. 159.

6113. Mon ame loe mon signeur
Qui par sus tous est le grigneur
Et mon esperit s'esjoït
En Dieu mon salut quand l'oït ...

"Magnificat" in rhymed couplets, part of the "Heures de Nostre
Dame."

LILLE, Bibl. mun., Godefroy 5 (147), fol. 82r°-83v°, XVc.,
Hours.

6114. Mon ame loe Nostre Seigneur et mon esperit se esjoïst en mon
Dieu qui est mon salut, car il a regardé ...

Hymn "Magnificat", in prose; not identical with nos. 1143 or
4689.

CHICAGO, Art Institute, 15.536, p. 273-4, c. 1400, Psalter.

6115.   Mon ame magnifie Dieu
        Et mon esperit se resjoye ...

        Hymn "Magnificat": Mystère de la Passion by Arnoul Gréban (vv.
        3607-16).

        CHANTILLY, Musée Condé, 614 (1691), fol. 20r°, XVc. Inc.: Mon
        ame magniffie en Dieu/En Dieu mon esperit s'esjoye ...

        LE MANS, Bibl. mun., 6, fol. 30v°, XVc.

        PARIS, Bibl. de l'Arsenal, 6431, fol. 14v°, XVc.

        PARIS, Bibl. nat., fr. 815, fol. 27v°-28r°, 1458.

        PARIS, Bibl. nat., fr. 816, fol. 26v°, 1473.

        PARIS, Bibl. nat., fr. 1550, fol. 70r°-70v°, XVIc.

        PARIS, Bibl. nat., fr. 15064, fol. 63r°, 1469.

        ROME, Accademia Nazionale dei Lincei, Bibl. Corsiniana, Rossi
        412 (44. A. 7), fol. 33r°, late XVc.

        Ed.: Paris-Raynaud, p. 46 (vv. 3625-34); Jodogne, p. 53 (vv.
        3607-16).

6116.   Mon ame magniffie en Dieu,
        En Dieu mon esperit s'esjoye ...

        Variant of the inc.: Mon ame magnifie Dieu ... (no. 6115).

6117.   Mon benoist Dieu, ainsy comment il est ycy contenu, tout cela
        que vous croist saincte Esglise en toutes choses je croy ...

        La second leçon du salut <eternel>; for the other two, see the
        inc.: La premiere lecon du salut eternel ...; and De cueur et
        de bouche je vous recongnois ...

        CAMBRIDGE, Harvard College Libr., Lat. 251, fol. 75r°, late
        XVc., Hours of Rome.

6118.   Mon benoist Dieu, je proteste que je veulx avoir douleur et
        deplaisance de tous les pechez que je filz (sic) jamaies
        (sic) principallement ...

        "Protestation a dire aven<t> recepvoir Nostre Seigneur."

        PARIS, Bibl. nat., fr. 13269, fol. 8v°-9r°, XVc.

6119.   Mon chier enfant, ma tres doulce portee,
        Mon bien, mon heur, mon seul avancement ...

        Chant royal to Jesus by the Virgin: Arnoul Gréban's Mystère de
        la   Passion   (vv. 5044-54, 5071-81, 5098-108).   Three
        eleven-line stanzas with refrain.

        Refr.: Mon doulx enfant, mon vray Dieu et mon pere.

CHANTILLY, Musée Condé, 614 (1691), fol. 32v°-33r°, XVc.

LE MANS, Bibl. mun., 6, fol. 51r°-52r°, XVc.

PARIS, Bibl. de l'Arsenal, 6431, fol. 25v°-26r°, XVc.

PARIS, Bibl. nat., fr. 815, fol. 39v°-40r°, 1458.

PARIS, Bibl. nat., fr. 816, fol. 35v°-36r°, 1473.

PARIS, Bibl. nat., fr. 1550, fol. 103r°-104r°, XVIc.

PARIS, Bibl. nat., fr. 15064, fol. 92r°-93r°, 1469.

PARIS, Bibl. nat., nouv. acq. fr. 12908, fol. 12r°-12v°, XVIc.

ROME, Accademia Nazionale dei Lincei, Bibl. Corsiniana, Rossi
    412 (44. A. 7), fol. 62v°-63v°, late XVc.

Ed.: Paris-Raynaud, pp. 65-66 (vv. 5068-78, 5095-106, 5122-32);
    Jodogne, p. 71 (5044-54, 5071-81, 5097-108).

6120. Mon chier seigneur, doulx benoist Jhesucrist, vray filz de Dieu
    le pere et ung mesmes Dieu avecques lui ...

    Orison to Jesus, in prose.

    PROVIDENCE, Brown Univ. Libr., C. 28. b. 4 (H.L. Koopman
    Collection), fol. 273r°-274r°, XVc., Hours.

6121. Mon createur Jhesucrist, je vous recongnoy et confesse estre
    vray et parfait Dieu et homme, filz du pere omnipotens et de
    la vierge Marie selonc vostre humanité ...

    "Confession a Dieu pour remission"; it includes the "Trois
    Verités" whose inc. are similar to but not identical with
    nos. 2372, 5198, 5199. See: Vray Dieu, je commande mon esprit
    ... (no. 6855); Vray est que Dieu nostre pere ... (no. 6871);
    Vray sire, j'ay bonne volenté ... (no. 6874).

    LUXEMBOURG, Bibl. nat., 28, fol. 134v°-136v°, XVIc.

6122. Mon Dieu, bien vous dois gracïer,
    Quant il vous plaist de vostre grace ...

    Christofle gives thanks to God: Mystère de saint Christofle
    (vv. 2094-9).

    Early Ed.: in 4° Gothic, Paris, Veuve Jean Trepperel and Jean
    Jehannot, n.d. (c. 1515). Ed.: Runnalls, p. 66.

6123. Mon Dieu, j'ay bonne voulenté de faire confession ...

    Third of the Trois Verités, with a special introduction: Nostre
    pere tres pieu ... (no. 6166).   Explicit attribution to
    Gerson.

BRUSSELS, Bibl. royale, II. 7604, fol. 35r°, XVc. Added by a later cursive hand.

6124. Mon Dieu, je ay bon propos et desirier, moyennant vostre ayde, ...

Second of the Trois Verités, with a particular introduction: Nostre pere tres pieu ... (no. 6166). Explicit attribution to Gerson.

BRUSSELS, Bibl. royale, II. 7604, fol. 35r°, XVc. Added in a later cursive hand.

6125. Mon dieu, je ay pechié contre vostre bonté souveraine ...

First of the Trois Verités, with a particular introduction: Nostre pere tres pieu ... (no. 6166). Explicit attribution to Gerson.

BRUSSELS, Bibl. royale, II. 7604, fol. 35r°, XVc. Added in a later cursive hand.

Ref.: Brayer, Livres d'heures, p. 70.

6126. Mon Dieu, j'ay pechié contre vostre bonté souveraine dont il me desplait ...

Variant incipit of no. 4706.

6127. Mon Dieu, mon createur de tes grés misericordes ...

"Autre oroison quant on a receu le corps Nostre Seigneur Jhesu Crist et se commence Gracias ago."

SUTTON COLDFIELD, Oscott College, 583, fol. 145v°-146v°, late XVc., Hours of Paris.

6128. Mon Dieu, mon createur, je me confesse a vous de tous mes pechiés que j'ay fait depuis ma jonesse jusques a l'heure de maintenant ...

"Trois Verités", unrubricated.

NEW YORK, Pierpont Morgan Libr., Morgan 198, fol. 10r°-10v°, XVc., Hours of Amiens. The text was added by a XVIc. hand.

6129. Mon Dieu, mon createur, je vous offre et presente la saincte oraison de la paternostre a intention de vois demander toutes les vertus ...

"S'ensuit pour demander a Dieu les sept petition<s> de la paternostre ce que on doit faire le jour du sainct dimenche, et premierement pour adreschier son intention." Prologue; only one petition has been transcribed, see the inc.: Nostre pere quy es es cieulx, nous enfans, nous suplions que ... (no. 6161).

NEW YORK, Pierpont Morgan Libr., Morgan 78, fol. 175r°-175v°, XVc., Hours of Rome. This text added by a XVIc. hand.

6130.   Mon Dieu, mon createur redempteur, mon glorificateur et mon
         tout, je vous adore de tout mon coeur, de toute mon ame ...

         "S'ensieut l'adoration en quoy est enclos ce que en faire (sic)
         le jour du saint dimenche."

         NEW YORK, Pierpont Morgan Libr., Morgan 78, fol. 1r°-2v°, XVc.,
         Hours of Rome. This text added by a XVIc. hand.

6131.   Mon Dieu, mon pere, mon seigneur,
         Moult me feistes trez granz honneur
         Quant de terre vous me formastes
         Et en paradis me posastes ...

         "Plainte" to God by Adam: "Mystère de la Nativité" (vv.
         387-413).

         LONDON, British Libr., Additional 38860, fol. 6v°-7r°, XVIIIc.
         copy of a lost codex.

         PARIS, Bibl. Sainte-Geneviève, 1131, fol. 4r°, XVc.

         Ed.: Whittredge, pp. 107-8.

6132.   Mon Dieu, si j'ay pechié encontre vous, si suis je creé par
         vous; se j'ay perdu ma purité, si me fyeie en vostre
         misericorde ...

         "Oraison que feist sainct Ancelme", in prose.

         NEW YORK, New York Public Libr., 57, fol. 8r°, first quarter
         XVIc., Book of Hours for a certain Yolène, perhaps of the
         Héricourt family.

6133.   Mon Dieu tres benin, mon Seigneur et mon createur, je, creature
         pecheresse, me presente aujourd'huy ...

         "Oraison pour dire tous les dimenches": Manuel de dévotion de
         prêtre Pierre.

         NEW HAVEN, Yale Univ. Libr., 498, fol. 106v°-107v°, last
         quarter XVIc.

6134.   Mon glorieux angle, l'un des nobles princes de la cité de
         paradis ...

         Variant of the inc.: Glorieux angle, l'un des nobles princes
         ... (no. 5839).

6135.   Mon Jesus prince de largesse
         Aquitte toy de ta promesse ...

         Prayer to Jesus, in paired octosyllables.

         NEW YORK, New York Public Libr., 39, fol. 83, XVc., Hours of
         Tournai; this orison added in a 16th century hand.

6136.   Mon pere, je sçay bien que mes pechiés sont infinis et que mes
         maulx sont innumerables et que por la grande qualité de mes
         pechiés veritablement ...

"Confession generale, des dis de saint Augustin ou livre des confessions, et le doibt on dire aprés la confession particulier (sic)."

LUXEMBOURG, Bibl. nat., 28, fol. 127r°-127v°, XVIc.

6137. Mon puissant createur et amoureus redempteur je congnois avoir offensé ta maiesté en ces pechés ...

"Recollection de l'esperit a faire ung chacun jour ... dire ce qui s'ensuit".

NEW YORK, New York Public Libr., 57, fol. 13r°, first quarter XVIc., Book of Hours for a certain Yolène, perhaps of the Héricourt family.

6138. Mon seigneur, je me confesseré a toi pour ce que t'es courrouciez a moy; ta fourcenerie est convertie ...

Canticle of Isaiah, in prose.

CHICAGO, Art Institute, 15.536, p. 253-4, c. 1400, Psalter.

6139. Mon tres doulz Creatour, doucement vous
                                    mercie
De vostre recepcion, mais humblement vous
                                    prie ...

Orison "aprés la recepcion" du corpz Nostre Seigneur; copied as prose, but really two quatrains of monorhymed alexandrines.

MANCHESTER, John Rylands Univ. Libr., French 143, fol. 176v°, early XVc., Hours.

6140. Mon tres doulz Creatour, vrais et tous
                                    puissans,
Je vien a vostre table et come povre et
                                    negligens,
Je ne suis mie digne, bonne ne sofizans
De recevoir vostre corps et vostre precieux
                                    sanc ...

"Quant on vuet recevoir le corpz Nostre Seigneur"; monorhymed quatrains copied as prose; not the same as no. 1220.

MANCHESTER, John Rylands Univ. Libr., Fr. 143, fol. 176r°-176v°, early XVc., Hours.

6141. Mon tres doulx Dieu, mon createur, je me mez en ta sainte misericorde et en ta pitié. Je suis ta povre creature, laquelle tu as cree<e> ...

Orison to God, in prose.

CAMBRIDGE, Harvard College Libr., Typ. 304, fol. 14v°-15r°, c. 1470, Hours.

6142. Mon tres doulx Dieu, puis que ne sçay que m'est expediant tant que je suis en ce povre monde ...

"L'oroison S. Augustin a Dieu le pere."

ROUBAIX, Archives Municipales, no shelf-mark, fol. 92r°, XVc., Prayer-book of Jacques de Luxembourg.

6143. Mon tres doulx et reverant creatour, je ne suy rienz de moy et par toy ja estre rienz je ne suiz ...

Meditation, or 'Cogitatio', in prose.

METZ, Bibl. mun., 600, fol. 102v°, XVc., Hours of Paris and Prayer-book.

Ref.: Rézeau, p. 168.

6144. Mon tres puissant createur (ms. creature) et tres amoureux redempteur, moy, povre creature et tres fragille pecheresse, proteste soubz ton ayde ...

"Protestation a faire le matin devant toute oeuvre."

NEW YORK, New York Public Libr., 57, fol. 13r°-13v°, first quarter XVIc., Book of Hours for a certain Yolène, perhaps of the Héricourt family.

6145. Mon tres souverain seygneur, mon benoist et pytoux redempteur ...

"Orayson pour pryer pour les ames de purgatoyre."

OXFORD, Lincoln College, Lat. 152, fol. 188v°, early XVc., Hours of Paris. This prayer added in XVIc.

6146. Mon vray Dieu, Kyrie eleyson!
Pouvres gens sont fort esbahis,
Il n'est justice ne raison
Qui s'oise tenir au païs ...

"Letania minor" by Jean Molinet; 29 quatrains and 10 sizains.

ARRAS, Bibl. mun., 619 (692), fol. 126v°-128r°, c. 1520.

PARIS, Bibl. nat., Rothschild 471, fol. 161r°-163v°, XVIc.

TOURNAI, Bibl. de la Ville, 105, fol. 179v°-183r°, XVIc.

Ed.: Dupire, Faictz et Dictz, II, 1937, pp. 548-554; III, 1939, p. 1032. Extracts reproduced by P. Eluard, La Poésie du passé, Verviers, 1960, pp. 174-6. Ref.: Champion, Histoire poétique du XV^{e}s., II, pp. 346-7; Monique Santucci in Senefiance no. 10, pp. 498 and 510.

6147. Moult est bien monstree l'amour de mon pere envers moy qui doy estre sa fille, quant tele dignité ...

"Oroison sus la seconde demande de la patenostre" in the Mendicité spirituelle by Jean Gerson.

BRUSSELS, Bibl. royale, IV. 111, fol. 209v°, XVc.

LYON, Bibl. de la Ville, 1249 (1121), fol. 32r°-32v°, XVc.

PARIS, Bibl. de l'Arsenal, 2113, fol. 72r°-72v°, XVc.

PARIS, Bibl. de l'Arsenal, 2121, fol. 20r°-20v°, XVc.

VIENNA, Oesterreichische Nationalbibl., 2574, fol. 239r°-239v°, XVc.

Screening of mss. is incomplete.

Ed.: Glorieux, Gerson: Oeuvres complètes, VII, 1, pp. 243-44.

N

6148. N'est pas a reciter le mal ou je suy enlassee et la necessité
qui me contraint chascun jour en mainte guise ...

"Oroison sus la septiesme demande de la patenostre", in the
Mendicité spirituelle by Jean Gerson.

BRUSSELS, Bibl. royale, IV. 111, fol. 211v°-212r°, XVc.

LYON, Bibl. de la Ville, 1249 (1121), fol. 35r°, XVc.

PARIS, Bibl. de l'Arsenal, 2113, fol. 79r°-79v°, XVc.

PARIS, Bibl. de l'Arsenal, 2121, fol. 25r°-25v°, XVc.

VIENNA, Oesterreichische Nationalbibl., 2574, fol. 242r°-242v°,
XVc.

Screening of mss. is incomplete.

Ed.: Glorieux, Gerson: Oeuvres complètes, VII, 1, pp. 248-9.

6149. Ne m'i fail, sire sainz Oiens,
Tent mei ennuit tes beles mains! ...

Orison to S. Ouen by the sacristan of the Abbey of Saint-Ouen:
Chronique des ducs de Normandie, by Benoît (vv. 28033-8).

LONDON, British Libr., Harley 1717, fol. 159v°, XIIIc.

TOURS, Bibl. mun., 903, fol. 137v°, late XIIc.

Ed.: Fahlin, II, p. 174.

6150. Ne nous delaissiez pas en desconfort, vous, pere de toute
consolation ...

Variant of the inc.: Ne nous laissez pas de desconfort, vous,
pere ... (no. 6151).

6151. Ne nous laissez pas de desconfort, vous, pere de toute
       consolation. Soyez nous refuge en toutes adversités ...

       Prayer to Jesus: Sermon sur la Passion: Ad Deum vadit, by Jean
       Gerson.

       BRUSSELS, Bibl. royale, IV. 111, fol. 255r°, XVc. Inc.: Ne nous
       delaissiez pas en desconfort ...

       LONDON, British Libr., Harley 4331, fol. 72r°, XVc.

       LYON, Bibl. de la Ville, 1182, fol. 52r°, XVc.

       PARIS, Bibl. nat., fr. 24841, fol. 40v°, XVc.

       Screening of mss. is incomplete.

       Ed.: Carnahan, p. 119; Frénaud, p. 104; Glorieux, Gerson:
       Oeuvres complètes, VII, 2, p. 511.

6152. Noble chevalier defensable,
       Gentil capitaine notable ...

       "Oraison de saint Maurice", 8 sizains rhyming aabaab.

       PARIS, Bibl. nat., Rés. D. 5616 and Ye 831, Louenges des
       benoistz sainctz et sainctes de paradis, fol. zz4v°-zz5r°,
       Paris, Vérard.

       VERSAILLES, Bibl. mun., M. 129 (Lacombe 109 quater).

       Ed.: Rézeau, Saints, II, pp. 377-9.

6153. Noble dame du redempteur ...

       Variante de l'inc.: Noble mere du redempteur ... (no. 1241).

6154. Nostre Dieu et nostre seigneur, le pain de vie celestiel, j'ay
       peché davent (sic) vous en terre et ne suy pas digne de
       revoir ...

       Orison to God, in prose.

       BALTIMORE, Walters Art Gallery, Walters 261, fol. 127v°, c.
       1400, Hours.

6155. Nostre Dieu, je proteste devant vostre saincte maiesté que
       veulx vivre et mourir en vostre saincte foy catholique en
       croiant tout ...

       Profession of Faith or "Protestation", in prose.

       NEW YORK, Pierpont Morgan Libr., Morgan 159, fol. 135v°-136v°,
       XVc., Hours of Rome, executed for Eleanor de Bourbon,
       duchesse de Nemours.

6156. Nostre duz seyngnur Jhesu Crist nus doint issi Deu honurer,
       nostre prome amer ...

Orison to Jesus in prose, at the end of the Mirour de seinte
Eglyse, a translation of the Speculum Ecclesiae by S. Edmund
of Abingdon. The texts of A and B versions are very close.

CAMBRIDGE, Emmanuel College, I. 4. 31, fol. 105r°, XIVc. (A
version).

DURHAM, Durham Univ. Libr., Cosin V.V. 15, fol. 43v., XIVc. (B
version). Inc.: Nostre tres duz seignur ...

LINCOLN, Chapter Libr., B. 5. 1, fol. 178r°, XIVc. (B version).

LONDON, British Libr., Arundel 288, fol. 122r°, XIIIc. (B
version).

LONDON, British Libr., Harley 1121, fol. 155v°, early XIVc. (B
version).

LONDON, British Libr., Royal 12. C. XII, fol. 30r°, early XIVc.
(A version).

LONDON, British Libr., Royal 20. B. XIV, fol. 65v°, early XIVc.
(A version).

MADRID, Bibl. nac., 18253, fol. 147v°, XIVc. (A version). Inc.:
Nostre tres douz seignor Jhesu Crist ...

NEW HAVEN, Yale Univ. Libr., 492, fol. 99v°, early XIVc. (A
version).

OXFORD, Bodleian Libr., Digby 20, fol. 157v°, XIIIc. (B
version).

OXFORD, Bodleian Libr., Digby 98, fol. 255r°, early XIVc. (B
version).

OXFORD, Bodleian Libr., Douce 210, fol. 43r°, early XIVc. (A
version).

OXFORD, Bodleian Libr., Rawlinson Poetry 241, p. 189, late
XIIIc. (B version).

OXFORD, Bodleian Libr., Selden Supra 74, fol. 59r°, XIIIc. (A
version).

OXFORD, St. John's College, 190, fol. 199r°, late XIIIc. (A
version).

PARIS, Bibl. nat., fr. 13342, fol. 44v°, early XIVc. (A
version). Inc.: Nostre tres dous seignor Jhesucrist ...

PARIS, Bibl. nat., nouv. acq. fr. 11200, fol. 23v°, XIIIc. (A
version).

Ed.: Robbins, p. 78 (base ms. Oxford, Digby 20); Wilshere, p.
88 (A version, base ms. Oxford, St. John's College, 190); p.
89 (B version, base ms. London, Arundel 288). Ref.: Same as
the Ref. section of the inc. Aprés ço devez saver queus sunt
les set prieres ... (no. 5431).

6157. Nostre pere celeste, nous constituez en terre, lesquelz vostre
      bonté a honorez de nom d'enfans, vous prions que par nostre
      doctri<ne> et par nostre vie ...

      Brefve Explanation du Pater Noster, by the chevalier Louis de
      Berquin, 1525.

      Ed.: Brefve admonition de la maniere de prier selon la doctrine
      de Jesuchrist, avec une brefve explanation du Pater Noster,
      Extraict des Paraphrases de Erasme, Paris, Simon Dubois (?),
      1525; Telle, pp. 17-22.

6158. Nostre pere qui es es cieulx, combien que je, vostre povre
      creature, ne sois pas digne ...

      Oroison des vifs pour les morts, a section, often rubricated
      separately, of Gerson's "Complainte des ames du purgatoire",
      inc. Priés pour nous, o vous qui estes vivans ... (no. 5004).

      DOUAI, Bibl. mun., 516, fol. 115r⁰-115v⁰, XVc.

      METZ, Bibl. mun., 530, fol. 94r⁰-94v⁰, XVc.

      PARIS, Bibl. nat., fr. 25552, fol. 28v⁰-29r⁰, XVc.

      ROUBAIX, Archives Municipales, sans cote, fol. 130v⁰-131r⁰,
      XVc., Prayer-book of Jacques de Luxembourg.

      Ed.: Glorieux, Gerson: Oeuvres complètes, VII, 1, pp. 366-7.

6159. Nostre pere qui es es cieulx et en la terre, sanctifié soit ton
      nom; ton royaume nous adviengne ...

      Pater Noster, in prose, as part of the Heures de Nostre Dame en
      françois (no. 3658).

      PROVIDENCE, Brown Univ. Libr., C. 28. b. 4 (H.L. Koopman
      Collection), fol. 9r⁰, XVc. Hours.

6160. Nostre pere qui es es cieulz et en la terre ton nom soit
      saintiffié, adveigne nous ton royaume ...

      Pater Noster in prose, as part of the Heures de Nostre Dame.
      The text is not the same as 1252 or 1253.

      CAMBRIDGE, Fitzwilliam Museum, McClean 76, fol. 20r⁰-20v⁰,
      XIV-XVc., Hours of Paris.

6161. Nostre pere quy es es (ms. est) cieulx, nous enfans, nous
      suplions que par vostre honte vostre nom soit sainctifiét en
      nous ...

      First petition of "Pour demander a Dieu les sept petitions de
      la paternostre". The prologue begins: Mon Dieu, mon createur,
      je vous offre ... (no. 6129).

      NEW YORK, Pierpont Morgan Libr., Morgan 78, fol. 175v⁰-176v⁰,
      XVc., Hours of Rome. This text by a XVIc. hand.

6162. Nostre pere qui es ez cieulz, soit sanctifié ton nom, adviengne
ton regne, soit faicte ta voulenté ...

"La Patenostre contient sept petitions", as part of Jean
Gerson's ABC des simples gens.

HAGUE (THE), Koninkl. Bibl., 78. J. 49, fol. 485r°, XVc.

LONDON, British Libr., Additional 29279, fol. 50r°, XVc.

PARIS, Bibl. de l'Arsenal, 3386, fol. 52v°, XVc.

PARIS, Bibl. Mazarine, 966, fol. 129v°, XVc.

PARIS, Bibl. Sainte-Geneviève, 2440, fol. 43r°, XVc.

Screening of mss. is incomplete.

Ed.: Glorieux, Gerson: Oeuvres complètes, VII, 1, p. 155.

6163. Nostre pere qui es es cieulx, sanctifié soit ton nom, ton
royaume nous advienne ...

Pater Noster in prose by Guillaume Farel, 1524. The text is not
identical with no. 1252.

Ed.: Le Pater Noster et le Credo en françoys avec une tresbelle
et tresutile exposition et declaration sur chascun, Bâle, A.
Cratander, 1524; Higman, p. 39.

6164. Nostre pere qui es es cieulx; ton nom soit sainctifié; adviegne
nous ton regne; ta voulenté soit faicte aussi ...

Variant of the inc.: Nostre pere qui es es ciaux, tes nons soit
sanctifiez, adviegne tes roiaumes ... (no. 4743).

6165. Nostre pere qui est es ciex,
Ton nom sy soit saintefiez
Ton royaume aviegne, Sire Diex,
Ton vouloir saint et ardefiez ...

Paraphrase of the Pater Noster uttered by Seth: "Mystère de la
Nativité" (vv. 530-44).

LONDON, British Libr., Additional 38860, fol. 9r°, XVIIIc. copy
of a lost codex.

PARIS, Bibl. Saint-Geneviève, 1131, fol. 5v°, XVc.

Ed.: Whittredge, p. 111-12.

6166. Nostre pere tres pieu et tres misericordieux, congnoissant
nostre tres grant fragilité et promptitude a pechié ...

Introduction to a particular version of the Trois Verités, with
attribution to Gerson.

BRUSSELS, Bibl. royale, II. 7604, fol. 34v°-35r°, XVc. Added in a later cursive hand.

Ref.: Brayer, Livres d'heures, p. 70.

6167. Nostre Seigneur a demené le juste par les droictes voyes et luy a monstré le royaulme de Dieu ...

Suffrage to S. Francis, in prose.

PARIS, Private Collection, LF 13, fol. 171v°-172r°, early XVIc., Prayer-book.

Ref.: Rézeau, Saints, II, pp. 220-1.

6168. Nostre seigneur Jhesucrist, fil de Dieu le vif, je te presente ces .xv. pater noster et .xv. ave maria en l'onneur et gloire des plaies ...

Variant of the Inc.: Seigneur Jhesu Crist, filz de Dieu vivant, je te presente ... (no. 1902).

6169. Nostre Seigneur Jesus Christ, l'aigneau qui a esté occis, qui nous a rachapté de son sang, est digne ...

"Action de graces pour le beneffice de la redemption": Manuel de dévotion de prêtre Pierre.

NEW HAVEN, Yale Univ. Libr., 498, fol. 39v°-40r°, last quarter XVIc.

6170. Nostre Seigneur, reçoive se sacrifice de tes mains a la louenge et gloire de son nom a nostre proufit et de toute la saincte Eglise. Amen.
                    (Complete Text).

"Quant le preste (sic) dit a la messe Orate pro me fratres, vous devez dire ceste oroison".

NEW YORK, New York Public Libr., 52, fol. 200r°-200v°, XVc., Hours of Paris.

6171. Nostre Sires est benoit, car il nous visita et feist la redempcion de son peuple, et esdreça a nous la corne ...

Canticle of Zechariah, in prose.

CHICAGO, Art Institute, 15.536, p. 272-3. c. 1400, Psalter.

6172. Nostre Sire, ke en cel manez, tun nun seit seintefiez, tun regne nus veigne, ceo devon requere ...

Pater Noster, copied as prose, but probably once rhymed; now part of the Heures de Nostre Dame.

STUTTGART, Württembergische Landesbibl., Brev. 75, fol. 15r°-15v°, XIVc., Hours of Sarum.

6173. Nostre tres duz seignor Jhesu Crist nus doint issi Deu honurer
...

Variant of the inc.: Nostre duz seygnur Jhesu Crist ... (no. 6156).

6174. Nous loons toy, Dieu; nous regehissons toy, Seigneur. Toute
terre te honnoure, pere pardurable ...

Hymn "Te Deum", not identical with nos. 1266 or 3238.

CHICAGO, Art Institute, 15.536, p. 268-70, c. 1400, Psalter.

6175. Nus rendum a tei loenge et honur, ki es Nostre Sire et Nostre
Seignur. Tei, pere omnipotent ...

"Te Deum" copied as prose but once rhymed; part of the Heures
de Nostre Dame.

STUTTGART, Württembergische Landesbibl., Brev. 75, fol.
18v°-19v°, XIVc., Hours of Sarum.

6176. Nus requerums la misericorde Deu, nostre dame seynte Marie, e
la vostre, ke vus priez pur nus, ke nus pusums ...

Novices request the Brethren attending their profession to pray
for them: Customary of the Benedictine Monastery of Saint
Augustine, Canterbury.

LONDON, British Libr., Cotton, Faustina C. XII, fol. 179r°,
XIVc.

Ed.: Thompson, I, p. 384.

6177. Nus requerums la misericorde Deu, nostre dame sainte Marie,
saint Pere, saint Pol, saint Augustin ...

Prayer of novices to be allowed to make their profession:
Customary of the Benedictine Monastery of Saint Augustine,
Canterbury.

LONDON, British Libr., Cotton, Faustina C. XII, fol. 122v°, and
another transcription fol. 178v°, XIVc.

Ed.: Thompson, I, p. 264 and 383-4.

6178. Nous requerons, seigneur Dieu, que de ce feu par le sainct
Esprit soions enflammés ...

"La nuyct de la Trinité, iij^e oraison".

NEW YORK, Pierpont Morgan Libr., Morgan 78, fol. 151r°, XVc.,
Hours of Rome. This text added in XVIc.

6179. Nous te loons mere et ancelle,
Toi confessons vierge pucelle,
Toi estoille clere marine
La clarté du pere enlumine ...

"Te matrem laudamus", in rhyme.

BALTIMORE, Walters Art Gallery, Walters 89, fol. 31r°-36r°, last quarter XIVc., Hours of Isabelle de Coucy (d. 1413).

SAN MARINO (Calif.), Huntington Libr., HM 1129, fo. 30v°-33r°, c. 1450, Hours of Paris.

6180.   Nous te prions, o sainct pere, pour les ames des fidelles trespassez qu'ilz puyssent jouyr du salut eternel et de la joye ...

"Oraison pour les ames de tous fidelles": Manuel de dévotion de prêtre Pierre.

NEW HAVEN, Yale Univ. Libr., 498, fol. 126r°-126v°, last quarter XVIc.

6181.   Nous te prions, Seigneur, pour ta saincte Eglise laquelle tu as acquis par le sang precieux de ton filz ...

"Oraison pour l'Eglise catholique et pour tous peuples" = Prone prayers: Manuel de devotion de prêtre Pierre.

NEW HAVEN, Yale Univ. Libr., 498, fol. 101v°-103r°, last quarter XVIc.

6182.   Nous te prions, sire Dieu, que l'affliction de nostre devotion soit faicte par la grace vertueuse ...

"Dimence de la Passion, oraison".

NEW YORK, Pierpont Morgan Libr., Morgan 78, fol. 92v°-93r°, XVc., Hours of Rome. The prayer was added in XVIc.

6183.   Nous te prions, vray Dieu, qui les offices et ministeres des anges et des hommes par merveilleuse ordre ...

Prayer to God, in prose.

BALTIMORE, Walters Art Gallery, Walters 293, fol. 178r°, early XVc., Hours.

6184.   Nous te requeron, doulz Sire, que nous soion tousjours joieux en toy par les merites de monseigneur saint George martir ...

Orison for S. George (on feast-day).

PARIS, Bibl. de l'Arsenal, 2162, fol. 139r°-139v°, XVc., Hours of Paris.

6185.   Nous te requerons que tu nous concede, tout puissant Dieu, que nous qui hantons la solemnité du don du sainct Esprit ...

"La veille de pentecouste, vij^e, oraison".

NEW YORK, Pierpont Morgan Libr., Morgan 78, fol. 147r°, XVc., Hours of Rome. The prayer in a XVIc. hand.

6186.   Nous te requerons, sire Dieu, que tu ottroies a tes sergens que nous nous puissons esjoïr de pardurable santé de corps ...

Orison to God in prose, at Terce of the Heures de Nostre Dame.

CAMBRIDGE, Fitzwilliam Museum, McClean 76, fol. 43v°-44r°, XIV-XVc., Hours of Paris.

6187. Nous te supplions, sire Dieu, regarde ta famille pour laquelle Nostre Seigneur Jhesucrist ne doubta point ...

"Le jour de merquedi sainct et du vendre<di> sainct", first of ten prayers.

NEW YORK, Pierpont Morgan Libr., Morgan 78, fol. 153r°, XVc., Hours of Rome. Orison added in XVIc.

6188. Nous te venerons
Louons, adorons,
Enffant de hault pris,
Car nous esperons ...

"Motet" to the Child Jesus by the angels: Arnoul Gréban's Mystère de la Passion (vv. 4984-5019). Six stanzas of six pentasyllabic lines, rhyming aabaab.

CHANTILLY, Musée Condé, 614 (1691), fol. 32r°, XVc.

LE MANS, Bibl. mun., 6, fol. 50r°-50v°, XVc.

PARIS, Bibl. de l'Arsenal, 6431, fol. 25r°, XVc.

PARIS, Bibl. nat., fr. 815, fol. 39r°-39v°, 1458.

PARIS, Bibl. nat., fr. 816, fol. 35r°-35v°, 1473.

PARIS, Bibl. nat., fr. 1550, fol. 101v°-102v°, XVIc.

PARIS, Bibl. nat., fr. 15064, fol. 91r°-91v°, 1469.

PARIS, Bibl. nat., nouv. acq. fr. 12908, fol. 3r°, XVIc.

ROME, Accademia Nazionale dei Lincei, Bibl. Corsiniana, Rossi 412 (44. A. 7), fol. 61v°-62r°, late XVc.

Ed.: Paris-Raynaud, pp. 64-5 (vv. 5009-43); Jodogne, p. 70 (vv. 4984-5019).

6189. Nous trouvons es escriptures que nostre benoit sauveur ...

Variant of no. 4758.

O

6190. O benois angeles de lasus,
Ki m'avés a garder cha jus ...

Prayer to Guardian Angel, 60 vv. rhyming pairs.

CAMBRAI, Bibl. mun., 87 (88), fol. 190v°-192v°, early XIVc.

SENS, Bibl. mun., 39, rouleau, XVc., lines 1280-1322.

Ed.: Tarbé, Romancero de Champagne, I, pp. 80-2 (ms. Sens);
Rézeau, Saints, II, pp. 515-18 (base ms. Cambrai).

6191. O benois angeles des cieux ...

Variant of the inc.: Benois angelz des cieulx ... (no. 241).

6192. O benoist archange Michiel,
Ange de paix, qui l'estandart ...

Prayers to several saints placed in the customary order of
Books of Hours; 98 vv. in 14 stanzas.

PARIS, Bibl. nat., Rés. B. 2941, fol. hlv°-h8r°, Hours of Rome,
Paris, Vérard, 1490.

Ed.: Rézeau, Saints, I, pp. 71-5, who refers also to other
incunabula.

6193. O benoit archange Michel,
Qui portes de Dieu l'estandart ...

Series of prayers to several saints; 68 vv. arranged in twelve
stanzas, on varying rhymes.

PARIS, Bibl. Mazarine, Rés. 34964, fol. 12v° - 18v°, Hours of
Rome, Paris, Vérard, c. 1488.

Ed.: Rézeau, Saints, I, pp. 76-9, who records another
incunabulum of the same text.

6194. O benoist Jesus, qui es couronne et loyer de tous les benoistz
       saincts martyrs ...

       "Oraison de l'apostre monseigneur saint Andry/Qui par torment
       ne peut oncques estre attendry"; in prose.

       PARIS, Bibl. Ecole Nat. Sup. des Beaux-Arts, Masson, impr. 29,
       fol. B2v°-B3r°, XVIc.

       PARIS, Bibl. nat., fr. 19243, fol. 166v°-167r°, XVIc.

       Ref.: Rézeau, Saints, II, pp. 7-8.

6195. O benoist sainct Denis, que ta foy est grande. Prie pour nous
       Nostre Seigneur Jesus Christ ...

       "Antienne de sainct Denis", in prose.

       PARIS, Bibl. Ecole Nat. Sup. des Beaux-Arts, Masson, impr. 480,
       1543, Hours of Rome.

       Ref.: Rézeau, Saints, II, pp. 188-9 who mentions other early
       imprints of the XVIc.

6196. O benoite vierge Marie, mere de Dieu tres debonnaire, ma dame,
       m'esperance, ma doulceur, ma consolacion, a toy premiere ...

       Orison to the Virgin, in prose.

       PROVIDENCE, Brown Univ. Libr., C. 28. b. 4 (H.L. Koopman
       Collection), fol. 187r°-188r°, XVc., Hours.

6197. O bieneureux acomplisseur des oeuvres de misericorde,
       monseigneur saint Julian, qui par le merite ...

       Suffrage to S. Julian the Hospitaller, in prose.

       PARIS, Bibl. Ecole Nat. Sup. des Beaux-Arts, Masson, impr. 29,
       fol. D5v°-D6r°, XVIc.

       Ref.: Rézeau, Saints, II, p. 297.

6198. O bien auerouse vierge, saincte Katherine, plus fust odorans
       que n'est balmes ...

       Prayer to S. Catherine of Alexandria, in prose.

       METZ, Bibl. mun., 600, fol. 117v°, XVc., Hours of Paris and
       Prayer-book.

       Ed.: Rézeau, p. 171; Rézeau, Saints, II, p. 126.

6199. O bon Dieu, qui par ta servante
       Catherine, en grace abondante ...

       "Oraison de saincte Katherine"; one dizain in rhyming couplets.

BESANCON, Bibl. mun., 121, fol. 94v°-95r°, late XVc., Hours of Besançon.

Ed.: Rézeau, Saints, II, pp. 153-4.

6200.   O bon Jesus de qui la magnificence est si grande qu'aucune creature ne le sauroit declairer que le ciel et la mer ...

"Institution catholique de la verité et dignité du corps et du sang de Jesus Christ au s. Sacrement": Manuel de dévotion de prêtre Pierre.

NEW HAVEN, Yale Univ. Libr., 498, fol. 82r°-83v°, last quarter XVIc.

6201.   O bon Jesus, o tres doux Jesus, tres debonnaire Jesus, o Jesus enfant de la pure Vierge Marie, vray Dieu, plein de misericorde ...

"Oraison a Nostre Seigneur Jesus Christ sauveur du monde": Manuel de dévotion de prêtre Pierre. The text of the prayer is close to but not identical with that of no. 1295.

NEW HAVEN, Yale Univ. Libr., 498, fol. 42v°-44v°, last quarter XVIc.

6202.   O bon Jesus, vray marchant tres prudent,
Qui m'as du pris de ton sang acheté ...

"Oraison a Dieu le filz", decasyllables rhyming abab.

NEW YORK, New York Public Libr., 39, fol. 83v°, XVc., Hours of Tournai; this prayer added by a 16th century hand.

6203.   O certaine esperance et darrien refuges des ames, Jhesucrist, nostre redempteur, et vous, Vierge, sa mere glorieuse ...

"Oroison a Jhesucrist et a Nostre Dame", part of the Mendicité spirituelle by Jean Gerson.

BRUSSELS, Bibl. royale, IV. 111, fol. 217v°, XVc. Inc.: O tres certaine esperance ...

LYON, Bibl. de la Ville, 1249 (1121), fol. 41v°, XVc. Only the first eight words remain.

PARIS, Bibl. de l'Arsenal, 2113, fol. 96r°-97r°, XVc.

PARIS, Bibl. de l'Arsenal, 2121, fol. 38r°-38v°, XVc.

VIENNA, Oesterreichische Nationalbibl., 2574, fol. 250r°-250v°, XVc.

Screening of mss. is incomplete.

Ed.: Glorieux, Gerson: Oeuvres complètes, VII, 1, pp. 261-2.

6204.   O createur, tronc de l'ault habitaige,
Le formateur de nature angelicque ...

Prayer to God by Severin on the point of being martyred: Mystère des Trois Doms, by chanoine Siboud Pra de Grenoble with the assistance of Claude Chevalet de Vienne, and performed at Romans in 1509 (vv. 9098-9105).

COLLECTION UNKNOWN (olim Giraud of Lyons), no shelf-mark, fol. not indicated, early XVIc.

Ed.: Giraud and Chevalier, p. 482.

6205.   O creature raisonnable, se tu veulz estre a la semblance de la glorieuse Trinité a l'image de laquelle tu ez formee ...

Exhortation to love of the Trinity, in prose.

METZ, Bibl. mun., 600, fol. 37r°, XVc., Hours of Paris and Prayer-book.

Ref.: Rézeau, pp. 159-60.

6206.   O dame de gloire, o royne des angelz, o royne de joie ...

Variante de l'inc.: O dame de glore, o royne de joie, o fontaine ... (no. 1307).

6207.   O Dieu, benoiste Trinité,
A ta pucelle, a ta meschine ...

Orison to the Trinity by the heroine: Miracles de sainte Geneviève (vv. 248-55).

PARIS, Bibl. Sainte-Geneviève, 1131, fol. 186r°, XVc.

Ed.: Sennewaldt, p. 69.

6208.   O Dieu eternel quant tu commandes que chascun de nous ait soin d'avancer le profit de son prochain ...

"Oraison pour un pere de famille": Manuel de dévotion de prêtre Pierre.

NEW HAVEN, Yale Univ. Libr., 498, fol. 135v°-137r°, last quarter XVIc.

6209.   O Dieu eternel, tout puissant et misericordieux, pere celeste, combien que par nostre vie meschante et tres grandz pechés n'ayons tant seulement merité ...

Oraison pour dire en temps de guerre ou autre persecution: Manuel de dévotion de prêtre Pierre.

NEW HAVEN, Yale Univ. Libr., 498, fol. 133v°-134v°, last quarter XVIc.

6210.   O Dieu le roys, je congnois que je suis indigne de recevoir ce precieux et digne sacrement et n'ai point ...

Prayer before the Communion, in prose.

NEW YORK, Pierpont Morgan Libr., Morgan 261, fol. 23r°, early XVIc., Hours of Rouen.

6211. O Dieus, les gentilz et les nations barbares et infidelles, qui n'ont poinct de foy ne cognoissance de ton nom, sont entrés en ton heritage ...

"Oraison pour l'Eglise affligee des heretiques": Manuel de dévotion de prêtre Pierre.

NEW HAVEN, Yale Univ. Libr., 498, fol. 103r°-106v°, last quarter XVIc.

6212. O Dieu misericordieux et debonnaire, qui selon la multitude de tes misericordes est ..., et pardonnes les pechés des penitens, regardes benignement moy ton serviteur ...

Oraison pour les malades a l'article de la mort: Manuel de dévotion de prêtre Pierre.

NEW HAVEN, Yale Univ. Libr., 498, fol. 114r°-115r°, last quarter XVIc.

6213. O Dieu, octroie nous que non seullement nous adherions a ta parolle et doctrine mais que puissions murrir ...

"Oraison que les enfans soient instruitz en la crainte de Dieu": Manuel de dévotion de prêtre Pierre.

NEW HAVEN, Yale Univ. Libr., 498, fol. 137v°-138r°, last quarter XVIc.

6214. O Dieu, prens moy a mercy par ta grande benignité, et selon la multitude de tes compassions efface mes pechés enormes. Lave moy et me relave ...

Fourth of the Penitential Psalms, prose version: Manuel de dévotion de prêtre Pierre.

NEW HAVEN, Yale Univ. Libr., 498, fol. 50r°-53r°, last quarter XVIc.

6215. O Dieu puyssant, gracieux et misericordieux, tous les citoyens de Paradis te chantent gloire et honneur ...

"Oraison pour acquerir devotion": Manuel de dévotion de prêtre Pierre.

NEW HAVEN, Yale Univ. Libr., 498, fol. 24v°-26v°, last quarter XVIc.

6216. O Dieu, qui es offencé par le peché et apaisé par penitence, nous te prions que tu regardes les prieres de ton peuple ...

"Oraison aprés les litanies": Manuel de dévotion de prêtre Pierre.

NEW HAVEN, Yale Univ. Libr., 498, fol. 63r°, last quarter XVIc.

6217.   O Dieu, recteur du ciel et de la terre, qui regnes
eternellement et seul domines sur toutes choses a la volonté
...

"Oraison pour estre justifié de Dieu": Manuel de dévotion de
prêtre Pierre.

NEW HAVEN, Yale Univ. Libr., 498, fol. 108vº-111rº, last
quarter XVIc.

6218.   O Dieu, roy souverain, voicy mon ame bien deliberee a ce coup
de se presenter a ton celeste banquet ...

"Priere pour le poinct de la Communion": Manuel de dévotion de
prêtre Pierre.

NEW HAVEN, Yale Univ. Libr., 498, fol. 76rº-77vº, last quarter
XVIc.

6219.   O Dieu, soiez propice a moy, pauvre pecheur, a l'heure derniere
de ma vie, ainsi qu'en celle presente, Seigneur, je remets en
voz mains ...

"Au son de la cloche quand l'heure frappe."

CHICAGO, Newberry Libr., 43, fol. 162vº, XVIc., Hours of Rouen.

6220.   O Dieu tout puyssant et eternel createur de toutes choses,
empereur des anges, roy des roys et seigneur des seigneurs
...

"Oraison pour le roy tres chrestien": Manuel de dévotion de
prêtre Pierre.

NEW HAVEN, Yale Univ. Libr., 498, fol. 129vº-130vº, last
quarter XVIc.

6221.   O Dieu tout puissant et eternel, fontaine de tous biens, je
remerchie vostre clemence de ce qu'indigne, vous m'avez
conservé ceste nuict ...

"Aprés que vous serez levé, continuez a prier en ceste
maniere."

CHICAGO, Newberry Libr., 43, fol. 160rº-160vº, XVIc., Hours of
Rouen.

6222.   O Dieu tout puyssant et eternel, je, pouvre homme, sujet a
peché, renouvelle aujourd'uy l'aliance ...

"Oraison avec la confession de la foy chrestienne": Manuel de
dévotion de prêtre Pierre.

NEW HAVEN, Yale Univ. Libr., 498, fol. 85vº-87vº, last quarter
XVIc.

6223.   O Dieu tout puyssant et eternel, je te rends graces de ce qu'il
t'a pleu me preserver aujourd'huy de mal ...

"Oraison quant on va dormir": Manuel de dévotion de prêtre Pierre.

NEW HAVEN, Yale Univ. Libr., 498, fol. 27r°, last quarter XVIc.

6224. O Dieu tout puissant et pardurable qui eliz les choses malades du monde affin que toutes les fortes ...

Orison to God, in prose.

PARIS, Bibl. nat., fr. 13167, fol. 136r°-136v°, late XVc., Hours of Paris.

6225. O Dieu tres clement, je te prie, donne moy vraye contrition de coeur et une fontaine de larmes a ce que je puisse incessement plourer ...

"Autre confession de pechez": Manuel de dévotion de prêtre Pierre.

NEW HAVEN, Yale Univ. Libr., 498, fol. 69r°-70r°, last quarter XVIc.

6226. O douce dame glorieuse ...

Variant inc. for no. 478: Douce dame tres gloriouse ...

6227. O doulce manne du ciel, o plaisante gloire, embrase et enflamme en moy ta grace et la saincte charité ...

"Oraison du sainct Sacrement".

NEW YORK, Pierpont Morgan Libr., Morgan 78, fol. 11r°-11v°, XVc., Hours of Rome.

6228. O doulx Jesucrist, redempteur de l'humain lignaige, qui es l'espoux des ames ...

"Oraison de saincte Katherine de Siene/Que Jesucrist ayma d'amour entiere et seine", in prose.

PARIS, Bibl. Ecole Nat. Sup. des Beaux-Arts, Masson, impr. 29, fol. F5v°-F6r°, XVIc.

PARIS, Bibl. Ecole Nat. Sup. des Beaux-Arts, Masson, impr. 351, fol. M4v°, XVIc.

PARIS, Bibl. nat., fr. 19243, fol. 191r°-194v°, XVIc.

Ref.: Rézeau, Saints, II, p. 154.

6229. O doulz Jhesu, per nulle voie
Rienz ne trueve ou que si bien voie ...

Prologue of 20 vv. to a Meditation on the Passion with inc.: Comme il soit vray, si comme on di ... (no. 5556).

METZ, Bibl. mun., 600, fol. 177r°, XVc., Hours of Paris and Prayer-book.

Ref.: Rézeau, p. 178.

6230. O doulz Jhesus, vray espoux de virginité et loyal ami de chasteté, doulz Jhesus sans malice, sans ire ...

Concluding prayer of the Sermon Poenitemini: De la chasteté conjugale, by Gerson. Although the opening words are identical with those of no. 998, the remainder of the text is not.

PARIS, Bibl. nat., fr. 24840, fol. 87r°-87v°, XVc.

PARIS, Bibl. nat., fr. 24842, fol. 36r°, XVc.

Ed.: Glorieux, Gerson: Oeuvres complètes, VII, 2, p. 868.

6231. O doulx Messÿas debonnaire,
En qui est nostre seul recours,
Approuche et viens si nous secours
Temps est que ta promesse tiennes ...

Ezechiel's prayer to God: Mystère de la Passion by Arnoul Gréban (vv. 1978-97).

CHANTILLY, Musée Condé, 614 (1691), fol. 6v°-7r°, XVc.

LE MANS, Bibl. mun., 6, fol. 7r°-7v°, XVc.

PARIS, Bibl. de l'Arsenal, 6431, fol. 3r°-3v°, XVc.

PARIS, Bibl. nat., fr. 815, fol. 16r°-16v°, 1458.

PARIS, Bibl. nat., fr. 816, fol. 16r°, 1473.

PARIS, Bibl. nat., fr. 1550, fol. 39v°, XVIc.

PARIS, Bibl. nat., fr. 15064, fol. 35v°-36r°, 1469.

ROME, Accademia Nazionale dei Lincei, Bibl. Corsiniana, Rossi 412 (44. A. 7), fol. 4v°, late XVc.

Ed.: Paris-Raynaud, p. 28 (vv. 1994-2013); Jodogne, p. 36 (vv. 1978-97).

6232. O doulx pere de misericorde, qui es le redempteur du monde ...

"Oraison de la glorieuse abbesse/Saincte Gertrud plain d'humblesse", in prose.

PARIS, Bibl. Ecole Nat. Sup. des Beaux-Arts, Masson, impr. 29, fol. F6v°-F7r°, XVIc.

PARIS, Bibl. nat., fr. 19243, fol. 192r°-192v°, XVIc.

Ref.: Rézeau, Saints, II, p. 248.

6233. O doulx redempteur Jesuchrist, facteur et createur du ciel et de la terre ...

Suffrage to S. Claire, in prose.

PARIS, Bibl. Ecole Nat. Sup. des Beaux-Arts, Masson, impr. 29, fol. F4v°-F5r°, XVIc.

PARIS, Bibl. nat., fr. 19243, fol. 190v°-191r°, XVIc.

PARIS, Private Collection, LF 13, fol. 181r°-181v°, XVIc., Prayer-book.

Ref.: Rézeau, Saints, II, p. 171.

6234. O excellent chevalier de Dieu, monseigneur sainct Sebastien ...

Suffrage to S. Sebastian, in prose.

PARIS, Bibl. Ecole Nat. Sup. des Beaux-Arts, Masson, impr. 29, fol. B5v°-B6r°, XVIc.

PARIS, Bibl. Ecole Nat. Sup. des Beaux-Arts, Masson, impr. 351, fol. M2r°, XVIc.

PARIS, Bibl. nat., fr. 19243, fol. 168v°-169r°, XVIc.

Ref.: Rézeau, Saints, II, p. 448.

6235. O Felicien angellicque,
       En martiremant paciffique ...

Orison to S. Felicien: Mystère des Trois Doms, by chanoine Siboud Pra de Grenoble with assistance from Claude Chevalet de Vienne, and performed at Romans in 1509 (vv. 11238-49).

COLLECTION UNKNOWN (olim Giraud of Lyons), no shelf-mark, fol. not indicated, early XVIc.

Ed.: Giraud and Chevalier, pp. 588-9.

6236. O fontaine de vie, Sire Dieu tout puissant, je suy la povre, lassee, dechassee et traveillee qui a l'exemple du cerf ...

"Oroison sus ce mot Sicut cervus etc.", in the Mendicité spirituelle by Jean Gerson.

BRUSSELS, Bibl. royale, IV. 111, fol. 210r°-210v°, XVc.

LYON, Bibl. de la Ville, 1249 (1121), fol. 33r°, XVc.

PARIS, Bibl. de l'Arsenal, 2113, fol. 74r°-74v°, XVc.

PARIS, Bibl. de l'Arsenal, 2121, fol. 21v°, XVc.

VIENNA, Oesterreichische Nationalbibl., 2574, fol. 240r°, XVc.

Screening of mss. is incomplete.

Ed.: Glorieux, Gerson: Oeuvres complètes, VII, 1, p. 245.

*   O glorieuse ...

Sometimes scribes omitted 'O', so it is necessary to consult also the alphabetical order: Glorieuse ...

6237.   O glorieuse amye de Dieu, ma dame saincte Marthe, qui au preterit temps ...

Prayer to S. Martha, in prose.

PARIS, Bibl. Ecole Nat. Sup. des Beaux-Arts, Masson, impr. 29, fol. E2v°-E3r°, XVIc.

PARIS, Bibl. nat., fr. 19243, fol. 183r°-183v°, XVIc.

Ref.: Rézeau, Saints, II, pp. 359-60.

6238.   O glorieuse amye de Dieu, saincte Marie Egyptienne, qui par l'espace ...

Prayer to s. Mary the Egyptian, in prose.

PARIS, Bibl. Ecole Nat. Sup. des Beaux-Arts, Masson, impr. 29, fol. F3v°-F4r°, XVIc.

PARIS, Bibl. nat., fr. 19243, fol. 190r°-190v°, XVIc.

Ref.: Rézeau, Saints, II, p. 336.

6239.   O glorieuse de Dieu mere
        Tousjours virge, sainte Marie,
        Qui deservis porter ton pere
        Signeur de toute no lignie ...

"O gloriosa dei genitrix virgo", in rhyme; part of the "Heures de Nostre Dame."

LILLE, Bibl. mun., Godefroy 5 (147), fol. 52v°-53r°, XVc., Hours.

6240.   O glorieuse espouse du benoit Jesuchrist, ma damme saincte Agnes, qui par le commandement ...

"Oraison de sainte Agnes vierge et martire/Qui du tres cruel tyrant ne douta oncques l'yre" or "De saincte Agnes anthienne"; in prose.

PARIS, Bibl. Ecole Nat. Sup. des Beaux-Arts, Masson, impr. 29, fol. E4v°-E5r°, XVIc.

PARIS, Bibl. Ecole Nat. Sup. des Beaux-Arts, Masson, impr. 351, fol. M4v°, c. 1527, Heures de Rome.

PARIS, Bibl. nat., fr. 19243, fol. 184v°-185r°, XVIc., Hours.

PARIS, Bibl. nat., Rés. p. Ye. 433, fol. A8r°, XVIc.

PARIS, Private Collection, LF 13, fol. 179r°-180r°, XVIc., Prayer-book.

Ref.: Rézeau, Saints, II, p. 5.

6241. O glorieuse Magdalaine,
Priez pour nous, gens de Verneil ...

Prayer to S. Mary Magdalene; 12 lines in rondeau structure.

PARIS, Bibl. nat., lat. 3335, fol. 1r°, added late XVc.

Ed.: Rézeau, Saints, II, p. 339.

6242. O glorieuse mere de Dieu, nous te requerons de ton ayde et secours; ne desprise noz oraisons, nos necessités ...

"Oraison a la Vierge Marie": Manuel de dévotion de prêtre Pierre.

NEW HAVEN, Yale Univ. Libr., 498, fol. 91v°-92r°, last quarter XVIc.

6243. O glorieuse pure vierge pucelle, fille et mere du redempteur et sauveur de tout le monde; O excellente dame, princesse, royne et domination de tout le monde ...

Prayer to the Virgin, in prose.

NEW YORK, Pierpont Morgan Libr., Morgan 292, fol. 33r°-34r°, early XVIc., Prayer-book.

6244. O glorieuse qui fais ta residence,
Residammant en paradis benigne ...

Prayer by Severin to the Virgin: Mystère des Trois Doms, by chanoine Siboud Pra de Grenoble with the aid of Claude Chevalet de Vienne, and performed at Romans in 1509 (vv. 8936-43).

COLLECTION UNKNOWN (olim Giraud of Lyons), no shelf-mark, no fol. indicated, early XVIc.

Ed.: Giraud and Chevalier, p. 473.

6245. O glorieuse qui le peché deffaict,
De fet a toy mon vouloyr se pourmeyne ...

Orison by Severin to Nostre Dame: Mystère des Trois Doms, by chanoine Siboud Pra de Grenoble with the help of Claude Chevalet de Vienne, and performed at Romans in 1509 (vv. 9070-7).

COLLECTION UNKNOWN (olim Giraud of Lyons), no shelf-mark, fol. not indicated, early XVIc.

Ed.: Giraud and Chevalier, pp. 480-1.

6246. O glorieuse Trinité,
Une essence en vraie unité,

En trois singulieres personnes
O glorieuse deïté ...

Variants of v. 2 are
  (i) Une essence en une unité
 (ii) Une essence en vraie bonté
(iii) Uns seulz Dieux en vraie unité

"Les sept articles de la foi", par Jean Chapuis; other titles
  occurring in the mss. are "Les vij articles de la foy
  catholique que maistre Jehan de Meun compila au lit de la
  mort", "Le tresor maistre Jehan de Meun", "Le premier
  codicile maistre Jehan de Mehun", "Le grant codicile maistre
  Jehan de Meung". The totally unscientific Méon ed. offers 135
  twelve-line stanzas, rhyming aabaab, bbabba.

ARRAS, Bibl. mun., 532 (845), fol. 66r°-73r°, XIVc.

BESANCON, Bibl. mun., 553, fol. 158r°-163v°, late XIVc.

BRUSSELS, Bibl. royale, 10394-414, fol. 105r°-110r°, XVc.

BRUSSELS, Bibl. royale, 11000-3, fol. 222r°-233v°, XVc..

BRUSSELS, Bibl. royale, 11244-51, fol. 85r°-97r°, XVc.

BRUSSELS, Bibl. royale, IV. 601, fol. 136r°-150v°, c. 1390.

CAMBRAI, Bibl. mun., 403 (379), fol. 79r°-112r°, XVc.

CARPENTRAS, Bibl. mun., 408 (L. 404), fol. 3r°-29v°, XVc. This
  copy lacks first four strophes.

CHANTILLY, Musée Condé, 485 (570), fol. 97r°-107r°, XIVc.

CHANTILLY, Musée Condé, 486 (1479), fol. 1r°-36v°, XVc.

CHICAGO, Art Institute of Chicago, 1957.162, one detached
  folio, c 1470. The fragment begins: Donc est droiz que nous
  doions dire ... and breaks off: Car mort de toute part le
  lance.

CHICAGO, Newberry Libr., 28, fol. 32r°-43v°, XIVc.

COPENHAGEN, Kongel. Bibl., Ny kgl. Saml., 124 in 8°, fol.
  1r°-35r°, XVc.

DUBLIN, Chester Beatty Libr., West. 82, fol. 321r°-364r°, XVc.
  Hours of Paris, owned once by Prigent de Coëtivy.

FALAISE, Bibl. mun., 37, pp. 318-41, 1423. Ms. destroyed in
  World War II.

HEIDELBERG, Heidelberg Univ. Libr., Pal. Germ. 354, fol.
  49r°-50v°, XVc. Copy is a fragment commencing in Méon's
  stanza 113.

LENINGRAD, Publichnaya Bibl., Fr. Q. v. XIV. 2, fol. 30r°-40v°,
  XVc.

LENINGRAD, Publishnaya Bibl., Fr. Q. v. XIV. 8, fol. 1r°-25v°, XVc.

LONDON, British Libr., Egerton 940, fol. 3r°-41r°, XVc.

LONDON, British Libr., Harley 3999, fol. 1r°-24r°, XVc.

LONDON, British Libr., Landsdowne 214, fol. 196r°-200r°, XVc.

LONDON, British Libr., Royal 19. A. XXII, fol. 1r°-31v°, XVc.

LONDON, British Libr., Royal 19. B. XII, fol. 181r°-194r°, XVc.

LONDON, British Libr., Royal 19. C. XI, fol. 79r°-89r°, early XVc.

MADRID, Bibl. nac., Res. 4a, 14, fol. 185r°-196r°, XIVc.

NEW HAVEN, Yale Univ. Libr., 406, fol. 135v°-141v°, XIVc.

PARIS, Bibl. de l'Arsenal, 2680, fol. 162v°-168r°, XVc.

PARIS, Bibl. de l'Arsenal, 3339, fol. 187r°-193r°, XVc.

PARIS, Bibl. Mazarine, 3872, fol. 185r°-189v°, late XIVc.

PARIS, Bibl. nat., fr. 380, fol. 154r°-159v°, XIVc.

PARIS, Bibl. nat., fr. 576, fol. 83r°-93r°, 1383.

PARIS, Bibl. nat., fr. 804, fol. 153r°-164r°, XVc.

PARIS, Bibl. nat., fr. 806, fol. 166r°-172v°, XVc.

PARIS, Bibl. nat., fr. 808, fol. 38r°-51r°, XVc.

PARIS, Bibl. nat., fr. 1556, fol. 43r°-77v°, XVc.

PARIS, Bibl. nat., fr. 1557, fol. 1r°-12r°, XVc.

PARIS, Bibl. nat., fr. 2197, fol. 73r°-end, XVc. The copy breaks off in stanza 61 of Méon.

PARIS, Bibl. nat., fr. 9345, fol. 62r°-71r°, XVc.

PARIS, Bibl. nat., fr. 12460, fol. 101v°-114r°, XVc.

PARIS, Bibl. nat., fr. 12595, fol. 169r°-200r°, XVc.

PARIS, Bibl. nat., fr. 12596, fol. 206r°-212v°, XVc.

PARIS, Bibl. nat., fr. 22551, fol. 91r°-97r°, 1428.

PARIS, Bibl. nat., fr. 24392, fol. 208r°-214r°, XVc.

PARIS, Bibl. nat., nouv. acq. fr. 10047, fol. 52r°-60v°, XIVc.

PHILADELPHIA, Philadelphia Museum of Art, 45. 65. 3, fol. 180r°-200v°, 1450.

PRIVAS, Archives départementales, I. 4, fol. 150r°-155v°, XVIc.

STOCKHOLM, Kungl. Bibl., Vu 39, fol. 181r°-192r°, XVc.

TURIN, Bibl. naz. univ., L. III. 14, fol. 142r°-147v°, XIVc.
Copy mutilated and lacks the ending.

VATICAN CITY, Bibl. apost., Reg. lat. 1492, fol. 216r°-227r°,
XVc.

VATICAN CITY, Bibl. apost., Reg. lat. 1518, fol. 119v°-133v°,
XVc. Abridged copy.

VATICAN CITY, Bibl. apost., Reg. lat. 1683, fol. 88r°-113v°,
XVc. Ends in stanza 127 of Méon.

VIENNA, Oesterreichische Nationalbibl., 2568, fol. 191r°-203r°,
c. 1420.

Screening of the mss. is incomplete.

Ed.: D.M. Méon, Le Roman de la Rose, Paris, 1813-1814, III, pp.
331-95. Ref.: Keller, p. 322; Naetebus, XXXVI, 12; E.
Langlois, Manuscrits français de Rome, 1889, pp. 183-4,
216-17; Delisle, BEC, 61 (1900), pp. 188-9; Omont, BEC, 64
(1903), p. 228; M. Schiff, Bibliothèque du marquis de
Santillane, Paris, 1905, p. 369; E. Langlois, Manuscrits du
Roman de la Rose, Paris, 1911, passim; A. Långfors, Roman de
Fauvel, Paris, 1914-1919, pp. xvii-xviii; K. Christ,
Altfranzösischen Handschriften der Palatina, Leipzig, 1916,
p. 113; Långfors, Romania, 45 (1918-1919), p. 63; W.
Söderhjelm, in Bok och Biblioteks-historiske Studier
tillägnade Isak Collijn, Uppsala, 1925, pp. 78-9; Sismarev,
pp. 186-88; Långfors, Notices et extraits, XLII (1933), pp.
171-2; Wahlgren, Studier i modern Språkvetenskap, 12 (1934),
p. 101; Laborde, pp. 116-17; Brayer, Manuscrits français de
Leningrad, p. 28; Borodina and Mal'kevic, p. 112.

6247. O glorieuse vierge et espouse de Dieu, ma dame saincte Agathe,
qui pour la foy ...

Prayer to S. Agatha, in prose.

PARIS, Bibl. de l'Arsenal, 8° T. 2560, fol. v8r°-xlr° (Lacombe
498).

PARIS, Bibl. Ecole Nat. Sup. des Beaux-Arts, Masson, impr. 29,
fol. F1, XVIc.

PARIS, Bibl. Ecole Nat. Sup. des Beaux-Arts, Masson, impr.
1012, fol. V8v°-Xlr°, XVIc.

PARIS, Bibl. nat., fr. 19243, fol. 187v°-188r°, XVIc.

PARIS, Private Collection, LF 13, fol. 180r°-181r°, XVIc.,
Prayer-book.

Ref.: Rézeau, Saints, II, p. 5.

6248.   O glorieuse vierge, ma dame saincte Geneviefve, qui des ton
        jeune aage fuz par le benoist sainct ...

        Prayer to S. Geneviève, in prose.

        PARIS, Bibl. Ecole Nat. Sup. des Beaux-Arts, Masson, impr. 29,
        fol. F2v°-F3r°, XVIc.

        PARIS, Bibl. Ecole Nat. Sup. des Beaux-Arts, Masson, impr. 351,
        fol. M4, XVIc.

        PARIS, Bibl. nat., fr. 19243, fol. 189r°-189v°, XVIc.

        Ref.: Rézeau, Saints, II, p. 232, who also mentions early
        imprints at the Arsenal Library.

6249.   O glorieuse vierge Marie, mere de Jhesucrist, je vous prie
        merchi ...

        Variant inc. of no. 678: Glorieuse vierge Marie ...

*   O glorieux ...

        Sometimes scribes omitted 'O', so it is necessary to consult
        also the alphabetical order: Glorieux ...

6250.   O glorieulx, a toy retire
        Le pouvre doulant qui trespasse ...

        Orison to God by Felicien just before decapitation: Mystère des
        Trois Doms, by chanoine Siboud Pra de Grenoble with the aid
        of Claude Chevalet de Vienne, and performed at Romans in 1509
        (vv. 9314-23).

        COLLECTION UNKNOWN (olim Giraud of Lyons), no shelf-mark, fol.
        not indicated, early XVIc.

        Ed.: Giraud and Chevalier, pp. 496-7.

6251.   O glorieux amy de Dieu, monseigneur saint Gregoire, qui par la
        grant humilité de charité ...

        Prayer to S. Gregory the Great, in prose.

        PARIS, Bibl. Ecole Nat. Sup. des Beaux-Arts, Masson, impr. 29,
        fol. D1v°-D2r°, XVIc.

        PARIS, Bibl. nat., fr. 19243, fol. 177v°-178r°, XVIc.

        Ref.: Rézeau, Saints, II, p. 253.

6252.   O glorieux augmentateur de la foy catholique, monseigneur saint
        Jherosme ...

        "Oraison du glorieux sainct Jherosme/Qui en sa vie fit maint
        cantique et pseaulme", in prose.

        PARIS, Bibl. de l'Arsenal, 8° T. 2560, fol. V7r°-v°, XVIc.

PARIS, Bibl. Ecole Nat. Sup. des Beaux-Arts, Masson, impr. 29, fol. C3v°-C4r°, XVIc.

PARIS, Bibl. Ecole Nat. Sup. des Beaux-Arts, Masson, impr. 351, fol. M2r°, XVIc.

PARIS, Bibl. Ecole Nat. Sup. des Beaux-Arts, Masson, impr. 1012, fol. V7r°-v°, XVIc.

PARIS, Bibl. nat., fr. 19243, fol. 173r°-173v°, XVIc.

Ref.: Rézeau, Saints, II, p. 295.

6253. O glorieux chevalier et amy de Dieu, monseigneur saint Eustache, qui tant de tribulations souffris ...

"Oraison a monseigneur sainct Eustache/Qui en luy n'eut oncques villaine tasche", in prose.

PARIS, Bibl. Ecole Nat. Sup. des Beaux-Arts, Masson, impr. 29, fol. C1v°-C2r°, XVIc.

PARIS, Bibl. nat., fr. 19243, fol. 171v°-172r°, XVIc.

Ref.: Rézeau, Saints, II, p. 209.

6254. O glorieux martyr et amy de Dieu, monseigneur sainct Adrien, qui voyant plusieurs crestiens ...

"Oraison du benoist sainct Adrien/qui Dieu ayma sur toute rien", en prose.

PARIS, Bibl. Ecole Nat. Sup. des Beaux-Arts, Masson, impr. 29, fol. B6v°-B7r°, XVIc.

PARIS, Bibl. nat., fr. 19243, fol. 169r°-169v°, XVIc., Hours.

Ref.: Rézeau, Saints, II, p. 1.

6255. O glorieulx pere et confesseur, monseigneur saint Martin, je te prie et requiers ...

Orison to S. Martin, in prose.

PARIS, Bibl. Ecole Nat. Sup. des Beaux-Arts, Masson, impr. 29, fol. C8v°, XVIc.

PARIS, Bibl. nat., fr. 19243, fol. 177r°-177v°, XVIc.

Ref.: Rézeau, Saints, II, p. 372.

6256. O glorieulx precurseur martir ...

Variant of: O glorieulx cursur martir ... (no. 1375).

6257. O glorieux qui volus estre homme,
Coeternel qui creas tout le monde ...

Orison to Jesus by Severin: Mystère des Trois Doms, by chanoine Siboud Pra de Grenoble with the assistance of Claude Chevalet de Vienne, and performed at Romans in 1509 (vv. 7513-20).

COLLECTION UNKNOWN (olim Giraud of Lyons), no shelf-mark, fol. not indicated, early XVIc.

Ed.: Giraud and Chevalier, p. 407.

6258. O glorieux roy de droicture,
       Formateur de toute creature ...

Prayer to God by a tortured Christian: Mystère des Trois Doms, by chanoine Siboud Pra de Grenoble with the aid of Claude Chevalet de Vienne, and performed at Romans in 1509 (vv. 3430-5).

COLLECTION UNKNOWN (olim Giraud of Lyons), no shelf-mark, fol. not indicated, early XVIc.

Ed.: Giraud and Chevalier, p. 186.

6259. O glorieulx sains ou sainte, N., j'é heu fiance en vous en ma vie; ne me faillés pas a ce dernier besoing ...

Prayer to a saint: Medecine de l'ame, alias Science de bien mourir, by Gerson.

BRUSSELS, Bibl. royale, 10394-414, fol. 123r°, XVc.

HAGUE (THE), Koninkl. Bibl., 78. J. 49, fol. 477r°, XVc. Inc.: Glorieux saint ou saincte, N., j'ay eu ...

LONDON, British Libr., Additional 29279, fol. 48v°, XVc.

LONDON, British Libr., Harley 1310, fol. 87v°, XVc.

LYON, Bibl. de la Ville, 1249 (1121), fol. 49v°, XVc.

PARIS, Bibl. Mazarine, 966, fol. 121v°, XVc.

ROUBAIX, Archives Municipales, no shelf-mark, fol. 78v°, XVc., Prayer-book of Jacques de Luxembourg.

VIENNA, Oesterreichische Nationalbibl., 3391, fol. 436r°, XVc.

Screening of mss. is incomplete.

Ed.: Glorieux, Gerson: Oeuvres complètes, VII, 1, p. 406.

6260. O glorieux sainct Hubert d'Ardenne,
       Qui de Dieu es le loyer tel ...

Prayer to S. Hubert; fourteen octosyllabic lines, abab.

EVREUX, Bibl. mun., 121, one printed fol. pasted inside cover.

PARIS, Musée nat. des Thermes et de l'Hotel de Cluny, 1850 (inv. 1247), a printed prelim. fol. 2v°, XVIc.

Ed.: Rézeau, Saints, II, pp. 265-66.

6261. O haulte nativité,
        O tres noble enfant ...

Rondeau to the Child Jesus: Mystère de la Passion by Arnoul Gréban (vv. 5607-19 of the Paris-Raynaud ed.). The piece is also termed a fatras.

PARIS, Bibl. nat., fr. 816, fol. 39r°, 1473.

Ed.: Paris-Raynaud, p. 72 (vv. 5607-19); L.C. Porter, La Fatrasie et le fatras, Geneva, 1960, p. 167; the lines are not included in the text published by Jodogne.

6262. O je, malavisee, nice et maleureuse, par quel oultrage m'ose je souvent esloingner de la bonne deffense de mon pere ...

Orison to Jesus and the Virgin, part of the Mendicité spirituelle by Jean Gerson.

BRUSSELS, Bibl. royale, IV. 111, fol. 217v°-218r°, XVc.

LYON, Bibl. de la Ville, 1249 (1121), fol. 41v°, XVc.

PARIS, Bibl. de l'Arsenal, 2113, fol. 97r°-97v°, XVc.

PARIS, Bibl. de l'Arsenal, 2121, fol. 38v°-39r°, XVc.

VIENNA, Oesterreichische Nationalbibl., 2574, fol. 250v°, XVc.

Screening of mss. is incomplete.

Ed.: Glorieux, Gerson: Oeuvres complètes, VII, 1, p. 262.

6263. O Jhesucrist, abisme de tres parfonde misericorde, je te prie par le merite de la profondité ...

Eleventh orison of S. Bridget; not identical with no. 1388.

PARIS, Bibl. nat., lat. 1393, fol. 140v°-141v°, XVc., Hours of Paris.

6264. O Jhesucrist, fontaine de charité qui jamais ne tarit, qui par affection piteable ...

Seventh prayer of S. Bridget.

PARIS, Bibl. nat., lat. 1393, fol. 138r°-138v°, XVc., Hours of Paris.

6265. O Jhesucrist, lyon tres fort, roy immortel et invicible (sic), aies memoire de la douleur ...

Thirteenth orison of S. Bridget; not identical with no. 1402.

PARIS, Bibl. nat., lat. 1393, fol. 142r°-143r°, XVc., Hours of Paris.

6266.   O Jhesucrist, m<e>decin celestiel, je te prie, aies memoire des grans douleurs ...

Fourth prayer of S. Bridget.

PARIS, Bibl. nat., lat. 1393, fol. 134v°-136r°, XVc., Hours of Paris.

6267.   O Jhesucrist, mirouer de clarté pardurable, aies memoire de la clarté que tu euz ...

Fifth orison of S. Bridget; not the same as no. 1403.

PARIS, Bibl. nat., lat. 1393, fol. 136r°-137r°, XVc., Hours of Paris.

6268.   O Jhesucrist, mirouer de verité, signe d'union et d'amour et lien de charité ...

Twelfth prayer of S. Bridget; not the same as no. 1404.

PARIS, Bibl. nat., lat. 1393, fol. 141v°-142r°, XVc., Hours of Paris.

6269.   O Jhesucrist qui es eternel sans commancement et sans fin, aies memoire ...

Tenth Orison of S. Bridget.

PARIS, Bibl. nat., lat. 1393, fol. 139v°-140v°, XVc., Hours of Paris.

6270.   O Jhesucrist, qui metz grande doulceur et suavité es cueurs et pensees ...

Eighth Prayer of S. Bridget.

PARIS, Bibl. nat., lat. 1393, fol. 138v°139r°, XVc., Hours of Paris.

6271.   O Jhesucrist, roy des sieclez, je ay a dire a toy parole secrete, l'ouvrage de tes mains, le desir de mon cuer amans ...

Meditation, in prose, attributed by the scribe to S. Augustine.

METZ, Bibl. mun., 600, fol. 62r°-73v°, XVc., Hours of Paris and Prayer-book.

Ref.: Rézeau, p. 165.

6272.   O Jhesucrist, roy tres aimable auquel chascun desire avoir amour entiere ...

Sixth Prayer of S. Bridget.

PARIS, Bibl. nat., lat. 1393, fol. 137r°-138r°, XVc., Hours of Paris.

6273.   O Jhesucrist, saulveur de tout le monde qui es inestimable sans fin ...

Third orison of S. Bridget.

PARIS, Bibl. nat., lat. 1393, fol. 134r°-134v°, XVc., Hours of Paris.

6274.   O Jhesucrist, seul filz et lumiere de Dieu tres hault et puissant, ton pere ...

Fourteenth of the orisons of S. Bridget.

PARIS, Bibl. nat., lat. 1393, fol. 143r°-143v°, XVc., Hours of Paris.

6275.   O Jhesucrist, vertu royale et jubilacion cordiale, aies souvenance et memoire ...

Ninth Prayer of S. Bridget.

PARIS, Bibl. nat., lat. 1393, fol. 139r°-139v°, XVc., Hours of Paris.

6276.   O Jhesucrist, vraie et plaine charité, aies memoire de la grande effusion de sang que tu espandis ...

Last of S. Bridget's fifteen prayers.

PARIS, Bibl. nat., lat. 1393, fol. 144r°-144v°, XVc., Hours of Paris.

6277.   O Jhesucrist, vraye franchise et liberté des anges et paradis de tous delices ...

Second orison of S. Bridget; not identical with no. 1412.

PARIS, Bibl. nat., lat. 1393, fol. 133r°-134r°, XVc., Hours of Paris.

6278.   O Jesus, fontaine de toute suavité, pardonne moy que jusques a present je n'ay soffisament cognneu ton incomprehensible douceur ...

"Oraison a nostre sauveur Jesus Christ": Manuel de dévotion de prêtre Pierre.

NEW HAVEN, Yale Univ. Libr., 498, fol. 41v°-42v°, last quarter XVIc.

6279.   O Jhesus, je te cry mercy ...

Variant of the inc.: O Jhesus, je te prie mercy ... (no. 6279).

6280.   O Jhesus, je te prie mercy
        De tant que je t'ay offensé;

Ne jamais n'avoye penssé
Que tu feusses si haulte chose ...

Prayer to Jesus by Longinus: Mystère de la Passion by Arnoul
   Gréban (vv. 26543-63).

CHANTILLY, Musée Condé, 614 (1691), fol. 224r°, XVc. Inc.: O
   Jhesus, je te cry mercy ...

PARIS, Bibl. de l'Arsenal, 6431, fol. 200r°, XVc.

PARIS, Bibl. nat., fr. 815, fol. 215r°-215v°, 1458.

PARIS, Bibl. nat., fr. 816, fol. 187r°-187v°, 1473. Inc.: O
   Jhesus, je te cry mercy ...

ROME, Accademia Nazionale dei Lincei, Bibl. Corsiniana, Rossi
   412 (44. A. 7), fol. 519v°, late XVc. Inc. O Jhesus, je te
   cry mercy ...

Ed.: Paris-Raynaud, p. 348 (vv. 26685-705); Jodogne, p. 356
   (vv. 26543-63).

6281. O juge tres doutable, je ne me puiz soustenir ne prenre
        contenance. O mon cuer, mon confort, je te prie ...

Orison to God, in prose.

METZ, Bibl. mun., 600, fol. 166v°, XVc., Hours of Paris and
   Prayer-book.

Ref.: Rézeau, p. 176.

6282. O l'excellence de toulx les saintz et benoistz docteurs,
        glorieux amy de Dieu ...

"Oraison du benoist saint Augustin docteur/Qui fut de la foy
   catholicque augmentateur", in prose.

PARIS, Bibl. Ecole Nat. Sup. des Beaux-Arts, Masson, impr. 29,
   fol. D2v°-D3r°, XVIc.

PARIS, Bibl. Ecole Nat. Sup. des Beaux-Arts, Masson, impr. 351,
   fol. M2v°, XVIc.

Ref.: Rézeau, Saints, II, p. 62.

6283. O Magdelainne par celle grant liesse
        Que heux ou temps con estoye pecheresse ...

"Oryson de la Magdelainne"; 15 twelve-line stanzas rhyming
   aabaabbbabba.

MANCHESTER, John Rylands Univ. Libr., Fr. 143, fol. 1r°-4v°,
   early XVc., Hours.

6284. O Marie, de mer estelle,
        Sanz pareille meire novelle ...

Hymn "O Maria stella maris"; 38 vv. arranged as 5 sizains and 2 quatrains.

METZ, Bibl. mun., 600, fol. 169r°-169v°, XVc., Hours of Paris and Prayer-book.

Ref.: Rézeau, p. 177.

6285. O Marie, mere tres piteuse
Par la grande affliction ...

Orison to the Virgin; 12 vv. effaced in places.

MANCHESTER, Chetham's Libr., 27971 (Mun. A. 3. 132), fol. 120v°, XVc., Hours of Coutances. This piece added in XVIc.

6286. O Marie, sainne et entiere,
Vierge du roy David yssant,
Qui de glorieuse lumiere
Tu es dame resplendissant ...

"O quam glorifica luce coruscas" in 24 octosyllables, grouped in 7 quatrains, of which the second and fourth are deficient. The hymn is part of the Heures de Notre Dame.

METZ, Bibl. mun., 600, fol. 34r°-34v°, XVc., Hours of Paris and Prayer-book.

Ref.: Rézeau, p. 159.

6287. O martir saint Sebastien,
De tout mon cueur a toy je vien ...

Prayer to S. Sebastian; 40 vv. rhymed in pairs.

AVIGNON, Bibl. mun., 1904, fol. 83v°-84v°, XVIc., Prayer-book.

Ed.: Rézeau, Saints, II, pp. 486-88.

6288. O mere et fille, Anne et Marie,
Secourés m'ame tres fort mar<r>ie
Pour l'ennemi qui la garie,
De tout mon sens si se varie ...

Orison to Anne and the Virgin; 20 monorhymed quatrains.

MANCHESTER, John Rylands Univ. Libr., Fr. 143, fol. 158v°-160v°, early XVc., Hours.

6289. O misericordieux seigneur Jesus Christ, je te prie par ton effable misericorde que tu espendes en mon ame une simple et vraye foy, ferme esperance ...

"Oraison pour impetrer parfaicte foy, esperance et charité": Manuel de dévotion de prêtre Pierre.

NEW HAVEN, Yale Univ. Libr., 498, fol. 111v°-112v°, last quarter XVIc.

6290.   O mon ame, prie tant humblement, devotement, tant
        affectueusement et tant reveremment ...

        "Une devote meditacion aprez la communion."

        METZ, Bibl. mun., 600, fol. 185r°, XVc., Hours of Paris and
        Prayer-book.

        Ref.: Rézeau, p. 180.

6291.   O mon ame, remembre toy de la tres grant benigneté de ton
        createur, la dilection que il a a toy; son amour ne puet
        souffrir de nul vice ...

        "Autre oroison bonne <de Nostre Seigneur>."

        PARIS, Bibl. nat., fr. 927, fol. 182r°-183r°, XVc.

6292.   O mon benoit Dieu, ja çoit ce que tu cognois le secret de mon
        cueur, et que je ne puis avoir sy petit desyr a toy ...

        "L'exposition tresutille <sur le Credo> pour enflamber la foy
        en Dieu, faicte en forme d'oraison", by Guillaume Farel,
        1524.

        Ed.: Le Pater Noster et le Credo en françoys avec une tresbelle
        et tresutile exposition et declaration sur chascun, Bâle, A.
        Cratander, 1524; Higman, pp. 49-63.

6293.   O mon bon ange, qui es ma defense par la pitié supernelle ...

        Prayer to Guardian Angel, in prose.

        BRUSSELS, Bibl. royale, II, 6334, fol. 40r°-40v°, 1555,
        Prayer-book.

        OXFORD, Keble College, 44, fol. 163v°, XVIc.

        Ed.: Rézeau, Saints, II, pp. 513 and 611.

6294.   O mon bon angele, qui me gardez
        Par la bonté du createur ...

        Prayer to Guardian Angel, 14 vv. some with paired, others with
        alternating rhymes.

        PARIS, Private Collection, LF 13, fol. 56r°-56v°, early XVIc.,
        Prayer-book.

        Ed.: Rézeau, Saints, II, pp. 523-4.

6295.   O mon Dieu, tres amoureux createur et piteux redempteur, moy,
        vostre povre creature et pecheresse ...

        Thanksgiving to God, or Action de grâces.

        STOCKHOLM, Kungl. Bibl., A. 87, pp. 75-85, late XVc.,
        Prayer-book.

6296. O mon saint ange! je te prie que nonobstant ma grande
       ingratitude tu me contregardes a jamais de tous perilz ...

       "Autre oraison au s. ange": Manuel de dévotion de prêtre
       Pierre.

       NEW HAVEN, Yale Univ. Libr., 498, fol. 95v°, last quarter XVIc.

6297. O mon Seigneur, mon Dieu misericordieux par dessus toutes
       choses, me voicy qui maintenant assiste devant toy, plain de
       calamités ...

       "Autre confession de pechés": Manuel de dévotion de prêtre
       Pierre.

       NEW HAVEN, Yale Univ. Libr., 498, fol. 70r°-71r°, last quarter
       XVIc.

6298. O mon tres digne et amoreux seigneur Jhesucrist, O mon tres
       puissant Dieu Jhesus, O tres benigne pasteur Jhesus, O mon
       tres chier et loya<l> espoux ...

       Orison to Jesus in prose.

       BALTIMORE, Walters Art Gallery, Walters 191, fol. 147v°-148v°,
       early XVc., Hours.

6299. O noble glorieux confez,
       Sainct Guillaume ou j'ay esperance ...

       Prayer to S. Guillaume of Bourges; seven huitains, rhyming
       ababbcbc.

       PARIS, Bibl. nat., Rés. D. 5616 and Ye 831, Louenges des
       benoistz sainctz et sainctes de paradis, fol. xxlr°-v°,
       Paris, Vérard.

       VERSAILLES, Bibl. mun., M. 129 (Lacombe 109 quater).

       Ed.: Rézeau, Saints, II, pp. 254-6.

6300. O nostre Dieu, pain celeste, vie de l'univers, j'ay peché au
       ciel et devant toy, et ne suys digne d'estre ...

       "Oraison pour dire avant que aller a la reception du sainct
       Sacrement": Manuel de dévotion de prêtre Pierre.

       NEW HAVEN, Yale Univ. Libr., 498, fol. 77v°-78v°, last quarter
       XVIc.

6301. O omnipotent misericors Dieu, par ta benignité fourclos toutes
       choses contraires affin que d'ame et de corps ...

       "Dimence xvij^e, oraison."

       NEW YORK, Pierpont Morgan Libr., Morgan 78, fol. 53r°, XVc.,
       Hours of Rome. This text added in XVIc.

6302.   O pere celeste, Dieu tout puissant, je te prie et rends graces
        cordiallement, louuenge (<u>sic</u>) eternelle, honneur et gloire
        ...

        Orison after the Communion.

        CHICAGO, Newberry Libr., 43, fol. 159r°-159v°, XVIc., Hours of
        Rouen.

6303.   O Pere tres puyssant qui as tant aymé le monde que tu as livré
        ton filz unique afin que chascun qui croit ...

        "Oblation de Jesus Christ a son Pere": Manuel de dévotion de
        prêtre Pierre.

        NEW HAVEN, Yale Univ. Libr., 498, fol. 40r°-41v°, last quarter
        XVIc.

6304.   O precieuse vierge Marie, en l'heure presente et en toutes noz
        tribulacions, plaise toy nous aider et conforter ...

        Orison to the Virgin, in prose.

        NEW YORK, Pierpont Morgan Libr., Morgan 292, fol. 34r°-34v°,
        early XVIc., Prayer-book.

6305.   O precieux corps sant Loÿs
        Alemant, cardinal de pris ...

        Prayer to S. Louis Aleman; 3 neuvains and one dizain.

        CARPENTRAS, Bibl. mun., 50, fol. 2v°-3r°, XVc., Hours of Rome.

        <u>Ed.</u>: Rézeau, Saints, II, pp. 306-8.

6306.   O que je suys grandement tenu a nostre commun Seigneur et pere
        qui m'a donné a toy afin que toy qui es clairvoyant ...

        "Oraison au s. ange, nostre protecteur": Manuel de dévotion de
        prêtre Pierre.

        NEW HAVEN, Yale Univ. Libr., 498, fol. 94r°-95r°, last quarter
        XVIc.

6307.   O qui est cil qui heurte a mon huys? Que demande il? Que veut
        il? Pour vray, c'est mon Dieu, mon seigneur ...

        "Meditacion de l'ame ...", part of the Mendicité spirituelle by
        Jean Gerson.

        BRUSSELS, Bibl. royale, IV. 111, fol. 224v°-225v°, XVc.

        LYON, Bibl. de la Ville, 1249 (1121), fol. 45v°-47r°, XVc.

        PARIS, Bibl. de l'Arsenal, 2113, fol. 115v°-119v°, XVc.

        PARIS, Bibl. de l'Arsenal, 2121, fol. 54r°-56v°, XVc.

        VIENNA, Oesterreichische Nationalbibl., 2574, fol. 259v°-261r°,
        XVc.

Screening of mss. is incomplete.

<u>Ed</u>.: Glorieux, Gerson: Oeuvres complètes, VII, 1, pp. 277-9.

6308.   O redempteur Jesus, qui non seulement nous as aymés, ains
        desires que nous pour l'honneur qui t'est deu ...

        "Oraison pour dire avant ou pendant le sacrifice de la messe":
        Manuel de dévotion de prêtre Pierre.

        NEW HAVEN, Yale Univ. Libr., 498, fol. 83vº-85vº, last quarter
        XVIc.

6309.   O Redempteur, qui soubstiens l'eslemant,
        Reparateur de l'humayne nature ...

        Orison to Jesus by Exupère under torture: Mystère des Trois
        Doms, by chanoine Siboud Pra de Grenoble with the aid of
        Claude Chevalet de Vienne, and performed at Romans in 1509
        (vv. 9134-9).

        COLLECTION UNKNOWN (olim Giraud of Lyons), no shelf-mark, no
        fol. indicated, early XVIc.

        <u>Ed</u>.: Giraud and Chevalier, p. 485.

6310.   O Roy des cieulx, regnant en Trinité,
        Trine en personne, seullet en unité ...

        Prayer to God and the Virgin by Exupère about to be executed:
        Mystère des Trois Doms, by chanoine Siboud Pra de Grenoble
        with the aid of Claude Chevalet de Vienne, and performed at
        Romans in 1509 (vv. 9174-85).

        COLLECTION UNKNOWN (olim Giraud of Lyons), no shelf-mark, fol.
        not indicated, early XVIc.

        <u>Ed</u>.: Giraud and Chevalier, p. 488.

6311.   O royne de dyvine escense
        Vierge mere d'aulte clemence ...

        Prayer to the Virgin: Mystère des Trois Doms, by chanoine
        Siboud Pra de Grenoble with the aid of Claude Chevalet de
        Vienne, and performed at Romans in 1509 (vv. 10428-39).

        COLLECTION UNKNOWN (olim Giraud of Lyons), no shelf-mark, fol.
        not indicated, early XVIc.

        <u>Ed</u>.: Giraud and Chevalier, pp. 550-1.

6312.   O sacré corps, o saincte hostie
        De Jesus mon sauveur ...

        Orison to the Sacrament; two six-line stanzas, rhyming ababbb;
        copy badly rubbed.

CAMBRIDGE, Harvard College Libr., Typ. 614, fol. 1r°, c. 1500, Hours of Rouen (this prayer added in XVIc. hand).

6313.   O sains anges de paradis,
        Vueilliez moy deffendre et conduire ...

Orison to Angels by the heroine: Miracles de sainte Geneviève (vv. 264-71).

PARIS, Bibl. Sainte-Geneviève, 1131, fol. 186r°, XVc.

Ed.: Sennewaldt, p. 69.

6314.   O saint André tres glorieux,
        Apostre saint, de Dieu amy ...

Oraison a saint André; six eight-line stanzas, rhyming ababbcbc.

PARIS, Bibl. nat., Rés. D. 5616 and Ye 831, Louenges des benoictz sainctz et sainctes de paradis, fol. zz 7, Paris, Vérard.

VERSAILLES, Bibl. mun., M. 129 (Lacombe 109 quater).

Ed.: Rézeau, Saints, II, pp. 10-11.

6315.   O saint Esprit, doulz oste tres clement,
        Benis, decore et garde ton logis ...

"Oraison au saint Esprit", decasyllables rhyming abab.

NEW YORK, New York Public Libr., 39, fol. 83v°, XVc., Hours of Tournai; this prayer added in 16th century.

6316.   O saint Esperit, souverain maistre et docteur de l'ame, viens,
        viens, nous te prions ...

Paraphrase of the Veni sancte spiritus, inserted by Gerson into his Sermon pour la Pentecôte: Accipietis virtutem.

PARIS, Bibl. nat., fr. 974, fol. 1r°, XVc.

PARIS, Bibl. nat., fr. 1029, fol. 1r°, XVc.

Ed.: Glorieux, Gerson: Oeuvres complètes, VII, 2, p. 431.

6317.   O sainct Esprit, viens visiter noz cueurs
        Et imprimer en nous nouvelles meurs
        Viens, remply nous de grace supernelle,
        Fay nous gouster de ta gloire eternelle ...

Hymn "Veni Creator", 7 quatrains of decasyllables, rhyming aabb.

PARIS, Bibl. nat., fr. 2206, fol. 248r°-248v°, XVIc.

Ref.: Rézeau, p. 159.

6318. O saint et beneuré loyer
De nostre actente desiree ...

Rondeau to Jesus: Mystère de la Passion by Arnoul Gréban (vv.
16122-37).

CHANTILLY, Musée Condé, 614 (1691), fol. 136r°, XVc.

PARIS, Bibl. de l'Arsenal, 6431, fol. 114r°-114v°, XVc.

PARIS, Bibl. nat., fr. 815, fol. 129r°-129v°, 1458.

PARIS, Bibl. nat., fr. 816, fol. 112v°, 1473.

PARIS, Bibl. nat., fr. 15065, fol. 128v°, 1469.

ROME, Accademia Nazionale dei Lincei, Bibl. Corsiniana, Rossi
412 (44. A. 7), fol. 313r°, late XVc.

Ed.: Paris-Raynaud, p. 210 (16161-76); Jodogne, p. 214 (vv.
16122-37).

6319. O saint Michel, des chrestiens lumiere,
Resplendissant par tes faiz glorieux ...

Prayer to S. Michael; ballade form composed of three onzains
and a sizain as envoy.

Refr.: Pour secourir ou royaume de France.

PARIS, Bibl. nat., Rés. D. 5616 and Ye 831, Louenges des
benoistz sainctz et sainctes de paradis, fol. zz6v°, Paris,
Vérard.

VERSAILLES, Bibl. mun., M. 129 (Lacombe 109 quater).

Ed.: Rézeau, Saints, II, pp. 543-4.

6320. O saint Piere Celestin,
Tres begnin,
De sainte vie exemplaire ...

Prayer to S. Peter Celestinus; 7 douzains of complex structure.

METZ, Bibl. mun., 571, fol. 205r°, XVc., Prayer-book.

Ed.: Rézeau, Saints, II, pp. 423-6.

6321. O sainct Thibault tres glorieux,
En paradis lassus regnant ...

Prayer to S. Thibaud of Provins; eleven quatrains, rhyming
abab.

VATICAN CITY, Bibl. apost., Reg. lat. 182, fol. 294r°-294v°,
XIV-XVc., Breviary of Saint-Quiriace of Provins. This text
added in XVc.

Ed.: Rézeau, Saints, II, pp. 497-9.

6322. O sainte crois, par ta poissance
       Dont je voy cy la ramenbrance ...

       Orison to the Cross by the first of the Living Men: anon. Dit
       des trois mors et des trois vis (vv. 179-88).

       ARRAS, Bibl. mun., 532 (845), fol. 157v°, XIVc.

       BRUSSELS, Bibl. royale, 10749-50, fol. 32v°, XVc.

       CHANTILLY, Musée Condé, 502 (1920), fol. 24v°, XVc.

       LILLE, Bibl. mun., 364 (139), fol. 12r°, XVc.

       OXFORD, Bodleian Libr., Douce 252, fol. 29r, XVc.

       PARIS, Bibl. nat., fr. 995, fol. 18v°-19r°, XVc.

       PARIS, Bibl. nat., fr. 1555, fol. 219v°-220r°, XIVc.

       Ed.: A. de Montaiglon, l'Alphabet de la mort de Hans Holbein,
       Paris, 1856, ⟨pp. 75-6⟩, (ms. B. N. fr. 995); A. de
       Montaiglon, Recueil de poésies françoises des XVe et XVIe
       siècles, Paris, 1856, V, pp. 64-5 (gothic ed.); M. Caron, in
       Mémoires de l'Académie des sciences, lettres et arts d'Arras,
       30 (1858), pp. 208-9 (Arras ms.); S. Glixelli, Les cinq
       poèmes des trois morts et des trois vifs, Paris, 1914, pp.
       101-2 (base ms. arras; no mention of the Douce codex). Ref.:
       Kathleen Chesney, in Studies ... presented to Mildred K.
       Pope, Manchester, 1939, pp. 69-70 (Douce ms).

6323. O saincte digne vraye croix aoree ...

       Variant of inc. no. 1876.

6324. O saincte et pure vierge Marie, mere de Dieu et mere de Nostre
       Seigneur Jesus Christ, ne prens en male part ...

       "Oraison a tous les saintz": Manuel de dévotion de prêtre
       Pierre.

       NEW HAVEN, Yale Univ. Libr., 498, fol. 96v°-100r°, last quarter
       XVIc.

6325. O saincte Marthe glorieuse,
       Hostesse de Dieu et amie ...

       Prayer to S. Martha; 114 vv.

       AVIGNON, Bibl. mun., 1904, fol. 58r°-60r°, XVIc., Prayer-book.

       Ed.: Rézeau, Saints, II, pp. 368-72.

6326. O saincte Trinité, je te loue de ma bouche, de mon cueur et de
       toute ma puyssence, je te beny et t'adore ...

       First of three prayers to the Trinity: Manuel de dévotion de
       prêtre Pierre.

NEW HAVEN, Yale Univ. Libr., 498, fol. l4r°-l5v°, last quarter
XVIc.

6327. O saincte, vraye, immaculee,
Franche de toute iniquité ...

"Oraison a saincte Opportune"; 65 vv.

PARIS, Bibl. nat., Rés. D. 5616 and Ye 831, Louenges des
benoistz sainctz et sainctes de paradis, fol. zz5v°-zz6r°,
Paris, Vérard.

VERSAILLES, Bibl. mun., M. 129 (Lacombe 109 quater).

Ed.: Rézeau, Saints, II, pp. 411-14.

6328. O sapience <tres> saintime,
Qui vins dou peire tres hautisme,
Attengnant fort de fin a fin
Et faisans toute soueif et fin ...

Orison to God, in rhyme but copied as prose.

NEW YORK, Pierpont Morgan Libr., Morgan 90, fol. 22lr°-223v°,
XIVc., Hours of Verdun.

6329. O Sauveur de tout le monde
Et toy en qui tout bien habunde
Qui par ta grant humilité
Nostre povre humanité ...

"Oroison quant l'en voit le corps Jhesucrist"; 14 lines, aabb.

BALTIMORE, Walters Art Gallery, Walters 261, fol. 12lv°-122r°,
c. 1400, Hours.

6330. O savoureuse royne du firmemant,
Dame de pais, chief de toute droicture ...

Orison to the Virgin by Exupère under torture: Mystère des
Trois Doms, by chanoine Siboud Pra de Grenoble with the aid
of Claude Chevalet de Vienne, and performed at Romans in 1509
(vv. 9150-7).

COLLECTION UNKNOWN (olim Giraud of Lyons), no shelf-mark, fol.
not indicated, early XVIc.

Ed.: Giraud and Chevalier, p. 486.

6331. O Seigneur, ayes semblablement pitié de moy, ton indigne
serviteur selon la multitude de tes misericordes; pardonne
moy mes pechez ...

"Oraison en memoire des saintz": Manuel de dévotion de prêtre
Pierre.

NEW HAVEN, Yale Univ. Libr., 498, fol. 96r°, last quarter XVIc.

6332.   O Seigneur debonnaire, Dieu tout puyssant, je te prie
         humblement que tu vueilles recevoir en gré le service que
         j'ay faict ...

         "Oraison aprés que la messe est achevee": Manuel de dévotion de
         prêtre Pierre.

         NEW HAVEN, Yale Univ. Libr., 498, fol. 89v°-90v°, last quarter
         XVIc.

6333.   O Seigneur des misericordes qui es le plus offencé par moy en
         ceste multitude presque infinie de mes pechés ...

         "Priere avant que aller a confession": Manuel de dévotion de
         prêtre Pierre.

         NEW HAVEN, Yale Univ. Libr., 498, fol. 63r°-65r°, last quarter
         XVIc.

6334.   O seigneur Dieu de nos peres, regarde maintenant le camp des
         Egiptiens quant ilz couroient tous armez aprés tes serviteurs
         ...

         "Oraison pour dire en temps de guerre ou autre persecution":
         Manuel de dévotion de prêtre Pierre.

         NEW HAVEN, Yale Univ. Libr., 498, fol. 130v°-132r°, last
         quarter XVIc.

6335.   O seigneur Dieu eternel qui gouvernes, regis et ordonnes toutes
         choses, je reclame ta bonté paternelle et te requiers que tu
         me vuilles ...

         "Oraison pour acquerir ung estat de vye qui soit agreable a
         Dieu": Manuel de dévotion de prêtre Pierre.

         NEW HAVEN, Yale Univ. Libr., 498, fol. 26v°, last quarter XVIc.

6336.   O Seigneur Dieu, mon redempteur, je souspire aprés toy de
         toutes mes affections; je m'encline totalement ...

         "Autre <oraison> de la passion Nostre Seigneur": Manuel de
         dévotion de prêtre Pierre.

         NEW HAVEN, Yale Univ. Libr., 498, fol. 39r°-39v°, last quarter
         XVIc.

6337.   O seigneur Dieu, pere sainct, de qui la misericorde est grande,
         de qui la misericorde dure tousjours, je te prie, ayes
         souvenance des ames ...

         "Oraison en memoire des trespassés": Manuel de dévotion de
         prêtre Pierre.

         NEW HAVEN, Yale Univ. Libr., 498, fol. 123r°-123v°, last
         quarter XVIc.

6338.   O seigneur Dieu qui entre et par dessus touts les saints as
         merveilleusement esleu tes bienhureux apostres ...

"Oraison a saint Pierre mon patron": Manuel de dévotion de prêtre Pierre.

NEW HAVEN, Yale Univ. Libr., 498, fol. 100r°-100v°, last quarter XVIc.

6339.   O Seigneur eternel qui as la vie et la mort en ta main et devant le trosne redoubtable duquel il nous fault tous comparoistre ...

"Oraison pour les trespassés": Manuel de dévotion de prêtre Pierre.

NEW HAVEN, Yale Univ. Libr., 498, fol. 124r°-124v°, last quarter XVIc.

6340.   O Seigneur eternel, qui es seigneur des mortz et des vivans et fais misericorde a tous ceulx lesquelz tu cognois ...

Oraison pour les vivans et trespassez: Manuel de dévotion de prêtre Pierre.

NEW HAVEN, Yale Univ. Libr., 498, fol. 127v°-128r°, last quarter XVIc.

6341.   O Seigneur, exauce ma priere, entens a ma supplication et par la fidelité et constance laquelle tu tiens en tes promesses ...

Seventh of the Penitential Psalsm, prose version; Manuel de dévotion de prêtre Pierre.

NEW HAVEN, Yale Univ. Libr., 498, fol. 57v°-59v°, last quarter XVIc.

6342.   O Seigneur, fontaine de toute bonté et clemence qui n'as esté contant (sic) d'avoir pourté le fais de nos pechez innumerables ...

"Priere avant que se presenter a la sainte communion": Manuel de dévotion de prêtre Pierre.

NEW HAVEN, Yale Univ. Libr., 498, fol. 71r°-76r°, last quarter XVIc.

6343.   O Seigneur, je me cognois indigne d'estre participant de ton tres pur corps et de ton sang precieux, mais me confiant de tes misericordes ...

Prayer before receiving the Holy Sacrament: Manuel de dévotion de prêtre Pierre.

NEW HAVEN, Yale Univ. Libr., 498, fol. 78v°-79r°, last quarter XVIc.

6344.   O Seigneur Jesus Christ, donne nous que ton precieux sacrement nous soit a la vie eternelle et en la remission de nos pechez ...

Prayer after receiving the Holy Sacrament: Manuel de dévotion de prêtre Pierre.

NEW HAVEN, Yale Univ. Libr., 498, fol. 80r°-82r°, last quarter XVIc.

6345. O seigneur Jesus Christ, filz de Dieu vivant, qui pour la redemption du genre humain as en l'arbre de la croix gousté ...

"Oraison a nostre sauveur Jesus Christ": Manuel de dévotion de prêtre Pierre.

NEW HAVEN, Yale Univ. Libr., 498, fol. 36r°-37v°, last quarter XVIc.

6346. O seigneur Jesus Christ, filz de Dieu vivant, redempteur et sauveur des honmes, je croy et confesse que, vous estant faict honme, vous avez offert ...

"A Jesus Christ redempteur."

CHICAGO, Newberry Libr., 43, fol. 160v°-161r°, XVIc., Hours of Rouen.

6347. O seigneur Jesus Christ, qui es la sapience eternelle de Dieu le pere celeste qui par toy as creé toutes choses ...

"Oraison pour nostre sainct pere le pape": Manuel de dévotion de prêtre Pierre.

NEW HAVEN, Yale Univ. Libr., 498, fol. 128r°-129r°, last quarter XVIc.

6348. O seigneur Jesus Christ, qui, estant obeÿssant a ton pere celeste jusques a la mort, de la croix nous as delivré ...

"Oraison du signe de la croix": Manuel de dévotion de prêtre Pierre.

NEW HAVEN, Yale Univ. Libr., 498, fol. 34r°-35r°, last quarter XVIc.

6349. O Seigneur, ne me reprens point en ta fureur et ne me chastie point en ton yre, car je sens en moy les fleches de ton courroux bien avant assises ...

Third of the Penitential Psalms, prose version: Manuel de dévotion de prêtre Pierre.

NEW HAVEN, Yale Univ. Libr., 498, fol. 47v°-50r°, last quarter XVIc.

6350. O Seigneur, ne me reprens poinct en ta fureur et ne me chastie poinct en ton yre, mais plustost, o Seigneur, aye pitié ...

First of the Penitential Psalms, prose version: Manuel de dévotion de prêtre Pierre.

NEW HAVEN, Yale Univ. Libr., 498, fol. 44v°-45v°, last quarter XVIc.

6351.   O Seigneur, nous te recommandons l'ame de ton serviteur afin que celluy qui est maintenant trespassé de ce monde vive en toy ...

"Recommandation de l'ame trespassee": Manuel de dévotion de prêtre Pierre.

NEW HAVEN, Yale Univ. Libr., 498, fol. 124v°-125v°, last quarter XVIc.

6352.   O Seigneur, pardonne a tous ceulx qui nous hayent et nous traitent outraigeusement; rendz bien a ceux qui nous font du bien ...

"Oraison pour les vivans et trespassez": Manuel de dévotion de prêtre Pierre.

NEW HAVEN, Yale Univ. Libr., 498, fol. 126v°-127v°, last quarter XVIc.

6353.   O Seigneur, previens mes oeuvres par ta benediction et les acompaigne de ta faveur ...

"Oraison pour le commensement de mon oeuvre": Manuel de dévotion de prêtre Pierre.

NEW HAVEN, Yale Univ. Libr., 498, fol. 5v°, last quarter XVIc.

6354.   O Seigneur, remply nostre bouche de ta louange, remply nos levres de ta joye afin que tout au long du jour nous louons ta gloire ...

"Oraison aprés la reception du s. sacrement": Manuel de dévotion de prêtre Pierre.

NEW HAVEN, Yale Univ. Libr., 498, fol. 79v°-80r°, last quarter XVIc.

6355.   O Seigneur, roy tout puyssant, toutes choses sont en ta puyssance et commandement, et n'y a celluy qui puysse resister ...

"Oraison pour dire en temps de guerre ou autre persecution": Manuel de dévotion de prêtre Pierre.

NEW HAVEN, Yale Univ. Libr., 498, fol. 132r°-133v°, last quarter XVIc.

6356.   O Seigneur tout puyssant, de qui toute puyssance et dignité procede, nous te requerons par ceste humble priere ...

"Oraison pour l'empereur": Manuel de dévotion de prêtre Pierre.

NEW HAVEN, Yale Univ. Libr., 498, fol. 129r°-129v°, last quarter XVIc.

6357.   O Seigneur tout puyssant et misericordieux, il m'ennuye fort de
        ceste vie et de ce miserable pelerinage, car ceste vie est
        une vie caduque ...

        Oraison to God on the Sorrows of this Life: Manuel de dévotion
        de prêtre Pierre.

        NEW HAVEN, Yale Univ. Libr., 498, fol. 116r°-118r°, last
        quarter XVIc.

6358.   O Seigneur tres benin, seulle esperance de mon ame, tu es la
        consolation eternelle qui te donnes tant seullement ...

        "Oraison consolatoire, nous exortant ...": Manuel de dévotion
        de prêtre Pierre.

        NEW HAVEN, Yale Univ. Libr., 498, fol. 118r°-120v°, last
        quarter XVIc.

6359.   O sempiternel Dieu, donne nous acroissement de foy, d'esperance
        et de charité et affin que desirons ...

        "Dimence xj^e, oraison."

        NEW YORK, Pierpont Morgan Libr., Morgan 78, fol. 43r°, XVc.,
        Hours of Rome. This text added in XVIc.

6360.   O seul et seigneur souverain ...

        Variant of the inc.: O seul et souverain recours ... (no.
        6361).

6361.   O seul et souverain recours
        A qui seul au besoing recours ...

        Adam give thanks to God: Arnoul Gréban's Mystère de la Passion
        (vv. 23205-10).

        CHANTILLY, Musée Condé, 614 (1691), fol. 197r°, XVc. Inc.: O
        seul et seigneur souverain ...

        PARIS, Bibl. de l'Arsenal, 6431, fol. 173r°, XVc.

        PARIS, Bibl. nat., fr. 815, fol. 187v°, 1458.

        PARIS, Bibl. nat., fr. 816, fol. 163v°, 1473.

        ROME, Accademia Nazionale dei Lincei, Bibl. Corsiniana, Rossi
        412 (44. A. 7), fol. 449r°, late XVc.

        Ed.: Paris-Raynaud, p. 304 (vv. 23242-7); Jodogne, p. 311 (vv.
        23205-10).

6362.   O Severin, ta face benigne,
        Logerey en lieu qui ne fine ...

        Orison to S. Severin: Mystère des Trois Doms, by chanoine
        Siboud Pra de Grenoble with the aid of Claude Chevalet de
        Vienne, and performed at Romans in 1509 (vv. 10440-50).

COLLECTION UNKNOWN (olim Giraud of Lyons), no shelf-mark, fol. not indicated, early XVIc.

Ed.: Giraud and Chevalier, p. 550-1.

6363. O sire Dieu, o vray pere, oyés les voiz de mes adversaires; ne vous eslongés de moy, entendez a mon aide ...

Orison to God, part of the Mendicité spirituelle by Jean Gerson.

BRUSSELS, Bibl. royale, IV. 111, fol. 224r°, XVc.

LYON, Bibl. de la Ville, 1249 (1121), fol. 45r°, XVc. Inc.: Retournez, sire, retournez, car depuis vostre departie ...

PARIS, Bibl. de l'Arsenal, 2113, fol. 114v°-115v°, XVc.

PARIS, Bibl. de l'Arsenal, 2121, fol. 53r°-53v°, XVc.

VIENNA, Oesterreichische Nationalbibl., 2574, fol. 259r°, XVc.

Screening of mss. is incomplete.

Ed.: Glorieux, Gerson: Oeuvres complètes, VII, 1, p. 276.

6364. O sire Dieu, ou gist provision,
N'obliez pas ce povre champion,
Maiz le tirez ou hault mont de Syon
De vous veoir qui est souverain bien ...

Orison to God by Nathalie: Mystère de saint Adrien (vv. 6081-96).

CHANTILLY, Musée Condé, 620 (1603), fol. 121v°, 1485.

Ed.: Picot, p. 117.

6365. O sire Jesucrist, qui es des sainctz splendeur admirable, toute leur joye et leur desir ...

"Oraison du benoist sainct Françoys/Le vray amateur de la croix", in prose.

PARIS, Bibl. Ecole Nat. Sup. des Beaux-Arts, Masson, impr. 29, fol. C7v°-C8r°, XVIc.

PARIS, Bibl. nat., fr. 19243, fol. 176v°-177r°, XVIc.

Ref.: Rézeau, Saints, II, p. 221.

6366. O Sire, laisse desormais
Ton servant reposer en paix ...

Canticle of Simeon: Arnoul Gréban's Mystère de la Passion (vv. 7006-22).

CHANTILLY, Musée Condé, 614 (1691), fol. 49v°, XVc.

LE MANS, Bibl. mun., 6, fol. 80r°, XVc.

PARIS, Bibl. de l'Arsenal, 6431, fol. 42v°, XVc.

PARIS, Bibl. nat., fr. 815, fol. 55v°, 1458.

PARIS, Bibl. nat., fr. 816, fol. 49r°, 1473.

PARIS, Bibl. nat., fr. 1550, fol. 151v°-152r°, XVIc.

PARIS, Bibl. nat., fr. 15064, fol. 132r°-132v°, 1469.

PARIS, Bibl. nat., nouv. acq. fr. 14043, fol. 10r°, XVc.

ROME, Accademia Nazionale dei Lincei, Bibl. Corsiniana, Rossi 412 (44. A. 7), fol. 115r°, late XVc.

Ed.: Paris-Raynaud, pp. 90-1 (vv. 7044-60); Jodogne, p. 96 (vv. 7006-22).

6367. O souverain maistre Jhesucrist, Nostre Seigneur et protecteur singulier, comment et pour quoy nous laissez vous ...

"Humble priere et piteuse complainte" by apostles, part of the Sermon pour la Pentecôte: Accipietis virtutem by Jean Gerson.

PARIS, Bibl. nat., fr. 974, fol. 1v°-2r°, XVc.

PARIS, Bibl. nat., fr. 1029, fol. 1v°-2r°, XVc.

Ed.: Glorieux, Gerson: Oeuvres complètes, VII, 2, p. 432.

6368. O souverain, qui de moy pris naissance,
De tes servans veullies avoir memoire ...

Prayer to God by Nostre Dame: Mystère des Trois Doms, by chanoine Siboud Pra de Grenoble with the assistance of Claude Chevalet de Vienne, and performed at Romans in 1509 (vv. 5966-73).

COLLECTION UNKNOWN (olim Giraud of Lyons), no shelf-mark, fol. not indicated, early XVIc.

Ed.: Giraud and Chevalier, p. 321.

6369. O souvereyne royne de joye,
Joyeusemant a toy envoye ...

Prayer to the Virgin by a tortured Christian: Mystère des Trois Doms, by chanoine Siboud Pra de Grenoble with the assistance of Claude Chevalet de Vienne, and performed at Romans in 1509 (vv. 3440-5).

COLLECTION UNKNOWN (olim Giraud of Lyons, no shelf-mark, fol. not indicated, early XVIc.

Ed.: Giraud and Chevalier, p. 186.

6370. O tres benyn seigneur Jesus Christ, qui avec si precieux gaige as abondamment satisfaict ...

"Oraison devant l'ymaige du crucifix": Manuel de dévotion de prêtre Pierre.

NEW HAVEN, Yale Univ. Libr., 498, fol. 35r°, last quarter XVIc.

6371. O tres certaine esperance et darrien refuges ...

Variant of the inc.: O certaine esperance et darrien refuges des ames ... (no. 6203).

6372. O tres chere ame en Jesus Christ marquee de l'image de semblance de la venerable Trinité, rachaptee du sang precieux ...

"Recommandation de l'ame des trespassez": Manuel de dévotion de prêtre Pierre.

NEW HAVEN, Yale Univ. Libr., 498, fol. 115r°-115v°, last quarter XVIc.

6373. O tres debonnaire et aimable sire Jhesucrist, roy des siecles, filz eternel de Dieu le pere, moyen de paix entre Dieu et les hommes ...

"Contemplacion le venredi a la benoite passion Nostre Seigneur."

PARIS, Bibl. nat., fr. 927, fol. 228r°-230r°, XVc.

6374. O tres doulce vierge Marie, ayes pitié de ceste dolante, quy a grant tort ay (sic) desloyalment esté traÿe.
(Complete Text)

Prayer to the Virgin by Euryant: Gérard de Nevers, in prose.

BRUSSELS, Bibl. royale, 9631, fol. 18r°, XVc.

PARIS, Bibl. nat., fr. 24378, p. 52, XVc.

Ed.: L.F.H. Lowe, Gérard de Nevers, prose version of the Roman de la Violette, Paris and Princeton, 1928, p. 22.

6375. O tres doulce Vierge Marie,
Pour mon salut vueilliez ourer ...

Prayer to the Virgin by the heroine: Miracles de sainte Geneviève (vv. 256-63).

PARIS, Bibl. Sainte-Geneviève, 1131, fol. 186r°, XVc.

Ed.: Sennewaldt, p. 69.

6376. O tres doulx createur et redempteur du genre humain, qui despuis le commensement du monde as assemblé ...

"Oraison pour les mariez": Manuel de dévotion de prêtre Pierre.

NEW HAVEN, Yale Univ. Libr., 498, fol. 137r°-137v°, last quarter XVIc.

6377. O tres doulz Dieu, je vous crie mercy et vous prie que vous me
       donnez memoire dez pechiez que je ay mis ...

       Orison to God, in prose, for confession.

       METZ, Bibl. mun., 600, fol. 45v°-46r° and conclusion on 37r°,
       XVc., Hours of Paris and Prayer-book.

       Ref.: Rézeau, p. 161.

6378. O tres doulx Dieu, peire tres digne et amiable, tres graciou et
       amorou, tres debonnaire ...

       "Une devote oroison aprez la messe a preste", in prose.

       METZ, Bibl. mun., 600, fol. 86r°-89v°, XVc., Hours of Paris and
       Prayer-book.

       Ref.: Rézeau, p. 167.

6379. O tres doux et tres aimable seigneur Jesus Christ, donne moy
       que je puysse reposer en toy ...

       "Oraison pour se reposer en Dieu": Manuel de dévotion de prêtre
       Pierre.

       NEW HAVEN, Yale Univ. Libr., 498, fol. 120v°-123r°, last
       quarter XVIc.

6380. O tres doulx et tres begnin saint Esperit, protecteur certain
       et conforteur des desolez ...

       "Plainte" to the Holy Spirit, part of the Sermon pour le jour
       de la Pentecôte, by Jean Gerson.

       BRUSSELS, Bibl. royale, 11065-73, fol. 38v°-39v°, XVc.

       CAMBRAI, Bibl. mun., 578, fol. 59r°-59v°, XVc.

       PARIS, Bibl. nat., fr. 974, fol. 14v°-15r°, XVc.

       PARIS, Bibl. nat., fr. 1029, fol. 13r°-14r°, XVc.

       PARIS, Bibl. nat., fr. 24839, fol. 75r°-77r°, XVc.

       Ed.: L. Mourin, Six Sermons, 1946, p. 74; Glorieux, Gerson:
       Oeuvres complètes, VII, 2, p. 681.

6381. O tres doulz roy de paradis,
       Vueilliez la cité de Paris ...

       Orison to God, the Virgin and Saints by the heroine: Miracles
       de sainte Geneviève (vv. 382-95).

       PARIS, Bibl. Sainte-Geneviève, 1131, fol. 187v°, XVc.

       Ed.: Sennewaldt, p. 73-4.

6382.   O tres doulz roys du firmament,
        Aide nous par ton plaisir ...

        "Prayer" to God by Isaiah: "Mystère de la Nativité" (vv.
          712-717).

        LONDON, British Libr., Additional 38860, fol. 12v°, XVIIIc.
          copy of a lost codex.

        PARIS, Bibl. Sainte-Geneviève, 1131, fol. 7r°, XVc.

        Ed.: Whittredge, p. 116.

6383.   O tres doulx saint Sebastien,
        Martir de Dieu, je te supplie ...

        Orison to S. Sebastian; 12 huitains with varying rhyme
          patterns.

        AVIGNON, Bibl. mun., 1904, fol. 80r°-82r°, XVIc., Prayer-book.

        Ed.: Rézeau, Saints, II, pp. 488-91.

6384.   O tres doulz, tres amiaublez et tres desiraubles Jhesucrist, tu
        siés sor la hautesse des cielz et sur la hautesse de tous les
        aingles ...

        Praise of Jesu beginning in prose, but concluding with 26
          octosyllabic lines rhymed in pairs.

        NEW YORK, Pierpont Morgan Libr., Morgan 90, fol. 205r°-221r°,
          XIVc., Hours of Verdun.

6385.   O tres glorieux et tres innocent anges de Dieu, qui estez
        deputez et ordonné ...

        Prayer to Guardian Angel, in prose.

        VATICAN CITY, Bibl. apost., Pal. lat. 537, fol. 25v°-26v°,
          XVc., Hours of Sarum.

        Ref.: Rézeau, Saints, II, p. 512 and p. 643 suggests the
          content is close to that of nos. 242-243.

6386.   O tres hault et tres debonnaire createur, et sauveur et
        gouverneur de toutes creatures, a tes piteuses oreilles je
        accuse et confesse ...

        "Autre oroison bonne <a Nostre Seigneur>".

        PARIS, Bibl. nat., fr. 927, fol. 182r°, XVc.

6387.   O tres saincte et noble compaignee des unze (sic) mille
        martyrs, nous vous supplyons ...

        Prayer to the Ten Thousand Martyrs, in prose.

        PARIS, Bibl. nat., Réserve p. B. 22, text added in a XVc. hand.

        Ref.: Rézeau, Saints, II, p. 196.

6388. O tresoriere de grace et de misericorde, veilles mon cuer
       amollier en grant compassion ...

       Orison to the Virgin, in prose.

       STUTTGART, Württembergische Landesbibl., Brev. 9, fol.
       116vº-125vº, XVc., Hours of Troyes.

6389. O tu angre de paradis qui es ma garde par la pitié souverainne,
       moy qui te suis commise ...

       "Oroison devote a son bon ange", in prose.

       NEW YORK, New York Public Libr., 52, fol. 190vº-191vº, XVc.,
       Hours of Paris.

6390. O tu benignes Sire, nous te prions que tu veulles enluminer ton
       eglise a ce que celle enluminee de la doctrine ...

       Orison in honour of St. John the Evangelist; prose.

       PROVIDENCE, Brown Univ. Libr., C. 28. b. 4 (H.L. Koopman
       Collection), fol. 193rº, XVc., Hours.

6391. O tu bons eurez sainz Jaques, si ço est veritez que tu te
       apareusses a moi, outroie moi que je la prengie!
                          (Complete Text)

       "Le oreison Karle a monsenhor saint Jaque" (B. N., fr. 124):
       Chronicle   of   Pseudo-Turpin   in   the   Chronique   dite
       saintongeaise.

       ABERYSTWYTH, Nat. Libr. of Wales, 5005 B, p. 74, XIIIc.

       PARIS, Bibl. nat., fr. 124, fol. 1vº, XIVc.

       PARIS, Bibl. nat., fr. 5714, fol. 43rº, XIIIc.

       Ed.: T.M. Auracher, ZRP, 1 (1877), p. 265 (base ms. B. N., fr.
       5714, variants from B. N., fr. 124); Mandach, p. 259
       (Aberystwyth codex).

6392. O tu dame de gloire et royne de toute liesse, fontaine de pitié
       et de misericorde voie de saincteté ...

       "Une oroison de la Vierge Marie qui est bien devote et
       prouffitable."

       PROVIDENCE, Brown Univ. Libr., C. 28. b. 4 (H.L. Koopman
       Collection), fol. 158vº-159rº, XVc., Hours.

6393. O tu, Dieu, ne m'argue pas,
       En ta fureur ynel le pas
       N'en ton ire ne corrige
       Tu es mon Dieu, a toy m'oblige ...

       Third of the Seven Penitential Psalms, version in rhymed
       couplets.

LILLE, Bibl. mun., Godefroy 5 (147), fol. 96v°-99v°, XVc., Hours.

6394.   O tu Dieu qui as donnee la loy a Moyse en la haultesse du mont de Synaÿ et en ce propre lieu ...

Orison in honour of S. Catherine on the feast-day; prose.

PROVIDENCE, Brown Univ. Libr., C. 28. b. 4 (H.L. Koopman Collection), fol. 194v°-195r°, XVc., Hours.

6395.   O tu Dieu, qui la benoite vierge Marie ou concepvement et en l'enfantement, sa virginité gardee de doubles joies, as esjouy ...

Orison to God, in prose.

PROVIDENCE, Brown Univ. Libr., C. 28. b. 4 (H.L. Koopman Collection), fol. 202r°-202v°, XVc., Hours.

6396.   O tu Dieu qui nous as faicte ceste presente et honnourable journee en l'onneur de saint Jehan baptiste ...

Orison in honour of S. John the Baptist on the feast-day; prose.

PROVIDENCE, Brown Univ. Libr., C. 28. b. 4 (H.L. Koopman Collection), fol. 192r°-192v°, XVc., Hours.

6397.   O tu Dieu qui nous donne chascun an joie pour la sollennité de tes appostres saint Philippe et saint Jacques, nous te deprions ...

Orison in honour of SS. Philip and James; prose.

PROVIDENCE, Brown Univ. Libr., C. 28. b. 4 (H.L. Koopman Collection), fol. 196r°-196v°, XVc., Hours.

6398.   O tu Dieu qui par la priere de saint Anthoine, ton noble confesseur, ottroie le feu portant mort estre estaint ...

Orison in honour of S. Antony on the feast-day; prose.

PROVIDENCE, Brown Univ. Libr., C. 28. b. 4 (H.L. Koopman Collection), fol. 193v°, XVc., Hours.

6399.   O tu Dieu qui saincte Marguerite es cieulx as faicte venir par la victoire de son martire, nous prions que ...

Orison in honour of S. Margaret on the feast-day; prose.

PROVIDENCE, Brown Univ. Libr., C. 28. b. 4 (H.L. Koopman Collection), fol. 195r°, XVc., Hours.

6400.   O tu Dieu tout puissant, nous te prions qu'il te plaise ottroier que ta famille voise par voie de salut ...

Orison in honour of S. John the Baptist on the feast-day; prose.

PROVIDENCE, Brown Univ. Libr., C. 28. b. 4 (H.L. Koopman Collection), fol. 192r°, XVc., Hours.

6401. O tu perpetuel et puissant Dieu qui as donné a ton varlet, saint Cristofle, grace de baptesme et victoire de son martire ...

Orison in the honour of S. Christopher on the feast-day; prose.

PROVIDENCE, Brown Univ. Libr., C. 28. b. 4 (H.L. Koopman Collection), fol. 194r°-194v°, XVc., Hours.

6402. O tu, sains aingrez de Dieu, qui par la vertu soverainne m'ez donné por garder ...

Prayer to Guardian Angel, in prose.

METZ, Bibl. mun., 600, fol. 115v°, XVc., Hours of Paris and Prayer-book.

Ed.: Rézeau, pp. 170-1; Rézeau, Saints, II, p. 513.

6403. O tu Sire debonnaire, nous te prions qu'il te plaise a regarder tous les pechez que nous avons fais ...

Orison in honour of All Saints on the feast-day; prose.

PROVIDENCE, Brown Univ. Libr., C. 28. b. 4 (H.L. Koopman Collection), fol. 195v°, XVc., Hours.

6404. O tu Sire et Dieu, qui es souverains prestres devant tous autres, je me confesse a toy, car j'ay peché devant toy en terre et devant tes anges ...

"La Confession qui se fait a Dieu."

PROVIDENCE, Brown Univ. Libr., C. 28. b. 4 (H.L. Koopman Collection), fol. 190r°-191r°, XVc., Book of Hours.

6405. O tu tres certaine esperance et defenderresse ...

Variant of no. 1538: O tres certaine esperance ...

6406. O venerable et glorieux martir
Je te supply, fay peché departir ...

Prayer to S. Antony hermit; 34 lines in Ballade form, 3 ten-line and one four-line stanza.

PARIS, Bibl. nat., Rés. D. 5616 and Ye 831, Louenges des benoistz sainctz et sainctes de paradis, fol. zz3r°-zz3v°, Paris, Vérard.

VERSAILLES, Bibl. mun., M. 129 (Lacombe 109 quater).

Ed.: Rézeau, Saints, II, pp. 51-3.

6407. O vie eternelle, o pais amiable, o celeste Jerusalem, qu'est ce que l'on escript de toy? Que dict on de toy? Qu'en escript on? ...

"De la joye de paradis": Manuel de dévotion de prêtre Pierre.

NEW HAVEN, Yale Univ. Libr., 498, fol. 151r°-153v°, last quarter XVIc.

6408. O vieillesse,
Estat de rudesse ...

Plainte to God by Simeon: Arnoul Gréban's Mystère de la Passion (vv. 6810-59).

CHANTILLY, Musée Condé, 614 (1691), fol. 48r°-48v°, XVc.

LE MANS, Bibl. mun., 6, fol. 77r°-77v°, XVc.

PARIS, Bibl. de l'Arsenal, 6431, fol. 41r°, XVc.

PARIS, Bibl. nat., fr. 815, fol. 54r°-54v°, 1458.

PARIS, Bibl. nat., fr. 816, fol. 47v°-48r°, 1473.

PARIS, Bibl. nat., fr. 1550, fol. 147v°-148r°, XVIc.

PARIS, Bibl. nat., fr. 15064, fol. 128v°-129r°, 1469.

PARIS, Bibl. nat., nouv. acq. fr. 14043, fol. 8r°-8v°, XVc.

ROME, Accademia Nazionale dei Lincei, Bibl. Corsiniana, Rossi 412 (44. A. 7), fol. 111r°-111v°, late XVc.

Ed.: Paris-Raynaud, pp. 88-9 (vv. 6848-97); Jodogne, p. 94 (vv. 6810-59).

6409. O vierge d'humilité remplie, ma dame saincte Avoye, qui par la grant amour ...

"Oraison de saincte Avoye/Qui son serf gard de malle voye", in prose.

PARIS, Bibl. Ecole Nat. Sup. des Beaux-Arts, Masson, impr. 29, fol. F1v°-F2r°, XVIc.

PARIS, Bibl. nat., fr. 19243, fol. 188v°-189r°, XVIc.

Ref.: Rézeau, Saints, II, p. 63.

6410. O Vierge, en tout temps mere de Dieu et de Jesus Christ, porte en hault nostre oraison vers les esleuz ...

"Oraison a la Vierge Marie": Manuel de dévotion de prêtre Pierre.

NEW HAVEN, Yale Univ. Libr., 498, fol. 92r°-93r°, last quarter XVIc.

6411. O virge Katherine, de Deu parfaite amie,
Que fuis de noble sang et de royal lignie
...

"Orison de sainte Katherine", 4 stanzas of 4 alexandrines, each monorhyme.

CAMBRIDGE, Fitzwilliam Museum, Fitzwilliam 9-1951, fol. 115r°-116r°, Hours of Toul.

Ed.: Rézeau, Saints, II, p. 131.

6412. O vierge souveraigne,
        Humblement te suplye:
        Deffens que mort soudaigne
        Ne viegne sus ma vie!
                    (Complete Text)

Quatrain to the Virgin by Philippe de Vigneulles, featuring on a needlepoint cloth hung in front of Metz Cathedral in 1507.

PARIS, Bibl. nat., nouv. acq. fr. 6720, pp. 223-4, XVIc.

Ed.: Gedenkbuch des Metzer Bürgers Philippe von Vigneulles, ed. H. Michelant, Stuttgart, 1852, p. 154; V.L. Saulnier, in Mélanges d'histoire littéraire, de linguistique et de philologie romane offers à Charles Rostaing, Liège, 1974, II, pp. 965-991.

6413. O Vierge tres digne, Vierge glorieuse, Vierge toute doulce et tres benigne ...

Prayer to the Virgin: Sermon en la fête de l'Immaculée Conception, by Jean Gerson.

BRUSSELS, Bibl. royale, 11065-73, fol. 73r°-73v°, XVc.

CHANTILLY, Musée Condé, 145 (869), fol. 88r°-88v°, XVc.

PARIS, Bibl. nat., fr. 13318, fol. 52v°-53r°, XVc.

PARIS, Bibl. nat., fr. 24839, fol. 130r°, XVc.

TOURS, Bibl. mun., 386, fol. 72v°-73v°, XVc.

Ed.: Mourin, Six Sermons, 1946, p. 427; Glorieux, Gerson: Oeuvres complètes, VII, 2, p. 1079. Ref.: L. Mourin, RBPH, 27 (1949), pp. 561-98 (plan and style of the sermon).

6414. O Vierge tres pure et tres nette, de tous bienz environnee, a tousjourz maix bieneurouze ...

"O intemerata", in prose.

METZ, Bibl. mun., 600, fol. 76r°-77v°, XVc., Hours of Paris and Prayer-book.

Ref.: Rézeau, p. 166-7.

6415. O vous, glorieus confesseurs,
        Qui avez, par grant penitence ...

Orison to Confessors; 8 vv. rhyming ababbcbc.

PARIS, Bibl. nat., Rés. D. 5616 and Ye 831, Louenges des benoistz sainctz et sainctes de paradis, fol. zz7v°, Paris, Vérard.

Ed.: Rézeau, Saints, I, pp. 213-14.

6416. O vous, troys personnes egales et coeternelles, un Dieu, vray pere, filz et le sainct Esprit qui seul habitez ...

"Oraison troysiesme a la saincte Trinité": Manuel de dévotion de prêtre Pierre.

NEW HAVEN, Yale Univ. Libr., 498, fol. 17r°-18v°, last quarter XVIc.

6417. O vray Baptiste vertuable (var. venerable)
Affin que ses griefz n'encourons ...

Rondeau to S. John Baptist: Mystère de la Passion by Arnoul Gréban (vv. 10223-44).

CHANTILLY, Musée Condé, 614 (1691), fol. 78r°, XVc. Inc.: O vray Baptiste venerable ...

PARIS, Bibl. de l'Arsenal, 6431, fol 69r°, XVc.

PARIS, Bibl. nat., fr. 815, fol. 82r°, 1458.

PARIS, Bibl. nat., fr. 816, fol. 71v°, 1473.

PARIS, Bibl. nat., fr. 15065, fol. 6r°-6v°, 1469.

ROME, Accademia Nazionale dei Lincei, Bibl. Corsiniana, Rossi 412 (44. A. 7), fol. 194r°-194v°, late XVc.

Ed.: Paris-Raynaud, p. 134 (vv. 10257-78); Jodogne, p. 138 (vv. 10223-44).

6418. O vray Dieu et eternel pere
Qui de riens ciel et terre fis ...

Plainte to God by the Virgin: Arnoul Gréban's Mystère de la Passion (vv. 27016-22).

CHANTILLY, Musée Condé, 614 (1691), fol. 227v°, XVc.

PARIS, Bibl. de l'Arsenal, 6431, fol. 203r°, XVc.

PARIS, Bibl. nat., fr. 815, fol. 219r°, 1458.

PARIS, Bibl. nat., fr. 816, fol. 190v°, 1473.

ROME, Academia Nazionale dei Lincei, Bibl. Corsiniana, Rossi 412 (44. A. 7), fol. 529r°, late XVc.

Ed.: Paris-Raynaud, p. 355 (vv. 27170-76); Jodogne, p. 362 (vv. 27016-22).

6419. O vray Dieu, tout juste et tout puissant, monstrez envers moy, vostre povre creature, la doulceur de vostre misericorde ...

Orison to God: Sermon en la fête de la sainte Trinité, by Jean Gerson.

BRUSSELS, Bibl. royale, 11065–73, fol. 47v°–48r°, XVc.

CAMBRAI, Bibl. mun., 578, fol. 78v°–79r°, XVc.

CHANTILLY, Musée Condé, 140 (699), fol. 103v°–105r°, XVc.

PARIS, Bibl. nat., fr. 13318, fol. 174r°–175v°, XVc.

PARIS, Bibl. nat. fr. 24839, fol. 274r°–274v°, XVc.

PARIS, Bibl. nat., nouv. acq. fr. 1975, fol. 104r°–104v°, XVc.

Ed.: L. Mourin, Six Sermons, 1946, p. 164–5; Glorieux, Gerson: Oeuvres complètes, VII, 2, pp. 1131–2.

6420.   O vray espoux et saincte garde de la royne des cieulx, je te requier humblement ...

"Oraison tres devote de monsieur sainct Joseph", in prose.

PARIS, Bibl. nat., Rés. p. B. 22, fol. C3r°–C4r°, Hours of Paris published 1537.

Ref.: Rézeau, Saints, II, pp. 295–6.

6421.   O vraye viande angelique, o vray pain celeste des humains miserables au desert de ceste valee de misere ...

Prayer after the Communion.

CHICAGO, Newberry Libr., 43, fol. 159v°, XVIc., Hours of Rouen.

*   Octroye ...

See the alphabetical order: Ottroye ...

6422.   Ohi! Deus, sire chier, ki es veir creatur,
Par ki devisé vait e la nut e li jor,
Dune mei veeir tens dunt joe su preecheur
         ...

Prayer to God by Gudmod: Roman de Horn by Thomas (vv. 2897–904).

CAMBRIDGE, Cambridge Univ. Libr., Ff. 6. 17, fol. 59v°, XIIIc.

LONDON, British Libr., Harley 527, fol. 66v°, XIIIc.

Ed.: Pope, I, p. 99.

6423.   Oy! Dex, qui fais vertuz et an ciel et an
                              terre,
Sire, ja te vig je outre la mer requerre;
Car me gitez, biau sire, de la prison de
                              terre,

Et secor cest chatif qui si souvant
                                    t'apelle.

Prayer to God by Orson in prison: Orson de Beauvais (vv. 1751-4).

PARIS, Bibl. nat., nouv. acq. fr. 16600 (olim Phillipps 222), fol. 28r°, XIIIc.

Ed.: Paris, p. 58.

6424. Omnipotens, veirs Dex autisme,
      Qui des hauz ceus jusqu'en abisme,
      Maines ta puissance e estenz
      Que si com vait li firmamenz ...

      "La premiere oreisun que Rous fait vers l'autisme/Qu'il le jette del torment e del parfunt abisme:" Chronique des ducs de Normandie, by Benoît (vv. 4271-336).

      LONDON, British Libr., Harley 1717, fol. 25v°-26r°, XIIIc.

      TOURS, Bibl. mun., 903, fol. 27r°-27v°, late XIIc.

      Ed.: Fahlin, I, p. 125-7 (base ms. is Tours).

6425. Omnipotent Dieu qui es (ms. estes) la force de ceulx quy ont esperance en toy, soyes propice ...

      Prayer for the Sunday following "le jour de la Trinité".

      NEW YORK, Pierpont Morgan Libr., Morgan 78, fol. 28r°, XVc., Hours of Rome. This text by a XVIc. hand.

6426. Omnipotent et misericors Dieu duquel don vient que tes serviteurs dignement et loablement ...

      "Dimence x^e, oraison."

      NEW YORK, Pierpont Morgan Libr., Morgan 78, fol. 43r°, XVc., Hours of Rome. This prayer by a XVIc. hand.

6427. Omnipotent et sempiternel Dieu qui a<s> donné a tes serviteurs par confession de vraye foy ...

      "Le jour de la Trinité, oraison."

      NEW YORK, Pierpont Morgan Libr., Morgan 78, fol. 28r°, XVc., Hours of Rome. This prayer in a XVIc. hand.

6428. Omnipotent et sempiternel Dieu qui a<s> moderé les choses celestes et terriennes, exauce ...

      "Aprés les octaves <des Roys>, oraison."

      NEW YORK, Pierpont Morgan Libr., Morgan 78, fol. 80r°, XVc., Hours of Rome. This prayer copied in XVIc.

6429. Omnipotent sempiternel Dieu, maine nos oeuvres en ton bon
       plaisir affin que au nom de ton tres chier filz meritons
       habonder en bonnes oeuvres.
                           (Complete Text)

       "Le jour de l'an, oraison."

       NEW YORK, Pierpont Morgan Libr., Morgan 78, fol. 79v°, XVc.,
       Hours of Rome. This text by a XVIc. hand.

6430. Omnipotent sempiternel Dieu qui a<s> fais nostre saulveur
       prendre char humaine et soustenir la croix ...

       "Dimence des Palmes, oraison."

       NEW YORK, Pierpont Morgan Libr., Morgan 78, fol. 93r°, XVc.,
       Hours of Rome. This prayer by a XVIc. hand.

6431. On dist que par commun usage
       Parole recordee au saige
       Une seule fie souffist,
       Car il est en si hault estage ...

       "L'Escole de foy que fist J. Brisebare l'an mccccxxvii." 262
       twelve-line stanzas.

       PARIS, Bibl. nat., fr. 576, fol. 93r°-113v°, XIVc.

       Ref.: Naetebus, XXXVI, 4; Gröber, Grundriss, II, p. 818;
       Långfors, p. 248; A. Thomas in H.L.F., XXXVI, 1927, pp. 44-7.

6432. On treuve es histoires escript
       Que Nostre Seigneur Jesuchrist
       Qui est dict par grant dignité
       Le prophete de verité ...

       "Devote contemplation sur la tres excellente beaulté, gestes,
       forme et figure estans au precieux corps de Nostre Seigneur
       Jesuchrist"; 64 lines rhymed in pairs.

       LONDON, British Libr., Additional 17446, fol. 34r°-35r°, XVc.

6433. Or delesses, Sire, ton sergent selonc ta parole en pais, car
       mes yeux ont veu ton sauveur (sic) par qui ...

       Canticle of Simeon in prose, as part of Compline in the Heures
       de Nostre Dame.

       CAMBRIDGE, Fitzwilliam Museum, McClean 76, fol. 62v°-63r°, XIV
       - XVc., Hours of Paris.

6434. Ore delaisses ton serf, Sire,
       Em paix selonc qu'as voulu dire,
       Car mes yeux ont veu ton salut
       Qui a bone gent moult valut ...

       Canticle of Simeon, in rhymed couplets, as part of the "Heures
       de Nostre Dame."

LILLE, Bibl. mun., Godefroy 5 (147), fol. 89v°-90r°, XVc., Hours.

6435.   Ore il eide a sercher quant de bien celui fait a lui mesmes q'aherde a bountee. Demandé est entre homes que soit purqei lez saintz de Dieu ...

Libellus beati anselmi episcopi de XIV partibus beatitudinis, in Anglo-Norman prose. The copy breaks off near the end of the work.

LICHFIELD, Lichfield Cathedral Chapter Libr., 6, fol. 233r°-247v°, early XVc.

6436.   Ore nus duinst Deu, li veir sauvere,
Pur amur de sa chere mere
Itele essanple a cesti prendre,
Ke nos almes li pussum rendre!
                    (Complete Text)

Concluding Invocation: Miracles de Nostre Dame by Adgar, called Willame (vv. 89-92 of miracle no. 9, found in one ms. only).

LONDON, British Libr., Additional 38664, fol. 9r°, c. 1240.

Ed.: J.A. Herbert, Romania, 32 (1903), p. 412. Ref.: Vising, p. 43, no. 13 (this prayer not recorded).

6437.   Or nous doint Dex si bien ouvrer ...

Variant of the inc.: Jhesucrist nos doint si ouvrer ... (no. 6019).

6438.   Or requier je a la parclose
Au tres doulz, gracieux, tres sade
Qu'au mien chief qui tant est malade,
Et a ja longuement esté ...

Orison by the author to the Saint: anon. Vie de S. Jean Baptiste (vv. 7749-7774).

PARIS, Bibl. nat., fr. 2182, fol. 137v°-138r°, 1322.

PARIS, Bibl. nat., nouv. acq. fr. 7515, fol. 136v°, XIVc. This copy contains only vv. 1-5, of which 2-5 offer a variant reading: Au tres gracious S. Johan/Qu'a mon corps qui ha grant ahan/De maladie et de pechié/Et de tous vices entechié.

Ed.: Gieber, pp. 223-4 (base ms. fr. 2182).

6439.   Or prion le Segnour qui maint en Orient,
Que paradis aion par no deservement ...

Closing invocation: Gaufrey (vv. 10728-31).

MONTPELLIER, Bibl. Fac. Ecole de Médecine, H. 247, fol. 88v°, XIVc.

Ed.: Guessard and Chabaille, p. 322.

6440.   Or vueilliez, Vierge pucelle saincte et sacree, vueilliez
empetrer grace envers vostre chier et doulx enfant ...

Concluding Prayer, to the Virgin: "Considerations sur saint
Joseph", by Jean Gerson.

PARIS, Bibl. nat., fr. 24841, fol. 150r°, XVc.

Ed.: Anne-Louise Masson, Jean Gerson: sa vie, son temps, ses
oeuvres, Lyon, 1894, p. 298; Glorieux, Gerson: Oeuvres
complètes, VII, 1, p. 94.

*   Ore ...

See the alphabetical order: Or ...

6441.   Ottrie nous, sire Dieu, s'il te plaist, nous esjouir des
solennités de ton benoist apostre saint Thomas affin que par
ses prieres ...

Orison for S. Thomas the Apostle (on feast-day).

PARIS, Bibl. de l'Arsenal, 2162, fol. 127v°-128r°, XVc., Hours
of Paris.

6442.   Ottroie nous, Sire tous puissans, que nous remembrons la
commemoracion monsignour s. Cristophe, le benoy martir ...

Orison to God in prose, preceding a transcription of a prayer
to S. Christopher (no. 1816).

MANCHESTER, John Rylands Univ. Libr., Fr. 143, fol. 174r°,
early XVc., Hours.

6443.   Octroye, nous te prions, Dieu omnipotent, que l'intercession de
la sainte mere Dieu et tousjours vierge, Marie, et de toutes
les saintes ...

"Oraison de Toussains."

NEW HAVEN, Yale Univ. Libr., 425, fol. 337v°-338r°, c. 1475,
Missal.

6444.   Ottroies nous, Dieu pietables, deffendement de nostre fragilité
que nous qui faisons memoire de la sainte mere ...

Orison to God in prose, at Sext of the Heures de Nostre Dame.

CAMBRIDGE, Fitzwilliam Museum, McClean 76, fol. 47v°-48r°, XIV
- XVc., Hours of Paris.

PROVIDENCE, Brown Univ. Libr., C. 28. b. 4 (H.L. Koopman
Collection), fol. 274v°-275r°, XVc., Hours. The rubric reads:
"Nous devons dire, quant la beneïçon de la messe est dicte,
l'oroison qui s'ensuit."

*   Oy! ...

See the alphabetical order: Oi! ...

P

6445. Pape Benedic donna a tous vrays catholicques qui diront ceste
oroison qui s'ensuit entre la elevation ...

Rubric at the head of a copy of no. 3029: Je te pri tres
debonnaire sire ... The rubric's statement is related to, but
not identical with that printed for no. 3027.

LEEDS, Leeds Univ. Libr., Brotherton 5, fol. 211v°-212r°, XVc.,
Hours of Paris.

6446. Pape Benoit composa et donna a tous singulierement que autant
de fois que ilz le pourroient dire ...

Rubric at the head of the prose Orison to Jesus, inc. Je te
prie, sire Dieux Jhesucrist ... (no. 3027). See another
version of the rubric with the wording: Pape Benedic donna a
tous vrays catholicques ... (no. 6445).

PARIS, Bibl. nat., fr. 927, fol. 198r°, XVc.

Ed.: Sinclair, FDTMA, no. 3027.

6447. Per ung ajournant trouvay en ung prey
Pastorel seant, de si biau (ms. bliau)
                              semblent,
Je le (ms. lez) salua (sic) mout tres
                              doucement.
Il me respondit de sa courtoizie ...

Poem in a 'pastourelle' mode, in honor of Jesus; 26
decasyllabic and 3 hexasyllabic lines; some rhyme in pairs
but a regular stanzaic pattern is not at first evident.

MANCHESTER, John Rylands Univ. Libr., Fr. 143, fol.
163v°-164r°, early XVc., Hours.

6448. Par une verge fleurissant
Fist Dieu Marie a Josep prendre

"Ballade" in honor of the Nativity, attributed to René d'Anjou; three eight-line stanzas rhyming ababbcbc, with refrain.

Refr.: Voiez quel joyeuse nouvelle.

LENINGRAD, Publichnaia Bibl., Fr. F. v. III. 2, fol. 1v°, XVc.

Ed.: Sismarev, pp. 175-6. Ref.: Laborde, p. 45.

6449. Parfonde tristesse enserree,
       Comment soustenir te pourray?
       Ou yray?
       Que feray? ...

       Plainte by the Virgin in front of the Cross: Mystère de la Passion by Arnould Gréban (vv. 25163-356).

       CHANTILLY, Musée Condé, 614 (1691), fol. 214r°-215v°, XVc.

       PARIS, Bibl. de l'Arsenal, 6431, fol. 188v°-190r°, XVc.

       PARIS, Bibl. nat., fr. 815, fol. 204r°-205r°, 1458.

       PARIS, Bibl. nat., fr. 816, fol. 177v°-179r°, 1473.

       ROME, Accademia Nazionale dei Lincei, Bibl. Corsiniana, Rossi 412 (44. A. 7), fol. 490r°-493r°, late XVc.

       Ed.: Paris-Raynaud, pp. 330-2 (vv. 25308-501); Jodogne, pp. 338-40 (vv. 25163-356).

6450. Pater Noster est la plus digne oraison et la meilleur qui soit, car elle contient vij peticions es quelles nous requerons a Dieu ...

       Explanation of the Pater Noster.

       LONDON, Lambeth Palace, 456, fol. 215v°, XVc.

6451. Pater Noster. O perfonde divine charité, je suy tres ville et tres povre creature et le roy de tout le monde ...

       "Cy est bonne doctrine sus la Paternostre."

       METZ, Bibl. mun., 600, fol. 134r°-137r°, XVc., Hours of Paris and Prayer-book.

       Ref.: Rézeau, p. 174.

6452. Pater Noster qui es in celis. Ce senefie loenge et reconciliation a Nostre Signor. Quant Dex oit ses fils qui le loent au commencement, il les oit plus tost ...

       Exposition of the Pater Noster in prose.

       OPORTO, Bibl. publ. mun., 619, fol. 135v°-136r°, XVc. Copied into spaces between spokes of a wheel that encompasses both folios.

6453. Pater noster qui es in celis sanctificetur nomen tuum. Nostres
       peres qui es es cieulz saintefiés soit li tiens nons ...

       Prose Pater Noster in Latin and French that precedes an
       Exposition which opens: De toutes les orisons ... (no. 5589).

       BRUSSELS, Bibl. royale, 10574-85, fol. 116r°, XIIIc.

6454. Pater Noster, tu n'es pas sos,
       Car tu t'es mis en grant repos,
       Qui es montés hault in celis,
       Car desor(e)mais en cest païs ...

       Paraphrase of the Pater Noster; 80 lines.

       NEW YORK, Pierpont Morgan Libr., Glazier 32, fol. 143v°, late
       XIVc.

*   Per ...

       See the alphabetical order: Par ...

6455. Pere de sapience, verité divine, doulz Jhesu, vous fuste pris a
       heure de matines ...

       Hymn "Patris sapientia" in the Heures de la Croix.

       MANCHESTER, John Rylands Univ. Libr., Fr. 143, fol. 82v°-83r°,
       early XVc., Hours.

6456. Et dist: Peres des chius, qui tous nous a
                              creés,
       Tu estoras Adam et Eve a l'autre lés;
       Tout leur habandonnas; et les euis menés
       En paradis terrestre. La leur fu devaés ...

       Orison to God the Father by the hero: Baudouin de Sebourc: (vv.
       314-401 of Chant XI).

       PARIS, Bibl. nat., fr. 12552, fol. 52v°, XIVc.

       PARIS, Bibl. nat., fr. 12553, fol. 153v°-154v°, XVc.

       Ed.: Boca, I, pp. 314-16. Ref.: Scheludko, ZFSL, 58 (1934), p.
       178; Wels, p. 7 n. 18 and p. 11 n. 25; Labande, pp. 71-3, 76
       n. 6, 77 n. 5, 78; Saly, p. 52.

6457. Disant: Pere doulx et piteux,
       De tous forvoyez la retraicte,
       Si j'ay chose commise et faicte,
       Qui desrogue au mien saulvement ...

       Confession, by Octavien de Saint-Gelais in his Séjour d'honneur
       (vv. 8616-48).

       PARIS, Bibl. nat., fr. 1196, fol. 138r°-138v°, XVIc.

       PARIS, Bibl. nat., fr. 12783, fol. 166v°-167r°, late XVc.

Ed.: J.A. James, Octavien de Saint-Gelais Le Séjour d'honneur, Chapel Hill, 1977, p. 285 (base ms. B. N. fr. 12783).

6458.   Pere du ciel, ayés de nous mercy,
Filz redempteur du monde, Dieu aussi ...

Orison to several saints; 145 vv., grouped in 24 stanzas of varying length.

PARIS, Bibl. nat., Rés. D. 5616 and Ye 831, Louenges a Nostre Seigneur etc., Paris, Vérard.

VERSAILLES, Bibl. mun., M. 129 (Lacombe 109 quater).

Ed.: Rézeau, Saints, I, pp. 157-64.

6459.   Pere eternelz, facteur de tous humains
Qui m'a creé si tres notablement ...

"Oraison a Dieu le pere", decasyllables rhyming abab

NEW YORK, New York Public Libr., 39, fol. 83r°-83v°, XVc., Hours of Tournai, this prayer added in XVIc.

6460.   Pere nostre qui es es cieulx ...

Variant of the inc.: Nostre pere qui es en cieulx ... (no. 4741).

6461.   Pere nostre qui es es cielz. Regarde comment nostre douz avocaz et nostre bon mestre Jhesucrist qui est la sapience Dieu le pere et set toutes les loys ...

"Ci commance la patenostre et coment l'en espont pater noster", part of the treatise entitled: Le Livre du jardin de la sainte ame. The prologue to the explanation of the seven petitions begins: Quant l'en met .i. enfant ... (no. 6492).

VIENNA, Oesterreichische Nationalbibl., 2627, fol. 94v°-105r°, XVc.

6462.   Peres nostres qui yes lassus
El ciel et nous qui sons ça jus,
Saincteficés soit li tiens nons
Qu'en toy entirement creons ...

Pater Noster in rhyme, part of an anonymous rhymed version of Cato.

NEW YORK, Pierpont Morgan Libr., Morgan 947, fol. 68v°-70r°, c. 1390, Hours.

6463.   Pere puissant, par la teue merci ...

Variant of the inc.: Glorieus Deu, par la teue merci ... (no. 5842).

6464.   Pour acomplir des prophetes tres sains
La parolle par grace revelee ...

"Ballade" in honor of Jesus on the Cross, attributed to René d'Anjou; three ten-line stanzas rhyming ababbccdcd, with refrain.

Refr.: Loué en soit ou siecle pardurable.

LENINGRAD, Publichnaia Bibl., Fr. F. v. III, 2, fol. 2r°, XVc.

Ed.: Sismarev, pp. 176-77. Ref.: Laborde, p. 45.

6465. Pour bien mourir il est moult convenable dire de ceur ce que Nostre Seigneur et mestre dist a sa (ms. ssa) mort et passion; et pour ce que a dignement recepu le saint sacrement ...

Prologue to the group of Orisons 'selon les sept paroles de Jesus en croix', each beginning: Jesus ...

PARIS, Bibl. nat., fr. 13269, fol. 2r°-2v°, XVc.

6466. Pur ceo que tu es, les sunt/il sunt; pur ceo que tu es beaus, beles sunt ...

Variant of the inc.: Pur ço ke vus estes, pur ço sunt, pur ço ke beaus estes, beles sunt ... (no. 6467).

6467. Pur ço ke vus estes, pur ço sunt; pur ço ke beaus estes, beles sunt; e pur ço ke bon estes, bones sunt ...

Praise of God, in the Mirour de seinte Eglyse, a translation of the Speculum Ecclesiae by S. Edmund of Abingdon. The texts of A and B versions are close.

CAMBRIDGE, Emmanuel College, I. 4. 31, fol. 68v°, XIVc. (A version). Inc.: Pur ceo que tu es, les sunt; pur ceo que tu es beaus, beles sunt ...

CAMBRIDGE, Trinity College, O. 1. 17, fol. 281r°, XIVc. (A version).

DURHAM, Durham Univ. Libr., Cosin V. V. 15, fol. 25v°, XIVc. (B version). The scribe places the first phrase in third position.

LINCOLN, Chapter Libr., B. 5. 1, fol. 171r°-171v°, XIVc. (B version).

LONDON, British Libr., Arundel 288, fol. 107v°, XIIIc. (B version).

LONDON, British Libr., Harley 1121, fol. 144v°, early XIVc. (B version).

LONDON, British Libr., Royal 12. C. XII, fol. 20r°, early XIVc. (A version).

LONDON, British Libr., Royal 20. B. XIV, fol. 56r°, early XIVc. (A version).

MADRID, Bibl. nac., 18253, fol. 125v°, XIVc. (A version).

NEW HAVEN, Yale Univ. Libr., 492, fol. 88v°-89r°, early XIVc. (A version).

OXFORD, Bodleian Libr., Digby 20, fol. 146r°, XIIIc. (B version).

OXFORD, Bodleian Libr., Douce 210, fol. 37r°, early XIVc. (A version).

OXFORD, Bodleian Libr., Rawlinson Poetry 241, p. 169, late XIIIc. (B version).

OXFORD, Bodleian Libr., Selden Supra 74, fol. 47r°-47v°, XIIIc. (A version).

OXFORD, Corpus Christi College, 36, fol. 39r°, early XIVc. (A version).

OXFORD, St. John's College, 190, fol. 192r°, late XIIIc. (A version).

PARIS, Bibl. nat., fr. 13342, fol. 31v°-32r°, early XIVc. (A version). Inc.: Pur ço ke tu es, il sont; pur ço ke tu es bel, belles sont ...

PARIS, Bibl. nat., nouv. acq. fr. 11200, fol. 6r°, XIIIc. (A version). Inc.: Pur ceo ke tu es, sunt eles; pur ceo ke tu es beaus, beles sunt ...

Ed.: Robbins, pp. 14-15 (base ms. Oxford, Digby 20); Wilshere, p. 20 (A version, base ms. Oxford, St. John's College, 190); p. 21 (B version, base ms. London, Arundel 288). Ref.: Same as the Ref. section of the inc. Aprés ço devez saver queus sunt les set prieres ... (no. 5431).

6468.   Pour lou pueple resconforteir
        Ke tant ait jeut en tenebrour ...

        Chanson de Croisade: "Maistres Renas lai fist de Nostre Seignor."

        Refr.: Jerusalem plaint et ploure
               Lou secors, ke trop demoure.

        BERN, Bürgerbibl., 389, fol. 179r°, XIIIc.

        Ed.: A. Jubinal, Rapport à M. le Ministre de l'Instruction publique, suivi de quelques pièces inédites tirées des manuscrits de la Bibliothèque de Berne, Paris, 1838, p. 39-41; W. Wackernagel, Altfranzösische Lieder und Leiche, Bâle, 1846, p. 35-7; Bédier and Aubry, p. 75-83; Bec, Lyrique française, II, pp. 88-90. Ref.: A. Guesnon, Le Moyen Age, 15 (1902), p. 139-40; Van den Boogaard, refr. no. 1122.

6469.   Pour le peuple soies propice
        Et au clergié soies encline ...

        "Ora pro populo", 7 octosyllabic lines rhyming ababbcc.

BALTIMORE, Walters Art Gallery, Walters 89, fol. 30r°-30v°, last quarter XIVc., Hours of Isabelle de Coucy.

6470. Pour moy et pour mes amis et por toutes nos
                                gent
        Qui Dieu nous doint honneur et mette a
                                sauvement!
        Pour les salus des vif<s> et pour cil qui
                                mort sunt
        Que Dieu son paradis et sa grace lor dont!
                        (Complete Text)

        Orison to God, preceding the Seven Penitential Psalms in French
          verse; one quatrain of alexandrines aabb.

        MANCHESTER, John Rylands Univ. Libr., Fr. 143, fol. 88r°, early
          XVc., Hours.

6471. Pour moustrer que Dieus s'esbanie
        Par amour et par jalousie
        A l'ame qui a li se prent,
        Me vient a talent que je die ...

        "Dit   de   l'ame",   oeuvre   mystique   d'origine   béguine;   16
          twelve-line stanzas after Helinand model.

        BERLIN, Deutsche Staatsbibl., gall. oct. 28, fol. 126v°-131v°,
          early XIVc., Prayer-book (destroyed).

        Ed.: E. Bechmann, Z.R.P., 13 (1889), pp. 67-72. Ref.: Naetebus,
          XXXVI, 28; Långfors, p. 289; H.A. Hatzfeld, P.M.L.A., 61
          (1946), pp. 331-78; W. Rothwell, in Current Thoughts in
          French Literature: Essays in Memory of G.T. Clapton (ed. J.C.
          Ireson), Oxford, 1965, pp. 33-48; Brayer, GRLMA, VI, 2, no.
          1156.

6472. Pour venir de pechié au cor
        Et pour des biens faire restor
        Que j'ay perdus par ma folie
        Jou, Brisbare, ay tres or ...

        "Tresor   Nostre   Dame"   by   Jean   Brisebarre;   87   twelve-line
          stanzas.

        BRUSSELS, Bibl. royale, 11244-51, fol. 100r°-107v°, XVc.

        PARIS, Bibl. nat., fr. 576, fol. 113v°-120v°, XIVc.

        PARIS, Bibl. nat., fr. 994, fol. 101r° - end of codex, XIVc.
          This copy begins at second stanza: Je tieng a perilleux
          dommage ...

        Ref.: Naetebus, XXXVI, 46; Långfors, p. 187 (mentions only
          Paris, B. N. fr. 994); A Thomas in H.L.F., XXXVI, 1927, p.
          48.

6473. Precious Dieus, et misericors pere Jhesucrist, alme commans hui
          en ce jour en vostre douce garde ...

Orison to Jesus; the text appears to be related to those at nos. 748, 749, 750 and 4478.

NEW YORK, Pierpont Morgan Libr., Morgan 90, fol. 225r°-229v°, XIVc., Hours of Verdun.

6474. Precieuz Jhesucrist, fiuz Dieu le pere vif, qui pendis en la croiz et euz en droite heure de nonne ta douce sainte bouche abuvree de cruel boivre ...

Hours of the Cross in prose, nones.

VIENNA, Oesterreichische Nationalbibl., 1969, fol. 134r°-135r°, XIVc., Hours.

6475. Precios Sir, <u>dist il,</u> vos souiés mercïé
De si grant honor chun vos m'avez apresté
                        ...

Prayer to God by Roland: Entrée d'Espagne (vv. 13633-43).

VENICE, Bibl. Marciana, 257 (olim gall. XXI), fol. 263v°-264r°, XIVc.

<u>Ed.</u>: Thomas, II, p. 205-6.

6476. Preciose roïne, con ta sainte semblançe
Garde moi dou faus angle, q'il n'ait sor mi
                              posance.
Glorios Deu, ma coupe, puis qe me ensi
                              d'enfançe.
              (Complete Text)

Confession of a hermit about to expire: Entrée d'Espagne (vv. 15188-90).

VENICE, Bibl. Marciana, 257 (olim gall. XXI), fol. 291r°, XIVc.

<u>Ed.</u>: Thomas, II, p. 263.

6477. Premier on doit prier chou que on doit, c'est a dire ses matines, ses eures, et ce qu'on a de penance en commandement. Aprés on doit prier pour toute sainte Eglise ...

"En orison a iiij choses": section of the Beghine tract Règle des fins amants.

BERLIN, Deutsche Staatsbibl., Gall. oct. 28, fol. 89r°, early XIVc., Prayer-book (destroyed).

<u>Ed.</u>: Christ, p. 201.

6478. Premierement l'orateur ou celuy qui prie doibt dire a genoulx: Mon Dieu et mon vray createur (<u>ms</u>. creature), je te remerchye tres affectueusement et de tout mon coeur de tous les biens ...

"Trois condicions requises a parfaitement prie<r> Dieu."

LUXEMBOURG, Bibl. nat., 28, fol. 126r°, XVIc.

6479. Premierement on doibt penser et mediter en hault es grandes
      joyes de paradis qui sont innumerables, et que je puisse
      tellement vivre en ce monde, et que en la fin de mes jours
      ...

      "VIII Contemplacions des dis de s. Bernarde (sic) extrait au
      livre du condempnement du monde."

      LUXEMBOURG, Bibl. nat., 28, fol. 126r°-127r°, XVIc.

6480. Preste, nous te prions, tout puissant Dieu, que la splendeur de
      ta clareté luyse espandue sur nous ...

      "Vespres <de pentecouste, oraison>.

      NEW YORK, Pierpont Morgan Libr., Morgan 78, fol. 147r°, XVc.,
      Hours of Rome. This prayer added in XVIc.

6481. Preste nous, tout puissant Dieu, que la future solemnité de
      nostre redemption nous conferer les subsides ...

      "Le merquedi des quatre temps, <oraison>".

      NEW YORK, Pierpont Morgan Libr., Morgan 78, fol. 75r°, XVc.,
      Hours of Rome. This prayer in a XVIc. hand.

6482. Prie pour le peuple et intervien
      Pour la clergie qui te sert bien;
      Et si prye tres chiere dame
      Pour le devot sexe de femme ...

      "Ora pro populo", 17 octosyllabic lines, as part of the Heures
      de Nostre Dame.

      SAN MARINO (Calif.), Huntington Libr., HM 1129, fol. 30r°-30v°,
      c. 1450, Hours of Paris.

6483. Prion Dieu au commencement
      Que il nos doint avancement
      De bien faire a son plesir
      Que nos puisson le bien aprendre ...

      Orison to God as the Prologue of 48 vv. to the Isopet de
      Chartres.

      CHARTRES, Bibl. mun., 620, fol. 136v°., XIIIc. (MS destroyed in
      Second World War).

      Ed.: Julia Bastin, Recueil général des Isopets, Paris, 1929, I,
      pp. 115-16. Ref.: Naetebus, LXV, 12; P. Meyer, Bull.
      S.A.T.F., 20 (1894), p. 59; Langfors, p. 292.

6484. Prions donques nostre pere, dieu eternel, que par les merites
      de son filz unique, Jesuchrist, il nous voeulle laisser vivre
      ...

      Concluding Invocation by the chevalier Louis de Berquin to his
      Credo, or Symbole des apostres, 1525 (inc. Demande: Croyez
      vous en Dieu ... no. 5560).

Ed.: Brefve admonition de la maniere de prier salon la doctrine de Jesuchrist, avec une brefve explanation du Pater Noster, Extraict des Paraphrases de Erasme, Paris, Simon Dubois (?), 1525; Telle, p. 73.

6485. Prium por la pes de seinte Eglise et por la pes de la tere: Ke Deus, por le honur de sei memis ...

"Prière du prône" or bidding Prayers in Anglo-Norman, from Ramsey Benedictine Abbey.

CAMBRIDGE, Cambridge Univ. Libr., Hh. 6. 11, fol. 3r°, XIIIc.

Ed.: K.V. Sinclair, Mediaeval Studies, 42 (1980), p. 454-62.

6486. Protectur Dieu de ceulx quy ont esperance en toy sans lequel rien n'est ne fort ne sainct ...

Orison for "Dimence iij."

NEW YORK, Pierpont Morgan Libr., Morgan 78, fol. 34v°, XVc., Hours of Rome. Prayer by a XVIc. hand.

6487. Pucelle royne glorieuse,
Je te requier de cuer fin ...

Orison to the Virgin; one quatrain abab.

METZ, Bibl. mun., 600, fol. 46r°, XVc., Hours of Paris and Prayer-book.

Ed.: Rézeau, p. 161.

6488. Puis qu'il vous a pleu ordonner, mon Dieu, que ce corps fragille et mortel seroit sujet a recevoir repoz la nuict ...

"Oraison quant on se mect au lict": Manuel de dévotion de prêtre Pierre.

NEW HAVEN, Yale Univ. Libr., 498, fol. 27v°-28r°, last quarter XVIc.

*   Pur (= "Pour") ...

See the alphabetical order: Pour ...

6489. Pur et parfaict Saulveur de creature,
Puissant sus tous, chief de toute droicture
                      ...

Orison to God by Nostre Dame to admit all three Doms, Severin, Exupère and Felicien, into Heaven: Mystère des Trois Doms, by chanoine Siboud Pra de Grenoble with the aid of Claude Chevalet de Vienne, and performed at Romans in 1509 (vv. 9349-60).

COLLECTION UNKNOWN (olim Giraud of Lyons), no shelf-mark, fol. not indicated, early XVIc.

Ed.: Giraud and Chevalier, p. 499.

Q

6490. Quant fu en ma juvente
       E en ma volenté
       Molt mis ma entente (sic)
       Certes a jolifté ...

       Poem in honor of Jesus; 176 vv. of varying syllable count.

       LONDON, British Libr., Harley 2253, fol. 76vº-77rº, XIVc.

       Ed.: N.R. Ker, Facsimile of British Museum ms. Harley 2253,
         London, 1965 (EETS o.s. 255). Ref.: Långfors, p. 301.

6491. Quant jadis avec nous regnas,
       Doulx Jhesus, tu nous gouvernas ...

       Plainte to Jesus by S. Bartholomew: Arnoul Gréban's Mystère de
         la Passion (vv. 28519-30).

       PARIS, Bibl. de l'Arsenal, 6431, fol. 215rº, XVc.

       PARIS, Bibl. nat., fr. 815, fol. 230vº, 1458.

       PARIS, Bibl. nat., fr. 816, fol. 199rº, 1473.

       ROME, Accademia Nazionale dei Lincei, Bibl. Corsiniana, Rossi
         412 (44. A. 7), fol. 555vº-556rº, late XVc.

       Ed.: Paris-Raynaud, p. 376 (vv. 28666-77); Jodogne, p. 381 (vv.
         28519-30).

6492. Quant l'en met .i. enfant a letre, au commancement l'en li
       aprent sa patenostre. Qui de ceste clergie veut savoir, si
       deviengne humble comme enfant ...

       "Le prologue de la sainte patenostre", part of the treatise
         entitled: Le Livre du jardin de la sainte ame. The
         Paternoster and commentary begin: Pere nostre qui es es
         cielz. Regarde comment ... (no. 6461).

VIENNA, Oesterreichische Nationalbibl., 2627, fol. 94r°-94v°, XVc.

6493. Ky avoyr veut confession,
Devant sa mort cest oreyson,
Lui est bon a dire
Chascon jour par devocion ...

Rhymed rubric (two six-line stanzas, aabaab, ccdccd) to the Latin hymn Jesu princeps maiestatis ...

CAMBRIDGE, Fitzwilliam Museum, Fitzwilliam 7-1953, Roll of 3 membranes, XIVc.

Ed.: Wormald and Giles, II, p. 471.

6494. Qui bien ayme il ne doit mie
Le tiers de la nuyt dormir ...

Eighth of the "xij balades de Pasques": 13 heptasyllabic lines rhyming abaabaabbabab, the first and second are repeated as the third and last respectively.

VATICAN CITY, Bibl. apost., Reg. lat. 1728, fol. 118v°, XVc.

Ed.: Keller, p. 619.

6495. Ky cest oreyson chescoun jour dist en le honurance de les cink joyes ke Nostre Dame aveyt de son chier fiz, il avera xl jours ...

Rubric, partly in prose and rhyme, to the Cinq Joyes (no. 663) in this ms.

CAMBRIDGE, Fitzwilliam Museum, Fitzwilliam 7-1953, Roll of 3 membranes, XIVc.

Ed.: Wormald and Giles, II, p. 471.

6496. Qui conforteras ceste desconfortee, ceste qui est mise entre mille et mille las et trabuches de temptacions? En laquelle voye sont perilz ...

"Oroison sur la sixiesme demande de la patenostre", in the Mendicité spirituelle by Jean Gerson.

BRUSSELS, Bibl. royale, IV, 111, fol. 211v°, XVc.

LYON, Bibl. de la Ville, 1249 (1121), fol. 34v°-35r°, XVc.

PARIS, Bibl. de l'Arsenal, 2113, fol. 78v°-79r°, XVc.

PARIS, Bibl. de l'Arsenal, 2121, fol. 25r°, XVc.

VIENNA, Oesterreichische Nationalbibl., 2574, fol. 242r°, XVc.

Screening of mss. is incomplete.

Ed.: Glorieux, Gerson: Oeuvres complètes, VII, 1, p. 248.

6497.   Qui du tout son cueur met en Dieu
         Il a son cueur et si a Dieu,
         Et qui le met en aultre lieu,
         Il pert son cueur et si pert Dieu.
                         (Complete Text)

         Quatrain monorhyme: "Aultre devote meditation."

         MANCHESTER, Chetham's Libr., 8007 (Mun. A. 2. 161), fol. 101r°,
            XVc., Hours of Besançon.

6498.   Qui est celluy qui pourroit declairer les grandz tourmens qui
            sont aprestez aux malhureux et ceulx qui vivent meschantement
            ...

         "Project des peynes d'enfer": Manuel de dévotion de prêtre
            Pierre.

         NEW HAVEN, Yale Univ. Libr., 498, fol. 140v°-144r°, last
            quarter XVIc.

6499.   Qui sera mon loyal ami, mon feable secours a mon darrien
            besoing, a la destroite heure de mon departement ...

         "Meditacion de l'ame qui pense a son departement du corps ...",
            in the Mendicité spirituelle by Jean Gerson.

         BRUSSELS, Bibl. royale, IV. 111, fol. 221r°-222r°, XVc.

         PARIS, Bibl. de l'Arsenal, 2113, fol. 105v°-109v°, XVc.

         PARIS, Bibl. de l'Arsenal, 2121, fol. 46r°-49r°, XVc.

         VIENNA, Oesterreichische Nationalbibl., 2574, fol. 254v°-256v°,
            XVc.

         Screening of mss. is incomplete.

         Ed.: Glorieux, Gerson: Oeuvres complètes, VII, 1, pp. 269-72.

6500.   Qui veult avoir lyesse
         Et avecques Dieu part,
         Aux sainctz escriptz s'adresse,
         Desquelz tout bien despart ...

         Chanson en l'honneur de Jesus; 9 huitains, rhyming ababcdcd.

         Early Ed.: Plusieurs belles chansons nouvelles imprimées par
            Claude Nourry, Lyon, vers 1533. Ed.: Jeffery, II, pp. 99-101.

6501.   Quiconques ceste oroison dira chacun jour devotement a genoulx,
            l'annemy ne mal homme ...

         Rubric for the prose version of Bede's "Sept Paroles" with
            inc.: Biau sire Dieux Jhesucrist qui le derrenier jour de ta
            vie ... (no. 5468).

         EDINBURGH, Edinburgh Univ. Libr., 302, fol. 182r°-182v°, XVc.,
            Hours of Paris.

6502.   Quiconques de corage vray non faint ou mechemment prononchera
        ces dessus dites trois veritez en quelque lieu ...

    Explanation at the end of one version of the Trois Verités,
    with attribution to Gerson.

    BRUSSELS, Bibl. royale, II. 7604, fol. 35v°, XVc. Added in a
    later cursive hand.

6503.   Quiconque veult estre salvé, devant toutes choses il luy est de
        necessité tenir la saincte foy catholicque ...

    Athanasian Creed in prose; a Latin phrase precedes each section
    in French; not identical with no. 3529.

    VIENNA, Oesterreichische Nationalbibl., 3391, fol. 1r°-2v°,
    XVc.

6504.   Quiconques veult estre sauvé, il est mestier devant toutes
        choses que il tiengne la foy crestienne ...

    Athanasian Creed, in prose; not identical with the wording of
    no. 5032.

    CHICAGO, Art Institute, 15.536, p. 275-9, c. 1400, Psalter.

R

6505. Recongnoissant le bien de mort amere,
Doulx Jesuchrist né d'une vierge mere ...

Prayer to Jesus; one ten-line stanza, rhyming aabbccddee.

BALTIMORE, Walters Art Gallery, Walters 451, fol. 2r°, c. 1510,
Hours of Rome; made for Jehan Lallemant of Bourges. Poem
copied c. 1548.

6506. Requerum ore tut pecheur
La gloriuse par sa grant duçur,
Si cum ele est mere Jhesu,
E ki par sa seinte vertu ...

Exhortation to sinners to pray to the Virgin: Miracles de la
sainte Vierge, by an anon. Anglo-Norman poet (no. I, vv.
268-79).

LONDON, British Libr., Royal 20. B. XIV, fol. 104v°-105r°, late
XIIIc.

Ed.: Neuhaus, p. 27. Ref.: Vising, p. 53, no. 97 (no reference
to the exhortation).

6507. Restitute, vierge glorieuse
De Dieu fille et amye eureuse ...

Prayer to S. Restituta, in verse.

PARIS, Bibl. nat., fr. 19243, fol. 192v°-193r°, XVIc.

Ref.: Rézeau, Saints, II, p. 261.

6508. Resjoïs toy, Vierge Marie, de Dieu engenreresse senz nulle
taiche de pechiez ...

Hymn "Regina coeli", in prose.

METZ, Bibl. mun., 600, fol. 166v°, XVc., Hours of Paris and Prayer-book.

Ref.: Rézeau, p. 176.

6509.   Retournez, sire, retournez, car depuis vostre departie j'ay le cuer dur ...

Variant of the inc.: O sire Dieu, o vray pere ... (no. 6363).

6510.   Roy des cieulx, qui tout bien parfaiz,
Ouvre ma bouche a ta louenge ...

"Oraison de saint Estienne", 10 huitains each with identical eighth line.

PARIS, Bibl. nat., Rés. D. 5616 and Ye 831, Louenges des benoistz sainctz et sainctes de paradis, fol. ZZ5r°-v°, Paris, Vérard.

VERSAILLES, Bibl. mun., M. 129 (Lacombe 109 quater).

Ed.: Rézeau, Saints, II, pp. 204-7.

6511.   Royne de doulceur, plaine d'umilité
                                           parfonde,
An qui misericorde et toute grace habonde,
Vers Dieu nostre esperance es contre
                                       l'ennemi fonde,
Vierge, je te salue par qui sauf est le
                                          monde.

"Et devons aourer la mere de Dieu et dire ce qu'il s'ensuit: Salve regina"; four monorhyme quatrains of alexandrines.

PROVIDENCE, Brown Univ. Libr., C. 28. b. 4 (H.L. Koopman Collection), fol. 244r°-245r°, XVc., Hours.

6512.   Royne des cieulx et mere de misericorde et refuge des pecheurs, racordez moy a vostre filz ...

Orison to the Virgin, part of the Medecine de l'ame, alias Science de bien mourir, de Gerson.

BRUSSELS, Bibl. royale, 10394-414, fol. 122v°, XVc. Inc.: Haa! Nostre dame, royne des cieulx et mere de misericorde ...

HAGUE (THE), Koninkl. Bibl., 78. J. 49, fol. 476v°, XVc.

LONDON, British Libr., Additional 29279, fol. 48v°, XVc.

LONDON, British Libr., Harley 1310, fol. 87v°, XVc.

LYON, Bibl. de la Ville, 1249 (1121), fol. 49v°, XVc.

PARIS, Bibl. Mazarine, 966, fol. 121r°-121v°, XVc.

ROUBAIX, Archives Municipales, no shelf-mark, fol. 78r°, XVc. Prayer-book of Jacques de Luxembourg.

VIENNA, Oesterreichische Nationalbibl., 3391, fol. 436r°, XVc.

Screening of mss. is incomplete.

Ed.: Glorieux, Gerson: Oeuvres complètes, VII, 1, p. 406. Ref.: Anne-Louise Masson, Jean Gerson, sa vie, son temps, ses oeuvres, Lyon, 1894, p. 143.

6513. Royne des cieulx glorieuse, Vierge au jour d'uy tant dignement, tant haultement saluee ...

Orison to the Virgin, at the conclusion of the "Sermon pour l'Annonciation", by Jean Gerson.

CAMBRAI, Bibl. mun., 578, fol. 9v°, XVc.

PARIS, Bibl. nat., fr. 974, fol. 46r°, XVc.

PARIS, Bibl. nat., fr. 1029, fol. 39v°, XVc.

PARIS, Bibl. nat., fr. 24841, fol. 71r°, XVc.

PARIS, Bibl. nat., lat. 14974, fol. 357v°, XVc.

Ed.: L. Mourin, Scriptorium, 2 (1948), pp. 239-40; Glorieux, Gerson: Oeuvres complètes, VII, 2, p. 549. Ref.: L. Mourin, RBPH, 27 (1949), pp. 561-98 (plan et style du Sermon).

6514. Royne des cieulx qui tout peché efface
Tous trois de cueur te prions que ta face
...

Prayer to the Virgin by one of three Christians about to be martyred: Mystère des Trois Doms, by chanoine Siboud Pra de Grenoble with the assistance of Claude Chevalet de Vienne, and performed at Romans in 1509 (vv. 3261-72).

COLLECTION UNKNOWN (olim Giraud of Lyons), no shelf-mark, fol. not indicated, early XVIc.

Ed.: Giraud and Chevalier, p. 175.

6515. Royne du ciel, esjoy toy, Alleluya! vault autretant comme loenge soit ... <one word illegible> car cil que tu as pourtei ...

"Antene de Nostre Dame: Regina celi."

MANCHESTER, John Rylands Univ. Libr., Fr. 143, fol. 17v°, early XVc., Hours.

6516. Crioient hautement: Roïne tresoriere ...

Varient of the inc.: Crioient hautement: Hé! Vierge trezoriere ... (no. 5937).

S

6517. S'ensieult ung (<u>sic</u>) protestation pour obvier aux temptations malices et deceptions que l'annemy d'enfer s'efforce de faire a la creature ...

<u>Protestation,</u> in prose.

LUXEMBOURG, Bibl. nat., 28, fol. 133r°-133v°, XVIc.

6518. S'ensuyvent les commandemens
Qu'il nous fault garder et savoir,
Qui veult evader les tourmens
D'enfer et paradis avoir.
(Complete Text)

Introductory quatrain for the "Dix Commandements de la loy", rhymed version which begins: Ung seul Dieu, de tout createur ... (no. 2282).

PARIS, Bibl. nat., fr. 952, fol. 187v°, ms. dated 1478.

<u>Ed.</u>: A. Piaget, Annales du Midi, 5 (1893), p. 330. <u>Ref.</u>: Naetebus, LXX, 1; Langfors, p. 389.

6519. Sains angeles de Dieu a qui je suis baillie et rendue comme a bonne garde pour l'ame et pour le corps de moy ...

"Oroison a son propre angele."

LEEDS, Leeds Univ. Libr., Brotherton 4, fol. 202v°-205r°, XVc., Hours of Rome.

6520. Sainz corps, sainz sanc et tres sainz sire,
Ne me mettez paz en vostre ire ...

Orison to Jesus; 10 vv.

METZ, Bibl. mun., 600, fol. 75v°, XVc., Hours of Paris and Prayer-book.

<u>Ref.</u>: Rézeau, p. 166.

6521. Sainct Adrian, de Dieu amy,
        Vous estes en maintz lieux requis ...

        Orayson de sainct Adrian; one eight-line stanza, rhyming by pairs.

        PARIS, Private Collection, LF 56, fol. not indicated, XVIc. Hours of Raoul II de Refuge.

        <u>Ed.</u>: Rézeau, Saints, II, p. 2.

6522. Sainct Anatoille glorieux,
        Qui es soubdain monté aux cieux ...

        "Oraison a sainct Anatoille"; one ten-line stanza, rhyming aabb.

        BESANCON, Bibl. mun., 121, fol. 95v°, late XIVc., Hours of Besançon. This text added in XVIc.

        <u>Ed.</u>: Rézeau, Saints, II, pp. 6-7.

6523. Sainct Andreus, vray(e) prescheur de Dieu, escoute mes prieres
        ...

        Prayer to S. Andrew, in prose.

        NANCY, Bibl. mun., 35 (245), fol. 125v°-126r°, XVc.

        <u>Ed.</u>: Rézeau, Saints, II, p. 7.

6524. Saint Anthoine, confesseur glorieux,
        Devot hermite et vray religieux ...

        "Oraison a saint Anthoine l'ermite", 4 stanzas of twelve decasyllabic lines.

        PARIS, Bibl. nat., Rés. D. 5616 and Ye 831, Louenges des benoistz sainctz et sainctes de paradis, fol. zz3v°, Paris, Vérard.

        VERSAILLES, Bibl. mun., M. 129 (Lacombe 109 quater).

        <u>Ed.</u>: Rézeau, Saints, II, pp. 49-51.

6525. Seint Austin escrist cest oreisun e cele ke la portera ou la chantera, nul enemi ne li porra nure en icel jour ...

        Rubric or introduction to the Latin prayer: Deus propicius esto michi peccatrici ...

        CAMBRIDGE, Fitzwilliam Museum, McClean 123, fol. 109r°, late XIIIc.

Ref.: M.R. James, Descriptive Catalogue of the Manuscripts of the McClean Collection in the Fitzwilliam Museum, Cambridge, 1912, p. 266; Bouly de Lesdain, Manuscrits didactiques, 1964-1965, p. 75 (calls the text a charm); Betty Hill, Notes and Queries, n.s. 19 (1972), p. 46.

6526. Saint Augustin nous enseigne comment Dieu devons servir et la gloire de Dieu conquerre; et dit que nous devons penser et recorder en noz cueurs ...

"Comment homme et femme se pevent sauver et paradis conquerre si comme saint Augustin le dit."

PROVIDENCE, Brown Univ. Libr., C. 28. b. 4 (H.L. Koopman Collection), fol. 232v°-233v°, XVc., Hours.

6527. Seint Bernard, oez ke ben le dist:
Regardez en la face Jhesu Crist ...

Meditation on the Love of Jesus; varying number of lines.

LONDON, British Libr., Additional 11579, fol. 36v°, early XIVc. (six lines).

LONDON, British Libr., Egerton 613, fol. 6r°, XIIIc. (eight lines).

Ed.: Carleton Brown, English Lyrics of the XIIIth Century, Oxford, 2nd ed. 1950, p. 128 (Addit. ms. text along with Latin verses and Middle English lines on the same subject); Betty Hill, Notes and Queries, n.s. 25 (1978), p. 500 (Egerton text as part of an Anglo-Norman Epistle to a nun on the Sufferings of Jesus).

6528. Sainct Berthomeus tres misericors, saulve moy et ne souffre mie que je soie pris ...

Prayer to S. Batholomew; in prose.

NANCY, Bibl. mun., 35 (245), fol. 128v°-129r°, XVc.

Ed.: Rézeau, Saints, II, p. 112.

6529. Sainct Estienne, amy de dieu, qui pour le nom de Jesucrist, iceluy an mesme ...

"Oraison du benoist sainct Estienne/Faicte en maniere d'anthienne", in prose.

PARIS, Bibl. Ecole Nat. Sup. des Beaux-Arts, Masson, impr. 29, fol. B3v°-B4r°, XVIc.

PARIS, Bibl. Ecole Nat. Sup. des Beaux-Arts, Masson, impr. 351, fol. M1v°, XVIc.

PARIS, Bibl. nat., fr. 19243, fol. 167r°-167v°, XVIc.

Ref.: Rézeau, Saints, II, p. 202.

6530. Saint Gaond tres puissant,
       Baron excellent,
       Soyes nous en garend ...

       Prayer to S. Gond; irregular stanzas and length of lines.

       GENEVA, Bibl. publ. univ., lat. 31, fol. 217v°-218v°, XVc.,
       Hours of Paris.

       Ed.: Rézeau, Saints, II, pp. 251-3.

6531. Saint Gregoire luy estant vivant en chantant sa messe Nostre
       Seigneur luy apparut en semblance de sa passion, lequel, meu
       en devotion, a donné a tous vrays confés ...

       Explanatory rubric introducing S. Gregory's O Domine Jhesu
       Christe adoro te ...

       NEW YORK, Pierpont Morgan Libr., Morgan 175, fol. 119r°-119v°,
       late XVc., Hours.

6532. Sainct Jacquez, apostre et amis de Dieu, je te prie par celluy
       ...

       Prayer to S. James the Less, in prose.

       NANCY, Bibl. mun., 35 (245), fol. 127r°-128r°, XVc., Hours of
       Toul.

       Ed.: Rézeau, Saints, II, p. 270.

6533. Sainct Jaique, bien heureis apostre et amy de Dieu, je te prie
       ...

       Suffrage to S. James the Great, in prose.

       NANCY, Bibl. mun., 35 (245), fol. 126r°-126v°, XVc., Hours of
       Toul.

       Ref.: Rézeau, Saints, II, p. 267.

6534. Sainct Jean, humblement te suppli qu'il te plaise prier celluy
       pour moy que au fleuve Jourdain baptisas ...

       Orison to S. John the Baptist, in prose.

       CAMBRIDGE, Harvard College Libr., Typ. 617, fol. 147v°-148r°,
       XVc., Hours.

6535. Sainct Jehan precurseur
       Delivre nous d'erreur
       Noz bouches et noz cueurs,
       Et que tes serviteurs ...

       Paraphrase of Breviary Hymn "Ut queant laxis"; eleven
       seven-line stanzas, aabbccb.

       PARIS, Bibl. nat., fr. 2206, fol. 161r°-162r°, XVIc.

       Ed.: Rézeau, Saints, II, pp. 291-4.

6536.   Saint Leon le pape de Rome fist ceste lettre et dit: Qui la
        lira ja le jour de male morte ne morra ...

        Rubric to the Names of Jesus.

        LONDON, Westminster Abbey, 39, fol. 43r°, XVc., Prayer-book of
        Margaret Beaufort.

6537.   Sains Lyons aposteles de Rome escript ces lettres et dist:
        Quiconques les vera le jour, ne li estuet doubter son anemi
        ...

        Rubric to the Names of Jesus.

        LONDON, British Libr., Sloane 2356, fol. 58v°-59r°, XVc.,
        Prayer-book.

6538.   Sainct Mathie, precieulx apostre de Dieu, escouttes mes prieres
        ...

        Suffrage to S. Mathias, in prose.

        NANCY, Bibl. mun., 35 (245), fol. 130r°-130v°, XVc., Hours of
        Toul.

        Ed.: Rézeau, Saints, II, p. 376.

6539.   Sainct Mathieus, apostre et evvangeliste de Dieu, je te prie
        que aujourd'ui tu soie ...

        Suffrage to S. Matthew, in prose.

        NANCY, Bibl. mun., 35 (245), fol. 129r°-129v°, XVc., Hours of
        Toul.

        Ed.: Rézeau, Saints, II, p. 376.

6540.   Sains Nicholay, amis tres doulz,
        Priez au roy des royz pour nous
        Qu'en la fin ayons confession
        Et de paradis le vray dons.
                        (Complete Text)

        Orison to S. Nicholas.

        METZ, Bibl. mun., 600, fol. 46r°, XVc., Hours of Paris and
        Prayer-book.

        Ed.: Rézeau, p. 161.

6541.   Sainct Phelippe, apostre de Dieu, presentes mes prieres pour
        quoy qu'il ne prengne garde ...

        Suffrage to S. Philip; in prose.

        NANCY, Bibl. mun., 35 (245), fol. 128r°-128v°, XVc., Hours of
        Toul.

        Ed.: Rézeau, Saints, II, p. 418.

6542. Saint Pierre, gloriex martir,
       Qui dou monde te volz partir ...

       Orison to S. Peter the Martyr of Verona; 21 sizains rhyming
         aabaab.

       BRUSSELS, Bibl. royale, IV. 427, fol. 173r°-177v°, c. 1380,
         Hours.

       Ed.: Rézeau, Saints, II, pp. 427-32.

6543. Sainct Piere, noble pastours, qui ais poioir de loier ...

       Suffrage to S. Peter, in prose.

       NANCY, Bibl. mun., 35 (245), fol. 124v°-125r°, XVc., Hours of
         Toul.

       Ref.: Rézeau, Saints, II, p. 419.

6544. Sainctz Polz, vray (ms. vraye) apostre, regarder mon angoisses
       ...

       Suffrage to S. Paul, in prose.

       NANCY, Bibl. mun., 35 (245), fol. 125r°-125v°, XVc., Hours of
         Toul.

       Ed.: Rézeau, Saints, II, p. 414.

6545. Sainct Roch, benoist amy de Dieu,
       Devot confesseur glorieux ...

       Prayer to S. Roch; 6 eight-line stanzas rhyming ababbcbc.

       PARIS, Bibl. nat., Rés. D. 5616 and Ye 831, Louenges des
         benoistz sainctz et sainctes de paradis, fol. vvlr°, Paris,
         Vérard.

       VERSAILLES, Bibl. mun., M. 129 (Lacombe 109 quater).

       Ed.: Rézeau, Saints, II, pp. 439-441.

6546. Saint Sebastien de cuer piteux ...

       Variant of the inc.: O Sebastien, franc cuer piteux ... (no.
         1511).

6547. Saint Sebastien, franc cuer pieu ...

       Variant inc.: O Sebastien, franc cuer piteux ... (no. 1511).

6548. Saint Servan sere! dist Charlez le sené,
       Vroy martyr, cousin es Dammedé ...

       Orison to S. Servan by Charlemagne: Aquin (vv. 1985-2028).

       PARIS, Bibl. nat., fr. 2233, fol. 35v°-36v°, XVc.

Ed.: Joüon des Longrais, p. 77-9. Ref.: Dickman, p. 144; Koch, p. 39-40, 102.

6549.   Sainct Thomas, noble apostres, precheur de Dieu, gouverneur de saincte Eglise ...

Prayer to S. Thomas Apostle, in prose.

NANCY, Bibl. mun., 35 (245), fol. 126v°-127r°, XVc., Hours of Toul.

Ed.: Rézeau, Saints, II, p. 499.

6550.   Saincte Barbe, c'est chose voire
        Que de Dieu tu as grant merite ...

Prayer to S. Barbe; one eight-line stanza rhyming ababbcbc.

DIJON, Bibl. mun., 2555, fol. 168r°-168v°, XVc., Hours of Langres.

Ed.: Rézeau, Saints, II, p. 80.

6551.   Saincte Barbe de valeur,
        Vierge pleine de grant doulceur ...

"Oracio sancte Barbare"; one eight-line stanza, aabb etc.

PARIS, Private Collection, LF 56, fol. not indicated, XVIc., Hours of Raoul II de Refuge.

Ed.: Rézeau, Saints, II, pp. 96-7.

6552.   Sainte doulce benoiste Trinité, je te regracie et mercie quant t'a pleu me donner estre presente au mengier de ce saint sacrement ...

"Oroison quant la messe est dicte."

PROVIDENCE, Brown Univ. Libr., C. 28. b. 4 (H.L. Koopman Collection), fol. 275r°-275v°, XVc., Hours.

6553.   Saincte doulce benoiste vierge Marie, mere de Nostre Seigneur Jhesucrist, royne couronnee des anges, dame et maistresse de tout le monde, mere tuterresse ...

"Une moult devote oroison de la glorieuse benoiste vierge Marie que l'on dit au samedi."

PROVIDENCE, Brown Univ. Libr., C. 28. b. 4 (H.L. Koopman Collection), fol. 160v°-163v°, XVc., Hours.

6554.   Saincte Elyzabeth fut famme Zacharie, si compceut ung filz, grant sainct home, Jehan Baptiste ...

"De sainct Jehan Baptiste", in prose.

MILAN, Bibl. Naz. Braidense, Gerli 68, fol. 89v°-90r°, XVc., Hours of Rennes.

Ref.: Rézeau, Saints, II, p. 281.

6555.   Sainte Katherine vierge couronnee,
De royal lignee fustes engendree;
Vous estes de Dieu si enluminee
Que toute en est honnouree ...

"Oroison de sainte Katherine"; decasyllables.

BALTIMORE, Walters Art Gallery, Walters 261, fol. 120v°-121v°, c. 1400, Hours.

6556.   Sainte Marie, croys aouree ...

Variant inc. for no. 1876.

6557.   Seinte Marie, dame chere,
Serrai jo sul en tel maniere,
Refusez de vus e deguerpiz,
Ki tant m'afi en voz sainz diz ...

"Plainte" to the Virgin by an amputee: Miracles de Nostre Dame by Adgar called Willame (no. XII, vv. 33-67).

LONDON, British Libr., Egerton 612, fol. 17r°-17v°, c. 1300.

Ed.: Neuhaus, p. 64-5. Ref.: Vising, p. 43, no. 13 (the plainte not mentioned).

6558.   Sainte Marie, genitrix,
Mere Deu, dame, Isembart dist ...

Orison to the Virgin by Isembart: Gormont et Isembart (vv. 651-4).

BRUSSELS, Bibl. royale, II. 181, fol. 4v°, XIIIc.

Ed.: Scheler, p. 53-4; Bayot, 1906, fol. 4v°; Bayot, 3 ed. CFMA, p. 42-3; H. Gelzer, Altfranzösisches Lesebuch, Heidelberg, 1953, p. 11; P. Groult, V. Emond, G. Muraille, Anthologie de la littérature française du moyen âge, Gembloux, 3 ed. 1964 and 1967, I, p. 25 and II, p. 18. Ref.: Altona, p. 8; Dickman, p. 154; Ahsmann, p. 53-4; Koch, p. 20-1, 96; Bélanger, p. 40, 218; Combarieu in Senefiance no. 10, p. 99. Legros, ibid, pp. 363-73.

6559.   Seinte Marie, dit Renier en plorant,
Guerisiez lui Olivier le vaillant.
Que il n'i soit veincu ne recreant!
                    (Complete Text)

Prayer to the Virgin by Renier de Genvres: Girart de Vienne by Bertrand de Bar-sur-Aube (vv. 5330-2).

LONDON, British Libr., Harley 1321, fol. 28v°, XIIIc.

LONDON, British Libr., Royal 20. B. XIX, fol. 30v°, XIIIc.

LONDON, British Libr., Royal 20. D. XI, fol. 57v°, XIVc.

PARIS, Bibl. nat., fr. 1374, fol. 124v°, XIIIc.

PARIS, Bibl. nat., fr. 1448, fol. 31r°, XIIIc.

Ed.: Yeandle, p. 169; Van Emden, p. 236 (both used as base ms.
Royal 20. B. XIX). Ref.: Dickman, p. 195.

6560. Si dist: Sainte Marie, qui portas en tes
flans
Le digne creatour qui es chieulz est
manans;
Diex! puis qu'il t'a pleut que telz est mes
semblans,
Donne moy forche avoec, se c'est li tiens
commans ...

Prayer to the Virgin by Baudouin: Baudouin de Sebourc (vv.
602-19 of Chant III).

PARIS, Bibl. nat., fr. 12552, fol. 14r°, XIVc.

PARIS, Bibl. nat., fr. 12553, fol. 39v°-40r°, XVc.

Ed.: Boca, I, p. 80.

6561. Sainte Marie roïne, bonemant
Te cri merci par ton digne commant ...

Orison to the Virgin by a queen: Yon (vv. 762-6).

PARIS, Bibl. nat., fr. 1622, fol. 265v°, XIIIc.

Ed.: Mitchneck, p. 22-3.

6562. Sainte mere de nostre racheteur qui es la porte ouverte du ciel
et estoille de la mer, secourt au pueple ...

"Antene de Nostre Dame: Alma redemptoris."

MANCHESTER, John Rylands Univ. Libr., Fr. 143, fol. 18v°, early
XVc., Hours.

6563. Sainte mere, secours aux chetifz, aide aux foibles, conforte
les plourans ...

Prayer to the Virgin, in prose.

PARIS, Bibl. nat., fr. 13167, fol. 48r°, XVc., Hours.

6564. Sainte pucelle glorieuse
Sur les estoilles precieuse,
Regarde cil qui te forma,
Ta sainte mamelle t'alaicta ...

Hymn "O gloriosa domina" in Lauds of the Heures de Nostre Dame.

MANCHESTER, John Rylands Univ. Libr., Fr. 143, fol. 64v°-65r°, early XVc., Hours.

6565. Seinte pucele Katerine, vous pri pur icele honur ke Deu vous dona a icel jour kant vous venquistes les mestres (sic) et aprés miracles feistes de eus ...

"Oreison de seinte Katerine", in prose.

NORWICH, Castle Museum, 158.926/4 f., fol. 154r°-155r°, XIVc., Hours of Sarum.

6566. Saincte pucelle, per ta saincte merite
En icelle houre secour mon esperit ...

Prayer to the Virgin; 24 vv. rhyming in pairs.

METZ, Bibl. mun., 600, fol. 53r°-53v°, XVc., Hours of Paris and Prayer-book.

Ref.: Rézeau, p. 163.

6567. Sainte pucelle precieuse,
Qui portas la char precieuse ...

Orison to the Virgin; one six-line stanza, aabbcc.

BALTIMORE, Walters Art Gallery, Walters 247, fol. 158v°, c. 1440, Hours.

6568. Sainte veraie crois Dieu aouree ...

Variant inc. for no. 1876.

6569. Saincte Vierge Marie, meire de Dieu et
roÿgne,
Qui pourtaiste celuy a qui le ciel
s'encline ...

Orison to the Virgin, one monorhymed quatrain.

METZ, Bibl. mun., 600, fol. 52v°, XVc., Hours of Paris and Prayer-book.

Ed.: Rézeau, p. 163.

6570. Saincte Vierge, que es meire de Dieu,
Soyes a nous tous deffance encontre
l'aneminz ...

Orison to the Virgin, one quatrain, abab.

METZ, Bibl. mun., 600, fol. 99v°, XVc., Hours of Paris and Prayer-book.

Ref.: Rézeau, p. 168.

6571. Salut a toy, mon bon et loyal serviteur, pourtant que sur peu de choses tu as esté fidele ...

"Antienne de sainct Hierome", in prose.

PARIS, Bibl. nat., Rés. B. 9098, fol. S6vº, XVIc.

Ref.: Rézeau, Saints, II, p. 295, who refers to other early editions.

6572.   Salve   doulce   vierge   Marie,   mere   de   misericorde,   mere d'esperance et mere de concorde, mere de Dieu et mere de grace, tu es vraiement mere ...

Orison to the Virgin, divided by the scribe into 98 paragraphs. Its colophon attributing the prayer to S. Augustine begins: Ceste oroison cy devant escripte ... (no. 5545).

PROVIDENCE, Brown Univ. Libr., C. 28. b. 4 (H.L. Koopman Collection), fol. 137rº-157vº, XVc., Hours.

6573.   Save nous Dieu, qui es tous poissans, et si nous ottroie la permenant lumiere ...

Benediction, in prose.

METZ, Bibl. mun., 600, fol. 53vº, XVc., Hours of Paris and Prayer-book.

Ref.: Rézeau, p. 163.

6574.   Salve royne de tout le monde, plaine de misericorde et de pitié. Ave dame des cieulx et des anges ...

"Oroison de Nostre Dame que l'on doit dire a genoulx".

PROVIDENCE, Brown Univ. Libr., C. 28. b. 4 (H.L. Koopman Collection), fol. 159rº-160vº, XVc., Book of Hours.

6575.   Salve, vierge gloriouse, qui estes Katherine apellee, fontainne de pitié selee par virginité ...

"Une devote orison de saincte Katherine, vierge." Text in prose, but was once rhymed, since one meets several octosyllabic lines.

METZ, Bibl. mun., 600, fol. 118rº-119rº, XVc., Hours of Paris and Prayer-book.

Ref.: Rézeau, p. 171; Rézeau, Saints, II, p. 126.

6576.   Sanz per estes, pucele,
Sur tutes suef et bele;
Nos pechez nus ostez
E chastes nus facez ...

"Virgo singularis inter omnes", in rhyme, as part of the Heures de Nostre Dame.

STUTTGART, Württembergische Landesbibl., Brev. 75, fol. 58vº-59vº, XIVc., Hours of Sarum.

6577.   Savés que j'apiel beghinage?
        Conscienche ne mie large,
        Pieue et devote affection.
        Oster son coer de tout herbage ...

        "Dit de l'ame", oeuvre mystique d'origine béguine; 21
        twelve-line stanzas.

        BERLIN, Deutsche Staatsbibl., gall. oct. 28, fol. 131v°-138r°,
        early XIVc., Prayer-book (destroyed).

        BRUSSELS, Bibl. roy., 9411-26, fol. 103r°-104r°, XIVc.
        (extracts beginning at tenth stanza: Amors ne crient mort ne
        torment ...)

        Ed.: E. Bechmann, Z.R.P., 13 (1889), pp. 72-8. Ref.: A.
        Scheler, Dits et contes de Baudouin de Condé, Brussels, 1866,
        I, p. xxiii; Naetebus, XXXVI, 2; Långfors, p. 363; H.A.
        Hatzfeld, P.M.L.A., 64 (1946), pp. 331-78; W. Rothwell, in
        Current Thoughts in French Literature: Essays in Memory of
        G.T. Clapton (ed. J.C. Ireson), Oxford, 1965, pp. 33-48;
        Brayer, GRLMA, VI, 2, no. 1176.

6578.   Se aucuns ha tribulation ou maladie ou pouvretey dont il soit
        en yre envers Dieu ...

        Introduction to the prayer to Jesus which opens: E! tres doulx
        sire Jhesucrist que ... (no. 5775). For another redaction,
        see no. 5094.

        MANCHESTER, Chetham's Libr., 8007 (Mun. A. 2. 161), fol. 115r°,
        XVc., Hours of Besançon.

6579.   Secorez mei, qu'or m'est mester,
        Tant que rentrez fusse eu moster ...

        Plainte to the Virgin by the sacristan of the Abbey of
        Sainte-Ouen: Chronique des ducs de Normandie, by Benoit (vv.
        28013-32).

        LONDON, British Libr., Harley 1717, fol. 159r°-159v°, XIIIc.

        TOURS, Bibl. mun., 903, fol. 137v°, late XIIc.

        Ed.: Fahlin, II, p. 173-4.

6580.   Seigneur, ayes mercy de nous; Christ, ayes pitié de nous;
        Seigneur, escoute nous; Christ exauce nous ...

        "Les Litanies ou supplications de l'Eglise catholique": Manuel
        de dévotion de prêtre Pierre.

        NEW HAVEN, Yale Univ. Libr., 498, fol. 59v°-63r°, last quarter
        XVIc.

6581.   Seigneur Dieu, je ne suis pas digne que tu loges et entre en ma
        conscience ...

        "Pour le Sacrement."

NEW YORK, Pierpont Morgan Libr., Morgan 78, fol. 11v°, XVc.,
Hours of Rome.

6582. Seigneur Dieu, pere nourrisier de toute creature, qui des le
ventre de nostre mere ...

Orison after a meal, in prose.

SAN MARINO (Calif.), Huntington Libr., HM 1170, fol. 100r°,
late XVc., Hours of Rome. This prayer added in 1561.

6583. Seigneur Dieu qui justifie le pecheur et ne veult point la mort
des pecheurs, je supplie a ta maiesté ...

"Devote oraison au Sacrement."

NEW YORK, Pierpont Morgan Libr., Morgan 78, fol. 163v°, XVc.,
Hours of Rome. This prayer by a XVIc. hand.

6584. Seigneur Dieu, qui nous as laissé la memoire de ta mort et
passion soubz ce sacrement admirable, donne nous la grace de
tellement l'adorer ...

"Autre oraison a mesme effect" = Prayer at the "elevation du
corps Nostre Seigneur": Manuel de dévotion de prêtre Pierre.

NEW HAVEN, Yale Univ. Libr., 498, fol. 88v°, last quarter XVIc.

6585. Seigneur Dieu saige et debonnaire, puys qu'il t'a pleu de me
prendre en sauvegarde et choisir parmy tant d'autres pour te
servir ...

"Prieres pour dire le matin devant toute(s) chose": Manuel de
dévotion de prêtre Pierre.

NEW HAVEN, Yale Univ. Libr., 498, fol. 22r°-24v°, last quarter
XVIc.

6586. Seigneur Dieu, sois propice a moy pecheresse et sois ma garde
...

Orison to God and the Angels, in prose.

OXFORD, Bodleian Libr., Rawlinson, liturg. f. 33, fol.
95r°-96r°, 1566.

Ref.: Rézeau, Saints, II, p. 530, who relates the text to no.
1994.

6587. Seigneur Dieu tout puyssant, qui n'estes venu en ce monde pour
perdre l'homme mais plustost pour le sauver ...

"Autre priere avant que aller a la confession": Manuel de
dévotion de prêtre Pierre.

NEW HAVEN, Yale Univ. Libr., 498, fol. 65r°-68v°, last quarter
XVIc.

6588. Seigneur, imbuez nos coeurs de vostre grace a ce qu'ayans cogneu par l'anonciation de l'ange l'incarnation de vostre filz ...

Prayer to God, in prose.

CHICAGO, Newberry Libr., 43, fol. 162r°-162v°, XVIc., Hours of Rouen.

6589. Seigneur Jesus Christ, fontaine de toute sapience et lumiere des coeurs, donnez moy, je vous supplie, l'illustration ...

"De celuy qui se prepare a lire et estudier."

CHICAGO, Newberry Libr., 43, fol. 162v°-163r°, XVIc., Hours of Rouen.

6590. Seigneur Jesus christ, qui pour la redemption du monde as voulu patiemment endurer angoisses, miseres, opobres, despitz ...

"Oraison a Jesus Christ crucifié" and "Oraison de la Passion de Nostre Seigneur": Manuel de dévotion de prêtre Pierre.

NEW HAVEN, Yale Univ. Libr., 498, fol. 35r°-36r° (second copy on 38v°-39r°), last quarter XVIc.

6591. Seigneur Jesus, en la main de qui nous confessons la playe et la santé, la mort et la vie et tout ce qui est en nous, vueiles interposer ta mort ...

"Oraison, estant en grand maladie": Manuel de dévotion de prêtre Pierre.

NEW HAVEN, Yale Univ. Libr., 498, fol. 112v°-113v°, last quarter XVIc.

6592. Seigneur, nous vous supplions de prevenir nos actions par vostre grace et les poursuivre en nous aydant, afin que ...

Orison to God, in prose.

CHICAGO, Newberry Libr, 43, fol. 163r°, XVIc., Hours of Rouen.

6593. Si com bone chos' est digne, juste et
                                leauls
      Remembrer les vertuz et les biens des feals
                        ...

Exhortation to the Love of God: Girart de Rossillon, Burgundian redaction (vv. 5653-78).

BRUSSELS, Bibl. royale, 11181, fol. 96r°, XVc.

MONTPELLIER, Bibl. Fac. Ecole de Médecine, H. 244, fol. 106r°-106v°, XVc.

MONTPELLIER, Bibl. Fac. Ecole de Médecine, H. 349, fol. 77r°, c. 1350.

PARIS, Bibl. nat., fr. 15103, fol. 115v°-116r°, 1417.

Ed.: Ham, p. 270-1 (base ms.: Montpellier H. 349).

6594.   Si cum jeo crai verament que vous preistes char ...

Orison at the Elevation, in prose.

LIVERPOOL, Liverpool Cathedral, Chapter Libr., 36, fly-leaves
        at the end, 1v°-2r°, late XIV - early XVc., Hours of Sarum.

6595.   Si com tu is par virité provee
        Li fil de Diex, qe as cele hostie aonbree
                          ...

Prayer at the Sacrement by Roland: Entrée d'Espagne (vv.
        2987-3013).

VENICE, Bibl. Marciana, 257 (olim gall. XXI), fol. 58r°-58v°,
        XIVc.

Ed.: Thomas, I, p. 111-2.

6596.   Si doulcement me demaine nature
        Que je ne say si je suis mors ou viz ...

Third of the "xij balades de Pasques": 13 decasyllabic lines
        rhyming abaabaabbabab, the first and second are repeated as
        the third and last respectively.

VATICAN CITY, Bibl. apost., Reg. lat. 1728, fol. 118r°, XVc.

Ed.: Keller, p. 616-17.

6597.   Si voirement cum je croi sanz dotance que tu conceus par la
        vertu deu seint Espir, sanz acointement d'omme, Nostre Segnor
        ...

Orison to the Virgin, at the end of a series of Salutations
        which begin: Dex te saut sainte Marie pleine de grace ...
        (no. 5706).

NEW YORK, Pierpont Morgan Libr., Morgan 92, fol. 130r°-130v°,
        late XIIIc., Hours.

6598.   Sy vous prie, Dame debonnaire,
        Qui a nulluy n'est contraire ...

Orison to the Virgin by Jaspar: "Geu des trois roys" (vv.
        759-65).

PARIS, Bibl. Sainte-Geneviève, 1131, fol. 28v°, XVc.

Ed.: Whittredge, p. 175.

6599.   Sire, a toy qui es net et mondes,
        Ay criey des choses profondes.
        Syre, ma voix ennuit exaulce,
        A toy me tray et me sohaulce (sic) ...

Sixth of the Seven Penitential Psalms; a version in rhymed couplets.

LILLE, Bibl. mun., Godefroy 5 (147), fol. 107r°-108r°, XVc., Hours.

6600. Sire beaus Deus Jhesu Cris, aies de ceaus merci qui per toi sunt martirizé, qu'il ne soient condampné ...

Prayer to God by S. Eutrope, on the point of death: Chronicle of Pseudo-Turpin in the Chronique dite saintongeaise.

ABERYSTWYTH, Nat. Libr. of Wales, 5005 B, p. 93, XIIIc.

PARIS, Bibl. nat., fr. 124, fol. 3v°, XIVc.

PARIS, Bibl. nat., fr. 5714, fol. 51v°, XIIIc.

Ed.: T.M. Auracher, ZRP, 1 (1877), p. 280 (base ms. B.N., fr. 5714, variants from B.N., fr. 124); Mandach, p. 274 (Aberystwyth codex).

6601. Sire beaus Deus Jhesu Cris per la cui foi ...

Variant of Sire Deus Jhesu Cris per la cui foi ... (no. 6607).

6602. Sire, bien puissiez vous venir qui estes le chastel de ma redemption. Sire, bien puissiez vous venir qui estes le commencement de ma creacion ...

"Ce doit on dire quant on voit le corps de Nostre Seigneur."

PROVIDENCE, Brown Univ. Libr., C. 28. b. 4 (H.L. Koopman Collection), fol. 271r°-271v°, XVc., Hours.

6603. Sire, bien soiez vous venus
A grant joie de cueur receuz
Qui cy me venez visiter
De vostre presence honnourer ...

Orison to Jesus; sixteen octosyllablic lines rhyming in pairs.

PROVIDENCE, Brown Univ. Libr., C. 28. b. 4 (H.L. Koopman Collection), fol. 272r°-272v°, XVc., Hours.

6604. Sire Dieu des vertus, qui repare les choses tresbuchies et conserve les réparés, augmente les poeuples ...

"<La veille de pentecouste>, oroison sixime."

NEW YORK, Pierpont Morgan Libr., Morgan 78, fol. 122r°, XVc., Hours of Rome. This prayer in a XVIc. hand.

6605. Sire Diex Jhesucrist, a qui pouer toutes choses celestiaus infernaux flechissent leurs genous et obeissent a tes commendemens ...

Vespers of the Hours of the Cross in prose.

VIENNA, Oesterreichische Nationalbibl., 1969, fol. 135v°-136r°, XIVc., Hours.

6606. Sire Dieu Jhesucrist, mon Dieu, mon createur, mon pere et mon seigneur, mon vray Dieu regnant divinement ...

Protestation de foi, in prose.

BRIGHTON, Brighton Public Libr., 2, fol. 159r°-159v°, XVc., Hours of Paris.

6607. Sire Deus Jhesu Cris per la cui foi e per la cui amor j'ai enpris ceste voie, done moi que je puisse prendre ceste cité a loenge e a l'enor de ton nom.
                    (Complete Text)

Orison to Jesus by Charlemagne for the capture of Pampelona: Chronicle of Pseudo-Turpin in the Chronique dite saintongeaise.

ABERYSTWYTH, Nat. Libr. of Wales, 5005 B, p. 74, XIIIc.

PARIS, Bibl. nat., fr. 124, fol. 1v°, XIVc. Inc.: Sire beaus Deus Jhesu Cris per la cui foi ...

PARIS, Bibl. nat., fr. 5714, fol. 43r°, XIIIc.

Ed.: T.M. Auracher, ZRP, 1 (1877), p. 265 (base ms. B.N., fr. 5714, variants from B.N., fr. 124); Mandach, p. 259 (Aberystwyth codex).

6608. Sire Dieux Jhesucrist, qui a heure de tierce feiz Adan le premier homme a ton ymage et a ta samblance et qui a icele heure meismes donnas la loy ...

Hours of the Cross in prose, terce.

VIENNA, Oesterreichische Nationalbibl., 1969, fol. 132r°-133r°, XIVc., Hours.

6609. Sire Dieu Jhesucrist, roy tout puyssant qui fis le ciel et la terre et m'as formé a ton ymage et a ta semblance ...

Orison to Jesus, in prose.

SAN MARINO (Calif.), Huntington Libr., HM 1129, fol. 144v°-145r°, c. 1450, Hours of Paris.

6610. Sire Dieu, merci te requier,
Doulz Jhesus Christ, vray Dieu entier ...

Prayer to several saints; 108 vv. arranged in twelve stanzas.

BERLIN, Deutsche Staatsbibl., Theol. lat. oct. 64, fol. 75v°-78r°, XVc., Hours.

Ed.: Rézeau, Saints, I, pp. 135-9.

6611. Sire Dieu, mez defautez cuevre
Mes levrez a toy loer oevre ...

Prayer to God, inspired by the opening lines of the Hours of the Virgin 'Domine labia mea'; one six-line stanza rhyming aabccb.

METZ, Bibl. mun., 600, fol. 8r°, XVc., Hours of Paris and Prayer-book.

Ed.: Rézeau, p. 157.

6612. Sire Dieus, dit Girart, mon pere n'oublier,
Qui chascun jor se poine de vo loi
                                essaucier.
Envoiez lui secors, que il se puist vengier
De l'amirant d'Espangne et son cuer
                                esclerier.
              (Complete Text)

Orison to God by Girart de Commarchis: Siège de Barbastre (vv. 4282-6).

LONDON, British Libr., Harley 1321, fol. 152v°, late XIIIc. Inc.: Gloriex sire Dex, mon pere n'oblier ...

LONDON, British Libr., Royal 20. B. XIX, fol. 134v°, mid XIIIc.

LONDON, British Libr., Royal 20. D. XI, fol. 230v°, XIVc. Inc.: Glorieux sire Diex, mon pere n'oublier ... This copy lacks v. 2.

PARIS, Bibl. nat., fr. 1448, fol. 139r°, mid XIIIc. Inc.: Gloriox sire Dex, mon pere n'oblier ...

PARIS, Bibl. nat., fr. 24369, fol. 140v°-141r°, XIVc.

Ed.: Perrier, p. 134 (base ms. London, Royal 20. B. XIX).

6613. Sire Dieu, ne me recevez mie en vostre indignacion, et ne me chastiez mie en vostre ire; Sire, ayez merci de moy ...

First of the Penitential Psalms, in a prose version. Wording is close to but not identical with that of no. 3646.

PARIS, Bibl. nat., fr. 13167, fol. 61v°-62v°, late XVc., Hours of Paris.

SAN MARINO (Calif.), Huntington Libr., HM 1129, fol. 84r°-85v°, c. 1450, Hours of Paris.

6614. Sire Dieu, nous requerons que la vertu du sainct Esprit nous assiste, laquelle par sa clemence ...

"Le mardy de la Pentecouste, oratio."

NEW YORK, Pierpont Morgan Libr., Morgan 78, fol. 149r°, XVc., Hours of Rome. This text in a XVIc. hand.

6615. Sire Dieux, nous te requeron humblement qu'il te plaise estre saintifieur et garde de ton peuple et nous, par les prieres et deffenses ...

Orison for S. James the Great (on feast-day).

PARIS, Bibl. de l'Arsenal, 2162, fol. 124v°, XVc., Hours of Paris.

6616. Sire Dieu, nous te requeron qu'il te plaise exaucier nos prieres lesquelles en l'honneur et solennité de saint Leu confesseur et evesque ...

Orison for S. Lupus (on feast-day).

PARIS, Bibl. de l'Arsenal, 2162, fol. 147r°, XVc., Hours of Paris.

6617. Sire Dex, oez m'oroison car je sei bien que mes jors est finés; done me sens et entendement et si enlumine mon cuer ...

Orison to God.

NEW YORK, Pierpont Morgan Libr., Morgan 92, fol. 132r°, late XIIIc., Hours.

6618. Sire Dieux, par vostre misericorde, prendez (sic) la douleur de noz cuers et si deffendez moy et luy .N. en touz temps ...

Orison to God in prose.

BALTIMORE, Walters Art Gallery, Walters 103, fol. 83r°-83v°, late XIVc., Hours of Paris (?).

6619. Sire Dex, pere pardurable,
Tous puissans, sage et veritable,
Qui mains en Sainte Trinité
En une meismes deÿté ...

Orison to God by a governess: Roman du comte d'Anjou by Jean Maillart (vv. 877-1020).

PARIS, Bibl. nat., fr. 146, fol. 43r°-44r°, XIVc. (as part of Chaillou de Pesstain's interpolation (vv. 1661-784) in the Roman de Fauvel by Gervais du Bus).

PARIS, Bibl. nat., fr. 765, fol. 5v°-6r°, XVc.

PARIS, Bibl. nat., nouv. acq. fr. 4531, fol. 10v°-11v°, early XIVc.

Ed.: Aubry, Fauvel, fol. 43v°-44r°; Långfors, Fauvel, pp. 191-4 (only Paris, B.N. fr. 146); Roques, Jehan Maillart, pp. 27-32. Ref.: M. Roques, Romania, 55 (1929), p. 551 (concerning the interpolation in Paris, B.N. fr. 146); Wels, p. 3, no. 5; p. 7, n. 18; Colliot, I, pp. 126-7.

6620. Sire Dieu, qui as mis tes mains, tes piés et tout ton corps en l'arbre de la crois pour nous pecheurs, et as soustenu la couronne d'espines ...

Orison to Jesus, in prose.

SAN MARINO (Calif.), Huntington Libr., HM 1129, fol. 143r°-143v°, c. 1450, Hours of Paris.

6621. Sire Dieu, qui d'an en an nous fais resjoïr de la feste et solennité de monseigneur saint Clement ton benoist evesque et martir ...

Orison for S. Clement (on feast-day).

PARIS, Bibl. de l'Arsenal, 2162, fol. 150r°-150v°, XVc., Hours of Paris.

6622. Sire Dex qui deis: om ne puet avoir gregnor charité en soi que metre s'ame por son ami ...

Orison to God, in prose.

NEW YORK, Pierpont Morgan Libr., Morgan 92, fol. 133v°-134v°, late XIIIc., Hours.

6623. Sire Dieu, qui donnas la foy a Moÿse en la montaigne de Synaï et en ycelui mesmes lieu fais transporter et colloquier par tes sains angels ...

Orison for S. Catherine (on feast-day).

PARIS, Bibl. de l'Arsenal, 2162, fol. 156v°-157r°, XVc., Hours of Paris.

6624. Sire Dieu, qui ensaignas et enluminas de ta sainte doctrine grant multitude de gent par la predicacion de saint Pol ...

Orison for S. Paul (on feast-day).

PARIS, Bibl. de l'Arsenal, 2162, fol. 127r°, XVc., Hours of Paris.

6625. Sire Dieux, qui, entre ces aultres miracles fais par ta puissance, voulus et ottrias que la sainte victoire de martire fut faicte ...

Orison for S. Agatha (on feast-day).

PARIS, Bibl. de l'Arsenal, 2162, fol. 161r°-161v°, XVc., Hours of Paris.

6626. Sire Dieux, qui es mout bening, veulles enluminer ton Eglise affin que icelle enluminee des doctrines de saint Jehan l'apostre ...

Orison for S. Jean the Evangelist (on feast-day).

PARIS, Bibl. de l'Arsenal, 2162, fol. 125v°-126r°, XVc., Hours of Paris.

6627. Sire Dieux, qui es tous puissans,
Qui gardes tes oubeïssans,
Dieu de nos peres Abraham,
Ysaac, Jacob qui maint ahan ...

Orison to God by Manasseh; adaptation by Guillaume de Machaut in his Confort d'ami (vv. 1453-1536).

BERN, Bürgerbibl., 218, fol. 62v°-63r°, XIVc.

PARIS, Bibl. de l'Arsenal, 5203, fol. 100r°-100v°, XIVc.

PARIS, Bibl. nat., fr. 843, fol. 130r°-130v°, XVc.

PARIS, Bibl. nat., fr. 1584, fol. 137v°-138r°, XIVc.

Screening of mss. is incomplete.

Ed.: Hoepffner, III, 1921, pp. 52-4.

6628. Sire Dieu, qui eslevas le benoit evangeliste saint Marc par grace de predicacion, donne nous et ottrie, nous le te requeron, que nous puisson ...

Orison for S. Mark (on feast-day).

PARIS, Bibl. de l'Arsenal, 2162, fol. 133v°, XVc., Hours of Paris.

6629. Sires Deus, qui estes fontainne de tous biens, de qui descendent tuit li russel de bonteit et de misericorde, je vos rans graice ...

"Li orisons c'on doit dire aprés la levation de Dieu."

LONDON, British Libr., Harley 2955, fol. 126v°-128r°, XIVc., Hours of Metz.

METZ, Bibl. mun., 600, fol. 111v°, XVc., Hours of Paris and Prayer-book.

Ref.: Rézeau, p. 170 (Metz codex).

6630. Sire Dieu qui fais monseigneur saint Yves ton confesseur resplendir par pluseurs nobles miracles, nous te requeron ...

Orison for S. Yves (on feast-day).

PARIS, Bibl. de l'Arsenal, 2162, fol. 147v°-148r°, XVc., Hours of Paris.

6631. Sire Dieu, qui fais venir avec toy en tes sains cieulx madame sainte Marguerite par la victoire de martire, nous te requeron ...

Orison for S. Margaret (on feast-day).

PARIS, Bibl. de l'Arsenal, 2162, fol. 157v°, XVc., Hours of Paris.

6632. Sire Dieu, qui nous as fait aujourd'huy esjoïr de la translacion de la benoiste virge, madame sainte Geneviefve, <qui> delivra la noble cité ...

Orison for the Translation of S. Geneviève (on feast-day).

PARIS, Bibl. de l'Arsenal, 2162, fol. 159v°-160r°, XVc., Hours of Paris.

6633.   Sire Dieu, qui nous as fait venir a la congnoissance de ton nom par tes benois apostres saint Symon et saint Jude, ottrie nous ...

Orison for SS. Simon and Jude (on feast-day).

PARIS, Bibl. de l'Arsenal, 2162, fol. 130v°, XVc., Hours of Paris.

6634.   Sire Dieu qui nous donnas le benoit confesseur saint Remy pour nous ensaignier la voie de nostre salvacion ...

Orison for S. Remi (on feast-day).

PARIS, Bibl. de l'Arsenal, 2162, fol. 148r°-148v°, XVc., Hours of Paris.

6635.   Sire Dieu, qui nous esjoïs par chascun an de la solennité de monseigneur saint .N., ton confesseur, accorde nous ...

Prayer for a single confessor (on feast-day).

PARIS, Bibl. de l'Arsenal, 2162, fol. 154v°, XVc., Hours of Paris.

6636.   Sire Dieu, qui nous sueffres et ottries honnorer les festes et solennités de tes sains martirs .N. et .N., fai nous esjoïr ...

Orison for several martyrs, unmitred (on feast-day).

PARIS, Bibl. de l'Arsenal, 2162, fol. 153r°-153v°, XVc., Hours of Paris.

6637.   Sire Dieu, qui ottrias au benoist confesseur, monseigneur saint Mor, diacre, que aujourd'juy il seroit a compaignie en ta grant gloire ...

Orison for S. Maur (on feast-day).

PARIS, Bibl. de l'Arsenal, 2162, fol. 150v°-151r°, XVc., Hours of Paris.

6638.   Sire Dieu, qui par ta largesse,
        Desis et fesis la promesse ...

Orison to God through the saints' intercession; 20 vv. rhyming in pairs.

NIORT, Bibl. mun., 7, fol. 174v°-175r°, XVc.

Ed.: Rézeau, Saints, I, pp. 217-18.

6639.   Sire Dex, qui par vostre sen et par vostre pooir merveillous feistes toutes creatures ...

Prayer to God, in prose; one of a large group the first of which is recorded at no. 2523.

METZ, Bibl. mun., 600, fol. 78v°, XVc., Hours of Paris and Prayer-book.

OPORTO, Bibl. publ. mun., 619, fol. 89r°-89v°, XVc.

Ref.: G. Moldenhauer, ASNS, 151 (1927), p. 74 (prayer not identified); Rézeau, p. 167 (Metz codex).

6640.   Sire Dex, qui por vostre pooir et vostre sen demonstrer feites el ciel les angles nobles creatures ...

Orison to God, in prose; one of a large group, the first of which is recorded at no. 2523.

METZ, Bibl. mun., 600, fol. 78r°, XVc., Hours of Paris and Prayer-book.

OPORTO, Bibl. publ. mun., 619, fol. 89r°, XVc.

Ref.: G. Moldenhauer, ASNS, 151 (1927), p. 74 (the orison is not mentioned); Rézeau, p. 167 (Metz codex).

6641.   Sire Dieu redempteur, tout veant merveilleusement, tout congnoissant, sapience de tous, je fay au jour de huy, en despit de l'ennemi, protestacion.

Variant inc. of no. 2007: Sire Dieu tout puissant, tout voyant ...

6642.   Sire Dieu tout puissant, nostre bon pere qui estez es cielx, vostre voulenté soit faitte telement en terre ...

"Oroison selonc la tierce demande de la patenostre" in the Mendicité spirituelle by Jean Gerson.

BRUSSELS, Bibl. royale, IV. 111, fol. 209v°-210r°, XVc.

LYON, Bibl. de la Ville, 1249 (1121), fol. 32v°, XVc.

PARIS, Bibl. de l'Arsenal, 2113, fol. 72v°-73v°, XVc.

PARIS, Bibl. de l'Arsenal, 2121, fol. 20v°-21r°, XVc.

VIENNA, Oesterreichische Nationalbibl., 2574, fol. 239v°, XVc.

Screening of mss. is incomplete.

Ed.: Glorieux, Gerson: Oeuvres complètes, VII, 1, p. 244.

6643.   Sire Dieu tout puissant, nous tes serviteurs subgetz a ta maiesté par ton benoist chier filz en la vertu ...

"La tierce oroison", last of three prayers to the Trinity, in prose.

PROVIDENCE, Brown Univ. Libr., C. 28. b. 4 (H.L. Koopman Collection), fol. 238r°-238v°, XVc., Hours.

6644. Sire Dieu, tout puissant pardurable, qui nous as donné
       aujourd'ui la sainte leesce de la feste de ton benoist
       apostre ...

       Orison for S. Bartholomew (on feast-day).

       PARIS, Bibl. de l'Arsenal, 2162, fol. 134r⁰-134v⁰, XVc., Hours
          of Paris.

6645. Sire Dieux tous poissans, pius et misericors, qui o cors d'une
          jovene ...

       Suffrage to S. Justine, in prose.

       PARIS, Bibl. de l'Arsenal, 288, fol. 98r⁰-98v⁰, XIVc. This text
          added by XVc. hand.

       Ref.: Rézeau, Saints, II, p. 300.

6646. Sire Dieu tout puissant, vostre prophete dit, et le fait
          monstre, que l'omme est comparé aux jumens ...

       "Oroison assés appartenant a ceste tierce demande <de la
          patenostre>, in the Mendicité spirituelle by Jean Gerson.

       BRUSSELS, Bibl. royale, IV. 111, fol. 210r⁰, XVc.

       LYON, Bibl. de la Ville, 1249 (1121), fol. 32v⁰-33r⁰, XVc.

       PARIS, Bibl. de l'Arsenal, 2113, fol. 73v⁰-74r⁰, XVc.

       PARIS, Bibl. de l'Arsenal, 2121, fol. 21r⁰-21v⁰, XVc.

       VIENNA, Oesterreichische Nationalbibl., 2574, fol. 239v⁰-240r⁰,
          XVc.

       Screening of mss. is incomplete.

       Ed.: Glorieux, Gerson: Oeuvres complètes, VII, 1, pp. 244-5.

6647. Sire, donne nous l'esprit de penser tousjours aux choses
          droictes et propices de faire ...

       "Dimence viij^e, oraison."

       NEW YORK, Pierpont Morgan Libr., Morgan 78, fol. 43r⁰, XVc.,
          Hours of Rome. Prayer by a XVIc. hand.

6648. Sire doulz Dieu, je te prie per le saint miracles de ton corpz
          et de ton saint sanc per quoy nous sommez peu ...

       "Ung preste puet dire cest oroison devant qu'il disse messe."

       METZ, Bibl. mun., 600, fol. 112r⁰-114r⁰, XVc., Hours of Paris
          and Prayer-book.

       Ref.: Rézeau, p. 170.

6649.   Sire dous Jhesucrist, filz de Dieu le vif, qui es vrai Dieu et
         vrai homme ...

         Prayer to Jesus, in prose.

         VATICAN CITY, Bibl. apost., Reg. lat. 315, fol. 10r°, XIVc.

6650.   Sire dous Jhesucrist, je commande en tes sainctes et honorables
         mains ...

         "Quant tu istras hors du moustier."

         VATICAN CITY, Bibl. apost., Reg. lat. 315, fol. 15r°, XIVc.

6651.   Sire dous Jhesucrist, je te recommande mon chief et te requier
         ...

         "Quant tu metras ton chaperon."

         VATICAN CITY, Bibl. apost., Reg. lat. 315, fol. 8r°, XIVc.

6652.   Sire doulx Jhesucrist, qui a heure de complie, puis que vous
         feustes mis hors de la croix par saint Joseph ...

         Compline of the Hours of the Cross; prose.

         PROVIDENCE, Brown Univ. Libr., C. 28. b. 4 (H.L. Koopman
         Collection), fol. 93r°-93v°, XVc., Hours.

6653.   Sire doulx Jhesucrist, qui a heure de midy, puis que vous
         feustes au lieu de vostre crucifiement, feustes despoillé ...

         Sext of the Hours of the Cross; prose.

         PROVIDENCE, Brown Univ. Libr., C. 28. b. 4 (H.L. Koopman
         Collection), fol. 89v°-91r°, XVc., Hours.

6654.   Sire doulx Jhesucrist, qui a heure de prime, aprés ce que vous
         aviez esté tout la nuit devant si honteusement demené ...

         Prime of the Hours of the Cross; prose.

         PROVIDENCE, Brown Univ. Libr., C. 28. b. 4 (H.L. Koopman
         Collection), fol. 87v°-88v°, XVc., Hours.

6655.   Sire doulx Jhesucrist, qui a heure de vespres, aprés ce que
         l'ame se fust partie de vostre benoit corps et que le costé
         vous fust ouvert ...

         Vespers of the Hours of the Cross; prose.

         PROVIDENCE, Brown Univ. Libr., C. 28. b. 4 (H.L. Koopman
         Collection), fol. 92r°-93r°, XVc., Hours.

6656.   Sire, encline tes oreilles a noz prieres par lesquelles nous,
         soupplians, deprions ta misericorde que les ames de tes
         serviteurs, hommes et femmes ...

         Orison to God: Inclina domine aurem tuam.

PROVIDENCE, Brown Univ. Libr., C. 28. b. 4 (H.L. Koopman Collection), fol. 104r°, XVc., Hours.

6657. Sires, enfes en humanité,
Roys des roys en divinité,
Nez sa jus de mere sanz pere,
Nez lassus de pere sanz mere ...

Orison to the Infant Jesus by Balthazar: "Geu des trois roys" (vv. 663-81).

PARIS, Bibl. Sainte-Geneviève, 1131, fol. 27v°-28r°, XVc.

Ed.: Whittredge, p. 173.

6658. Sire, enlumine mes yeulx affin que jamais ne me endorme en la mort, ne ja nul jour die mon ennemy: 'J'ay eu victoire contre luy!' ...

"Les sept vers saint Bernard", in prose.

SAN MARINO (Calif.), Huntington Libr., HM 1129, fol. 136r°-137v°, c. 1450, Hours of Paris.

6659. Sire, escoutés ma priere et ma clameur viegne devant vous; ne destournes mye vostre face et ...

Fifth of the Seven Penitential Psalms, in prose. Wording not identical with that of no. 3685.

SAN MARINO (Calif.), Huntington Libr., HM 1129, fol. 92r°-94v°, c. 1450, Hours of Paris.

6660. Syre, exaulce mon ouraison
Et ma clameur sans achaison
Jusquez a ton oreille avienne
A celle fin que bien m'en viengne ...

Fifth of the Seven Penitential Psalms; a version in rhymed couplets.

LILLE, Bibl. mun., Godefroy 5 (147), fol. 103r°-107r°, XVc., Hours.

6661. Sire, excite nos coeurs pour préparer les voyes a ton filz unique affin que par son advenement nous meritons le servir purement.
                    (Complete Text)

"Dimence second <des Avens>, oraison."

NEW YORK, Pierpont Morgan Libr., Morgan 78, fol. 70r°, XVc., Hours of Rome. This prayer in a XVIc. hand.

6662. Sire, fais nous avoir perpetuelle crainte de ton saint nom et samblement l'amour ...

Prayer for "Dimence second aprés la Pentecouste."

NEW YORK, Pierpont Morgan Libr., Morgan 78, fol. 34v°, XVc., Hours of Rome. Prayer in a XVIc. hand.

6663.   Sire, _fait il_, graces te rent,
Qui par ton saint commandement
M'as otreié que tel ovre oie!
Moct (_sic_) par en sent mis cuers grant joie
· · ·

Richard I, Duke of Normandy, gives thanks to Jesus: Chronique des ducs de Normandie, by Benoit (vv. 27937-48).

LONDON, British Libr., Harley 1717, fol. 159r°, XIIIc.

TOURS, Bibl. mun., 903, fol. 137r°, late XIIc.

_Ed._: Fahlin, II, p. 171-2 (base ms. is Tours).

6664.   Sire, j'ay crié a vous du plus parfont de mon cueur. Sire, entendés ce que je veil dire. Oyés ententivement ...

Sixth of the Seven Penitential Psalms, in prose; not completely identical with no. 3687.

SAN MARINO (Calif.), Huntington Libr., HM 1129, fol. 95v°-97r°, _c_. 1450, Hours of Paris.

6665.   Sire (_ms_. Cire), je ne suis pas digne que tu entres soubz mon tet, mais dy de ta parolle et mon ame sera sauvee avec la vierge Marie en la court celestre.
(Complete Text).

"Oroison devote que on doit dire par iij fois quant on reçoit le corps Nostre Seigneur"; an adaptation of the "Domine non sum dignus."

NEW YORK, New York Public Libr., 52, fol. 205v°-206r°, XVc., Hours of Paris.

6666.   Sire, jo vus pri ke vous priez pur moy, ke je puysse en teu manere receyvre le ordre de sacerdotlz ...

Novice requests the Brethren witnessing the conferral of the Seven Orders of the Priesthood to pray for him: Customary of the Benedictine Monastery of Saint Peter, Westminster.

LONDON, British Libr., Cotton, Otho C. XI, fol. 118r°, XIVc.

_Ed._: Thompson, II, p. 227.

6667.   Sire Jhesucrist, filz le Dieu vif, met ta passion, ta crois et ta mort entre ton jugement et mon ame ...

Orison to Jesus in prose, to be said after each of the Hours of the Cross.

SAN MARINO (Calif.), Huntington Libr., HM 1129, fol. 81v°-82r°, _c_. 1450, Hours of Paris.

6668.   Sire Jesus, par vo doulceur
        Vous m'avez cy reconforté ...

        Praise of Jesus by the hero: Mystère de saint Christofle (vv.
        533-552).

        Early Ed.: in 4° Gothic, Paris, Veuve Jean Trepperel and Jean
        Jehannot, n.d. (c. 1515). Ed.: Runnalls, p. 20-1.

6669.   Sire, l'infusion du sainct Esprit mondifie (sic) nos coeurs et
        les faice estre fecundes et fructifiant par l'interiore (sic)
        aspersion de la rousee!
                        (Complete Text)

        "Lundy a la messe, oraison."

        NEW YORK, Pierpont Morgan Libr., Morgan 78, fol. 147r°, XVc.,
        Hours of Rome. This text added in XVIc.

6670.   Sire, les oreilles de ta misericorde soient ouvertes aux
        prieres de tes supplicateurs ...

        "Dimence ix^e, oraison."

        NEW YORK, Pierpont Morgan Libr., Morgan 78, fol. 43r°, XVc.,
        Hours of Rome. Prayer by a XVIc. hand.

6671.   Sire, maine nos coeurs, nous te prions, par oeuvre de ta
        misericorde car sans toy ...

        "Dimence xvj^e, oraison.

        NEW YORK, Pierpont Morgan Libr., Morgan 78, fol. 53r°, XVc.,
        Hours of Rome. This text added in XVIc.

6672.   Syre, mon oraison exaulce.
        Oy ma proiere s'el n'est faulce,
        Et m'exaulce en ta verité
        En ta justice et equité ...

        Seventh of the Penitential Psalms; a version in rhymed
        couplets.

        LILLE, Bibl. mun., Godefroy 5 (147), fol. 108v°-110v°, XVc.,
        Hours.

6673.   Sire, ne me reprenez mie en vostre fureur; ne me chastiez en
        vostre ire, pour ce que les sayettes de voz peines ...

        Third of the Penitential Psalms; a prose version. The wording
        is close to but not identical with that of no. 3734.

        PARIS, Bibl. nat., fr. 13167, fol. 64r°-66r°, late XVc., Hours
        of Paris.

        SAN MARINO (Calif.), Huntington Libr., HM 1129, fol. 87v°-90r°,
        c. 1450, Hours of Paris.

6674.   Sire, nous prions, absoubz les pechiez de ton poeuple et si
        nous delivre par ta benignité ...

"Dimence xxj^e, oraison."

NEW YORK, Pierpont Morgan Libr., Morgan 78, fol. 65r°, XVc.,
Hours of Rome. This text is by a XVIc. hand.

6675. Sire, nous prions benignement, exauce nos prieres et nous qui
       sommez absoubz des liens de pechiés, garde nous de touttes
       adversités. Amen.
                    (Complete Text)

"Dimence de la quinquagesime, ⟨oraison⟩."

NEW YORK, Pierpont Morgan Libr., Morgan 78, fol. 85r°, XVc.,
Hours of Rome. This prayer added by a XVIc. hand.

6676. Sire, nous prions, excite ta puissance et viens affin que des
       perilz visibles de nos pechiés, par toy protecteur ...

"Oraison du premier dimence des Avens."

NEW YORK, Pierpont Morgan Libr. Morgan 78, fol. 70r°, XVc.,
Hours of Rome. This text by a XVIc. hand.

6677. Sire, nous prions, garde ta famille de ta pitié continuelle
       affin que elle qui en seul espoir ...

"Le quastrime dimence des Roys, ⟨oraison⟩."

NEW YORK, Pierpont Morgan Libr., Morgan 78, fol. 84v°, XVc.,
Hours of Rome. This prayer added in XVIc.

6678. Sire, nous prions, garde ta famille par ta continuelle pityé et
       de toutes adversités ...

"Dimence xixe, oraison."

NEW YORK, Pierpont Morgan Libr., Morgan 78, fol. 65r°, XVc.,
Hours of Rome. This text added in XVIc.

6679. Sire, ' nous prions, garde ton eglise de ta perpetuelle
       propiciation et pourtant que sans toy chiet ...

"Dimence xij^e, oraison."

NEW YORK, Pierpont Morgan Libr., Morgan 78, fol. 52v°, XVc.,
Hours of Rome. This prayer is by a XVIc. hand.

6680. Sire, nous prions, haste ta puissance et viens affin que ceulx
       qui ont confidence en ta pitié soient delivrés de toute
       adversité. Amen.
                    (Complete Text)

"Dimence quatrime ⟨des Avens⟩, oraison."

NEW YORK, Pierpont Morgan Libr., Morgan 78, fol. 70r°, XVc.,
Hours of Rome. This prayer by a XVIc. hand.

6681. Sire, nous prions par ta pitié celeste, poursieus les desirs de
       ton poeuple suppliant ...

"Dimence en l'octave des Roys, oraison."

NEW YORK, Pierpont Morgan Libr., Morgan 78, fol. 80r⁰, XVc.,
Hours of Rome. This prayer in a XVIc. hand.

6682. Sire (ms. Dire), nous prions que benignement exauce les prieres
de ton poeuple affin que nous ...

"Le dimence de la septuagesime, oraison."

NEW YORK, Pierpont Morgan Libr., Morgan 78, fol. 84v⁰-85r⁰,
XVc., Hours of Rome. This prayer by a XVIc. hand.

6683. Sire, nous prions, resveille les voluntés de tes fideles affin
que, exsecutant abondamment le fruict de divine oeuvre ...

"Dimence xxij^e, oraison."

NEW YORK, Pierpont Morgan Libr., Morgan 78, fol. 65r⁰, XVc.,
Hours of Rome. This text is by a XVIc. hand.

6684. Sire, nous prions tousjours que ta grace nous previenne (sic)
et poursieve et donne estre ententifz continuellement en
bonnes oeuvres. Amen.
                    (Complete Text)

"Dimence xiiij^e, oraison."

NEW YORK, Pierpont Morgan Libr., Morgan 78, fol. 52v⁰, XVc.,
Hours of Rome. This text added in XVIc.

6685. Sire, nous querons par nos prieres que preste ton aüye et les
tenebres (ms. et les t. twice) de nostre ame enlumine par
grace de ta visitation.
                    (Complete Text)

"Dimence troisime <des Avens>, oraison."

NEW YORK, Pierpont Morgan Libr., Morgan 78, fol. 70r⁰, XVc.,
Hours of Rome. This text added in XVIc.

6686. Sire, nous requerons que benignement infunde le sainct Esprit
en nos coeurs ...

"<La nuyct de la Trinité>, seconde oraison."

NEW YORK, Pierpont Morgan Libr., Morgan 78, fol. 149r⁰, Xc.,
Hours of Rome. This text added in XVIc.

6687. Sire, nous requerons que noz coeurs et pensees soient par le
paraclit de toy procedant ...

"Le merquedi <de la Pentecouste>, oraison."

NEW YORK, Pierpont Morgan Libr., Morgan 78, fol. 149r⁰, XVc.,
Hours of Rome. This prayer by a XVIc. hand.

6688. Sire, nous te prions, donne a tes serviteurs, toy apaisié,
       indulgence et paix, affin que emsamble (sic) soient purgiés
       ...

       "<Dimence> xviij^e, oraison."

       NEW YORK, Pierpont Morgan Libr., Morgan 78, fol. 53r°, XVc.,
       Hours of Rome. This text added in XVIc.

6689. Sire, nous te requerons que par ta pitié ne veulles pas
       delaisser tes serviteurs ...

       "La seconde oroison," second of three prayers to the Trinity,
       in prose.

       PROVIDENCE, Brown Univ. Libr., C. 28. b. 4 (H.L. Koopman
       Collection), fol. 238r°, XVc., Hours.

6690. Sire, oyes nous, ostes nous de soucy.
       Crist, oyes nous, ayes de nous mercy ...

       "La Letanie", in the Heures à l'usage de Rome, par Pierre
       Gringore;

       PARIS, Bibl. de l'Arsenal, 8° T. 2577, Rés., fol. k5r°-k7r°,
       1525.

       Ed.: Rézeau, Saints, I, pp. 164-70, who records many other
       early editions.

6691. Sire, or reçois m'orison, et mes criz vieingnent a toy! Nous te
       prions, Sire Jhesucrist, que ore et a l'eure de la mort ...

       Translation of the Domine exaudi orationem meam et clamor meus
       ad te veniat, to be recited at the end of each of the Heures
       de la Croix in prose in a redaction whose prologue begins: A!
       pour Dieu ... (no. 5379).

       LONDON, British Libr., Royal 16. E. XII, fol. 309r°, XIVc.

6692. Sire, par misericorde continuelle soit ton eglise purgie et
       munye ...

       "Dimence xiij^e, oraison."

       NEW YORK, Pierpont Morgan Libr., Morgan 78, fol. 52v°, XVc.,
       Hours of Rome. This text added in XVIc.

6693. Sire Peire tous poixant, donne nous vie
                                       pure
       Et si nous fay la voie xeure ...

       Orison to the Trinity; 7 vv. of irregular syllabic count.

       METZ, Bibl. mun., 600, fol. 165v°, XVc., Hours of Paris and
       Prayer-book.

       Ed.: Rézeau, p. 176.

6694.   Sir, que Diex is e desendis del tron,
        Si com la Vergne do lignas Salamon ...

        Orison to Jesus and S. James the Great by Roland during his
            combat with Ferragu: Entrée d'Espagne (1780-90).

        VENICE, Bibl. Marciana, 257 (olim gall. XXI), fol. 35r°, XIVc.

        Ed.: Thomas, I, p. 68.

6695.   Sire que nous voulsis commander
        Pere et mere a honnorer,
        De lor ame pitié te praingne
        C'un chascun a ta gloire mengne,
        Et que je les puisse esgarder
        En saint lieu precieux et cler!
                    (Complete Text)

        Prayer "Deus qui nobis patrem" rubricated "Orison pour pere et
            pour mere", as part of the Vigiles des Morts in rhyme.

        MANCHESTER, John Rylands Univ. Libr., French 143, fol. 120r°,
            early XVc., Hours.

6696.   Sire, quel que j'aie esté ne quel que je soye ne quelque chose
            me soit a venir, benoit soit Dieu le pere ...

        Prayer to God in prose, in Vespers of the Heures de Nostre
            Dame.

        CAMBRIDGE, Fitzwilliam Museum, McClean 76, fol. 58v°-59r°,
            XIV-XVc., Hours of Paris.

        PROVIDENCE, Brown Univ. Libr., C. 28. b. 4 (H.L. Koopman
            Collection), fol. 236v°-237v°, XVc., Hours.

6697.   Et dist: Sire, qui char presis
        En la Virge et de li nasquis ...

        Orison to Jesus by Joseph of Arimathea: Le Roman de l'Estoire
            dou Graal by Robert de Boron (vv. 2433-58).

        PARIS, Bibl. nat., fr. 20047, fol. 39r°, late XIIIc.

        Ed.: Nitze, p. 84-5. Ref.: Koch, p. 51-2, 109.

6698.   Sire, regarde tes sergens parfaitement de pais et nous frans
            essauce par la bieneuree vierge ...

        Orison to God in prose, at Nones of the Heures de Nostre Dame.

        CAMBRIDGE, Fitzwilliam Museum, McClean 76, fol. 51v°, XIV-XVc.,
            Hours of Paris.

6699.   Sire seinz pere, toz puissanz, parmanablez Dex, je te pri
            sopplement que tu me deignez delivrer de tout mes anemis ...

        Orison to God, in prose.

NEW YORK, Pierpont Morgan Libr., Morgan 92, fol. 135r⁰-135v⁰, late XIIIc., Hours.

6700.   Sire, si jo ai a nul frere trespassé, jo pri pur Deu ke y me soyt pardoné, _vel si plures fuerint, dicatur sic_: Sire, si nous eyum ...

Novice(s) pray(s) for forgiveness for any trespass against a Brother Monk: Customary of the Benedictine Monastery of Saint Peter, Westminster.

LONDON, British Libr., Cotton, Otho C. XI, fol. 118r⁰, XIVc.

Ed.: Thompson, II, p. 227.

6701.   Syre, si je ay, _vel_ si nus aiums, a nul frere trespassé, je pri _vel_ nus priums, pur Deu, ke il nus _vel_ moy, soyt pardoné.
(Complete Text)

Novice(s) Pray(s) for forgiveness for any trespass against a Brother Monk: Customary of the Benedictine Monastery of Saint Augustine, Canterbury.

LONDON, British Libr., Cotton, Faustina C. XII, fol. 127v⁰, XIVc.

Ed.: Thompson, I, p. 275.

6702.   Sire, si vraiement comme c'est voirs et comme je le croy, vous pri, tres doux sires, que vouz me gardés ...

Prayer to God in prose as part of Lauds in the Heures de Nostre Dame.

CAMBRIDGE, Fitzwilliam Museum, McClean 76, fol. 33v⁰-34v⁰, XIV - XVc., Hours of Paris.

6703.   Sire sainct Anthoine puyssant
Qui peulx estaindre feu ardent ...

"Oracio de sancto Anthonio"; one eight-line stanza, aabb.

PARIS, Private Collection, LF 56, fol. not given, XVIc. Hours of Raoul II de Refuge.

Ed.: Rézeau, Saints, II, pp. 48-9.

6704.   Sire saint Michiel l'ange, gracieux et
poissant,
Sur tous les autres bel, cler et
resplandissant ...

Prayer to S. Michael; 32 alexandrines rhyming in pairs.

BRUSSELS, Bibl. royale, IV. 427, fol. 29r⁰-31r⁰, c. 1380, Hours.

METZ, Bibl. mun., 600, fol. 142r⁰-142v⁰, XVc., Hours of Paris and Prayer-book.

Ed.: Rézeau, Saints, II, pp. 531-3. Ref.: Rézeau, p. 175.

6705. Sire, soies a nos supplications, et ordenne et dispose la voye de tes servans en la prosperité ...

Translation of the "Adesto Domine supplicationibus nostris."

PARIS, Bibl. nat., fr. 962, fol. 268v⁰, XIVc., Psalter.

Ref.: Berger, Bible fr., p. 342.

6706. Sire tout puissant et pardurable Dieu, es mains duquel sont les poestez et le poer de touz ...

"Pour la saincte Terre diras ceste oroison."

VATICAN CITY, Bibl. apost., Reg. lat. 315, fol. 17v⁰, XIVc.

6707. Sire tout puissant et roy victorieux, ostez nous tous les vestemens de nostre propre volonté ...

Prayer to Jesus by Jean Gerson, Sermon sur la Passion Ad Deum vadit.

BRUSSELS, Bibl. royale, IV. 111, fol. 251v⁰-252r⁰, XVc.

LONDON, British Libr., Harley 4331, fol. 63v⁰, XVc.

LYON, Bibl. de la Ville, 1182, fol. 46r⁰-46v⁰, XVc.

PARIS, Bibl. nat., fr. 24841, fol. 34v⁰, XVc.

Screening of mss. is incomplete.

Ed.: Carnahan, p. 109; Frénaud, p. 91; Glorieux, Gerson: Oeuvres complètes, VII, 2, pp. 503-4.

6708. Sire, tres dous et tres amoureus Diex, peres tous poissans, courtois et debonnaire, doulx Jhesu ...

Prayer to Jesus, in prose.

LONDON, St. Paul's Chapter Libr., 19, fol. 68r⁰-69r⁰ (another copy on fol. 75v⁰-76v⁰), XVc., Hours.

6709. Sire, tu delaisse maintenant ton sergent en paix selon ta parolle, car mes yeulx virent ton salut ...

Canticle of Simeon, in prose; not identical with no. 2085.

CHICAGO, Art Institute, 15.536, p. 274-5, c. 1400, Psalter.

6710. Sires vrais Dieux, Jhesucris, filz de Dieu le pere qui voulus pour le rachetement du monde estre tourmentez des Juis et par ung faux baisier de Judas ...

Prayer to Jesus, in prose.

TROYES, Bibl. mun., 1971, fol. 168r⁰-169r⁰, XVc., Prayer-book.

6711.   Soies (ms. soions) piteus et debonnaire a nos supplicacions,
        sire Dieux, nous le te requeron, affin que nous qui
        congnoisson que nous sommes coupables ...

Orison for S. Vincent (on feast-day).

PARIS, Bibl. de l'Arsenal, 2162, fol. 139v⁰-140r⁰, XVc., Hours
of Paris.

6712.   Souverain roy du hault empire,
        Mon Dieu, mon pere createur,
        Vueille en gré prandre le martire
        De ton pouvre humble serviteur ...

Orison to God and the Holy Spirit by the dying hero: Mystère de
saint Adrien (vv. 7868-927).

CHANTILLY, Musée Condé, 620 (1603), fol. 157r⁰-158r⁰, 1485.

Ed.: Picot, p. 152-3.

6713.   Souveraine et divine essence
        Qui tout sces en ta prescience ...

Plainte to God by Eve in limbo: Arnoul Gréban's Mystère de la
Passion (vv. 23155-66).

CHANTILLY, Musée Condé, 614 (1691), fol. 196v⁰, XVc.

PARIS, Bibl. de l'Arsenal, 6431, fol. 172v⁰, XVc.

PARIS, Bibl. nat., fr. 815, fol. 187v⁰, 1458.

PARIS, Bibl. nat., fr. 816, fol. 163v⁰, 1473.

ROME, Accademia Nazionale dei Lincei, Bibl. Corsiniana, Rossi
412 (44. A. 7), fol. 448r⁰-448v⁰, late XVc.

Ed.: Paris-Raynaud, p. 304 (vv. 23192 - 203); Jodogne, p. 310
(vv. 23155-66).

6714.   Sur piedz estoit la Vierge Marie
        Pres de la croix en douleur amere
        Quant Jhesu son filz il pendit (ms.
                                    pendoit)
        De laquelle l'ame dolente ...

"Une devote oroison de Nostre Dame "Stabat mater dolorosa";
six-line stanzas rhyming aabccb; ending is missing, only 41
vv. in this copy.

MANCHESTER, Chetham's Libr., 8007 (Mun. A. 2. 161), fol.
101r⁰-102r⁰, XVc., Hours of Besançon.

T

6715. Toy (ms. uoy) loons Dieu et toy creons,
       Ciel, terre et anges et lor chanssons.
       Sains Dieu, saint sire, saint sauverres,
       Ta gloire emplist ciel et terre ...

       "Cantique des anges: Te Deum laudamus", in the Heures de Nostre
          Dame.

       MANCHESTER, John Rylands Univ. Libr., French 143, fol. 61r°,
          early XVc., Hours.

6716. Toy, mon bon ange, qui me garde,
       De l'ennemy me vueil deffendre ...

       Orison to Guardian Angel; 8 vv., rhyming ababbcbc.

       PARIS, Bibl. nat., Rés. D. 5616 and Ye 831, Louenges des
          benoistz sainctz et sainctes de paradis, fol. zz7r°, Paris,
          Vérard.

       VERSAILLES, Bibl. mun., M. 129 (Lacombe 109 quater).

       Ed.: Rézeau, Saints, II, pp. 524-5.

6717. Toy qui es la lumiere et le jour tout
                                    ensemble,
       Clairté qui ne se void que des yeux de la
                                    foy ...

       "Parafraze sur l'hymne Christe qui lux es et dies"; 13
          quatrains, rhyming abab.

       CAMBRIDGE, Harvard College Libr., Typ. 617, fol. 150v°-151v°,
          XVc., Hours (the hymn added in a XVIc. hand).

6718. Tous cieuls, oés les choses que je parle; la terre, oes la
          parole de ma bouche; ma doctrine croisse aussi comme ...

Canticle of Moses (Audite coeli), in prose.

CHICAGO, Art Institute, 15.536, p. 263-8, c. 1400, Psalter.

6719.   Touz li seins dunt les nuns sunt escriz en le livre de vie ...

Prayer to All Saints, in prose.

OXFORD, Bodleian Libr., Bodley 9, fol. 47v°, XVc.

Ed.: Rézeau, Saints, I, p. 200.

6720.   Tous sainctz et sainctes glorieuses,
Defendez moy des ennemys ...

Prayer to All Saints; 8 vv. ababcdcd.

BESANCON, Bibl. mun., 121, fol. 97r°, late XVc., Hours of
Besançon. This text added in XVIc.

Ed.: Rézeau, Saints, I, p. 204.

6721.   Tous te loons, toy, Dieu de glore,
Toy confessons, signeur, encore
Toy pere par droit pardurable
Toute terre ta venerable ...

Hymn "Te Deum", in rhymed couplets, part of the "Heures de
Nostre Dame."

LILLE, Bibl. mun., Godefroy 5 (147), fol. 32v°-35v°, XVc.,
Hours.

6722.   Tout nostre pouvoir est en toy, Seigneur Dieu, par quoy nous
labourons pour neant et ne profitons aucunement ...

"Action de graces, ayant achevé le present manuel": Manuel de
dévotion de prêtre Pierre.

NEW HAVEN, Yale Univ. Libr., 498, fol. 153v°-154r°, last
quarter XVIc.

6723.   Tout puissant Dieu sempiternel, par le jugement duquel touttes
choses sont fondees, regarde propice a prieres ...

"<Le jour du vendredi sainct>, iij^e oraison."

NEW YORK, Pierpont Morgan Libr., Morgan 78, fol. 153r°, XVc.,
Hours of Rome. The prayer in a XVIc. hand.

6724.   Tout puissant Dieu sempiternel qui a<s> revelé en Christ ta
gloire aux gens, garde les oeuvres ...

"<Le jour du vendredi sainct>, ij^e <oraison>.

NEW YORK, Pierpont Morgan Libr., Morgan 78, fol. 153r°, XVc.,
Hours of Rome. This text in a XVIc. hand.

6725.   Tout puissant Dieu sempiternel, qui par ton filz t'es monstré
vigneron en ta vigne, l'eglise, affin que tous ceulx ...

"<La veille de pentecouste>, iiij^e oraison."

NEW YORK, Pierpont Morgan Libr., Morgan 78, fol. 121v°-122r°, XVc., Hours of Rome. This text by a XVIc. hand.

6726. Tout (<u>ms</u>. tres) puissant et misericordieux Dieu, noz requerons que tu ottroie que le sainct Esprit ...

"Le vendredy <de la Pentecouste>, oraison."

NEW YORK, Pierpont Morgan Libr., Morgan 78, fol. 149r°, XVc., Hours of Rome. The prayer was copied by a XVIc. hand.

6727. Tout puissant pardurable Dieu, donne nos celle grace du sainct Esperit, laquelle a tes disciples tu envoyas le jour de la saincte Penthecoste.
                    (Complete Text)

Orison to god in prose, as part of the Heures du Saint Esprit.

SAN MARINO (Calif.), Huntington Libr., HM 1129, fol. 78v°-79r°, <u>c</u>. 1450, Hours of Paris.

6728. Tout puissant sempiternel Dieu, consolation des plourans, force des labourans, nos prieres parviennent ...

"Le jour du saint Vendredi, vij^e oraison."

NEW YORK, Pierpont Morgan Libr., Morgan 78, fol. 155r°, XVc., Hours of Rome. Prayer in XVIc. hand.

6729. Tout puissant sempiternel Dieu, en la main duquel sont les puissances de drois de tous roiaulmes, regarde bening ...

"<Le jour du sainct vendredi>, la ve oraison."

NEW YORK, Pierpont Morgan Libr., Morgan 78, fol. 155r°, XVc., Hours of Rome. This prayer by a XVIc. hand.

6730. Tout puissant sempiternel Dieu, par l'esprit duquel tout le corps de l'eglise est sanctifié et regist ...

"Le jour du sainct vendredi, iiij^e oraison."

NEW YORK, Pierpont Morgan Libr., Morgan 78, fol. 155r°, XVc., Hours of Rome. This text added in XVIc.

6731. Tout puissant sempiternel Dieu qui meismes la judaïcque infidelité ne exclos point de ta misericorde ...

"<Le vendredy sainct>, oraison ix."

NEW YORK, Pierpont Morgan Libr., Morgan 78, fol. 157v°, XVc., Hours of Rome. Prayer by a XVIc. hand.

6732. Tout puissant sempiternel Dieu qui ne quiers point la mort des pecheurs mais plustot la vie ...

"<Le vendredy sainct>, oraison x^e."

NEW YORK, Pierpont Morgan Libr., Morgan 78, fol. 157v°, XVc.,
Hours of Rome. This text added in XVIc.

6733.   Tout puissans sempiternel Dieu qui saulve<s> tous et ne veulx
que nulz ne peris<s>ent, regarde aux armes decuptes ...

"Le vendredy sainct, viij^e oraison."

NEW YORK, Pierpont Morgan Libr., Morgan 78, fol. 157v°, XVc.,
Hours of Rome. This text by a XVIc. hand.

6734.   Tout puissant sempiternel Dieu qui, tousjours feconde, acroys
la foy et l'entendement ...

"<Le jour du sainct vendredi>, la vj^e oraison."

NEW YORK, Pierpont Morgan Libr., Morgan 78, fol. 155r°, XVc.,
Hours of Rome. The prayer by a XVIc. hand.

6735.   Toute riens out commencement,
Fors Diex, qui onc ne conmença,
Mes cil fu esperitelment
Adés, ne ja ne finera ...

"Chanson" to the Virgin; seven eight-line stanzas, rhyming
ababbaba.

BERN, Bürgerbibl., 389, fol. 36r°, XIIIc.

PARIS, Bibl. nat., fr. 24406, fol. 153v°, XIIIc.

Ed.: J. Brakelmann, ASNS, 42 (1868), p. 249; Järnström,
Recueil, pp. 62-4, no. XXII. Ref.: Spanke, no. 648.

6736.   Toutes oeuvres de Nostre Syre,
Beneissiez a son empire!
Loez son nom et sourauciez
Et en tous secles l'exauciez ...

Canticle of the Three Youths; part of the "Heures de Nostre
Dame."

LILLE, Bibl. mun., Godefroy 5 (147), fol. 40v°-44r°, XVc.,
Hours.

6737.   Toutes souffrites par martyre
Contre vous, unze mille vierges ...

Orison to Eleven Thousand Virgins; 8 vv.

BESANCON, Bibl. mun., 152, fol. 1r°, XVc., Hours of Rome.

Numerous early editions.

Ed.: Rézeau, Saints, II, pp. 409-10, who gives details of the
early imprints.

6738.   Tres certaine esperance, defenderesse, dame de tous ceulx qui
...

Variant of the inc.: O tres certaine esperance, deffenderesse et dame de tous ceulx ... (no. 1538).

6739. Tres certainne esperance et dame a tous ceulz qui si attendent ...

Variant of the inc.: O tres certaine esperance, deffenderesse et dame de tous ceux ... (no. 1538).

6740. Tres chers freres, quant nous sommes debout pour prier, il nous convient veiller et de tout nostre cueur nous donner a l'oraison ...

"Meditation, estant entré a l'eglise": Manuel de dévotion de prêtre Pierre.

NEW HAVEN, Yale Univ. Libr., 498, fol. 29r°-30r°, last quarter XVIc.

6741. Tres debonnaire, tres piteus et tres misericors Jhesucrist, mon Deu et mon Savour, si com je croy que cest precious corps ...

"Quant on se vuelt communier, on puet dire ceste orison."

CAMBRIDGE, Fitzwilliam Museum, Fitzwilliam 9-1951, fol. 109r°-109v°, XIVc., Hours of Toul.

6742. Tres digne princesse, dame de pitié, fontaine de misericorde, come le benoist sainct Esprit vous a arousee ...

Orison to the Virgin, in prose.

SAN MARINO (Calif.), Huntington Libr., HM 1172, fol. 77r°-77v°, early XVIc., Hours of Amiens.

6743. Tres diverses (sic) espris, angeles, archangeles, saint Michiel, et chascun d'eux du regne celestre, je me recoumande a chascun de vous; soyés a mon trespas et tres puissament me defendeis ...

"Dictés aux angeles."

LUXEMBOURG, Bibl. nat., 28, fol. 136v°, XVIc.

6744. Tres doulce dame que portas
Le filz de Dieu et enfantas ...

Prayer to the Virgin; 28 vv. paired rhymes, one line missing.

METZ, Bibl. mun., 600, fol. 178r°-178v°, XVc., Hours of Paris and Prayer-book.

Ref.: Rézeau, p. 179.

6745. Tres doulce et tres debonnaire dame, empetreiz a vostre tres chier enfant ...

Orison to the Virgin, in prose.

METZ, Bibl. mun., 600, fol. 167v°, XVc., Hours of Paris and Prayer-book.

Ref.: Rézeau, p. 177.

6746.   Tres doulce Vierge glorieuse,
Qui partout puez pardouner,
Vueillez nous estre gracieuse
Et pour nous grace demander ...

Prayer to the Virgin; one eight-line stanza, rhyming abab.

BALTIMORE, Walters Art Gallery, Walters 261, fol. 99v° and a second copy on 127r°, c. 1400, Hours.

6747.   Tres doulche vierge Katherine,
En bien parfaite et enterine ...

Prayer to S. Catherine of Alexandria; 106 octosyllabic lines, rhyming in pairs.

SOISSONS, Bibl. mun., 110, fol. 108v°-111r°, XVc., Hours of Rome.

Ed.: Rézeau, Saints, II, pp. 146-50.

6748.   Tres doulz ange, en qui garde suys commise par la grace et pitié ...

Prayer to Guardian Angel, in prose.

ROUEN, Bibl. mun., 339 (A 553), fol. 28r°-28v°, XVc.

Ed.: Rézeau, Saints, II, p. 513.

6749.   Tres doulx benoist Jhesucrist, de qui sont les bieus desirs, les droiz conceuz, les justes euvres que, quant tu deuz passer de cest monde ...

"Orison pour la paix."

PROVIDENCE, Brown Univ. Libr., C. 28. b. 4 (H.L. Koopman Collection), fol. 176r°-178r°, XVc., Hours.

6750.   Tres doulx benoist Jhesucrist qui as dit de ta bouche, qui oncques ne mentit, que que mengue ton precieux sang ...

Variant of the inc.: Tres doulx benoist Jhesus qui onques ne menti, qui a dit de ta bouche que quiconque mengue ... (no. 2159).

6751.   Tres doulx benois Jhesucrist qui es nostre commencement et nostre fin, sans qui nulle chose ne peut venir a perfection ...

"Ceste oroison doit dire femme qui a conceu, jusques a son enfanter."

PROVIDENCE, Brown Univ. Libr., C. 28. b. 4 (H.L. Koopman Collection), fol. 178r°-179r°, XVc., Hours.

6752.   Tres doulx benoist Jhesucrist qui es venu en ce monde pour nous
approuchier pres de Dieu de qui nous estions ...

"Oroison quant l'en demande au curé chose en especial."

PROVIDENCE, Brown Univ. Libr., C. 28. b. 4 (H.L. Koopman
Collection), fol. 180v°-181v°, XVc., Hours.

6753.   Tres doulx benoist Jhesucrist qui, quanques tu as prins du
nostre, tu as tout converty a nostre sauvement ...

Variant of the incipit: Tres doulx benoist Jhesus, tout ce que
tu as prins du nostre, tu as tout converti ... (no. 2160).

6754.   Tres doulz Dieu, de cuer et de voiz
Graces vous rend tant com je puis ...

Geneviève gives thanks to God: Miracles de sainte Geneviève
(vv. 789-93).

PARIS, Bibl. Sainte-Geneviève, 1131, fol. 191v°, XVc.

Ed.: Sennewaldt, p. 84.

6755.   Tres doulz Dieus debonnaire,
Tres puissant, donne nous faire ...

"Commemoration de saint Michiel", 18 vv., paired lines.

OXFORD, Keble College, 15, fol. 92v°-93r°, late XIvc., Hours of
Rome.

Ed.: Rézeau, Saints, II, p. 526.

6756.   Tres doulx Dieu, donnés moy science
Que je vous puisce bien amer
Et me vueillés de vostre grace
En ce monde cy ordrenner (sic) ...

Orison to God; one eight-line stanza.

BALTIMORE, Walters Art Gallery, Walters 261, fol. 127v°, c.
1400, Hours.

6757.   Tres doulz Dieu piteux, qui as tant amé ma povre ame que pour
elle sauver tu as voulu estre enfant ...

Orison to Jesus by Jean Gerson: Sermon pour le jour de Noël
'Puer natus est'.

CHANTILLY, Musée Condé, 145 (869), fol. 90r°-90v°, XVc.

LONDON, British Libr., Additional 12215, fol. 200r°-200v°, XVc.

PARIS, Bibl. nat., fr. 936, fol. 43v°-44r°, XVc.

PARIS, Bibl. nat., fr. 974, fol. 68v°-69r°, XVc.

PARIS, Bibl. nat., fr. 1029, fol. 55v°-56r°, XVc.

PARIS, Bibl. nat., fr. 13318, fol. 54v°-55r°, XVc.

PARIS, Bibl. nat., fr. 24841, fol. 77r°-77v°, XVc.

PARIS, Bibl. nat., lat. 14974, fol. 363v°-364r°, XVc.

TOURS, Bibl. mun., 386, fol. 75r°-75v°, XVc.

Ed.: Glorieux, Gerson: Oeuvres complètes, VII, 2, p. 949.

6758. Tres doulx et piteux Jhesus, je vous rends graces et loenges
        des peines, doleurs et tribulations ...

        "S'ensuivent quinze articles principaulx de la benoite passion
        de nostre sauveur Jhesucrist pour conformer sa vie et ses
        meurs a sa saincte conversation en laquelle consiste toute
        perfection de vie humaine."

        ROUBAIX, Archives Municipales, no shelf-mark, fol. 104v°-108r°,
        XVc., Prayer-book of Jacques de Luxembourg.

6759. Tres doulz Jhesucrist, miel en bouche, melodie en oraille, joie
        en cuer, vie de l'ame ...

        "Une devoite oroison a Nostre Savor Jhesucrist quant on vuelt
        recevoir le saint sacrement ou celebrer."

        METZ, Bibl. mun., 600, fol. 105r°-107v°, XVc., Hours of Paris
        and Prayer-book.

        Ref.: Rézeau, p. 169.

6760. Tres doulz Jhesucrist, roy de gloire,
        Bien devons avoir en memoire ...

        Prayer to Jesus by the heroine: Miracles de sainte Geneviève
        (vv. 2005-26).

        PARIS, Bibl. Sainte-Geneviève, 1131, fol. 204v°, XVc.

        Ed.: Sennewaldt, p. 124.

6761. Tres doulz Jhesus de Nazaret
        Qui de toute pitié es rempli ...

        Orison to Jesus; 38 vv. in paired rhymes, for the most part.

        METZ, Bibl. mun., 600, fol. 75r°-75v°, XVc., Hours of Paris and
        Prayer-book.

        Ref.: Rézeau, p. 166.

6762. Tres doulz Jhesus, leurs biens, leurs viez
        De vous dependent et descendent ...

        Orison to Jesus by the Virgin: Miracles de sainte Geneviève
        (vv. 673-90).

PARIS, Bibl. Sainte-Geneviève, 1131, fol. 190r°, XVc.

Ed.: Sennewaldt, p. 80-1.

6763. Tres doulx Jhesus, pere tout puissant, je vous rens graces et
       merciz de tous biens que vous m'avez donnez ...

       Thanksgiving to Jesus, in prose.

       NEW YORK, New York Public Libr., 52, fol. 226r°-228v°, XVc.,
       Hours of Paris.

6764. Tres doulz Jhesu, vueilliez me consentir et ottroier que, je,
       qui suiz entre le<z> pecheurs le plus bas ...

       Prayer to Jesus, in prose.

       METZ, Bibl. mun., 600, fol. 167r°, XVc., Hours of Paris and
       Prayer-book.

       Ed.: Rézeau, p. 177.

6765. Tres doulx pere a tous pardonne
       Les pechez a tous ceulx qui cy sont ...

       Orison to God for the forgiveness of Sins; 24 heptasyllabic
       lines, rhyming abab.

       SAN MARINO (Calif.), Huntington Libr., HM 1139, fol.
       157r°-157v°, c. 1500, Hours of Rome.

6766. Tres doulz prophete gracieux,
       Sueffre que ton chief precieux
       Avecques moy porter en puisse,
       Et pourtant que nul ouvrier truisse ...

       Orison by the Emperor Theodosius to the Saint: anon. Vie de S.
       Jean Baptiste (vv. 6941-63).

       PARIS, Bibl. nat., fr. 2182, fol. 123r°-123v°, 1322.

       PARIS, Bibl. nat., nouv. acq. fr. 7515, fol. 118r°-118v°, XIVc.

       Ed.: Gieber, p. 199 (base ms. fr. 2182).

6767. Tres doulx sauveur Jhesus, plain de
                                    misericorde,
       Ensaigne moi comment a toi je me racorde
                          ...

       "Tres devote orison" to Jesus, in 54 alexandrines.

       LIVERPOOL, Liverpool Public Libr., D. 435, fol. 74v°-78r°,
       early XVc., Hours of Paris.

6768. Tres duz sire et tres duz Jhesu Crist, tres duz et tres
       delitables e tres confortans est vostre nun, kar Jhesu dit
       autant cum sauveres ...

       Orison to Jesus, in prose, but metrical in places.

LONDON, British Libr., Additional 40675, fol. 109r°-110v°, XIIIc., Psalter.

Ref.: Bouly de Lesdain, Manuscrits didactiques, 1966, p. 54.

6769. Tres doulx syre Jhesu Crist qui as voulu prendre ta tres saincte char cy presente du tres saint et tres glorieux ventre ...

"Oroison a Jhesu Crist", in prose.

BALTIMORE, Walters Art Gallery, Walters 268, fol. 25r°-26r°, c. 1450, Hours.

6770. Tres doulx sire Jhesus, ta benoite crois nos honorons et devotement aourons et par icelle en nos cuers nous fichons le memoire et recort de ta benoite passion ...

"Une tres belle et devote oroison a Nostre Seigneur Jhesu Crist faisant memoire de sa passion ..."

NEW YORK, Pierpont Morgan Libr., Morgan 239, fol. 67r°-68r°, XVc., Hours of Orleans.

6771. Tres excellent apostre glorieux,
Cousin germain par le noble lignage ...

Prayer to S. James the Great; ballade form of 3 stanzas of eight lines and an envoy of 4 lines.

Refr.: Que bonnement puisse vivre et morir.

PARIS, Bibl. nat., Rés. D. 5616 and Ye 831, Louenges des benoistz sainctz et sainctes de paradis, fol. xx2r°, Paris, Vérard.

VATICAN CITY, Bibl. apost., Reg. lat. 182, fol. 295r°-295v°, XVc., Breviary of St. Quiriace de Provins.

VERSAILLES, Bibl. mun., M. 129 (Lacombe 109 quater).

Ed.: Rézeau, Saints, II, pp. 267-9.

6772. Tres excellent et inestimable bonté de Dieu, o pere de misericorde et de toute consolacion ...

"Meditacion de l'ame ... pour rendre graces a Dieu", in the Mendicité spirituelle by Jean Gerson.

BRUSSELS, Bibl. royale, IV. 111, fol. 220v°-221r°, XVc.

PARIS, Bibl. de l'Arsenal, 2113, fol. 104v°-105v°, XVc.

PARIS, Bibl. de l'Arsenal, 2121, fol. 45v°-46r°, XVc.

VIENNA, Oesterreichische Nationalbibl., 2574, fol. 254r°-254v°, XVc.

Screening of mss. is incomplete.

Ed.: Glorieux, Gerson: Oeuvres complètes, VII, 1, pp. 268-9.

6773. Tres glorieuse dame haulte,
       Par dessus les estoilles belles,
       Celuy qui terre crea sans faulte
       As alaité de tes mamelles ...

       "O gloriosa domina" in rhyme, as part of the Heures de Nostre
       Dame.

       SAN MARINO (Calif.), Huntington Libr., HM 1129, fol. 42v°-43r°,
       c. 1450, Hours of Paris.

6774. Tres glorieux martyr nommé Baudelle,
       Vray medecin des pouvres langoreux ...

       "Oraison a monsieur sainct Baudelle", decasyllabic lines in a
       complexity of stanzaic arrangements.

       PARIS, Bibl. nat., Rés. D. 5616 and Ye 831, Louenges des
       benoistz sainctz et sainctes de paradis, fol. xxlv°-xx2r°,
       Paris, Vérard.

       VERSAILLES, Bibl. mun., M. 129 (Lacombe, 109 quater).

       Ed.: Rézeau, Saints, II, pp. 113-115.

6775. Tres glorieux martir saint Clair,
       Amy de Dieu tres glorieux ...

       Prayer to S. Clair; three eight-line stanzas and a quatrain.

       PARIS, Bibl. nat., fr. 2206, fol. 252r°-252v°, XVIc.

       Ed.: Rézeau, Saints, II, pp. 170-1.

6776. Tres glorieux sainct Germain confesseur,
       D'Auxerre evesque par revelation ...

       Orison to S. Germain; ballade form with 3 stanzas of eight
       lines and an envoy of 4.

       Refr.: Car j'en ay bien grande necessité.

       PARIS, Bibl. nat., fr. 2206, fol. 251v°-252r°, XVIc.

       Ed.: Rézeau, Saints, II, pp. 247-8.

6777. Tres precieuse et glorieuse vierge Marie, mere de Dieu, plainne
       de graces et de vertus, Vierge tres piteable, benigne et
       secourable ...

       Oroison de Nostre Dame.

       CAMBRIDGE, Harvard College Libr., Lat. 251, fol. 69r°-69v°,
       late XVc., Hours of Rome.

6778. Tres puissant Dieu, nous prions que tu nous preste ainsy
       abstenir des viandes du corps que aussy puissons juner des
       impetueux vices.
                         (Complete Text)

       "<La nuyct de la Trinité>, vj^e oraison."

       NEW YORK, Pierpont Morgan Libr., Morgan 78, fol. 151r°, XVc.,
       Hours of Rome. This text copied by a XVIc. hand.

6779. Tres puissant Dieu nous prions que tu ottroie que nous, estans
       inst<r>uis par les junes salutaires ...

       "<La nuyct de la Trinité>, v^e oraison."

       NEW YORK, Pierpont Morgan Libr., Morgan 78, fol. 151r°, XVc.,
       Hours of Rome. This text by a XVIc. hand.

6780. Tres poissans et debonaire Dieu lou peire et lou fil et lou
       saint Esperit, qui es une gloriouse deïté ...

       Orison to the Trinity and the Virgin, in prose.

       METZ, Bibl. mun., 600, fol. 110r°-111v°, XVc., Hours of Paris
       and Prayer-book.

       Ref.: Rézeau, p. 170.

6781. Tres saincte Trinité, a moy soyez aidant! Tu es mon Dieu vif et
       vray; tu es mon pere saint ...

       "Aprés vous devez dire ceste oroison qui commence: Auxiliatrix,
       laquelle s'ensuit en françois."

       PROVIDENCE, Brown Univ. Libr., C. 28. b. 4 (H.L. Koopman
       Collection), fol. 247r°-247v°, XVc., Hours.

6782. Tres savoureuse dame, je vos saluerai en l'aneur de cele grant
       douleur qu'i vous covint sofrir quant vous aidastes ...

       Orison to the Virgin in prose.

       NEW YORK, New York Public Libr., Spencer 56, fol. 369v°-370r°,
       XIVc., Hours of Blanche de France, Duchess of Orleans.

6783. Tres savoreuse dame, je vous saluerai en l'aneur de cele joie
       que vos eustes quant Nostre Sires entra en Jerusalem ...

       Orison to the Virgin in prose.

       NEW YORK, New York Public Libr., Spencer 56, fol. 369r°, XIVc.,
       Hours of Blanche de France, Duchess of Orleans.

6784. Tres savoreuse dame, je vous saluerai en l'aneur de cele joie
       que vous eustes quant vous retrovastes vostre chier fil ...

       Orison to the Virgin in prose.

       NEW YORK, New York Public Libr., Spencer 56, fol. 368v°, XIVc.,
       Hours of Blanche de France, Duchess of Orleans.

6785. Tres savoureuse dame, je vous saluerai en l'aneur de la sainte
Pentecoste quant vostre chier fil envoia le saint Esperit a
ces deciples ...

Orison to the Virgin in prose.

NEW YORK, New York Public Libr., Spencer 56, fol. 370v⁰-371r⁰,
XIVc., Hours of Blanche de France, Duchess of Orleans.

6786. Tres savoreuse dame, je vous saluerai en l'aneur de le (sic)
vostre glorieuse assumption quant vostre chier fiuz vous osta
de ce monde ...

Orison to the Virgin in prose.

NEW YORK, New York Public Libr., Spencer 56, fol. 371r⁰-371v⁰,
XIVc., Hours of Blanche de France, Duchess of Orleans.

6787. Tres savoureuse dame, je vous saluerai en l'aneur de toutes les
pitiez que vous eustes de vostre precieux fil et quanque vous
en eustes ...

Orison to the Virgin in prose.

NEW YORK, New York Public Libr., Spencer 56, fol. 369v⁰, XIVc.,
Hours of Blanche de France, Duchess of Orleans.

6788. Tres vertueux victorieux,
Benois martirs tres glorieux,
Sains dix mil martirs triumphans
En vrais miracles tres puissans ...

Prayer to the Ten Thousand Martyrs; fifty octosyllabic lines,
rhymed in pairs.

BRUSSELS, Bibl. royale, IV. 193, fol. 187r⁰-188v⁰, XVc., Hours.

6789. Triumphateur tres precieux et digne,
De te prier de moy me sens indigne ...

Orison to S. Claude; in the form of a Ballade, 3 stanzas and an
envoy.

Refr.: Santé de corps et salut de mon ame.

PARIS, Bibl. nat., Réserve D. 5616 and Ye 831, Louenges des
benoistz ainctz at sainctes de paradis, fol. vv2r⁰-v⁰, Paris,
Vérard.

VERSAILLES, Bibl. mun., M. 129 (Lacombe 109 quater).

Ed.: Rézeau, Saints, II, pp. 181-3.

6790. Tronc paternel, le Dieu de tout humain,
Chief de vertu, de tout le vray facteur ...

Orison to God by Nostre Dame: Mystère des Trois Doms, by
chanoine Siboud Pra de Grenoble with the assistance of Claude

Chevalet de Vienne, and performed at Romans in 1509 (vv. 2502-9).

COLLECTION UNKNOWN (olim Giraud of Lyons), no shelf-mark, fol. not indicated, early XVIc.

Ed.: Giraud and Chevalier, p. 133.

6791.   Tu dois croire et sçavoir que Nostre Signeur Jhesucrist est venu et descendu du ciel pour nostre sauvement de corps et ame ...

"Exortation por fortifier le malaide en ferme foy."

LUXEMBOURG, Bibl. nat., 28, fol. 133vº-134vº, XVIc.

6792.   Tu es le roy de tout le monde
Et tel te croyons ...

Rondeau to Jesus: Mystère de la Passion by Arnoul Gréban (vv. 5571-83). The piece is also termed a fatras.

CHANTILLY, Musée Condé, 614 (1691), fol. 37rº, XVc.

LE MANS, Bibl. mun., 6, fol. 58vº, XVc.

PARIS, Bibl. de l'Arsenal, 6431, fol. 30rº, XVc.

PARIS, Bibl. nat., fr. 815, fol. 44rº, 1458.

PARIS, Bibl. nat., fr. 816, fol. 39rº, 1473.

PARIS, Bibl. nat., fr. 1550, fol. 115vº, XVIc.

PARIS, Bibl. nat., fr. 15064, fol. 102vº, 1469.

ROME, Accademia Nazionale dei Lincei, Bibl. Corsiniana, Rossi 412 (44. A. 7), fol. 79vº, late XVc.

Ed.: Paris-Raynaud, p. 72 (vv. 5594-606); L.C. Porter, La Fatrasie et le fatras, Geneva, 1960, p. 167; Jodogne, p. 77 (vv. 5571-83).

6793.   Tu es le sauveur du monde,
Enfant ou tout bien habonde ...

Praise of Infant Jesus by Joseph: Arnoul Gréban's Mystère de la Passion (vv. 5055-70, 5082-97, 5109-24). Three sixteen-line stanzas.

CHANTILLY, Musée Condé, 614 (1691), fol. 32vº-33rº, XVc. Inc.: Tu es souverain du monde ...

LE MANS, Bibl. mun., 6, fol. 51rº-52rº, XVc. Inc.: Tu es vray sauveur du monde ...

PARIS, Bibl. de l'Arsenal, 6431, fol. 25vº-26rº, XVc.

PARIS, Bibl. nat., fr. 815, fol. 39vº-40rº, 1458.

PARIS, Bibl. nat., fr. 816, fol. 35v°-36r°, 1473.

PARIS, Bibl. nat., fr. 1550, fol. 103r°-104r°, XVIc.

PARIS, Bibl. nat., fr. 15064, fol. 92r°-93v°, 1469.

PARIS, Bibl. nat., nouv. acq. fr., 12908, fol. 12v°-13r°, XVIc.

ROME, Accademia Nazionale dei Lincei, Bibl. Corsiniana, Rossi 412 (44. A. 7), fol. 63r°-64r°, late XVc.

Ed.: Paris-Raynaud, pp. 65-6 (vv. 5079-94, 5106-21, 5133-52); Jodogne, pp. 71-2 (vv. 5055-70, 5082-97, 5109-24).

6794. Tu es souverain du monde ...

Variant of the inc.: Tu es le sauveur du monde ... (no. 6793).

6795. Tu es vray sauveur du monde ...

Variant of the inc.: Tu es le sauveur du monde ... (no. 6793).

6796. Tu juneras pour le bien de ton ame:
Premierement, la veille Nostre Dame ...

"Les junes de l'Eglise"; ten decasyllabic lines rhyming in pairs.

ROUBAIX, Archives Municipales, no shelf-mark, fol. 4v°, XVc., Prayer-book of Jacques de Luxembourg.

6797. Amont regarde et dist: Tu qui penas
Sor sainte croz, quant Longis perdonas ...

Orison to Jesus by Roland: Entrée d'Espagne (vv. 1632-65).

VENICE, Bibl. Marciana, 257 (olim gall. XXI), fol. 32r°-32v°, XIVc.

Ed.: Thomas, I, p. 63-4.

6798. Tu repentaunt fist homage
A Nostre Dame; si fist ke sage ...

Epilogue in 8 lines to a copy of the "Cinq Joies Nostre Dame" (no. 2681).

BOSTON, Boston Public Libr. 124, fol. 58r°, XIVc., Hours of Sarum.

6799. Dist autemant: Tu soies merceé,
Ch'is Diex et home e fus de vergne né ...

Roland gives thanks to God, on slaying Ferragu: Entrée d'Espagne (vv. 4140-4).

VENICE, Bibl. Marciana, 257 (olim gall. XXI), fol. 79r°, XIVc.

Ed.: Thomas, I, p. 152.

U

6800. Ung chastel say ou droit fief de l'empire
Dont venus est de son droit chastellaine
...

Sixth of the "xij balades de Pasques": 13 decasyllabic lines
rhyming abaabaabbabab, the first and second are repeated as
the third and last respectively.

VATICAN CITY, Bibl. apost., Reg. lat. 1728, fol. 118r°, XVc.

Ed.: Keller, p. 618.

6801. Ung seul Dieu de tout creatour
Croyras, craindras et serviras;
Sur toutes choses nuit et jour
T'amour, force et pensee mectras ...

"Les .x. commandemens de la loy"; 10 quatrains.

PARIS, Bibl. nat., fr. 1843, fol. 47r°-50r°, XVc.

Ed.: Glorieux, Gerson, Oeuvres Complètes, VII, 1, 1966, pp.
423-4; Ref.: A. Piaget, Annales du Midi, 5 (1893), p. 330, n.
2.

6802. Une petite parole, seigneurs, escotez!
De ce que je vus counterai ne me blamerez
(sic) ...

Poem in honor of Jesus; 126 vv., seemingly rhymed in pairs; of
uneven length, as transcribed.

LONDON, British Libr., Harley 2253, fol. 78v°-79r°, XIVc.

Ed.: T. Wright, Specimens of Lyric Poetry, London, 1842, no.
26; N.R. Ker, Facsimile of British Museum ms. Harley 2253,
London, 1965 (EETS o.s. 255). Ref.: Bouly de Lesdain,
Manuscrits didactiques, 1966, p. 76.

V

6803. Vaillans chevaliers et preux
Tres eureux,
Je vous salue humblement ...

"De X mille martirs. Lay."

METZ, Bibl. mun., 571, fol. 206v°, XVc. Prayer-book.

Ed.: Rézeau, Saints, II, pp. 197-99.

6804. Vecy l'omme qui pour amender mes meffaiz et pour moi acquitter
envers vous a souffert ...

Orison to God, by Jean Gerson, Sermon sur la Passion Ad Deum
vadit.

BRUSSELS, Bibl. royale, IV. 111, fol. 246v°, XVc.

LONDON, British Libr., Harley 4331, fol. 50r°, XVc.

LYON, Bibl. de la Ville, 1182, fol. 36r°, XVc.

PARIS, Bibl. nat., fr. 24841, fol. 26v°, XVc.

Screening of mss. is incomplete.

Ed.: Carnahan, p. 93; Frénaud, p. 69; Glorieux; Gerson: Oeuvres
complètes, VII, 2, p. 490.

6805. Veez cy la croix Nostre Seigneur Jhesucrist! Fuyez vous en,
mauvaises et contrarieuses parties que le lion de la lignee
Juda, racine de David ...

Orison in prose, unrubricated, preceded by the sign of the
Cross. Text is not identical with that of nos. 3832, 3833,
5305, but there are common passages. Each of the others is
considered an Oroison contre la tempête.

PROVIDENCE, Brown Univ. Libr., C. 28. b. 4 (H.L. Koopman Collection), fol. 224v°-225v°, XVc., Hours.

6806.   Voyez qu'aprés que humanité
Par Adam cheut en dampnement ...

"Ballade" in honor of the Incarnation of Jesus, attributed to René d'Anjou; three eight-line stanzas rhyming ababbcbc, with refrain.

Refr.: La venue de Jhesu Crist.

LENINGRAD, Publichnaia Bibl., Fr. F. v. III. 2, fol. 1v°, XVc.

Ed.: Sismarev, p. 175; Ref.: Laborde, p. 45.

6807.   Veillez, car vous ne sçavez heure ne jour. Bienhureuse est l'ame laquelle pense a l'heure derniere lors que toutes les choses ...

"Meditation contenant la briesveté de nostre vye": Manuel de dévotion de prêtre Pierre.

NEW HAVEN, Yale Univ. Libr., 498, fol. 30r°-34r°, last quarter XVIc.

*   Veirs Deu ...

See the alphabetical order: Voirs Deu ...

6808.   Venez avant cueur et ame; esjouyssons nous en Nostre Seigneur; chantons a Dieu, nostre saulveur ...

"Venite exultemus domino" in prose, as part of the Heures de Nostre Dame en françois (no. 3658); not identical with no. 5314.

PROVIDENCE, Brown Univ. Libr., C. 28. b. 4 (H.L. Koopman Collection), fol. 1v°, XVc., Book of Hours.

6809.   Venez, o sainct Esprit, remplissez les coeurs de voz fideles et allumez en eux le feu de vostre amour qui par la diversité des langues ...

"Celuy qui veut faire quelque bon (sic) oeuvre doit dire."

CHICAGO, Newberry Libr., 43, fol. 163r°, XVIc., Hours of Rouen.

6810.   Venez si nous esjoisons
A Nostre Signour et chantons.
Deprions li devant sa face
Que en chantant merci nous face ...

Hymn "Venite exultemus" occurring in the Heures de Nostre Dame; rhyme aabb ...

MANCHESTER, John Rylands Univ. Libr., French 143, fol. 56v°-57r°, and again 101r°-102r°, early XVc., Hours.

6811.   Veni creator sains Esperis,
        Gardes nos corps de tous peris,
        Rampli de grace souverainne
        Les cuers de creature humainne ...

        "Oroison du saint Esperit", paraphrase of the "Veni creator" in
           seven quatrains, with a few lines in common with no. 2301.

        CHICAGO, Chicago Univ. Libr., 26, fol. 117r°-118r°, early XVc.,
           Hours of Châlons-sur-Marne.

*   Verais Diex ...

        See the alphabetical order: Vrais Diex ...

*   Verge ...

        See the alphabetical order: Vierge ...

6812.   Vien a nous li saint Esprit
        Les pensees de tes amis
        visite et les ampli de grace;
        Enlumine les de ta face ...

        Hymn "Veni creator" in Sext of the Heures de Nostre Dame.

        MANCHESTER, John Rylands Univ. Libr., French 143, fol. 71v°,
           early XVc., Hours.

6813.   Vien saint Esperit remplir les cueurs de tes fielz, et de ton
           amour en eulx le feu alume ...

        "Veni creator spiritus" in prose, as part of the Heures du
           Saint Esprit.

        SAN MARINO (Calif.), Huntington Libr., HM 1129, fol. 78v°, c.
           1450, Hours of Paris.

6814.   Vierge Barbe, c'est chose vraye (read
                                        veire)
        Que de Dieu tu as grant merite ...

        Orison to S. Barbara; one eight-line stanza, rhyming ababbcbc.

        BALTIMORE, Walters Art Gallery, Walters 448, fol. 22r°, early
           XVIc., Book of Hours of Maistre Jehan de Launay.

6815.   Vierge de Dieu mere en ton ventre s'enclost cellui que tout le
           monde ne pot comprendre tant comme dure Dieu ...

        Hymn "Virgo dei genitrix", an unrhymed version, as part of
           Compline of the Heures de Nostre Dame en françois (no. 3658).

        PROVIDENCE, Brown Univ. Libr., C. 28. b. 4 (H.L. Koopman
           Collection), fol. 57v°-58r°, XVc., Hours.

6816.   Verge de tous biens exemplaire
        Et a tes servans douche mere ...

        Oroison de S. Barbe; 24 octosyllabic lines, ababbcbc.

FORT AUGUSTUS, Abbey Libr., A. 3, fol. 176v°-177r°, XVc. Hours of Thérouanne.

MANCHESTER, Chetham's Libr., 8007 (Mun. A. 2. 161), fol. 125r°, XVc., Hours of Besançon. This copy has the last 13 vv.

TOURS, Bibl. mun., 231, fol. 202r°, XVc. This copy lacks its beginning.

Ed.: Rézeau, Saints, II, p. 86-87 (no mention of the Manchester codex).

6817.   Virgne glorieuse et mere Diu clamee
        Sour toutes les autres dames hiestes
                          houneree ...

        "Chanson" to the Virgin, composed c. 1265 by a Canon of an unidentified church; 12 alexandrines for the most part, and mainly monorhymed.

        BOULOGNE-SUR-MER, Bibl. mun., 119, fol. 91r°, XIIIc.

        Ed.: Aubry, Les plus anciens monuments, p. 9 and pl. VII.

6818.   Virge glorieuse qui au salut saint Gabrihel, l'angle en
        Nazareth ...

        Prayer to the Virgin, in prose.

        OPORTO, Bibl. publ. mun., 619, fol. 72v°, XVc.

        Ref.: G. Moldenhauer, ASNS, 151 (1927), p. 74 (the prayer is not recorded).

6819.   Virge honoree, qui en vostre enfance fustes presentee au temple
        cum acceptable offrande ...

        Orison to the Virgin, in prose.

        OPORTO, Bibl. publ. mun., 619, fol. 72r°, XVc.

        Ref.: G. Moldenhauer, ASNS, 151 (1927), p. 74 (the prayer is not recorded).

6820.   Virge honoree, qui le jor de l'ascension veistes vostre douz
        fil en la char qu'il prist de vous glorieusement monter ...

        Prayer to the Virgin, in prose.

        OPORTO, Bibl. publ. mun., 619, fol. 74v°, XVc.

        Ref.: G. Moldenhauer, ASNS, 151 (1927), p. 74 (this text not identified).

6821.   Il se mist a genous si dist: Virge loee,
        Qui portas Jhesucrist qui fist chiel et
                          rosee,

Si voir que tu en fus que vierge delivrée,
S'aies de moi merchi, douche Virge sauvee!
                    (Complete Text)

Prayer to the Virgin by Polibant: Baudouin de Sebourc (vv.
    453-6 of Chant XIV).

PARIS, Bibl. nat., fr. 12552, fol. 66v°, XIVc.

PARIS, Bibl. nat., fr. 12553, fol. 195v°, XVc.

Ed.: Boca, II, p. 14.

6822. Vierge Marie tres sacree
        Nous qui avons ferme creance
        Que tu es vierge inviolee
        Et mere de Dieu sans doubtance ...

        "O sacratissima" in rhyme; 12 octosyllabic lines, ababcdcdefef.

        BALTIMORE, Walters Art Gallery, Walters 89, fol. 28v°-29v°,
            last quarter XIVc., Hours of Isabelle de Coucy.

        SAN MARINO (Calif.), Huntington Libr., HM 1129, fol. 29v°, c.
            1450, Hours of Paris.

6823. Virge martire glorieuse,
        Precieuse,
        Couronnee es cieulx haultement,
        Je te offre mon ame doleureuse ...

        Ballade to S. Barbe; three ten-line stanzas and an envoi of
            four lines.

        Refr.: Ne perir par desesperance.

        ROUEN, Bibl. mun., 350 (Y 152), fol. 101r°-102r°, Hours of
            Lisieux.

        Ed.: Rézeau, Saints, II, pp. 88-9.

6824. Vierge mere Dieu laquelle
        Tout le monde ne conprent,
        Dedans tes entrailles se mist
        Jhesu Crist quant homme se fist ...

        Hymn "Virgo dei genitrix", 16 rhymed lines (of which the first
            two are here manifestly corrupt), as part of Lauds of the
            Heures de Nostre Dame en françois (no. 3658).

        PROVIDENCE, Brown Univ. Libr., C. 28. b. 4 (H.L. Koopman
            Collection), fol. 22v°-23r°, XVc., Hours.

6825. Vierge pucelle nette et pure,
        Vierge de tres plaisant figure
        Et de sainte protection ...

        Orison to the Virgin; 5 six-line stanzas rhyming aabaab.

MANCHESTER, John Rylands Univ. Libr., French 143, fol. 181r°-181v°, early XVc., Hours.

6826. Vierge royalle, tres preciouse,
Que en majesté gloriouse ...

Prayer to the Virgin; 12 vv., rhyming in pairs.

METZ, Bibl. mun., 600, fol. 56v°, XVc., Hours of Paris and Prayer-book.

Ref.: Rézeau, p. 164.

6827. Vierge seule sens paire,
Sur toute debonnaire,
Fay soyens desloié
De courpe (sic) et de pichié (sic) ...

Hymn "Virgo singularis" in Compline, Heures de Nostre Dame.

MANCHESTER, John Rylands Univ. Libr., French 143, fol. 80v°-81r°, early XVc., Hours.

6828. Virge tres doulce, virge benigne ...

Variant of the inc.: Vierge doulce, vierge benigne ... (no. 2314).

*   Virge ..., Virgne ...

See the alphabetical order: Vierge ...

*   Voiez ..., Voyez ...

See the alphabetical order: Veez ...

6829. Ve⟨i⟩rs Deu, ço dist la damaisele,
Qui char preīs en la pucele,
Que onques home ne conut
E del saint Esperit con⟨ç⟩ut ...

A maiden prays to God: Yder (vv. 4686-707).

CAMBRIDGE, Cambridge Univ. Libr., Ee. 4. 26, fol. 37v°, late XIIIc.

Ed.: Gelzer, p. 134-5. Ref.: Koch, p. 72, 120, 144.

6830. Voir rois celestre, font li baron menbré,
Vos en soiez come Deu aoré,
Qant nos avez tel mesaje mendé
Par le vostre angre, qui a a nos parlé.
                    (Complete Text)

Praise to God by noblemen: Girart de Vienne by Bertrand de Bar-sur-Aube (vv. 5924-7).

LONDON, British Libr., Harley 1321, fol. 32r°, XIIIc.

LONDON, British Libr., Royal 20. B. XIX, fol. 34r°, XIIIc.

LONDON, British Libr., Royal 20. D. XI, fol. 59v°, XIVc.

PARIS, Bibl. nat., fr. 1374, fol. 127v°, XIIIc.

PARIS, Bibl. nat., fr. 1448, fol. 34v°, XIIIc. Inc.: Vrais Deus celestres, tu soies aoré ...

Ed.: Yeandle, p. 188; Van Emden, p. 262 (both used as base ms. Royal 20. B. XIX). Ref.: Altona, 1883, p. 34 (citing the version in Paris, B.N., fr. 1448).

6831. Vous angelz, annoncez moy que chacun jour m'est mestier a faire ou cognoistre pour moy ou pour autruy ...

Last of the nine orisons to the angelic orders. The wording is almost identical to the version included by Jean Gerson in his Mendicité spirituelle.

ROUBAIX, Archives Municipales, no shelf-mark, fol. Cr°-Cv°, XVc., Prayer-book of Jacques de Luxembourg.

Ed.: Glorieux, Gerson: Oeuvres complètes, VII, 1, p. 251.

6832. Vous archangelz, denoncez moy en tant (ms. entact) que besoing me fait le hault mistere ...

Eighth of nine orisons to the angelic orders. The wording is almost identical to the version included by Jean Gerson in his Mendicité spirituelle.

ROUBAIX, Archives Municipales, no shelf-mark, fol. Bv°, XVc., Prayer-book of Jacques de Luxembourg.

Ed.: Glorieux, Gerson: Oeuvres complètes, VII, 1, p. 251.

6833. Vous avés voulu, Sire tout puissant, que en nostre priere nous vous nonmons et appellons nostre pere ...

"Oroison sus la premiere partie de la patenostre", in the Mendicité spirituelle by Jean Gerson.

BRUSSELS, Bibl. royale, IV. 111, fol. 209r°-209v°, XVc.

LYON, Bibl. de la Ville, 1249 (1121), fol. 31v°-32r°, XVc.

PARIS, Bibl. de l'Arsenal, 2113, fol. 70v°-72r°, XVc.

PARIS, Bibl. de l'Arsenal, 2121, fol. 19r°-20r°, XVc.

VIENNA, Oesterreichische Nationalbibl., 2574, fol. 238v°-239r°, XVc.

Screening of mss. is incomplete.

Ed.: Glorieux, Gerson: Oeuvres complètes, VII, 1, pp. 242-3.

6834. Vous cherubins, plains de science et sapience, enseignez ceste fole male aprise qui souvent juge le bien mal et le mal bien ...

Second of the nine prayers to the angelic orders. The wording is almost identical to the version included by Jean Gerson in his Mendicité spirituelle.

ROUBAIX, Archives Municipales, no shelf-mark, fol. Ar°-Av°, XVc., Prayer-book of Jacques de Luxembourg.

Ed.: Glorieux, Gerson: Oeuvres complètes, VII, 1, p. 250.

6835. Vous dame, tres benigne et religieuse, Marie Magdalayne, nous estes l'exemplaire attraiant l'ame chrestienne ...

"Oroison de tierce" of the Heures de saincte Marie Magdalayne; the prologue of the group commences: En l'onneur de nostre doulx sauveur ... (no. 5788).

ROUBAIX, Archives Municipales, no shelf-mark, fol. 10v°-11r°, XVc., Prayer-book of Jacques de Luxembourg.

Ref.: Chanoine Looten, in Bulletin du comité flamand de France, VI (1920), p. 160.

6836. Vous dominations, faites moy telle seignourie sur mon corps ainsi qu'il appartient que de riens ne me mecte en sa subjection.
                    (Complete Text)

Fourth of nine prayers to the angelic orders. The wording is almost identical to the version included by Jean Gerson in his Mendicité spirituelle.

ROUBAIX, Archives Municipales, no shelf-mark, fol. Br°, XVc., Prayer-book of Jacques de Luxembourg.

Ed.: Glorieux, Gerson: Oeuvres complètes, VII, 1, p. 251.

6837. Vous, doncques, Jhesus, qui avez soif de nostre salut, donnez tousjours ceste soif pour nous ...

Orison to Jesus: Sermon sur la Passion Ad Deum vadit, by Jean Gerson.

BRUSSELS, Bibl. royale, IV. 111, fol. 255r°, XVc. Inc.: Jhesus qui avez soif ...

LONDON, British Libr., Harley 4331, fol. 72v°, XVc.

LYON, Bibl. de la Ville, 1182, fol. 52v°, XVc.

PARIS, Bibl. nat., fr. 24841, fol. 40v°, XVc. Inc.: Jhesus qui avez soif ...

Screening of mss. is incomplete.

Ed.: Carnahan, p. 119; Frénaud, p. 105; Glorieux, Gerson: Oeuvres complètes, VII, 2, p. 512.

6838. Vous en especial, Vierge tres digne, qui confroissastes la teste du vielz serpent, l'ennemy, selon la promesse ...

Orison to the Virgin: Sermon pour la fête de saint Michael, by Jean Gerson.

PARIS, Bibl. de l'Arsenal, 2109, fol. 42v°, XVc.

Screening of mss. is incomplete.

Ed.: L. Mourin, Recherches de théologie ancienne et médiévale, 16 (1949), p. 134; Glorieux, Gerson: Oeuvres complètes, VII, 2, p. 622.

6839. Vous estes celle dame tres glorieuse qui a la parfin, apres la tres merveilleuse ascension de nostre sauveur ...

Oroison de complyes, Heures de saincte Marie Magdalayne; the inc. of the whole series is: En l'onneur de nostre doulx sauveur ... (no. 5788).

ROUBAIX, Archives Municipales, no shelf-mark, fol. 12r°-13v°, XVc., Prayer-book of Jacques de Luxembourg.

Ref.: Chanoine Looten, in Bulletin du comité flamand de France, VI (1920), p. 161.

6840. Vous estes celle dame tres honoree, qui par soingneusement querir le jour de Pasques ...

"Oroison de vespres" of the Heures de saincte Marie Magdalayne; the prologue of the series opens: En l'onneur de nostre doulx sauveur ... (no. 5788).

ROUBAIX, Archives Municipales, no shelf-mark, fol. 12r°, XVc., Prayer-book of Jacques de Luxembourg.

Ref.: Chanoine Looten, in Bulletin du comité flamand de France, VI (1920), p. 161.

6841. Vous estes, dame, celle qui tousdis accompaignastes jusques a la mort de la croix, voir jusques a la sepulture ...

"Oroison de none" of the Heures de saincte Marie Magdalayne; the inc. of the prologue to the series reads: En l'onneur de nostre doulx sauveur ... (no. 5788).

ROUBAIX, Archives Municipales, no shelf-mark, fol. 11v°-12r°, XVc., Prayer-book of Jacques de Luxembourg.

Ref.: Chanoine Looten, in Bulletin du comité flamand de France, VI (1920), pp. 160-1.

6842. Vous estes, dame Marie Magdalayne, la bienamee de Jhesucrist pour l'amour de laquelle il resuscita son bon amy ...

"Oroison de sexte" of the Heures de saincte Marie Magdalayne; the prologue of the series begins: En l'onneur de nostre doulx sauveur ... (no. 5788).

ROUBAIX, Archives Municipales, no shelf-mark, fol. 11r°-11v°, XVc., Prayer-book of Jacques de Luxembourg.

Ref.: Chanoine Looten, in Bulletin du comité flamand de France, VI (1920), p. 160.

6843. Vous glorieux saincts patriarches,
       Les secretz Dieu avez ouvers ...

       Orison to Patriarchs and Prophets; 8 vv. rhyming ababbcbc.

       PARIS, Bibl. nat., Rés. D. 5616 and Ye 831, Louenges des benoistz sainctz et sainctes de paradis, fol. zz7v°, Paris, Vérard.

       Ed.: Rézeau, Saints, I, pp. 205-6.

6844. Vous, Marie Magdalayne, dame enluminee, nous estes exemplaire de contemplation ou de la vie contemplative ...

       "Oroison de prime" of the Heures de saincte Marie Magdalayne; the prologue to the series commences: En l'onneur de nostre doulx sauveur ... (no. 5788).

       ROUBAIX, Archives Municipales, no shelf-mark, fol. 9v°-10v°, XVc., Prayer-book of Jacques de Luxembourg.

       Ref.: Chanoine Looten, in Bulletin du comité flamand de France, VI (1920), p. 160.

6845. Vous potestats, delivrez moy de tous mes adversaires qui ont telle puissance que pareille n'est point trouvee sur terre.
                          (Complete Text)

       Sixth of nine orisons to the angelic orders. The wording is almost identical to the version included by Jean Gerson in his Mendicité spirituelle.

       ROUBAIX, Archives Municipales, no shelf-mark, fol. Br°, XVc., Prayer-book of Jacques de Luxembourg.

       Ed.: Glorieux, Gerson: Oeuvres complètes, VII, 1, p. 251.

6846. Vous principats, donne<z> moy que je soye subjecte a mes souverains sans murmur, sans desobeir et sans detraction.
                          (Complete Text)

       Fifth of nine orisons to the angelic orders. The wording is almost identical to the version included by Jean Gerson in his Mendicité spirituelle.

       ROUBAIX, Archives Municipales, no shelf-mark, fol. Br°, XVc., Prayer-book of Jacques de Luxembourg.

       Ed.: Glorieux, Gerson: Oeuvres complètes, VII, 1, p. 251.

6847. Vous seraphins, qui estes tous embrasez de plaisant feu de l'amour divine, envoyez moy ...

       First of nine prayers to the angelic orders. The wording is almost identical to the version included by Jean Gerson in his Mendicité spirituelle.

ROUBAIX, Archives Municipales, no shelf-mark, fol. Ar°, XVc., Prayer-book of Jacques de Luxembourg.

Ed.: Glorieux, Gerson: Oeuvres complètes, VII, 1, p. 250.

6848.   Vous thrones, esquelz pour la tres profonde humilité et reverence que vous avez a Dieu, il repose et siet ...

Third of nine orisons to the angelic orders. The wording is almost identical to the version included by Jean Gerson in his Mendicité spirituelle.

ROUBAIX, Archives Municipales, no shelf-mark, fol. Av°-Br°, Prayer-book of Jacques de Luxembourg.

Ed.: Glorieux, Gerson: Oeuvres complètes, VII, 1, p. 251.

6849.   Vous vertus, ouvrez dedans moy miracles en mon resuscitant quant je suys morte par peché ...

Seventh of nine prayers to the angelic orders. The wording is almost identical to the version included by Jean Gerson in his Mendicité spirituelle.

ROUBAIX, Archives Municipales, no shelf-mark, fol. Br°-Bv°, XVc., Prayer-book of Jacques de Luxembourg.

Ed.: Glorieux, Gerson: Oeuvres complètes, VII, 1, p. 251.

6850.   Vray Dieu, ayes de nous merci; Pere du ciel aies de nous merci; Filz de Dieu racheteur du monde aiez merci de nous ...

Litany in prose.

MANCHESTER, John Rylands Univ. Libr., French 143, fol. 97r°-100v°, early XVc., Hours.

6851.   Vrais Dieux, bien trouvasmes en noz livres
Qu'encor serions nous racheté ...

"Plainte" to God by Daniel: "Mystère de la Nativité" (vv. 594-605).

LONDON, British Libr., Additional 38860, fol. 13r°, XVIIIc. copy of a lost ms.

PARIS, Bibl. Sainte-Geneviève, 1131, fol. 7v°, XVc.

Ed.: Whittredge, p. 113.

6852.   Vrais Deus celestres, tu soies aoré
Kant nos aveiz par mesaige mandé
Par le vostre aingle ki ait a nos parlé.
                    (Complete Text)

Variant of no. 6830: Voir rois celestre, font li baron menbré.

6853. Vrais Dieus, <u>dist la pucele</u>, con tu es
                                     presious!
       Tu fais croistre les arbres, porter foilles
                                    et flors ...

       Orison to God by Rosamunde, a secret convert to Christianity:
          Elie de Saint-Gille (vv. 1370-8).

       PARIS, Bibl. nat., fr. 25516, fol. 85v°, XIIIc.

       <u>Ed.</u>: Förster, p. 358; Raynaud, p. 45-6. <u>Ref.</u>: Merk, p. 12 n.
          11; 64 n. 10; 73 n. 20; 301 n. 4 etc.; Koch, pp. 69 and 119;
          Labande, pp. 67, 70 n. 2; Caluwé, p. 72.

6854. Vrais Diex en qui n'a point d'amer
       Vueilles nous secourir, sy te plaist!
       Perdu avons, dont nous desplaist,
       L'estoille qui nous conduisoit ...

       Orison to God by Jaspar: "Geu des trois roys" (vv. 622-37).

       PARIS, Bibl. Saint-Geneviève, 1131, fol. 27v°, XVc.

       <u>Ed.</u>: Whittredge, p. 172.

6855. Vray Dieu, je commande mon esprit en vous (<u>sic</u>) mains; pere de
          misericorde, ayés pitié de moy, voustre pauvre creature ...

       Last of the "Trois Verités" incorporated into the "Confession a
          Dieu pour remission."

       LUXEMBOURG, Bibl. nat., 28, fol. 136r°-136v°, XVIc.

6856. Vray Dieu, mon pere createur,
       De tout le monde redempteur ...

       Prayer to several saints, in rhyme.

       ROUEN, Bibl. mun., 362 (Y 143), fol. 94v°-98v°, XVIc., Hours of
          Paris.

       <u>Ref.</u>: Rézeau, Saints, I, p. 174.

6857. Vray Dieu, mon puissant createur,
       Et mon amoureux redempteur ...

       Orison to God, the Virgin, Angels and Saints.

       STUTTGART, Württembergische Landesbibl., Brev. 14, fol.
          110v°-112v°, late XIVc., Hours of Langres. This prayer added
          in XVc.

6858. Vrais Dieus, ne me voelle astenir
       De toy aourer et benir,
       Car par ta crois de mort secunde
       En morant rachatas le monde.
                          (Complete Text)

Orison to God; one octosyllabic quatrain copied as prose, rhyming aabb, repeated at the head of each of the Heures de la Croix which begin En l'eure de ...

NEW YORK, New York Public Libr., 28, fol. 127r°, 129r°, 130v°, 132r°, 133v°, 135r°, 136v°, XVc., Hours.

6859. Vray Dieux, nostre bon pere de misericorde qui savez nostre fragilité enclinee a pecher tost; qui estes tousjours apresté ...

"Confession a Dieu le pere", in prose.

BALTIMORE, Walters Art Gallery, Walters 261, fol. 127v°-128r°, c. 1400, Hours.

6860. Verais Diex, dist le duc, por ta vertu
                                    divine,
Qe feïs de ta mer celestial roïne,
Tu consoile celui por cui ma joie fine;
Tant qe jel reverai, n'avrai joie enterine.
              (Complete Text)

Plaint to God by Olivier: Entrée d'Espagne (vv. 11390-3).

VENICE, Bibl. Marciana, 257 (olim gall. XXI), fol. 222r°, XIVc.

Ed.: Thomas, II, p. 123.

6861. Vray Dieu puissant et roy celestre,
Cy nous lessiez longuement estre ...

"Plainte" to God by Isaiah: "Mystère de la Nativité" (vv. 1153-7).

LONDON, British Libr., Additional 38860, fol. 24r°, XVIIIc. copy of a lost ms.

PARIS, Bibl. Sainte-Geneviève, 1131, fol. 13r°, XVc.

Ed.: Whittredge, p. 129.

6862. Vrais Diex que (sic) le ciel establistes
Ou soleil et lune meistes,
les estoils i ordenastes,
Air, mer, terre et feu compassastes ...

Orison to God attributed to Simon de Montfort by Guillaume Guiart in his Branche des royaux lignages (vv. 5085-5254).

PARIS, Bibl. nat., fr. 5698, pp. 92-95, XIVc.

Ed.: Buchon, I, pp. 213-221. Ref.: Wels, p. 3, n. 7; p. 7, n. 19.

6863. Vrai Dieu qui en la croix pendy
Au jour du grant vendredy ...

Oraison to Jesus; one ten-line stanza, rhyming aabbccddee.

BALTIMORE, Walters Art Gallery, Walters 247, fol. 158r°-158v°, c. 1440, Hours.

6864. Vrais Dieu, qui es misericors
Et tout gouvernes par ta main ...

Orison to God by Daniel: "Mystère de la Nativité" (vv. 718-24).

LONDON, British Libr., Additional 38860, fol. 14r°, XVIIIc. copy of a lost codex.

PARIS, Bibl. Sainte-Geneviève, 1131, fol. 8r°, XVc.

Ed.: Whittredge, p. 117.

6865. Vrais Dex, qui le mont estoras
Et l'air de la tierre eslevas
Et el chiel les angeles mesis,
Esperitelment les fesis ...

Orison to God by Euriaut: Roman de la Violette by Gerbert de Montreuil (vv. 5182-331).

LENINGRAD, Publichnaia Bibl., Fr. Q. v. XIV, 3, fol. 36r°-37r°, c. 1400.

NEW YORK, Pierpont Morgan Libr., Morgan 36, fol. 84r°-87r°, XVc.

PARIS, Bibl. nat., fr. 1374, fol. 164r°-165r°, early XIIIc.

PARIS, Bibl. nat., fr. 1553, fol. 317 (318)r°-318 (319)r°, 1284.

Ed.: Buffum, pp. 207-13. Ref.: Scheludko, ZFSL, 58 (1934), pp. 83-4; Wels, p. 3, n. 7; p. 7, n. 19; Koch, pp. 57-60, 116; Whittredge, p. 50, n. 56; Colliot, I, pp. 124-5.

6866. Vrais Diex, qui me feistez nuncier
Par l'angle et dire le salu
Qui me vauldra et m'a valu
Vous reposez dedans mon corps ...

Orison to God by the Virgin: "Mystère de la Nativité" (vv. 1446-61).

LONDON, British Libr., Additional 38860, fol. 29v°-30r°, XVIIIc. copy of a lost ms.

PARIS, Bibl. Sainte-Geneviève, 1131, fol. 16r°, XVc.

Ed.: Whittredge, p. 137.

6867. Vray Dieux, saulve mon corps et garde que ce Sarrasin ne me occie, car ton noble champion Guillaume seroit en mortel dangier.
(Complete Text)

Orison to God by Rainouart: Bataille Loquifer in prose.

PARIS, Bibl. nat., fr. 796, fol. 292r°, early XVIc.

PARIS, Bibl. nat., fr. 1497, fol. 435r°, c. 1465.

Ed.: Castedello, p. 70 (base ms.: Paris, fr. 1497).

6868. Vray Dieu, veulle nous secourir!
        Cy ne faisons que lengourir ...

        "Plainte" to God by Adam: "Mystère de la Nativité" (vv.
        545-553).

        LONDON, British Libr., Additional 38860, fol. 9r°-9v°, XVIIIc.
        copy of a lost ms.

        PARIS, Bibl. Sainte-Geneviève, 1131, fol. 5v°, XVc.

        Ed.: Whittredge, p. 112.

6869. Vray Dieu, vray chief de nostre loy,
        Tous mes pechez confesse a toy
        Et sçay bien que ne suis pas digne
        De veoir personne tant divine ...

        Prayer to God by the prophetess Anna: Arnoul Gréban's Mystère
        de la Passion (vv. 7050-68).

        CHANTILLY, Musée Condé, 614 (1691), fol. 50r°, XVc.

        LE MANS, Bibl. mun., 6, fol. 80v°, XVc.

        PARIS, Bibl. de l'Arsenal, 6431, fol. 43r°, XVc.

        PARIS, Bibl. nat., fr. 815, fol. 56r°, 1458.

        PARIS, Bibl. nat., fr. 816, fol. 49v°, 1473.

        PARIS, Bibl. nat., fr. 1550, fol. 152v°-153r°, XVIc.

        PARIS, Bibl. nat., fr. 15064, fol. 133r°-133v°, 1469.

        PARIS, Bibl. nat., nouv. acq. fr. 14043, fol. 10v°, XVc.

        ROME, Accademia Nazionale dei Lincei, Bibl. Corsiniana, Rossi
        412 (44. A. 7), fol. 116r°, late XVc.

        Ed.: Paris-Raynaud, p. 91 (vv. 7088-106); Jodogne, p. 97 (vv.
        7050-68).

6870. Vray Dieu, vray pere omnipotens,
        Je suis au cuer triste et dolens ...

        "Plainte" to God by Joseph: "Mystère de la Nativité" (vv.
        1477-89).

        LONDON, British Libr., Additional 38860, fol. 30v°, XVIIIc.
        copy of a lost ms.

PARIS, Bibl. Sainte-Geneviève, 1131, fol. 14v°-15r°, XVc.,

Ed.: Whittredge, p. 138.

6871. Vray est que Dieu nostre pere de sa misericorde qui sceit et
       cognoit nostre fragille et humaine nature ...

       First of the "Trois Verités" incorporated into the "Confession
       a Dieu pour remission."

       LUXEMBOURG, Bibl. nat., 28, fol. 135r°, XVIc.

6872. Vray redempteur,
       Qui humaine lignie
       Getas jadis de paine et de servage,
       Qui par doulceur ...

       Orison by Barlaam: "Mystere du roy Advenir" by Jean du Prier
       (vv. 15560-83).

       PARIS, Bibl. nat., fr. 1042, fol. 266r°-266v°, XVc.

       Ed.: Meiller, p. 648.

6873. Vraiz sire Dieux, donnez a .N. grace et amour devant toutez
       personnez ainxi que vous donnastes a Joseph grace ...

       Orison to God in prose.

       BALTIMORE, Walters Art Gallery, Walters 103, fol. 83r°, late
       XIVc., Hours of Paris (?).

6874. Vray sire, j'ay bonne volenté et propos moyennant vostre aide
       de moy corrygier et amendeir et garderay ...

       Second of the "Trois Verités" incorporated into the "Confession
       a Dieu pour remission."

       LUXEMBOURG, Bibl. nat., 28, fol. 135v°-136r°, XVIc.

6875. Vraiement tu es le doulx benoit Jhesucrist, vray Dieu, filz de
       Dieu le pere et vray homme, filz de la benoiste vierge Marie
       ...

       "Oroison que l'on doit dire quant on lieve le corps de
       Jhesucrist."

       PROVIDENCE, Brown Univ. Libr., C. 28. b. 4 (H.L. Koopman
       Collection), fol. 270v°-271r°, XVc., Hours.

Index of Manuscripts

All references are to entry numbers. An asterisk indicates an early imprint.

Index of Individual Owners

Astor, v. OXFORD Bodleian Libr.

Blanche de France, Duchess of
        Orleans, v. NEW YORK, New
        York Public Libr., Spencer
        56

Buchanan, v. OXFORD, Bodleian
        Libr.

Didot, A. Firmin, v. CAMBRIDGE
        (Mass.), Harvard College
        Libr., Typ. 321 and
        LOUVAIN, Bibl. de l'Univ.,
        G. 170

Eleanor de Bourbon, v. NEW YORK,
        Pierpont Morgan Libr.,
        Morgan 159

Giraud, bibliophile de Lyon, v.
        COLLECTION UNKNOWN

Guillebert de Lannoy, v.
        WADDESDON MANOR, Collection
        James A. de Rothschild, 4

Holkham, v. OXFORD, Bodleian
        Libr.

Isabelle de Coucy, v. BALTIMORE,
        Walters Art Gallery,
        Walters 89

Jacques de Luxembourg, v.
        ROUBAIX, Archives
        Municipales

Jean de Launay, v. BALTIMORE,
        Walters Art Gallery,
        Walters 448

Jean Lallemant, v. BALTIMORE,
        Walters Art Gallery,
        Walters 451

Koopman, H.L., v. PROVIDENCE,
        Brown Univ. Libr., C. 28.
        b. 4

Kuosmanen, v. HELSINKI,
        Collection Kuosmanen

Margaret Beauchamp, v. CAMBRIDGE,
        Fitzwilliam Museum,
        Fitzwilliam 41/1950

Margaret Beaufort, v. LONDON,
        Westminster Abbey, 39

Marguerite de La Chaussée, v.
        BARNARD CASTLE, Bowes
        Museum, O91. MED. 8

Phillipps, Sir Thomas, v.
        BERKELEY, Univ. of Calif.
        Libr., 106 and PARIS, Bibl.
        nat., nouv. acq. fr. 16600

Index of Authors and Translators

Index of Saints,
Blessed and Biblical Personages

All references are to entry numbers. Well-known names are listed under their English forms; French graphies are employed for saints especially venerated in France.

Abel (in Mystère de la Passion), 5639

Abraham, mention, 5681, 5912, 5985, 6627

Adam (in Mystère de la Passion), 6361; – (in Mystère de la Nativité), 5382, 6131, 6868; – mention, 5416, 5579, 5657, 5767, 5860, 6608, 6806

Adrien, orison, 5540, 6254, 6521; – v. also Index of Subjects: Mystère

Agatha, orison 6247, 6625

Agnes, orison, 6240

All Hallows, All Saints, v. Saints

Anatole, orison, 6522

Andrew (in Mystère de la Passion) 5704; – orison, 6194, 6314, 6523

Angel, Guardian, orison, 5428, 5808, 5839, 5993, 5998-9, 6011, 6190, 6293-4, 6296, 6306, 6385, 6389, 6402, 6519, 6716, 6748

Angels in general: canticle, v. Index of Subjects: hymn "Te Deum"; – dictés aux anges, 6743; – mention, 6384, 6404; – orison, 5427, 6313, 6586, 6857; – as last of the nine in the Hierarchy, 5808, 6831

Anne, Mother of the Virgin, orison, 5570, 6096, 6288

Anselm, author, 5942, 6132, 6435

Anthony the Great, orison, 5840, 5868, 6398, 6406, 6524, 6703

Apostles, plainte, 6367

Archangels (as eighth of the nine in the Hierarchy), orison, 5811, 6832

Archedeclin, mention 5683, 5687

Athanasius, author, 6503-4

Augustine, author, 5545, 6136, 6142, 6271, 6525-6, 6572; – orison, 6282; – v. also Index of Subjects: Canterbury

Avia, Avoye, orison, 6409

George, Vie, 5625, 5633, 5634,
    5652; - orison, 6184

Gérard, orison, 6010

Germain, orison, 6776

Gertrude, orison, 5773, 6232

God (v. also Jesus, since authors
    often do not distinguish
    clearly between the two);
    orison in prose, 5412,
    5420, 5456, 5462, 5465,
    5467, 5472, 5475, 5484,
    5486, 5488, 5490, 5623,
    5630, 5640, 5667, 5668,
    5680, 5695, 5715, 5716,
    5789, 5849, 5850, 5851,
    5943, 6004, 6005, 6103,
    6109, 6111, 6141-2, 6154,
    6183, 6186, 6224, 6281,
    6341, 6363, 6377, 6386,
    6395, 6419, 6442, 6444,
    6586, 6588, 6592, 6600,
    6617-18, 6622, 6639-40,
    6698-9, 6702, 6727, 6804,
    6867, 6873; - orison in
    rhyme, 5380, 5414, 5416,
    5418, 5457, 5459, 5485,
    5550, 5552, 5572, 5574,
    5576, 5579, 5621, 5625,
    5629, 5632, 5633, 5634,
    5639, 5652, 5654, 5655,
    5656, 5657, 5659, 5660,
    5663, 5664, 5666, 5669,
    5685, 5699, 5700, 5702,
    5704, 5738, 5747, 5769,
    5770, 5801, 5803, 5843-47,
    5853, 5858, 5860-2, 5871,
    5876-7, 5881, 5905, 5907-8,
    5910, 5914, 5918, 5925,
    6231, 6250, 6258, 6310,
    6328, 6364, 6368, 6381,
    6382, 6422-4, 6456, 6459,
    6470, 6475, 6483, 6489,
    6611, 6612, 6619, 6627,
    6638, 6712, 6756, 6765,
    6790, 6829, 6853-4, 6857-8,
    6862, 6864-6, 6869; -
    plainte, 5476, 5559, 5573,
    5653, 5665, 5694, 5717,
    5718, 5741, 5768, 5771,
    5780, 5842, 5888, 5890,
    5911, 5912, 5939, 6069,
    6131, 6408, 6418, 6713,
    6851, 6860-1, 6868, 6870; -
    praise, 5906, 5944, 6086,
    6130, 6467, 6830; rondeau,
    6085; -

thanksgiving, 5382, 5493,
    5495, 5719, 5894, 5977,
    6122, 6295, 6361, 6754,
    6799

Gond, orison, 6530

Gregory the Great, antienne,
    5531; - author, 6531; -
    orison, 6251

Guillaume (of Bourges), orison,
    6299

Herod, mention, 5581

Hezekiah, canticle, 5962

Hubert, orison, 6260

Isaac, 5488, 6627

Isaiah (in Mystère de la
    Nativité), 5699, 5899,
    6382, 6861; - canticle,
    6138

Jacob, 5488, 6627

James the Great, orison, 5809,
    6391, 6533, 6615, 6694,
    6771

James the Less, orison, 6532

Jaspar (in Geu des trois roys),
    5867, 6598, 6854

Jeremiah (in Mystère de la
    Passion), 5760

Jerome, antienne, 6571; - orison,
    6252

Jesus (see also God, since
    authors often do not
    distinguish clearly between
    the two); ballade, 5549,
    5981, 6464; - chanson,
    6500; - chansonnette, 5432;
    - chant royal, 6119; -
    motet, 6188; - Names,
    6536-7; - orison to, or in
    honour of (prose): 5464,
    5466, 5754, 5759, 5775,
    5866, 5935, 5936, 5938,
    5941, 5976, 6012-17, 6032,

Virtues (as seventh of the nine
 in the Hierarchy), <u>orison</u>,
 6849

Youths, Three, <u>canticle</u>, 6736; –
 <u>mention</u>, 5676

Yves, <u>orison</u>, 6630

Zacharias, <u>mention</u>, 6554

Zechariah, <u>canticle</u>, 5522, 5523,
 6171

Index of Subjects and Titles

All references are to entry numbers. Titles of French texts appear mainly in their medieval forms without grave or circumflex accents. O = orison.

A.B.C. des simple gens, by Jean Gerson, 5956, 5987, 6162

Absolution, 5517

Aceline (in Orson de Beauvais), 5579

Actions de graces, 6007, 6169, 6722

Adesto Domine supplicationibus nostris (in Fr.), 6705

Advent, v. Dimence

Agnus Dei (in Fr.), 5421-2

Alisandrine (in Vie de s. Georges), 5625

Alma redemptoris (in Fr.), 6562

Altar of S. Peter's, Rome, 5539, 5544

Ame, desir a la vie eternelle, 5557

Ame, Dit de l', 6471

Ame, Livre du jardin de la s., 6461, 6492

Ames de purgatoyre, o. pour pryer les, 6145

Ames de tous fidelles, o. pour les, 6180

Ame des trespassez, or Ame trespassee, Recommandation de l', 6351, 6372

Ami (in Ami et Amile), 5660, 5663

Ami et Amile, 5655, 5660, 5663, 5912-3

Amiens, v. Heures

Amile (in Ami et Amile), 5655

Amilun (in Amis e Amilun), 5926

Amis e Amilun, 5926

An, o. pour le jour de l', 6429

Angels, v. Index of Saints

Angers, v. Heures

Annunciation, mention, 5401, 5499, 5597, 5602-3, 5680, 5833, 5996, 6588, 6866; - v. also Sermon

Anseïs d'Auvergne (in Moniage Guillaume), 6103

Ante thronum trinitatis, 5590

About the Compiler

KEITH V. SINCLAIR is Professor of French and Chairman of the Department of Modern Languages at James Cook University of North Queensland in Australia. A noted expert in the fields of medieval French language and literature, he has written *Melbourne Livy*, *Descriptive Catalogue of Medieval Manuscripts in Australia*, *Tristan de Nanteuil*, and *Prieres en Ancien Francais*, as well as the first volume and supplement of *French Devotional Texts of the Middle Ages* (Greenwood Press, 1979, 1982).